Survival Communications
in Florida: Treasure Coast Region

John E. Parnell, KK4HWX

10 ISBN 1479135933
13 ISBN 978-1479135936

Cover design by:
Lynda Colón
FREELANCE GRAPHIC DESIGN &
MARKETING COMMUNICATIONS
www.hirelynda.webs.com

I do wish to acknowledge the hard work of **Angie Shirley** in putting together the database required for this book. Without her efforts, this book could not have been done.

Titles available in this series:

Survival Communications in Alabama
Survival Communications in Alaska
Survival Communications in Arizona
Survival Communications in Arkansas
Survival Communications in California
Survival Communications in Colorado
Survival Communications in Connecticut
Survival Communications in Delaware
Survival Communications in Florida
Survival Communications in Georgia
Survival Communications in Hawaii
Survival Communications in Idaho
Survival Communications in Illinois
Survival Communications in Indiana
Survival Communications in Iowa
Survival Communications in Kansas
Survival Communications in Kentucky
Survival Communications in Louisiana
Survival Communications in Maine
Survival Communications in Maryland
Survival Communications in Massachusetts
Survival Communications in Michigan
Survival Communications in Minnesota
Survival Communications in Mississippi
Survival Communications in Missouri
Survival Communications in Montana

Survival Communications in Nebraska
Survival Communications in Nevada
Survival Communications in New Hampshire
Survival Communications in New Jersey
Survival Communications in New Mexico
Survival Communications in New York
Survival Communications in North Carolina
Survival Communications in North Dakota
Survival Communications in Ohio
Survival Communications in Oklahoma
Survival Communications in Oregon
Survival Communications in Pennsylvania
Survival Communications in Rhode Island
Survival Communications in South Carolina
Survival Communications in South Dakota
Survival Communications in Tennessee
Survival Communications in Texas
Survival Communications in Utah
Survival Communications in Vermont
Survival Communications in Virginia
Survival Communications in Washington
Survival Communications in West Virginia
Survival Communications in Wisconsin
Survival Communications in Wyoming

The above titles are available from your favorite online or brick-and-mortar bookstore or directly from the publisher at Tutor Turtle Press LLC, 1027 S. Pendleton St. – Suite B-10, Easley, SC 29642.

TABLE OF CONTENTS

Survival Communications in Florida 1
General Mobile Radio Service / Family Radio Service 1
Citizens Band Radio 1
Ham / Amateur Radio 2
Standardized Amateur Radio Prepper Communications Plan 2
Nets and Network Etiquette 3
Topics for Technician Amateur License Exam 4
Call Sign Numbers 6
Topics for General Amateur License Exam 7
Topics for Extra Amateur License Exam 9
Canadian Call Sign Prefixes 13
Common Radio Bands in the United States 14
Common Amateur Radio Bands in Canada 14
Call Sign Phonics 21
Morse Code and Ham Radio 23
International Call Sign Prefixes 24
Third Party Communications 31

Appendix A – Florida Ham Radio Clubs

ARRL Affiliated Amateur and Ham Radio Clubs – By City

Arcadia .... App A – 3
Big Pine .... App A – 3
Boca Raton .... App A – 3
Bradenton .... App A – 3
Brandon .... App A – 3
Bronson .... App A – 3
Brooksville .... App A – 4
Clearwater .... App A – 4
Clewiston .... App A – 4
Cocoa .... App A – 4
Coconut Creek .... App A – 4
Dade City .... App A – 4
Davenport .... App A – 5
Davie .... App A – 5
Daytona Beach .... App A – 5
Deland .... App A – 5
Eaton Park .... App A – 5
Englewood .... App A – 5
Fort Lauderdale .... App A – 5
Fort Myers .... App A – 6
Fort Pierce .... App A – 6

Fort Walton Beach .... App A – 6
Freeport .... App A – 6
Gainesville .... App A – 6
Geneva .... App A – 7
Goldenrod .... App A – 7
Green Cove Springs .... App A – 7
Gulfport .... App A – 7
Hillard .... App A – 7
Hollywood .... App A – 7
Holt .... App A – 8
Homestead .... App A – 8
Hudson .... App A – 8
Interlachen .... App A – 8
Jacksonville .... App A – 8
Jupiter .... App A – 9
Key West .... App A – 9
Lake City .... App A – 9
Lake Wales .... App A – 9
Largo.. App A – 9
Leesburg .... App A – 9
Lehigh Acres .... App A – 10
Loxahatchee .... App A – 10
Marianna .... App A – 10
Melbourne .... App A – 10
Merritt Island .... App A – 11
Miami .... App A – 11
Milton .... App A – 11
Mims .... App A – 11
Myakka City .... App A – 11
Naples .... App A – 11
Navarre .... App A – 11
New Port Richey .... App A – 12
Newberry .... App A – 12
North Palm Beach .... App A – 12
North Port .... App A – 12
Ocala .... App A – 12
Okeechobee .... App A – 12
Oneco .... App A – 13
Orlando .... App A – 13
Palm Bay .... App A – 13
Palm Coast .... App A – 13
Panama City .... App A – 14
Pensacola .... App A – 14
Plantation .... App A – 14
Pompano Beach .... App A – 14
Port Saint Lucie .... App A – 14

Punta Gorda .... App A – 15
Saint Augustine .... App A – 15
Saint Petersburg .... App A – 15
Sarasota .... App A – 15
Sebring .... App A – 16
Silver Springs .... App A – 16
Spring Hill .... App A – 16
St. Cloud .... App A – 16
Starke .... App A – 16
Stuart .... App A – 16
Sun City Center .... App A – 16
Tallahassee .... App A – 17
Tampa .... App A – 17
Tavares .... App A – 18
The Villages .... App A – 18
Titusville .... App A – 18
Venice .... App A – 18
Vero Beach .... App A – 18
Wesley Chapel .... App A – 18
West Palm Beach .... App A – 19
Wewahitchka .... App A – 19

Appendix B – Florida: Treasure Coast Region Amateur Radio Licensees by City

Alva .... App B – 3
Arcadia .... App B – 3
Ave Maria .... App B – 8
Avon Park .... App B – 9
Boca Grande .... App B – 12
Bokeelia .... App B – 12
Bonita Springs .... App B – 13
Bowling Green .... App B – 17
Cape Coral .... App B – 18
Cape Haze .... App B – 39
Captiva .... App B – 39
Charlotte Habor .... App B – 39
Chokoloskee .... App B – 40
Clewiston .... App B – 40
East Fort Myers .... App B – 42
El Jobean .... App B – 42
Estero .... App B – 42
Everglades City .... App B – 44
Felda .... App B – 44
Fort Myers .... App B – 44
Fort Myers Beach .... App B – 69

Fort Ogden .... App B – 71
Golden Gate .... App B – 71
Goodland .... App B – 71
Grove City .... App B – 72
Harbor Heights .... App B – 72
Immokalee .... App B – 72
Labelle .... App B – 72
Lake Placid .... App B – 74
Lake Suzy .... App B – 80
Lakeport .... App B – 81
Lee .... App B – 81
Lehigh Acres .... App B – 81
Lorida .... App B – 88
Marco Island .... App B – 89
Matlacha .... App B – 92
Moore Haven .... App B – 93
Murdock .... App B – 94
Naples .... App B – 94
North Fort Myers .... App B – 122
North Naples .... App B – 135
Ochopee .... App B – 135
Ona .... App B – 135
Palmdale .... App B – 135
Pineland .... App B – 135
Placida .... App B – 136
Port Charlotte .... App B – 136
Punta Gorda .... App B – 154
Punta Gorda Isles .... App B – 172
Rotonda West .... App B – 172
Saint James City .... App B – 174
Sanibel .... App B – 175
Sebring .... App B – 177
South Punta Gorda .... App B – 187
Tice .... App B – 187
Venus .... App B – 187
Wauchula .... App B – 188
West Fort Myers .... App B – 188
Zolfo Springs .... App B – 188

Survival Communications in Florida

Perhaps you have prepared for WTSHTF or TEOTWAWKI with respect to food, water, self-defense and shelter. But what about communication?

Whenever there is a disaster (hurricane, earthquake, economic collapse, nuclear war, EMF, solar eruption, etc.), the normal means of communication that we're all reliant upon (cell phone, land line phone, the Internet, etc.) will probably be, at best, sporadic and at worst, non-existent.

As this author sees it, short of smoke signals and mirrors, there are three options for communication in "trying times": (1) GMRS or FRS radios; (2) CB radios; and (3) ham or amateur radio. Let's consider each of these options to come up with the most acceptable one.

GMRS (General Mobile Radio Service) / FRS (Family Radio Service)

GMRS (General Mobile Radio Service) / FRS (Family Radio Service) radios work optimally over short distances where there is minimal interference. Originally designed to be used as pagers, particularly inside a building or other such confined area, these radios are low-cost and convenient to carry. Unfortunately their small size and light weight comes with a trade-off – short range and short battery life. These radios are supposed to be able to communicate for up to 25-30 miles. Right. That's on level terrain, without buildings or trees getting in the way. While battery life technology is constantly improving, you will need spare batteries to keep communicating or someway of recharging the ones in the radio. In this author's opinion, GMRS/FRS radios are not first choice when concerned with medium or long range communication.

CB (Citizens Band)

CB (Citizens Band) radios operate in a frequency range originally reserved for ham or amateur radio operation. Because of the overwhelming number of people wishing quick, low-cost, regulation-free communication, the FCC (Federal Communication Commission) split off a portion of the frequency spectrum and allowed anyone to purchase a CB radio and start communicating. No test. No license. Just personal/business communication. Today, CB radios are readily available in such outlets as eBay and Craigslist. This author has seen them at yard/garage/tag sales and at flea markets.

CB radios come in a variety of "flavors." Fixed units, sometimes referred to as base units are intended for home use. For the most part, they derive their power from the utility company. In the event of loss of electricity, most base units can also be connected to a 12-volt battery, like that in your car/truck. If you choose to obtain a fixed unit, make sure you know how to connect the unit to the battery – ahead of time. Trying to figure this out when you're under extra stress is not a good situation.

A second type of CB radio is designed to be mobile, that is, installed in your car/truck. It gets its power from the vehicle's battery. You can either attach an antenna permanently to the vehicle or have a removable, magnetic type antenna.

The third type of CB radio is designed for handheld use. They are small and light. Most weigh less than a pound and operate on batteries. Yes, using batteries in a CB poses the same limitations as those by the GMRS/FRS radios, but have the added advantage that most handheld units come with a cigarette lighter adapter. Comes in handy when you are on the move and wish to be able to communicate both from a vehicle and also when you have to abandon it.

While they have a greater range than GMRS/FRS radios, CB radios are, legally, limited to operate on 40 channels, with a power rating of four (4) watts or less. Yes, it is possible to alter CB radios to get around these limitations, but not legally,

Ham/Amateur Radio

Ham/Amateur radio is very appealing. With a ham radio, you are not limited to less than 50 miles, but can communicate with anyone in the world (who also has access to a ham radio, of course).

Standardized Amateur Radio Prepper Communications Plan

In the event of a nationwide catastrophic disaster, the nationwide network of Amateur Radio licensed preppers will need a set of standardized meeting frequencies to share information and coordinate activities between various prepper groups. This Standardized Amateur Radio Communications Plan establishes a set of frequencies on the 80 meter, 40 meter, 20 meter, and 2 meter Amateur Radio bands for use during these types of catastrophic disasters.

Routine nets will not be held on all of these frequencies, but preppers are encouraged to use them when coordinating with other preppers on a routine basis. Routine nets may be conducted by The American Preparedness Radio Net (TAPRN) on these or other frequencies as they see fit. However, TAPRN will promote the use of these standardized frequencies by all Amateur Radio licensed preppers during times of catastrophic disaster. The promotion of this Standardized Amateur Radio Communications Plan is encouraged by all means within the prepper community, including via Amateur Radio, Twitter, Facebook, and various blogs.

Standardized Frequencies and Modes
80 Meters – 3.818 MHz LSB (TAPRN Net: Sundays at 9 PM ET)
40 Meters – 7.242 MHz LSB
40 Meters Morse Code / Digital – 7.073 MHz USB (TAPRN: Sundays at 7:30 PM ET on CONTESTIA 4/250)
20 Meters – 14.242 MHz USB
2 Meters – 146.420 MHz FM

Nets and Network Etiquette

In times of nationwide catastrophic disaster, the ability of any one prepper to initiate and sustain themselves as a net control may be limited by the availability of power and other resource shortages. However, all licensed preppers are encouraged to maintain a listening watch on these frequencies as often as possible during a catastrophic disaster. Preppers may routinely announce themselves in the following manner:

• This is [Your Callsign Phonetically] in [Your State], maintaining a listening watch on [Standard Frequency] for any preppers on frequency seeking information or looking to provide information. Please call [Your Callsign Phonetically]. Preppers exchanging information that may require follow up should agree upon a designated time to return to the frequency and provide further information. If other stations are utilizing the frequency at the designated time you return, maintain watch and proceed with your communications when those stations are finished. If your communications are urgent and the stations on frequency are not passing information of a critical nature, interrupt with the word "Break" and request use of the frequency.

For More Information

Catastrophe Network: http://www.catastrophenetwork.org or @CatastropheNet on Twitter The American Preparedness Radio Network: http://www.taprn.com or @TAPRN on Twitter

© 2011 Catastrophe Network, Please Distribute Freely

In order to use a ham radio, legally, one must be licensed to do so by the FCC (other countries have analogous governmental bodies to regulate ham radio). To obtain a license is quite easy – take a test and pay your license fee. There are currently three classes of license – Technician, General, and Amateur Extra. With each of these licenses come specific abilities.

Technician class is the beginning level. The exam consists of 35 multiple choice questions randomly drawn from a pool of 395 questions. The question pool is readily available online for free downloading (http://www.ncvec.org/downloads/Revised%20Element%202.Pdf) or in such publications at *Ham Radio License Manual Revised 2nd Edition* (ISBN 978-0-87259-097-7). The current Technician pool of questions is to be used from July 1, 2010 to June 30, 2014. Be sure the question pool you are studying from is current. You will need to score at least 26 correct to pass. (Do not worry, Morse Code is no longer on the test, although many ham operators use it anyway.) You do not need to take a formal class in order to qualify to take the exam. You can learn the material on your own. Most people spend 10-15 hours studying and then successfully take the exam. The cost of taking the exam is under $20. The exam is given in MANY locations throughout the US. Usually the exam is given by area ham clubs. You do not have to belong to the club to take the exam. Check Appendix A for a listing of clubs in Florida.

Topics for the Technician License in Amateur Radio

The Technician license exam covers such topics as basic regulations, operating practices, and electronic theory, with a focus on VHF and UHF applications. Below is the syllabus for the Technician Class.

Subelement T1 – FCC Rules, descriptions and definitions for the amateur radio service, operator and station license responsibilities

[6 Exam Questions – 6 Groups]

T1A – Amateur Radio services; purpose of the amateur service, amateur-satellite service, operator/primary station license grant, where FCC rules are codified, basis and purpose of FCC rules, meanings of basic terms used in FCC rules

T1B – Authorized frequencies; frequency allocations, ITU regions, emission type, restricted sub-bands, spectrum sharing, transmissions near band edges

T1C – Operator classes and station call signs; operator classes, sequential, special event, and vanity call sign systems, international communications, reciprocal operation, station license licensee, places where the amateur service is regulated by the FCC, name and address on ULS, license term, renewal, grace period

T1D – Authorized and prohibited transmissions

T1E – Control operator and control types; control operator required, eligibility, designation of control operator, privileges and duties, control point, local, automatic and remote control, location of control operator

T1F – Station identification and operation standards; special operations for repeaters and auxiliary stations, third party communications, club stations, station security, FCC inspection

Subelement T2 – Operating Procedures

[3 Exam Questions – 3 Groups]

T2A – Station operation; choosing an operating frequency, calling another station, test transmissions, use of minimum power, frequency use, band plans

T2B – VHF/UHF operating practices; SSB phone, FM repeater, simplex, frequency offsets, splits and shifts, CTCSS, DTMF, tone squelch, carrier squelch, phonetics

T2C – Public service; emergency and non-emergency operations, message traffic handling

Subelement T3 – Radio wave characteristics, radio and electromagnetic properties, propagation modes

[3 Exam Questions – 3 Groups]

T3A – Radio wave characteristics; how a radio signal travels; distinctions of HF, VHF and UHF; fading, multipath; wavelength vs. penetration; antenna orientation

T3B – Radio and electromagnetic wave properties; the electromagnetic spectrum, wavelength vs. frequency, velocity of electromagnetic waves

T3C – Propagation modes; line of sight, sporadic E, meteor, aurora scatter, tropospheric ducting, F layer skip, radio horizon

Subelement T4 - Amateur radio practices and station setup

[2 Exam Questions – 2 Groups]

T4A – Station setup; microphone, speaker, headphones, filters, power source, connecting a computer, RF grounding

T4B – Operating controls; tuning, use of filters, squelch, AGC, repeater offset, memory channels

Subelement T5 – Electrical principles, math for electronics, electronic principles, Ohm's Law

[4 Exam Questions – 4 Groups]

T5A – Electrical principles; current and voltage, conductors and insulators, alternating and direct current

T5B – Math for electronics; decibels, electronic units and the metric system

T5C – Electronic principles; capacitance, inductance, current flow in circuits, alternating current, definition of RF, power calculations

T5D – Ohm's Law

Subelement T6 – Electrical components, semiconductors, circuit diagrams, component functions

[4 Exam Groups – 4 Questions]

T6A – Electrical components; fixed and variable resistors, capacitors, and inductors; fuses, switches, batteries

T6B – Semiconductors; basic principles of diodes and transistors

T6C – Circuit diagrams; schematic symbols

T6D – Component functions

Subelement T7 – Station equipment, common transmitter and receiver problems, antenna measurements and troubleshooting, basic repair and testing

[4 Exam Questions – 4 Groups]

T7A – Station radios; receivers, transmitters, transceivers

T7B – Common transmitter and receiver problems; symptoms of overload and overdrive, distortion, interference, over and under modulation, RF feedback, off frequency signals; fading and noise; problems with digital communications interfaces

T7C – Antenna measurements and troubleshooting; measuring SWR, dummy loads, feedline failure modes

T7D – Basic repair and testing; soldering, use of a voltmeter, ammeter, and ohmmeter

Subelement T8 – Modulation modes, amateur satellite operation, operating activities, non-voice communications

[4 Exam Questions – 4 Groups]

T8A – Modulation modes; bandwidth of various signals

T8B – Amateur satellite operation; Doppler shift, basic orbits, operating protocols

T8C – Operating activities; radio direction finding, radio control, contests, special event stations, basic linking over Internet

T8D – Non-voice communications; image data, digital modes, CW, packet, PSK31

Subelement T9 – Antennas, feedlines

[2 Exam Groups – 2 Questions]

T9A – Antennas; vertical and horizontal, concept of gain, common portable and mobile antennas, relationships between antenna length and frequency

T9B – Feedlines; types, losses vs. frequency, SWR concepts, matching, weather protection, connectors

Subelement T0 – AC power circuits, antenna installation, RF hazards

[3 Exam Questions – 3 Groups]

T0A – AC power circuits; hazardous voltages, fuses and circuit breakers, grounding, lightning protection, battery safety, electrical code compliance

T0B – Antenna installation; tower safety, overhead power lines

T0C – RF hazards; radiation exposure, proximity to antennas, recognized safe power levels, exposure to others

Once your name and call sign are available in the FCC database, you have the privilege of operating on all VHF (2 m) and UHF (70 cm) frequencies above 30 megahertz (MHz) and HF frequencies 80, 40, and 15 meter, and on the 10 meter band using Morse code (CW), voice, and digital mode. For a Technician license in Florida, your call sign will consist of a two-letter prefix beginning with K or W, the number four (4), and a three-letter suffix. The single digit number in the call sign is determined according to which area of the US you obtain your first license. Even though you may move to another state, you keep this number in your call sign. This is also true should you upgrade to a higher license and get a new call sign. The numeral portion of your call sign stays the same.

Call Sign Numbers

Below is a chart showing the various numbers and the state(s) in which you would obtain the number.

Call Sign Number	State(s)
0	CO, IA, KS, MN, MO, NE, ND, SD
1	CT, ME, MA, NH, RI, VT
2	NJ, NY
3	DE, DC, MD, PA
4	AL, FL, GA, KY, NC, SC, TN, VA
5	AR, LA, MS, NM, OK, TX
6	CA
7	AZ, ID, MT, NV, OR, WA, UT, WY
8	MI, OH, WV
9	IL, IN, WI

Residents of Alaska may have any of the following call sign prefixes assigned to them: AL0-7, KL0-7, NL0-7, or WL0-7. Likewise, residents of Hawaii may have the prefix AH6-7, KH6-7, NH6-7, or WH6-7 assigned.

Once you obtain your Technician license, do not stop there. Go and get your General license.

General is the second of three ham license classes. Like the Technician license, to get a General license, you merely have to take a 35-question multiple choice exam and pay your license fee. Passing is still at least 26 correct answers and the fee is the same (less than $20). Again the question pool is available for free online (http://www.ncvec.org/page.php?id=358). It is also available in such print publications as *The ARRL General Class License Manual 7th Edition* (ISBN 978-0-87259-811-9). The current General pool of questions is to be used from July 1, 2011 to June 30, 2015. Be sure the question pool you are using is current. Being a bit more comprehensive than the Technician license, the General license usually requires 15-20 hours of study to learn the material. Check Appendix A for a listing of clubs in Florida where you might take your exam. Once your name and NEW call sign is listed in the FCC database, you're good to go. For a General license in Florida, your call sign will consist of a one-letter prefix beginning with K, N or W, the number four (4), and a three-letter suffix.

Topics for the General License in Amateur Radio

The General license exam covers regulations, operating practices and electronic theory. Below is the syllabus for the General Class.

Subelement G1 – Commission's Rules

(5 Exam Questions – 5 Groups)

G1A – General Class control operator frequency privileges; primary and secondary allocations

G1B – Antenna structure limitations; good engineering and good amateur practice, beacon operation; restricted operation; retransmitting radio signals

G1C – Transmitter power regulations; data emission standards

G1D – Volunteer Examiners and Volunteer Examiner Coordinators; temporary identification

G1E – Control categories; repeater regulations; harmful interference; third party rules; ITU regions

Subelement G2 – Operating procedures

(5 Exam Questions – 5 Groups)

G2A – Phone operating procedures; USB/LSB utilization conventions; procedural signals; breaking into a OSO in progress; VOX operation

G2B – Operating courtesy; band plans, emergencies, including drills and emergency communications

G2C – CW operating procedures and procedural signals; Q signals and common abbreviations; full break in

G2D – Amateur Auxiliary; minimizing interference; HF operations

G2E – Digital operating; procedures, procedural signals and common abbreviations

Subelement G3 – Radio wave propagation

(3 Exam Questions – 3 Groups)

G3A – Sunspots and solar radiation; ionospheric disturbances; propagation forecasting and indices

G3B – Maximum Usable Frequency; Lowest Usable Frequency; propagation

G3C – Ionospheric layers; critical angle and frequency; HF scatter; Near Vertical Incidence Sky waves

Subelement G4 – Amateur radio practices

(5 Exam Questions – 5 Groups)

G4A – Station Operation and setup

G4B – Test and monitoring equipment; two-tone test

G4C – Interference with consumer electronics; grounding; DSP

G4D – Speech processors; S meters; sideband operation near band edges

G4E – HF mobile radio installations; emergency and battery powered operation

Subelement G5 – Electrical principles

(3 Exam Questions – 3 Groups)

G5A – Reactance; inductance; capacitance; impedance; impedance matching

G5B – The Decibel; current and voltage dividers; electrical power calculations; sine wave root-mean-square (RMS) values; PEP calculations

G5C – Resistors; capacitors and inductors in series and parallel; transformers

Subelement G6 – Circuit components

(3 Exam Questions – 3 Groups)

G6A – Resistors; capacitors; inductors

G6B – Rectifiers; solid state diodes and transistors; vacuum tubes; batteries

G6C – Analog and digital integrated circuits (ICs); microprocessors; memory; I/O devices; microwave ICs (MMICs); display devices

Subelement G7 – Practical circuits

(3 Exam Questions – 3 Groups)

G7A – Power supplies; schematic symbols

G7B – Digital circuits; amplifiers and oscillators

G7C – Receivers and transmitters; filters, oscillators

Subelement G8 – Signals and emissions

(2 Exam Questions – 2 Groups)

G8A – Carriers and modulation; AM; FM; single and double sideband; modulation envelope; overmodulation

G8B – Frequency mixing; multiplication; HF data communications; bandwidths of various modes; deviation

---

Subelement G9 – Antennas and feed lines

(4 Exam Questions – 4 Groups)

G9A – Antenna feed lines; characteristic impedance and attenuation; SWR calculation, measurement and effects; matching networks

G9B – Basic antennas

G9C – Directional antennas

G9D – Specialized antennas

Subelement G0 – Electrical and RF safety

(2 Exam Questions – 2 Groups)

G0A – RF safety principles, rules and guidelines; routine station elevation

G0B – Safety in the ham shack; electrical shock and treatment, safety grounding, fusing, interlocks, wiring, antenna and tower safety

---

With a General license, you can use all VHF and UHF frequencies and most of the HF frequencies. You would have access to the 160, 30, 17, 12, and 10 meter bands and access to major parts of the 80, 40, 20, and 15 meter bands. Of course, this is in addition to all bands available to Technician license holders.

Amateur Extra is the third of three ham license classes. Like the Technician and General classes, you merely have to pass a test and pay your fee to get your Amateur Extra license. This class of license is more comprehensive than the lower license classes. The exam is longer – 50 questions – and the minimum passing score is higher – 37. However, once you get your Amateur Extra license, all ham frequencies, VHF, UHF and HF are available for your enjoyment. The Extra exam covers regulations, specialized operating practices, advanced electronics theory, and radio equipment design.

Like for the other license classes, the question pool for the Amateur Extra license is available online for downloading (http://www.ncvec.org/downloads/REVISED%202012-2016%20Extra%20Class%20Pool.doc). It is also available in print form in such publications as *The ARRL Extra Class License Manual Revised 9th Edition* (ISBN 978-0-87259-887-4).

Topics for the Extra License in Amateur Radio

Below is the syllabus for the Amateur Extra Class for July 1, 2012 to June 30, 2016.

Subelement E1 – Commission's Rules

[6 Exam Questions – 6 Groups]

E1A – Operating Standards: frequency privileges; emission standards; automatic message forwarding; frequency sharing; stations aboard ships or aircraft

E1B – Station restrictions and special operations: restrictions on station location; general operating restrictions, spurious emissions, control operator reimbursement; antenna structure restrictions; RACES operations

E1C – Station control: definitions and restrictions pertaining to local, automatic and remote control operation; control operator responsibilities for remote and automatically controlled stations

E1D – Amateur Satellite service: definitions and purpose; license requirements for space stations; available frequencies and bands; telecommand and telemetry operations; restrictions, and special provisions; notification requirements

E1E – Volunteer examiner program: definitions, qualifications, preparation and administration of exams; accreditation; question pools; documentation requirements

E1F – Miscellaneous rules: external RF power amplifiers; national quiet zone; business communications; compensated communications; spread spectrum; auxiliary stations; reciprocal operating privileges; IARP and CEPT licenses; third party communications with foreign countries; special temporary authority

Subelement E2 – Operating procedures

[5 Exam Questions – 5 Groups]

E2A – Amateur radio in space: amateur satellites; orbital mechanics; frequencies and modes; satellite hardware; satellite operations

E2B – Television practices: fast scan television standards and techniques; slow scan television standards and techniques

E2C – Operating methods: contest and DX operating; spread-spectrum transmissions; selecting an operating frequency

E2D – Operating methods: VHF and UHF digital modes; APRS

E2E – Operating methods: operating HF digital modes; error correction

Subelement E3 – Radio wave propagation

[3 Exam Questions – 3 Groups]

E3A – Propagation and technique, Earth-Moon-Earth communications; meteor scatter

E3B – Propagation and technique, trans-equatorial; long path; gray-line; multi-path propagation

E3C – Propagation and technique, Aurora propagation; selective fading; radio-path horizon; take-off angle over flat or sloping terrain; effects of ground on propagation; less common propagation modes

Subelement E4 – Amateur practices

[5 Exam Questions – 5 Groups]

E4A – Test equipment: analog and digital instruments; spectrum and network analyzers, antenna analyzers; oscilloscopes; testing transistors; RF measurements

E4B – Measurement technique and limitations: instrument accuracy and performance limitations; probes; techniques to minimize errors; measurement of "Q"; instrument calibration

E4C – Receiver performance characteristics, phase noise, capture effect, noise floor, image rejection, MDS, signal-to-noise-ratio; selectivity

E4D – Receiver performance characteristics, blocking dynamic range, intermodulation and cross-modulation interference; 3rd order intercept; desensitization; preselection

E4E – Noise suppression: system noise; electrical appliance noise; line noise; locating noise sources; DSP noise reduction; noise blankers

Subelement E5 – Electrical principles

[4 Exam Questions – 4 Groups]

E5A – Resonance and Q: characteristics of resonant circuits: series and parallel resonance; Q; half-power bandwidth; phase relationships in reactive circuits

E5B – Time constants and phase relationships: RLC time constants: definition; time constants in RL and RC circuits; phase angle between voltage and current; phase angles of series and parallel circuits

E5C – Impedance plots and coordinate systems: plotting impedances in polar coordinates; rectangular coordinates

E5D – AC and RF energy in real circuits: skin effect; electrostatic and electromagnetic fields; reactive power; power factor; coordinate systems

Subelement E6 – Circuit components

[6 Exam Questions – 6 Groups]

E6A – Semiconductor materials and devices: semiconductor materials germanium, silicon, P-type, N-type; transistor types: NPN, PNP, junction, field-effect transistors: enhancement mode; depletion mode; MOS; CMOS; N-channel; P-channel

E6B – Semiconductor diodes

E6C – Integrated circuits: TTL digital integrated circuits; CMOS digital integrated circuits; gates

E6D – Optical devices and toroids: cathode-ray tube devices; charge-coupled devices (CCDs); liquid crystal displays (LCDs); toroids: permeability, core material, selecting, winding

E6E – Piezoelectric crystals and MMICs: quartz crystals; crystal oscillators and filters; monolithic amplifiers

E6F – Optical components and power systems: photoconductive principles and effects, photovoltaic systems, optical couplers, optical sensors, and optoisolators

Subelement E7 – Practical circuits

[8 Exam Questions – 8 Groups]

E7A – Digital circuits: digital circuit principles and logic circuits: classes of logic elements; positive and negative logic; frequency dividers; truth tables

E7B – Amplifiers: Class of operation; vacuum tube and solid-state circuits; distortion and intermodulation; spurious and parasitic suppression; microwave amplifiers

E7C – Filters and matching networks: filters and impedance matching networks: types of networks; types of filters; filter applications; filter characteristics; impedance matching; DSP filtering

E7D – Power supplies and voltage regulators

E7E – Modulation and demodulation: reactance, phase and balanced modulators; detectors; mixer stages; DSP modulation and demodulation; software defined radio systems

E7F – Frequency markers and counters: frequency divider circuits; frequency marker generators; frequency counters

E7G – Active filters and op-amps: active audio filters; characteristics; basic circuit design; operational amplifiers

E7H – Oscillators and signal sources: types of oscillators; synthesizers and phase-locked loops; direct digital synthesizers

Subelement E8 – Signals and emissions

[4 Exam Questions – 4 Groups]

E8A – AC waveforms: sine, square, sawtooth and irregular waveforms; AC measurements; average and PEP of RF signals; pulse and digital signal waveforms

E8B – Modulation and demodulation: modulation methods; modulation index and deviation ratio; pulse modulation; frequency and time division multiplexing

E8C – Digital signals: digital communications modes; CW; information rate vs. bandwidth; spread-spectrum communications; modulation methods

E8D – Waves, measurements, and RF grounding: peak-to-peak values, polarization; RF grounding

Subelement E9 – Antennas and transmission lines

[8 Exam Questions – 8 Groups]

E9A – Isotropic and gain antennas: definition; used as a standard for comparison; radiation pattern; basic antenna parameters: radiation resistance and reactance, gain, beamwidth, efficiency

E9B – Antenna patterns: E and H plane patterns; gain as a function of pattern; antenna design; Yagi antennas

E9C – Wire and phased vertical antennas: beverage antennas; terminated and resonant rhombic antennas; elevation above real ground; ground effects as related to polarization; take-off angles

E9D – Directional antennas: gain; satellite antennas; antenna beamwidth; losses; SWR bandwidth; antenna efficiency; shortened and mobile antennas; grounding

E9E – Matching: matching antennas to feed lines; power dividers

E9F – Transmission lines: characteristics of open and shorted feed lines: 1/8 wavelength; 1/4 wavelength; 1/2 wavelength; feed lines: coax versus open-wire; velocity factor; electrical length; transformation characteristics of line terminated in impedance not equal to characteristic impedance

E9G – The Smith chart

E9H – Effective radiated power; system gains and losses; radio direction finding antennas

Once your new call sign is listed in the FCC database, you are good to go. For an Amateur Extra license in Florida, your call sign will consist of a prefix of K, N or W, the number four (4), and a two-letter suffix, or a two-letter prefix beginning with A, N, K or W, the number four (4), and a one-letter suffix, or a two-letter prefix beginning with A, the number four (4), and a two-letter suffix.

Ham radio equipment can be expensive or you can do it "on the cheap." The cost will run from a couple hundred dollars to well in the thousands, depending on what you have available. eBay, and Craigslist are good places to start looking. Most ham clubs do some sort of hamfest annually wherein club members or others are willing to part with older equipment. See Appendix A for a list of clubs in Florida.

Another excellent source of equipment, as well as advice on setting the equipment up and how to use it properly, is current ham operators. In Appendix B, the author has listed all the FCC licensed ham operators in Florida, listed by city, and then sorted by street and house number on the street. Who knows, maybe someone who lives close to you is a ham operator. Be a good neighbor, stop by and have a chat with him/her.

Like CB radios, ham radios come in three formats – base, mobile, and handheld. They can use the electric company for power, or operate off a car battery. In the opinion of this author, in spite of the slightly higher cost of the equipment and having to take a test to legally use the equipment, ham radio is the way to go when concerned about communication during times of crisis.

Canadian Call Sign Prefixes

Because of our proximity to Canada, many times ham contact is made with our northern neighbors. Below is a chart showing the origin of Canadian call sign prefixes.

Call Sign Prefix	Provence or Territory
CY0	Sable Island
CY9	St. Paul Island
VA1, VE1	New Brunswick, Nova Scotia
VA2, VE2	Quebec
VA3, VE3	Ontario
VA4, VE4	Manitoba
VA5, VE5	Saskatchewan
VA6, VE6	Alberta
VA7, VE7	British Columbia
VE8	North West Territories
VE9	New Brunswick
VO1	Newfoundland

VO2	Labrador
VY0	Nunavut
VY1	Yukon
VY2	Prince Edward Island

Common Radio Bands in the United States

Certain radio bands are more popular with ham radio enthusiasts than others. Below is a chart showing these bands and when they are most popular.

	Band (meter)	Frequency (MHz)	Use
HF	160	1.8 – 2.0	Night
	80	3.5 – 4.0	Night and Local Day
	40	7.0 – 7.3	Night and Local Day
	30	10.1 – 10.15	CW and Digital
	20	14.0 – 14.350	World Wide Day and Night
	17	18.068 – 18.168	World Wide Day and Night
	15	21.0 – 21.450	Primarily Daytime
	12	24.890 – 24.990	Primarily Daytime
	10	28.0 – 29.70	Daytime during Sunspot highs
VHF	6	50 – 54	Local to World Wide
	2	144 – 148	Local to Medium Distance
UHF	70 cm	430 – 440	Local

Common Amateur Radio Bands in Canada

160 Meter Band - Maximum bandwidth 6 kHz

1.800 - 1.820 MHz - CW
1.820 - 1.830 MHz - Digital Modes
1 830 - 1.840 MHz - DX Window
1.840 - 2.000 MHz - SSB and other wide band modes

80 Meter Band - Maximum bandwidth 6 kHz

3.500 - 3.580 MHz - CW
3.580 - 3.620 MHz - Digital Modes
3.620 - 3.635 MHz - Packet/Digital Secondary
3.635 - 3.725 MHz - CW
3.725 - 3.790 MHz - SSB and other side band modes*
3.790 - 3.800 MHz - SSB DX Window
3.800 - 4.000 MHz - SSB and other wide band modes

40 Meter Band - Maximum bandwidth 6 kHz

7.000 - 7.035 MHz - CW
7.035 - 7.050 MHz - Digital Modes
7.040 - 7.050 MHz - International packet

7.050 - 7.100 MHz - SSB
7.100 - 7.120 MHz - Packet within Region 2
7.120 - 7.150 MHz - CW
7.150 - 7.300 MHz - SSB and other wide band modes

30 Meter Band - Maximum bandwidth 1 kHz

10.100 - 10.130 MHz - CW only
10.130 - 10.140 MHz - Digital Modes
10.140 - 10.150 MHz - Packet

20 Meter Band - Maximum bandwidth 6 kHz

14.000 - 14.070 MHz - CW only
14.070 - 14.095 MHz - Digital Mode
14.095 - 14.099 MHz - Packet
14.100 MHz - Beacons
14.101 - 14.112 MHz - CW, SSB, packet shared
14.112 - 14.350 MHz - SSB
14.225 - 14.235 MHz - SSTV

17 Meter Band - Maximum bandwidth 6 kHz

18.068 - 18.100 MHz - CW
18.100 - 18.105 MHz - Digital Modes
18.105 - 18.110 MHz - Packet
18.110 - 18.168 MHz - SSB and other wide band modes

15 Meter Band - maximum bandwidth 6 kHz

21.000 - 21.070 MHz - CW
21.070 - 21.090 MHz - Digital Modes
21.090 - 21.125 MHz - Packet
21.100 - 21.150 MHz - CW and SSB
21.150 - 21.335 MHz - SSB and other wide band modes
21.335 - 21.345 MHz - SSTV
21.345 - 21.450 MHz - SSB and other wide band modes

12 Meter Band - Maximum bandwidth 6 kHz

24.890 - 24.930 MHz - CW
24.920 - 24.925 MHz - Digital Modes
24.925 - 24.930 MHz - Packet
24.930 - 24.990 MHz - SSB and other wide band modes

10 Meter Band - Maximum band width 20 kHz

28.000 - 28.200 MHz - CW
28.070 - 28.120 MHz - Digital Modes
28.120 - 28.190 MHz - Packet

28.190 - 28.200 MHz - Beacons
28.200 - 29.300 MHz - SSB and other wide band modes
29.300 - 29.510 MHz - Satellite
29.510 - 29.700 MHz - SSB, FM and repeaters

160 Meters (1.8-2.0 MHz)
1.800 - 2.000 CW
1.800 - 1.810 Digital Modes
1.810 CW QRP
1.843-2.000 SSB, SSTV and other wideband modes
1.910 SSB QRP
1.995 - 2.000 Experimental
1.999 - 2.000 Beacons

80 Meters (3.5-4.0 MHz)
3.590 RTTY/Data DX
3.570-3.600 RTTY/Data
3.790-3.800 DX window
3.845 SSTV
3.885 AM calling frequency

40 Meters (7.0-7.3 MHz)
7.040 RTTY/Data DX
7.080-7.125 RTTY/Data
7.171 SSTV
7.290 AM calling frequency

30 Meters (10.1-10.15 MHz)
10.130-10.140 RTTY
10.140-10.150 Packet

20 Meters (14.0-14.35 MHz)
14.070-14.095 RTTY
14.095-14.0995 Packet
14.100 NCDXF Beacons
14.1005-14.112 Packet
14.230 SSTV
14.286 AM calling frequency

17 Meters (18.068-18.168 MHz)
18.100-18.105 RTTY
18.105-18.110 Packet

15 Meters (21.0-21.45 MHz)
21.070-21.110 RTTY/Data

21.340 SSTV

12 Meters (24.89-24.99 MHz)
24.920-24.925 RTTY
24.925-24.930 Packet

10 Meters (28-29.7 MHz)
28.000-28.070 CW
28.070-28.150 RTTY
28.150-28.190 CW
28.200-28.300 Beacons
28.300-29.300 Phone
28.680 SSTV
29.000-29.200 AM
29.300-29.510 Satellite Downlinks
29.520-29.590 Repeater Inputs
29.600 FM Simplex
29.610-29.700 Repeater Outputs

6 Meters (50-54 MHz)
50.0-50.1 CW, beacons
50.060-50.080 beacon subband
50.1-50.3 SSB, CW
50.10-50.125 DX window
50.125 SSB calling
50.3-50.6 All modes
50.6-50.8 Nonvoice communications
50.62 Digital (packet) calling
50.8-51.0 Radio remote control (20-kHz channels)
51.0-51.1 Pacific DX window
51.12-51.48 Repeater inputs (19 channels)
51.12-51.18 Digital repeater inputs
51.5-51.6 Simplex (six channels)
51.62-51.98 Repeater outputs (19 channels)
51.62-51.68 Digital repeater outputs
52.0-52.48 Repeater inputs (except as noted; 23 channels)
52.02, 52.04 FM simplex
52.2 TEST PAIR (input)
52.5-52.98 Repeater output (except as noted; 23 channels)
52.525 Primary FM simplex
52.54 Secondary FM simplex
52.7 TEST PAIR (output)
53.0-53.48 Repeater inputs (except as noted; 19 channels)
53.0 Remote base FM simplex
53.02 Simplex
53.1, 53.2, 53.3, 53.4 Radio remote control

53.5-53.98 Repeater outputs (except as noted; 19 channels)
53.5, 53.6, 53.7, 53.8 Radio remote control
53.52, 53.9 Simplex

2 Meters (144-148 MHz)

144.00-144.05 EME (CW)
144.05-144.10 General CW and weak signals
144.10-144.20 EME and weak-signal SSB
144.200 National calling frequency
144.200-144.275 General SSB operation
144.275-144.300 Propagation beacons
144.30-144.50 New OSCAR subband
144.50-144.60 Linear translator inputs
144.60-144.90 FM repeater inputs
144.90-145.10 Weak signal and FM simplex (145.01,03,05,07,09 are widely used for packet)
145.10-145.20 Linear translator outputs
145.20-145.50 FM repeater outputs
145.50-145.80 Miscellaneous and experimental modes
145.80-146.00 OSCAR subband
146.01-146.37 Repeater inputs
146.40-146.58 Simplex
146.52 National Simplex Calling Frequency
146.61-146.97 Repeater outputs
147.00-147.39 Repeater outputs
147.42-147.57 Simplex
147.60-147.99 Repeater inputs

1.25 Meters (222-225 MHz)

222.0-222.150 Weak-signal modes
222.0-222.025 EME
222.05-222.06 Propagation beacons
222.1 SSB & CW calling frequency
222.10-222.15 Weak-signal CW & SSB
222.15-222.25 Local coordinator's option; weak signal, ACSB, repeater inputs, control
222.25-223.38 FM repeater inputs only
223.40-223.52 FM simplex
223.52-223.64 Digital, packet
223.64-223.70 Links, control
223.71-223.85 Local coordinator's option; FM simplex, packet, repeater outputs
223.85-224.98 Repeater outputs only

70 Centimeters (420-450 MHz)

420.00-426.00 ATV repeater or simplex with 421.25 MHz video carrier control links and experimental
426.00-432.00 ATV simplex with 427.250-MHz video carrier frequency

432.00-432.07 EME (Earth-Moon-Earth)
432.07-432.10 Weak-signal CW
432.10 70-cm calling frequency
432.10-432.30 Mixed-mode and weak-signal work
432.30-432.40 Propagation beacons
432.40-433.00 Mixed-mode and weak-signal work
433.00-435.00 Auxiliary/repeater links
435.00-438.00 Satellite only (internationally)
438.00-444.00 ATV repeater input with 439.250-MHz video carrier frequency and repeater links
442.00-445.00 Repeater inputs and outputs (local option)
445.00-447.00 Shared by auxiliary and control links, repeaters and simplex (local option)
446.00 National simplex frequency
447.00-450.00 Repeater inputs and outputs (local option)

33 Centimeters (902-928 MHz)

902.0-903.0 Narrow-bandwidth, weak-signal communications
902.0-902.8 SSTV, FAX, ACSSB, experimental
902.1 Weak-signal calling frequency
902.8-903.0 Reserved for EME, CW expansion
903.1 Alternate calling frequency
903.0-906.0 Digital communications
906-909 FM repeater inputs
909-915 ATV
915-918 Digital communications
918-921 FM repeater outputs
921-927 ATV
927-928 FM simplex and links

23 Centimeters (1240-1300 MHz)

1240-1246 ATV #1
1246-1248 Narrow-bandwidth FM point-to-point links and digital, duplex with 1258-1260.
1248-1258 Digital Communications
1252-1258 ATV #2
1258-1260 Narrow-bandwidth FM point-to-point links digital, duplexed with 1246-1252
1260-1270 Satellite uplinks, reference WARC '79
1260-1270 Wide-bandwidth experimental, simplex ATV
1270-1276 Repeater inputs, FM and linear, paired with 1282-1288, 239 pairs every 25 kHz, e.g. 1270.025, .050, etc.
1271-1283 Non-coordinated test pair
1276-1282 ATV #3
1282-1288 Repeater outputs, paired with 1270-1276
1288-1294 Wide-bandwidth experimental, simplex ATV
1294-1295 Narrow-bandwidth FM simplex services, 25-kHz channels
1294.5 National FM simplex calling frequency

1295-1297 Narrow bandwidth weak-signal communications (no FM)
1295.0-1295.8 SSTV, FAX, ACSSB, experimental
1295.8-1296.0 Reserved for EME, CW expansion
1296.00-1296.05 EME-exclusive
1296.07-1296.08 CW beacons
1296.1 CW, SSB calling frequency
1296.4-1296.6 Crossband linear translator input
1296.6-1296.8 Crossband linear translator output
1296.8-1297.0 Experimental beacons (exclusive)
1297-1300 Digital Communications

2300-2310 and 2390-2450 MHz

2300.0-2303.0 High-rate data
2303.0-2303.5 Packet
2303.5-2303.8 TTY packet
2303.9-2303.9 Packet, TTY, CW, EME
2303.9-2304.1 CW, EME
2304.1 Calling frequency
2304.1-2304.2 CW, EME, SSB
2304.2-2304.3 SSB, SSTV, FAX, Packet AM, Amtor
2304.30-2304.32 Propagation beacon network
2304.32-2304.40 General propagation beacons
2304.4-2304.5 SSB, SSTV, ACSSB, FAX, Packet AM, Amtor experimental
2304.5-2304.7 Crossband linear translator input
2304.7-2304.9 Crossband linear translator output
2304.9-2305.0 Experimental beacons
2305.0-2305.2 FM simplex (25 kHz spacing)
2305.20 FM simplex calling frequency
2305.2-2306.0 FM simplex (25 kHz spacing)
2306.0-2309.0 FM Repeaters (25 kHz) input
2309.0-2310.0 Control and auxiliary links
2390.0-2396.0 Fast-scan TV
2396.0-2399.0 High-rate data
2399.0-2399.5 Packet
2399.5-2400.0 Control and auxiliary links
2400.0-2403.0 Satellite
2403.0-2408.0 Satellite high-rate data
2408.0-2410.0 Satellite
2410.0-2413.0 FM repeaters (25 kHz) output
2413.0-2418.0 High-rate data
2418.0-2430.0 Fast-scan TV
2430.0-2433.0 Satellite
2433.0-2438.0 Satellite high-rate data
2438.0-2450.0 WB FM, FSTV, FMTV, SS experimental

3300-3500 MHz
3456.3-3456.4 Propagation beacons

5650-5925 MHz
5760.3-5760.4 Propagation beacons

10.00-10.50 GHz
10.368 Narrow band calling frequency 10.3683-10.3684 Propagation beacons 10.3640 Calling frequency

Now that you have your license (you do, don't you?), and your equipment, you are ready to go live. Below is a suggested start.

1) Assuming you have the HT set up to the appropriate frequency, and offset, press the mic button on the HT and say, "KK4HWX listening." Replace the KK4HWX with your own call sign, the one assigned to you by the FCC (it's the law). If no one responds to your call, you may wish to try again. Hopefully someone will respond to your call.

2) Once you get a response, it will be in the form of something like, "KK4HWX this is ??1??? in Eastport returning. My name is Florence. Back to you. ??1???" then a tone. Let us examine the response more closely. She first acknowledged your call sign (KK4HWX), then identified hers (??1???). From the 1 in her call sign, you know that she first got her license in Region 1, meaning she got it while a resident of CT, ME, MA, NH, RI, or VT. She then told you where she's transmitting from (Eastport). The term "returning" means that she is returning your call. Her name is Florence. The phrase, "Back to you" indicates that she is turning over the conversation to you. She then repeats her call sign. The tone indicates to you that it is okay to proceed with your response. BTW if she had used the term "Over" instead of "Back to you," it would mean the same thing, just fewer words.

3) At this point, press the mic button and continue with the conversation. You should restate your call sign often during the conversation (perhaps every 10 minutes or less and whenever you begin transmitting). Don't forget to say, "Over" or "Back to you" whenever you are giving Florence control of the conversation again.

4) When you are ready to stop the conversation, you should say goodbye or use the phrase "73", meaning "best wishes." Your conversation would end something like, "??1??? 73, this is KK4HWX clear and monitoring." The "clear and monitoring" indicates that you are going to continue to monitor the frequency. If you are not going to continue monitoring, you may wish to end the conversation with Florence with, "clear and QRT" instead. The QRT means that you are stopping transmissions.

Call Sign Phonics

Because of different accents of various people, sometimes it is difficult to understand call sign letters when spoken. For this reason, most ham operators verbalize their call sign using phonics. Below is a table listing the accepted phonics for letters and numbers.

A = ALFA	S = SIERRA
B = BRAVO	T = TANGO
C = CHARLIE	U = UNIFORM
D = DELTA	V = VICTOR
E = ECHO	W = WHISKEY
F = FOXTROT	X = X-RAY
G = GOLF	Y = YANKEE
H = HOTEL	Z = ZULU (ZED)
I = INDIA	1 = ONE
J = JULIETT	2 = TWO
K = KILO	3 = THREE (TREE)
L = LIMA	4 = FOUR
M = MIKE	5 = FIVE (FIFE)
N = NOVEMBER	6 = SIX
O = OSCAR	7 = SEVEN
P = PAPA (PA-PA')	8 = EIGHT
Q = QUEBEC (KAY-BEK')	9 = NINE (NINER)
R = ROMEO	0 = ZERO

The words in parentheses are the pronunciation or the alternate pronunciations for the words or numbers, but you will hear both used. With the letter Z, (ZED) is by far the most commonly used. With the number 9, NINER is the most common and easiest to understand ON THE AIR.

If you wish to use Morse code (CW) instead of voice communication, the "conversation" would follow the same steps, with a few modifications. To type out each word would require a lot of typing and translating. If you are like this author, more means more, i.e., more typing means more typos are likely. To help with this situation, CW enthusiasts have developed a language all their own – they use abbreviations for common phrases. Below is a chart showing some of these abbreviations.

Abbreviation	Use
AR	Over
de	From or "this is"
ES	And
GM	Good Morning
K	Go
KN	Go only
NM	Name
QTH	Location
RPT	Report

R	Roger
SK	Clear
tnx	Thanks
UR	Your, you are
73	Best Wishes

Morse Code and Amateur Radio

If you wish to use CW, but are concerned about accuracy, you might consider purchasing a Morse code translator. This is an electronic device that you place in front of your speakers. It takes the CW sounds and translates them into English and displays the transmission on an LCD display. For the reverse, you can pick up a CW keyboard. With the keyboard, you type in your message and it converts the text to Morse code. The translator does not need to be attached to your ham equipment, whereas the keyboard would.

For your convenience, below is a table showing the Morse code signals and their meaning.

Character	Code
A	· —
B	— · · ·
C	— · — ·
D	— · ·
E	·
F	· · — ·
G	— — ·
H	· · · ·
I	· ·
J	· — — —
K	— · —
L	· — · ·
M	— —
N	— ·
O	— — —
P	· — — ·
Q	— — · —
R	· — ·
S	· · ·
T	—
U	· · —
V	· · · —
W	· — —
X	— · · —
Y	— · — —
Z	— — · ·

0	— — — — —
1	• — — — —
2	• • — — —
3	• • • — —
4	• • • • —
5	• • • • •
6	— • • • •
7	— — • • •
8	— — — • •
9	— — — — •
Ampersand [&], Wait	• — • • •
Apostrophe [']	• — — — — •
At sign [@]	• — — • — •
Colon [:]	— — — • • •
Comma [,]	— — • • — —
Dollar sign [$]	• • • — • • —
Double dash [=]	— • • • —
Exclamation mark [!]	— • — • — —
Hyphen, Minus [-]	— • • • • —
Parenthesis closed [)]	— • — — • —
Parenthesis open [(]	— • — — •
Period [.]	• — • — • —
Plus [+]	• — • — •
Question mark [?]	• • — — • •
Quotation mark ["]	• — • • — •
Semicolon [;]	— • — • — •
Slash [/], Fraction bar	— • • — •
Underscore [_]	• • — — • —

An advantage of using Morse Code is that when broadcasting CW, you are using reduced power, thereby saving your battery. Your battery is used only while actually transmitting or receiving.

International Call Sign Prefixes

As was stated earlier, all ham radio call signs begin with letters (or numbers) taken from blocks assigned to each country of the world by the *ITU - International Telecommunications Union,* a body controlled by the United Nations. The following chart indicates which call sign series are allocated to which countries.

Call Sign Series	Allocated to
AAA-ALZ	**United States of America**
AMA-AOZ	Spain
APA-ASZ	Pakistan (Islamic Republic of)
ATA-AWZ	India (Republic of)

AXA-AXZ	Australia
AYA-AZZ	Argentine Republic
A2A-A2Z	Botswana (Republic of)
A3A-A3Z	Tonga (Kingdom of)
A4A-A4Z	Oman (Sultanate of)
A5A-A5Z	Bhutan (Kingdom of)
A6A-A6Z	United Arab Emirates
A7A-A7Z	Qatar (State of)
A8A-A8Z	Liberia (Republic of)
A9A-A9Z	Bahrain (State of)
BAA-BZZ	China (People's Republic of)
CAA-CEZ	Chile
CFA-CKZ	Canada
CLA-CMZ	Cuba
CNA-CNZ	Morocco (Kingdom of)
COA-COZ	Cuba
CPA-CPZ	Bolivia (Republic of)
CQA-CUZ	Portugal
CVA-CXZ	Uruguay (Eastern Republic of)
CYA-CZZ	Canada
C2A-C2Z	Nauru (Republic of)
C3A-C3Z	Andorra (Principality of)
C4A-C4Z	Cyprus (Republic of)
C5A-C5Z	Gambia (Republic of the)
C6A-C6Z	Bahamas (Commonwealth of the)
C7A-C7Z	World Meteorological Organization
C8A-C9Z	Mozambique (Republic of)
DAA-DRZ	Germany (Federal Republic of)
DSA-DTZ	Korea (Republic of)
DUA-DZZ	Philippines (Republic of the)
D2A-D3Z	Angola (Republic of)
D4A-D4Z	Cape Verde (Republic of)
D5A-D5Z	Liberia (Republic of)
D6A-D6Z	Comoros (Islamic Federal Republic of the)
D7A-D9Z	Korea (Republic of)
EAA-EHZ	Spain
EIA-EJZ	Ireland
EKA-EKZ	Armenia (Republic of)
ELA-ELZ	Liberia (Republic of)
EMA-EOZ	Ukraine
EPA-EQZ	Iran (Islamic Republic of)
ERA-ERZ	Moldova (Republic of)
ESA-ESZ	Estonia (Republic of)
ETA-ETZ	Ethiopia (Federal Democratic Republic of)
EUA-EWZ	Belarus (Republic of)

EXA-EXZ	Kyrgyz Republic
EYA-EYZ	Tajikistan (Republic of)
EZA-EZZ	Turkmenistan
E2A-E2Z	Thailand
E3A-E3Z	Eritrea
E4A-E4Z	Palestinian Authority
E5A-E5Z	New Zealand - Cook Islands (WRC-07)
E7A-E7Z	Bosnia and Herzegovina (Republic of) (WRC-07)
FAA-FZZ	France
GAA-GZZ	United Kingdom of Great Britain and Northern Ireland
HAA-HAZ	Hungary (Republic of)
HBA-HBZ	Switzerland (Confederation of)
HCA-HDZ	Ecuador
HEA-HEZ	Switzerland (Confederation of)
HFA-HFZ	Poland (Republic of)
HGA-HGZ	Hungary (Republic of)
HHA-HHZ	Haiti (Republic of)
HIA-HIZ	Dominican Republic
HJA-HKZ	Colombia (Republic of)
HLA-HLZ	Korea (Republic of)
HMA-HMZ	Democratic People's Republic of Korea
HNA-HNZ	Iraq (Republic of)
HOA-HPZ	Panama (Republic of)
HQA-HRZ	Honduras (Republic of)
HSA-HSZ	Thailand
HTA-HTZ	Nicaragua
HUA-HUZ	El Salvador (Republic of)
HVA-HVZ	Vatican City State
HWA-HYZ	France
HZA-HZZ	Saudi Arabia (Kingdom of)
H2A-H2Z	Cyprus (Republic of)
H3A-H3Z	Panama (Republic of)
H4A-H4Z	Solomon Islands
H6A-H7Z	Nicaragua
H8A-H9Z	Panama (Republic of)
IAA-IZZ	Italy
JAA-JSZ	Japan
JTA-JVZ	Mongolia
JWA-JXZ	Norway
JYA-JYZ	Jordan (Hashemite Kingdom of)
JZA-JZZ	Indonesia (Republic of)
J2A-J2Z	Djibouti (Republic of)
J3A-J3Z	Grenada
J4A-J4Z	Greece
J5A-J5Z	Guinea-Bissau (Republic of)

J6A-J6Z	Saint Lucia
J7A-J7Z	Dominica (Commonwealth of)
J8A-J8Z	Saint Vincent and the Grenadines
KAA-KZZ	**United States of America**
LAA-LNZ	Norway
LOA-LWZ	Argentine Republic
LXA-LXZ	Luxembourg
LYA-LYZ	Lithuania (Republic of)
LZA-LZZ	Bulgaria (Republic of)
L2A-L9Z	Argentine Republic
MAA-MZZ	United Kingdom of Great Britain and Northern Ireland
NAA-NZZ	**United States of America**
OAA-OCZ	Peru
ODA-ODZ	Lebanon
OEA-OEZ	Austria
OFA-OJZ	Finland
OKA-OLZ	Czech Republic
OMA-OMZ	Slovak Republic
ONA-OTZ	Belgium
OUA-OZZ	Denmark
PAA-PIZ	Netherlands (Kingdom of the)
PJA-PJZ	Netherlands (Kingdom of the) - Netherlands Antilles
PKA-POZ	Indonesia (Republic of)
PPA-PYZ	Brazil (Federative Republic of)
PZA-PZZ	Suriname (Republic of)
P2A-P2Z	Papua New Guinea
P3A-P3Z	Cyprus (Republic of)
P4A-P4Z	Netherlands (Kingdom of the) - Aruba
P5A-P9Z	Democratic People's Republic of Korea
RAA-RZZ	Russian Federation
SAA-SMZ	Sweden
SNA-SRZ	Poland (Republic of)
SSA-SSM	Egypt (Arab Republic of)
SSN-STZ	Sudan (Republic of the)
SUA-SUZ	Egypt (Arab Republic of)
SVA-SZZ	Greece
S2A-S3Z	Bangladesh (People's Republic of)
S5A-S5Z	Slovenia (Republic of)
S6A-S6Z	Singapore (Republic of)
S7A-S7Z	Seychelles (Republic of)
S8A-S8Z	South Africa (Republic of)
S9A-S9Z	Sao Tome and Principe (Democratic Republic of)
TAA-TCZ	Turkey
TDA-TDZ	Guatemala (Republic of)
TEA-TEZ	Costa Rica

TFA-TFZ	Iceland
TGA-TGZ	Guatemala (Republic of)
THA-THZ	France
TIA-TIZ	Costa Rica
TJA-TJZ	Cameroon (Republic of)
TKA-TKZ	France
TLA-TLZ	Central African Republic
TMA-TMZ	France
TNA-TNZ	Congo (Republic of the)
TOA-TQZ	France
TRA-TRZ	Gabonese Republic
TSA-TSZ	Tunisia
TTA-TTZ	Chad (Republic of)
TUA-TUZ	Côte d'Ivoire (Republic of)
TVA-TXZ	France
TYA-TYZ	Benin (Republic of)
TZA-TZZ	Mali (Republic of)
T2A-T2Z	Tuvalu
T3A-T3Z	Kiribati (Republic of)
T4A-T4Z	Cuba
T5A-T5Z	Somali Democratic Republic
T6A-T6Z	Afghanistan (Islamic State of)
T7A-T7Z	San Marino (Republic of)
T8A-T8Z	Palau (Republic of)
UAA-UIZ	Russian Federation
UJA-UMZ	Uzbekistan (Republic of)
UNA-UQZ	Kazakhstan (Republic of)
URA-UZZ	Ukraine
VAA-VGZ	Canada
VHA-VNZ	Australia
VOA-VOZ	Canada
VPA-VQZ	United Kingdom of Great Britain and Northern Ireland
VRA-VRZ	China (People's Republic of) - Hong Kong
VSA-VSZ	United Kingdom of Great Britain and Northern Ireland
VTA-VWZ	India (Republic of)
VXA-VYZ	Canada
VZA-VZZ	Australia
V2A-V2Z	Antigua and Barbuda
V3A-V3Z	Belize
V4A-V4Z	Saint Kitts and Nevis
V5A-V5Z	Namibia (Republic of)
V6A-V6Z	Micronesia (Federated States of)
V7A-V7Z	Marshall Islands (Republic of the)
V8A-V8Z	Brunei Darussalam
WAA-WZZ	**United States of America**

XAA-XIZ	Mexico
XJA-XOZ	Canada
XPA-XPZ	Denmark
XQA-XRZ	Chile
XSA-XSZ	China (People's Republic of)
XTA-XTZ	Burkina Faso
XUA-XUZ	Cambodia (Kingdom of)
XVA-XVZ	Viet Nam (Socialist Republic of)
XWA-XWZ	Lao People's Democratic Republic
XXA-XXZ	China (People's Republic of) - Macao (WRC-07)
XYA-XZZ	Myanmar (Union of)
YAA-YAZ	Afghanistan (Islamic State of)
YBA-YHZ	Indonesia (Republic of)
YIA-YIZ	Iraq (Republic of)
YJA-YJZ	Vanuatu (Republic of)
YKA-YKZ	Syrian Arab Republic
YLA-YLZ	Latvia (Republic of)
YMA-YMZ	Turkey
YNA-YNZ	Nicaragua
YOA-YRZ	Romania
YSA-YSZ	El Salvador (Republic of)
YTA-YUZ	Serbia (Republic of) (WRC-07)
YVA-YYZ	Venezuela (Republic of)
Y2A-Y9Z	Germany (Federal Republic of)
ZAA-ZAZ	Albania (Republic of)
ZBA-ZJZ	United Kingdom of Great Britain and Northern Ireland
ZKA-ZMZ	New Zealand
ZNA-ZOZ	United Kingdom of Great Britain and Northern Ireland
ZPA-ZPZ	Paraguay (Republic of)
ZQA-ZQZ	United Kingdom of Great Britain and Northern Ireland
ZRA-ZUZ	South Africa (Republic of)
ZVA-ZZZ	Brazil (Federative Republic of)
Z2A-Z2Z	Zimbabwe (Republic of)
Z3A-Z3Z	The Former Yugoslav Republic of Macedonia
2AA-2ZZ	United Kingdom of Great Britain and Northern Ireland
3AA-3AZ	Monaco (Principality of)
3BA-3BZ	Mauritius (Republic of)
3CA-3CZ	Equatorial Guinea (Republic of)
3DA-3DM	Swaziland (Kingdom of)
3DN-3DZ	Fiji (Republic of)
3EA-3FZ	Panama (Republic of)
3GA-3GZ	Chile
3HA-3UZ	China (People's Republic of)
3VA-3VZ	Tunisia
3WA-3WZ	Viet Nam (Socialist Republic of)

3XA-3XZ	Guinea (Republic of)
3YA-3YZ	Norway
3ZA-3ZZ	Poland (Republic of)
4AA-4CZ	Mexico
4DA-4IZ	Philippines (Republic of the)
4JA-4KZ	Azerbaijani Republic
4LA-4LZ	Georgia (Republic of)
4MA-4MZ	Venezuela (Republic of)
4OA-4OZ	Montenegro (Republic of) (WRC-07)
4PA-4SZ	Sri Lanka (Democratic Socialist Republic of)
4TA-4TZ	Peru
4UA-4UZ	United Nations
4VA-4VZ	Haiti (Republic of)
4WA-4WZ	Democratic Republic of Timor-Leste (WRC-03)
4XA-4XZ	Israel (State of)
4YA-4YZ	International Civil Aviation Organization
4ZA-4ZZ	Israel (State of)
5AA-5AZ	Libya (Socialist People's Libyan Arab Jamahiriya)
5BA-5BZ	Cyprus (Republic of)
5CA-5GZ	Morocco (Kingdom of)
5HA-5IZ	Tanzania (United Republic of)
5JA-5KZ	Colombia (Republic of)
5LA-5MZ	Liberia (Republic of)
5NA-5OZ	Nigeria (Federal Republic of)
5PA-5QZ	Denmark
5RA-5SZ	Madagascar (Republic of)
5TA-5TZ	Mauritania (Islamic Republic of)
5UA-5UZ	Niger (Republic of the)
5VA-5VZ	Togolese Republic
5WA-5WZ	Samoa (Independent State of)
5XA-5XZ	Uganda (Republic of)
5YA-5ZZ	Kenya (Republic of)
6AA-6BZ	Egypt (Arab Republic of)
6CA-6CZ	Syrian Arab Republic
6DA-6JZ	Mexico
6KA-6NZ	Korea (Republic of)
6OA-6OZ	Somali Democratic Republic
6PA-6SZ	Pakistan (Islamic Republic of)
6TA-6UZ	Sudan (Republic of the)
6VA-6WZ	Senegal (Republic of)
6XA-6XZ	Madagascar (Republic of)
6YA-6YZ	Jamaica
6ZA-6ZZ	Liberia (Republic of)
7AA-7IZ	Indonesia (Republic of)
7JA-7NZ	Japan

7OA-7OZ	Yemen (Republic of)
7PA-7PZ	Lesotho (Kingdom of)
7QA-7QZ	Malawi
7RA-7RZ	Algeria (People's Democratic Republic of)
7SA-7SZ	Sweden
7TA-7YZ	Algeria (People's Democratic Republic of)
7ZA-7ZZ	Saudi Arabia (Kingdom of)
8AA-8IZ	Indonesia (Republic of)
8JA-8NZ	Japan
8OA-8OZ	Botswana (Republic of)
8PA-8PZ	Barbados
8QA-8QZ	Maldives (Republic of)
8RA-8RZ	Guyana
8SA-8SZ	Sweden
8TA-8YZ	India (Republic of)
8ZA-8ZZ	Saudi Arabia (Kingdom of)
9AA-9AZ	Croatia (Republic of)
9BA-9DZ	Iran (Islamic Republic of)
9EA-9FZ	Ethiopia (Federal Democratic Republic of)
9GA-9GZ	Ghana
9HA-9HZ	Malta
9IA-9JZ	Zambia (Republic of)
9KA-9KZ	Kuwait (State of)
9LA-9LZ	Sierra Leone
9MA-9MZ	Malaysia
9NA-9NZ	Nepal
9OA-9TZ	Democratic Republic of the Congo
9UA-9UZ	Burundi (Republic of)
9VA-9VZ	Singapore (Republic of)
9WA-9WZ	Malaysia
9XA-9XZ	Rwandese Republic
9YA-9ZZ	Trinidad and Tobago

Third-Party Communications and Amateur Radio

If all of this information about ham radios is somewhat intimidating, do not despair. "You" can still use ham radios for communications without being a licensed operator. Yes, you do have to have a ham license in order to legally transmit by ham equipment (or be under the direct supervision of someone else who is licensed), but there is an alternative – third-party communication.

Third-party communications occur when a licensed operator sends either written or verbal messages on behalf of unlicensed persons or organizations. There are two "controls" on third-party communication.

First, the communication must be noncommercial and of a personal nature. Asking a ham operator to contact another ham operator located in an area just hit by tornados and, because of being without power, phones do not work in Grandma Sally's city so you can check up on her, is okay. Asking a ham to send a message out that you have an old Chevy for sale would not be okay.

Second, the message must be going to a permitted area. Transmitting from a US location to another US location is okay, but transmitting from the US to another country may not. Because third-party communications bypass a country's normal telephone and postal systems, many foreign governments forbid such communications. In order to transmit from one country to another, the other country must have signed a third-party agreement with the US. What follows is a list of those countries that do have third-party a communications agreement with the US.

V2	Antigua / Barbuda
LU	Argentina
VK	Australia
V3	Belize
CP	Bolivia
T9	Bosnia-Herzegovina
PY	Brazil
VE	Canada
CE	Chile
HK	Colombia
D6	Comoros (Federal Islamic Republic of)
TI	Costa Rica
CO	Cuba
HI	Dominican Republic
J7	Dominica
HC	Ecuador
YS	El Salvador
C5	Gambia, The
9G	Ghana
J3	Grenada
TG	Guatemala
8R	Guyana
HH	Haiti
HR	Honduras
4X	Israel
6Y	Jamaica
JY	Jordan
EL	Liberia
V7	Marshall Islands
XE	Mexico
V6	Micronesia, Federated States of

YN	Nicaragua
HP	Panama
ZP	Paraguay
OA	Peru
DU	Philippines
VR6	Pitcairn Island
V4	St. Christopher / Nevis
J6	St. Lucia
J8	St. Vincent and the Grenadines
9L	Sierra Leone
ZS	South Africa
3DA	Swaziland
9Y	Trinidad / Tobago
TA	Turkey
GB	United Kingdom
CX	Uruguay
YV	Venezuela
4U1ITUITU	Geneva
4U1VICVIC	Vienna

Remember, before TSHTF, keep your pantry well stocked, your powder dry, and your batteries fully charged. 73

APPENDIX A

American Radio Relay League

Affiliated Amateur Radio Clubs in

Florida

ARRL Affiliated Club	Desoto Amateur Radio Club, Inc.
City:	Arcadia, FL
Call Sign:	W4MIN
Section:	WCF
Links:	desotoarc.org/

ARRL Affiliated Club	Florida Keys Amateur Radio Club
City:	Big Pine Key, FL
Call Sign:	KB4GCZ
Section:	SFL
Links:	www.qsl.net/kb4gcz/

ARRL Affiliated Club	South Florida DX Association
City:	Boca Raton, FL
Call Sign:	K4FK
Section:	SFL
Links:	www.qsl.net/k4fk/

ARRL Affiliated Club	Florida Atlantic University Amateur Radio Club
City:	Boca Raton, FL
Call Sign:	K4FAU
Section:	SFL
Links:	www.k4fau.org

ARRL Affiliated Club	Boca Raton Amateur Radio Assoc.
City:	Boca Raton, FL
Call Sign:	N4BRF
Section:	SFL
Links:	www.brara.org

ARRL Affiliated Club	West Central Florida Group, Inc.
City:	Bradenton, FL
Call Sign:	NI4CE
Section:	WCF
Links:	www.ni4ce.org

ARRL Affiliated Club	Bradenton Amateur Radio Club
City:	Bradenton, FL
Call Sign:	K4BRC
Section:	WCF
Links:	www.qsl.net/k4brc/

ARRL Affiliated Club	Sheriff's Tactical Amateur Radio Club
City:	Brandon, FL
Call Sign:	W4HSO
Section:	WCF
Links:	www.w4hso-starc.org

ARRL Affiliated Club	Dixie Amateur Radio Klub
City:	Bronson, FL
Call Sign:	W4DAK
Section:	NFL
Links:	darklub.com

ARRL Affiliated Club	Hernando County Amateur Radio Association
City:	Brooksville, FL
Call Sign:	K4BKV
Section:	NFL
Links:	www.hcara.org

ARRL Affiliated Club	Clearwater Amateur Radio Society, Inc.
City:	Clearwater, FL
Call Sign:	K4JMH
Section:	WCF
Links:	www.carshamradio.org

ARRL Affiliated Club	Big Lake Amateur Radio Club
City:	Clewiston, FL
Call Sign:	KI4AYW
Section:	SFL

ARRL Affiliated Club	Cocoa Amateur Radio Society
City:	Cocoa, FL
Call Sign:	KI4URF
Section:	SFL
Links:	www.cocoaars.org

ARRL Affiliated Club	Indian River Amateur Radio Club
City:	Cocoa, FL
Call Sign:	W4NLX
Section:	SFL
Links:	irarc.ham-radio-op.net

ARRL Affiliated Club	Wynmoor Radio Club
City:	Coconut Creek, FL
Call Sign:	KW4ARC
Section:	SFL

ARRL Affiliated Club	Traveler's Rest Amateur Radio Club
City:	Dade City, FL
Call Sign:	K4TRR
Section:	WCF

ARRL Affiliated Club	Four Corners Amateur Radio Club
City:	Davenport, FL
Call Sign:	KK4HCV
Section:	WCF
Links:	www.nadxa.org

ARRL Affiliated Club	North Dade Repeater Assn.
City:	Davie, FL
Call Sign:	KE4YVQ
Section:	SFL

ARRL Affiliated Club	Daytona Beach Amateur Radio Association
City:	Daytona Beach, FL
Call Sign:	K4BV
Section:	NFL
Links:	www.dbara.org

ARRL Affiliated Club	Daytona Beach Cert Amateur Radio Club
City:	Daytona Beach, FL
Call Sign:	N4DAB
Section:	NFL
Links:	www.dbcertarc.org/

ARRL Affiliated Club	West Volusia Amateur Radio Sociey, Inc.
City:	Deland, FL
Call Sign:	WV4ARS
Section:	NFL
Links:	bellsouthpwp2.net/n/4/n4gmu/

ARRL Affiliated Club	Lakeland Amateur Radio Club Inc.
City:	Eaton Park, FL
Call Sign:	K4LKL
Section:	WCF
Links:	www.Lakelandarc.org

ARRL Affiliated Club	Englewood Amateur Radio Society
City:	Englewood, FL
Call Sign:	N4EAR
Section:	WCF
Links:	www.earsradioclub.org

ARRL Affiliated Club	Broward Amateur Radio Club
City:	Fort Lauderdale, FL
Call Sign:	W4AB
Section:	SFL
Links:	www.browardarc.org, www.eagle3.net/barc

ARRL Affiliated Club	Palmetto Amateur Radio Club, Inc.
City:	Fort Lauderdale, FL
Call Sign:	K4PAL
Section:	SFL
Links:	www.palmettoarc.org/, Palmetto Amateur Radio Club
ARRL Affiliated Club	Gulf Coast Area Repeater Club
City:	Fort Myers, FL
Section:	SFL
ARRL Affiliated Club	Fort Myers Amateur Radio Club
City:	Fort Myers, FL
Call Sign:	W4LX
Section:	SFL
Links:	www.fmarc.net
ARRL Affiliated Club	Fort Pierce Radio Club
City:	Fort Pierce, FL
Call Sign:	W4AKH
Section:	SFL
Links:	www.qsl.net/w4akh
ARRL Affiliated Club	Playground Amateur Radio Club
City:	Fort Walton Beach, FL
Call Sign:	W4ZBB
Section:	NFL
Links:	www.w4zbb.org
ARRL Affiliated Club	Walton County Amateur Radio Club
City:	Freeport, FL
Call Sign:	WF4X
Section:	NFL
Links:	www.wcflarc.com
ARRL Affiliated Club	North Florida DX Assn.
City:	Gainesville, FL
Call Sign:	W4ZR
Section:	NFL
Links:	www.nfdxa.com
ARRL Affiliated Club	Santa Fe College Amateur Radio Society
City:	Gainesville, FL
Call Sign:	K4EAC
Section:	NFL

ARRL Affiliated Club	Gator Amateur Radio Club at The University of Florida
City:	Gainesville, FL
Call Sign:	W4DFU
Section:	NFL
Links:	www.gatorradio.org

ARRL Affiliated Club	Gainesville Amateur Radio Society
City:	Gainesville, FL
Call Sign:	K4GNV
Section:	NFL
Links:	www.gars.net

ARRL Affiliated Club	Central Florida DX Assn.
City:	Geneva, FL
Call Sign:	N4SA
Section:	NFL
Links:	www.freewebs.com/cfdxa

ARRL Special Service Club	Lake Monroe Amateur Radio Society Inc.
City:	Goldenrod, FL
Call Sign:	N4EH
Section:	NFL
Links:	www.lmars.org

ARRL Affiliated Club	Orange Park Amateur Radio Club
City:	Green Cove Springs, FL
Call Sign:	K4BT
Section:	NFL
Links:	www.oparc.weebly.com

ARRL Affiliated Club	Honeywell Emergency Amateur Radio Team
City:	Gulfport, FL
Call Sign:	WD0DIA
Section:	WCF
Links:	qsl.net/heart/

ARRL Affiliated Club	Nassau County Amateur Radio Society NCARS
City:	Hillard, FL
Call Sign:	W4NAS
Section:	NFL

ARRL Affiliated Club	Hollywood Amateur Radio Club
City:	Hollywood, FL
Call Sign:	WB4TON
Section:	SFL

ARRL Affiliated Club	C3I Amateur Radio Group
City:	Hollywood, FL
Call Sign:	AC4XQ
Section:	SFL
Links:	www.ac4xq.net

ARRL Affiliated Club	North Okaloosa Amateur Radio Club
City:	Holt, FL
Call Sign:	W4AAZ
Section:	NFL
Links:	www.noarc.net

ARRL Affiliated Club	Centro La Salle Radio Club
City:	Homestead, FL
Call Sign:	KJ4GTA
Section:	SFL

ARRL Affiliated Club	Everglades Amateur Radio Club
City:	Homestead, FL
Call Sign:	W4SVI
Section:	SFL

ARRL Affiliated Club	East Coast Amateur Radio Service
City:	Hudson, FL
Section:	ME
Links:	www.ecars7255.com

ARRL Affiliated Club	Putnam County Amateur Radio Club
City:	Interlachen, FL
Call Sign:	W4SA
Section:	NFL

ARRL Affiliated Club	North Florida Amateur Radio Society
City:	Jacksonville, FL
Call Sign:	W4IZ
Section:	NFL
Links:	www.nofars.net

ARRL Affiliated Club	Beaches Amateur Radio Society
City:	Jacksonville, FL
Call Sign:	KB4ARS
Section:	NFL
Links:	www.kb4ars.net

ARRL Affiliated Club	North Florida Amateur Radio Society
City:	Jacksonville, FL
Call Sign:	W4IZ
Section:	NFL
Links:	www.nofars.net

ARRL Special Service Club	Jupiter Tequesta Repeater Group Inc.
City:	Jupiter, FL
Call Sign:	W4JUP
Section:	SFL
Links:	JTRG

ARRL Affiliated Club	Lighthouse Amateur Radio Alliance
City:	Jupiter, FL
Call Sign:	K4LRA
Section:	SFL
Links:	www.k4lra.org

ARRL Affiliated Club	Key West Amateur Radio Club Inc.
City:	Key West, FL
Call Sign:	W4LLO
Section:	SFL

ARRL Affiliated Club	Columbia Amateur Radio Society
City:	Lake City, FL
Call Sign:	NF4CQ
Section:	NFL
Links:	nf4cq.com

ARRL Affiliated Club	Lake Wales Repeater Assoc.
City:	Lake Wales, FL
Call Sign:	K4LKW
Section:	WCF
Links:	www.lwra.us

ARRL Affiliated Club	Thunder Bay Amateur Radio Association
City:	Largo, FL
Section:	WCF
Links:	www.freeradiobook.org

ARRL Affiliated Club	Lake Amateur Radio Association, Inc.
City:	Leesburg, FL
Call Sign:	K4FC
Section:	NFL
Links:	www.k4fc.org

ARRL Affiliated Club	Lehigh PSK31 Club
City:	Lehigh Acres, FL
Call Sign:	W2UXL
Section:	SFL
Links:	lehigh_psk31_club.home.att.net

ARRL Affiliated Club	K2UGH Kilowatt Club
City:	Lehigh Acres, FL
Call Sign:	K2UGH
Section:	SFL

ARRL Affiliated Club	Palm Beach Amateur Radio Council
City:	Loxahatchee, FL
Call Sign:	W4SS
Section:	SFL
Links:	PBARC

ARRL Special Service Club	Palms West Amateur Radio Club, Inc.
City:	Loxahatchee, FL
Call Sign:	K4EEX
Section:	SFL
Links:	www.palmswestarc.org

ARRL Affiliated Club	Palm Beach County ARES, Inc.
City:	Loxahatchee, FL
Call Sign:	W4PBC
Section:	SFL
Links:	www.pbdares.org

ARRL Affiliated Club	Major EH Armstrong Memorial Radio Club
City:	Loxahatchee, FL
Call Sign:	W2XMN
Section:	SFL

ARRL Affiliated Club	Chipola Amateur Radio Club
City:	Marianna, FL
Call Sign:	W4BKD
Section:	NFL
Links:	www.chipolaarc.org

ARRL Affiliated Club	Platinum Coast Amateur Radio Society
City:	Melbourne, FL
Call Sign:	W4MLB
Section:	SFL
Links:	www.pcars.org

ARRL Affiliated Club	Florida Weak Signal Society
City:	Merritt Island, FL
Section:	SFL
Links:	www.flwss.net

ARRL Affiliated Club	America Radio Club, Inc.
City:	Miami, FL
Call Sign:	WD4ARC
Section:	SFL
Links:	www.qsl.net/americaradioclub

ARRL Affiliated Club	Dade Radio Club of Miami Inc.
City:	Miami, FL
Call Sign:	W4NVU
Section:	SFL
Links:	w4nvu.org, www.daderadioclub.org

ARRL Affiliated Club	Milton Amateur Radio Club
City:	Milton, FL
Call Sign:	W4VIY
Section:	NFL
Links:	www.MiltonARC.org

ARRL Affiliated Club	Brevard Amateur Radio Society
City:	Mims, FL
Section:	SFL
Links:	www.brevardars.org

ARRL Affiliated Club	Florida Contest Group
City:	Myakka City, FL
Call Sign:	K4FCG
Section:	WCF
Links:	www.floridacontestgroup.org/

ARRL Affiliated Club	Amateur Radio Association of Southwest Florida, Inc.
City:	Naples, FL
Call Sign:	WB2QLP
Links:	www.araswf.org

ARRL Affiliated Club	Navarre Certified Amateur Radio Club
City:	Navarre, FL
Call Sign:	KC4ERT
Section:	NFL
Links:	navarrecert.org/commo/joomla, navarrecert.org/commo

ARRL Affiliated Club	Suncoast Amateur Radio Club
City:	New Port Richey, FL
Call Sign:	WA4T
Section:	WCF
Links:	www.sarcfl.com

ARRL Affiliated Club	Gulf Coast Amateur Radio Club
City:	New Port Richey, FL
Call Sign:	WA4GDN
Section:	WCF
Links:	www.gulfcoastarc.org

ARRL Affiliated Club	Timco Amateur Radio Club
City:	Newberry, FL
Section:	NFL

ARRL Special Service Club	West Palm Beach Amateur Radio Club, Inc.
City:	North Palm Beach, FL
Call Sign:	W4HAW
Section:	SFL
Links:	www.wpbarc.org, www.wpbarc.com

ARRL Affiliated Club	North Port Amateur Radio Club
City:	North Port, FL
Call Sign:	W4NPT
Section:	WCF
Links:	www.w4npt.org, www.qsl.net/k4npt/, www.k4npt.com/nparc, www.w4npt.org/

ARRL Affiliated Club	Central Florida D-Star Group
City:	Ocala, FL
Section:	NFL
Links:	www.cfldsg.org/

ARRL Affiliated Club	Friendship Amateur Radio Club
City:	Ocala, FL
Section:	NFL

ARRL Affiliated Club	Okeechobee Amateur Radio Club, Inc.
City:	Okeechobee, FL
Call Sign:	K4OKE
Section:	SFL
Links:	www.k4oke.com

ARRL Affiliated Club	Manatee Amateur Radio Club
City:	Oneco, FL
Call Sign:	K4GG
Section:	WCF
Links:	www.manatee-arc.org/

ARRL Special Service Club	Disney Emergency Amateur Radio Service
City:	Orlando, FL
Call Sign:	WD4WDW
Section:	NFL
Links:	www.WD4WDW.org

ARRL Affiliated Club	Orlando Amateur Radio Club
City:	Orlando, FL
Call Sign:	W4PLB
Section:	NFL
Links:	www.oarc.org

ARRL Affiliated Club	Lockheed Martin Amateur Radio Assoc.
City:	Orlando, FL
Section:	NFL
Links:	www.w4mfc.com

ARRL Affiliated Club	Palm Bay Community Charter School Amateur Radio Club
City:	Palm Bay, FL
Call Sign:	KI4ZUR
Section:	SFL
Links:	www.palmbaycharter.org/student/default.html

ARRL Affiliated Club	Harris Intersil Amateur Radio Club
City:	Palm Bay, FL
Call Sign:	K4HRS
Section:	SFL
Links:	www.qsl.net/hiarc/

ARRL Affiliated Club	Florida East Coast DX Club
City:	Palm Bay, FL
Section:	SFL
Links:	www.freewebs.com/fecdx

ARRL Affiliated Club	Flager-Palm Coast Amateur Radio Club, Inc.
City:	Palm Coast, FL
Call Sign:	W4FPC
Section:	NFL
Links:	www.fpcamateurradioclub.com

ARRL Affiliated Club	Flagler Emergency Communications Association
City:	Palm Coast, FL
Call Sign:	KG4TCC
Section:	NFL
Links:	www.flagleremcomm.org
ARRL Affiliated Club	Panama City Amateur Radio Club
City:	Panama City, FL
Call Sign:	W4RYZ
Section:	NFL
Links:	www.w4ryz.org
ARRL Affiliated Club	Five Flags Amateur Radio Association
City:	Pensacola, FL
Call Sign:	W4UC
Section:	NFL
Links:	www.w4uc.org
ARRL Affiliated Club	Pensacola Amateur Radio Club
City:	Pensacola, FL
Call Sign:	K4PNS
Section:	NFL
ARRL Affiliated Club	Motorola Amateur Radio Club
City:	Plantation, FL
Call Sign:	W4MOT
Section:	SFL
Links:	w4mot.org
ARRL Affiliated Club	WR4AYC Repeater Group
City:	Plantation, FL
Call Sign:	WR4AYC
Section:	SFL
Links:	wr4ayc.org
ARRL Special Service Club	Gold Coast Amateur Radio Association Inc.
City:	Pompano Beach, FL
Call Sign:	W4BUG
Section:	SFL
Links:	www.w4bug.org
ARRL Affiliated Club	Port St Lucie Amateur Radio Association
City:	Port Saint Lucie, FL
Call Sign:	K4PSL
Section:	SFL
Links:	www.pslara.com

ARRL Affiliated Club   Peace River Radio Assn.
City: Punta Gorda, FL
Call Sign: W4DUX
Section: WCF
Links: w4dux.net/

ARRL Affiliated Club   Charlotte Amateur Radio Society, Inc.
City: Punta Gorda, FL
Call Sign: WX4E
Section: WCF
Links: w4dux.net/CARSNEWSLETTER.aspx, charlotte-
                            florida.com/community/cars/htm

ARRL Affiliated Club   St Augustine Amateur Radio Society
City: Saint Augustine, FL
Call Sign: N4AUG
Section: NFL
Links: www.saarsham.net

ARRL Affiliated Club   The Glorious Society of The Wormhole
City: Saint Petersburg, FL
Call Sign: W4ORM
Section: WCF
Links: www.w4orm.org

ARRL Affiliated Club   Alphalpha Repeater Group
City: Saint Petersburg, FL
Call Sign: N4AAC
Section: WCF
Links: www.alphalpha.us

ARRL Affiliated Club   St Petersburg Amateur Radio Club
City: Saint Petersburg, FL
Call Sign: W4GAC
Section: WCF
Links: www.sparc-club.org, www.sparc-club.org

ARRL Affiliated Club   Sarasota Amateur Radio Association
City: Sarasota, FL
Call Sign: W4IE
Section: WCF
Links: www.saraclub.org

ARRL Affiliated Club   Sarasota Emergency Radio Club
City: Sarasota, FL
Call Sign: N4SER
Section: WCF
Links: www.n4ser.org

ARRL Affiliated Club   Highlands County Amateur Radio Club
City: Sebring, FL
Call Sign: W4HCA
Section: WCF
Links: www.strato.net/~hamradio

ARRL Affiliated Club   Silver Springs Radio Club Inc.
City: Silver Springs, FL
Call Sign: K4GSO
Section: NFL
Links: k4gso.us

ARRL Affiliated Club   Spring Hill Amateur Radio Club
City: Spring Hill, FL
Call Sign: KF4IXU
Section: NFL
Links: www.kf4ixu.org

ARRL Affiliated Club   Osceola City Repeater Assn. Inc.
City: St Cloud, FL
Call Sign: W4SIE
Section: SFL

ARRL Affiliated Club   Amateur Radio Club, Bradford Area
City: Starke, FL
Call Sign: K4BAR
Section: NFL
Links: www.arcba-fl.org

ARRL Affiliated Club   Martin County Amateur Radio Association
City: Stuart, FL
Call Sign: K4ZK
Section: SFL
Links: www.mcaraweb.com

ARRL Affiliated Club   Sun City Center Amateur Radio Club
City: Sun City Center, FL
Call Sign: KE4ZIP
Section: WCF
Links: www.sccarc.info

ARRL Affiliated Club	Kings Point Amateur Radio Club
City:	Sun City Center, FL
Call Sign:	W4KPR
Section:	WCF
Links:	www.W4KPR.org, www.kparc.org

ARRL Affiliated Club	Tallahassee Amateur Radio Society
City:	Tallahassee, FL
Call Sign:	K4TLH
Section:	NFL
Links:	www.k4tlh.net

ARRL Affiliated Club	Tampa Bay Amateur Radio Society - TBARS
City:	Tampa, FL
Call Sign:	N4TP
Section:	WCF
Links:	www.hamclub.org

ARRL Affiliated Club	Tampa Amateur Radio Club
City:	Tampa, FL
Call Sign:	W4DUG
Section:	WCF
Links:	www.hamclub.org

ARRL Affiliated Club	Baycare Emergency Amateur Radio Service
City:	Tampa, FL
Call Sign:	W4TCH
Section:	WCF
Links:	www.flbears.org

ARRL Special Service Club	Mid Florida DX Association
City:	Tampa, FL
Call Sign:	W4FDX
Section:	WCF
Links:	MFDXA web site

ARRL Affiliated Club	Museum of Science & Industry
City:	Tampa, FL
Call Sign:	KM0SI
Section:	WCF
Links:	www.mosihamradio.org

ARRL Affiliated Club	Florida Gulf Coast Amateur Radio Council
City:	Tampa, FL
Call Sign:	KF4CNH
Section:	WCF
Links:	www.fcgarc.org

ARRL Affiliated Club	Royal Harbor Amateur Radio Club
City:	Tavares, FL
Call Sign:	WX4RH
Section:	NFL

ARRL Affiliated Club	The Villages Amateur Radio Club
City:	The Villages, FL
Call Sign:	K4VRC
Section:	NFL
Links:	www.k4vrc.org

ARRL Affiliated Club	Titusville Amateur Radio Club
City:	Titusville, FL
Call Sign:	K4KSC
Section:	SFL
Links:	www.TitusvilleARC.Org

ARRL Affiliated Club	North Brevard Amateur Radio Club
City:	Titusville, FL
Call Sign:	K4NBR
Section:	SFL
Links:	www.northbrevardarc.org

ARRL Affiliated Club	Tamiami Amateur Radio Club
City:	Venice, FL
Call Sign:	W4AC
Section:	WCF
Links:	tamiamiarc.org

ARRL Affiliated Club	Vero Beach Amateur Radio Club
City:	Vero Beach, FL
Call Sign:	W4OT
Section:	SFL
Links:	www.vbarc.net

ARRL Affiliated Club	St Lucie Repeater Assn. Inc.
City:	Vero Beach, FL
Call Sign:	AF4CN
Section:	SFL

ARRL Affiliated Club	East Pasco Amateur Radio Society
City:	Wesley Chapel, FL
Call Sign:	K4EX
Section:	WCF
Links:	www.eparsonline.org

ARRL Affiliated Club   VA Medical Center Radio Club
City: West Palm Beach, FL
Call Sign: K4VMC
Section: SFL

ARRL Affiliated Club   Gulf Amateur Radio Society
City: Wewahitchka, FL
Section: NFL
Links: www.gulfars.net

APPENDIX B

Amateur Radio License Holders

in

Florida: Treasure Coast Region
(by City)

Call Sign: KG6CXP
Richard H Groetchen
17190 Broadway St
Alva FL 33920

Call Sign: KF6SM
David H Turkel
17651 Cypress Creek Rd
Alva FL 33920

Call Sign: WB8GQL
Ken J Riggs
1961 Goode Ave
Alva FL 339200862

Call Sign: WB8AMD
William O Hollenback
9 Hay St
Alva FL 33920

Call Sign: W4ZYV
Richard S Darling
12 Ilex St
Alva FL 339200444

Call Sign: KC3KX
John E Bickel
2005 Johns Ave
Alva FL 33920

Call Sign: W9FPO
Knoefel L Purlee
21580 N River Rd
Alva FL 33920

Call Sign: W4CER
Robert J Roper
22131 N River Rd
Alva FL 33920

Call Sign: KF4QAY
William S Beaty

15850 Old Olga Rd
Alva FL 33920

Call Sign: KI4LFF
Gustave R Fruauff
17810 Rancho 78 Dr
Alva FL 339203335

Call Sign: WA4DKD
Abbott Kagan II
18741 S River Rd
Alva FL 33920

Call Sign: KA8HPI
Robert E Carson
2131 Safe Harbour Ct
Alva FL 33920

Call Sign: WD4ORX
Baxter P Cochran
2151 Sebastian Ct
Alva FL 33920

Call Sign: KE4PQH
James D Miller
5520 SR 80
Alva FL 339209572

Call Sign: KI4GAJ
John W Moore
2110 Waylife Ct
Alva FL 33920

Call Sign: N1JWM
John W Moore
2110 Waylife Ct
Alva FL 33920

Call Sign: N3WCJ
Gay A Bennett
2121 Waylife Ct
Alva FL 339203829

Call Sign: KG4TZY
Brian B Roberts

2211 Waylife Ct
Alva FL 33920

Call Sign: WD8CQN
Mary Ann Taylor
Alva FL 33920

Call Sign: KB4RBW
Robert J Roper
Alva FL 33920

Call Sign: N4OIN
Sandra G Smith
Alva FL 33920

Call Sign: K8INX
Joker Memorial Radio
Club
Alva FL 339200757

Call Sign: KI4JKE
David W Lee
Alva FL 33920

Call Sign: N8HT
Hollie H Taylor
Alva FL 33920

Call Sign: KK4DEK
Linda F Admire
Alva FL 33920

Call Sign: W4HLH
William L Wells
Alva FL 33920

Call Sign: KG6II
Harry C Adams
Alva FL 33920

Call Sign: KE4SBS
Robert D Robbins

1662 Addison Ave
Arcadia FL 33821

Call Sign: KD4SES
Betty J Werner
Box 6 Thomas St
Arcadia FL 33821

Call Sign: KD4SET
Robert D Werner II
Box 6 Thomas St
Arcadia FL 33821

Call Sign: WD8LGK
Dorothy C Huff
Box 68
Arcadia FL 33821

Call Sign: KA4SEN
Fred C Pearce
Box 785
Arcadia FL 33821

Call Sign: KF4RJE
Jeanette L Witmer
43 Bridle Path
Arcadia FL 34266

Call Sign: KE4QCL
Richard J Witmer
43 Bridle Path
Arcadia FL 34266

Call Sign: K4RJW
Richard J Witmer
43 Bridle Path
Arcadia FL 34266

Call Sign: KF4ETY
Thomas H Anderson
170 Bridle Path
Arcadia FL 34266

Call Sign: N4XFR
Emilio Yero

5100 Hwy 31
Arcadia FL 33821

Call Sign: KA4SJI
Ralph F Mc Cannan
2230 Hwy 70 E
Arcadia FL 34266

Call Sign: KG4BWF
Marjorie A Ricker
89 Kentucky Ave
Arcadia FL 34266

Call Sign: KD4MEH
Ralph C Ricker
89 Kentucky Ave
Arcadia FL 34266

Call Sign: AI4VS
Ralph C Ricker
89 Kentucky Ave
Arcadia FL 34266

Call Sign: KI4WGL
Larry W Duisberg
332 La Solona Ave
Arcadia FL 34266

Call Sign: W4PML
George A Bruno Sr
318 Lasolona
Arcadia FL 33821

Call Sign: N8IGF
Arthur W Mc Coy
4 Maine St
Arcadia FL 34266

Call Sign: NY1M
Joseph P Kamen
13 Michigan Ave
Arcadia FL 33821

Call Sign: KE4SBU
Michael H Ward

113 N Dade
Arcadia FL 33821

Call Sign: KC8IGG
Monita K Clark
5905 NE Cubitis Ave Box
212
Arcadia FL 34266

Call Sign: W8BJC
James S Clark Sr
5905 NE Cubitis Ave Box
212
Arcadia FL 34266

Call Sign: KB9TFG
Martha A Gore
7895 NE Cubitis Ave D 21
Lot 515N
Arcadia FL 34266

Call Sign: N3UYV
Charles W Gore
7895 NE Cubitis Ave D21
Lot 515N
Arcadia FL 34266

Call Sign: W8UVI
Darrel J Hunter
1519 NE Grapefruit St
Arcadia FL 33821

Call Sign: KE4UTO
John A Ward
7895 NE Hwy 17 E21
Arcadia FL 34266

Call Sign: K4SMW
Norma R Adams
3831 NE Hwy 17 N
Arcadia FL 33821

Call Sign: WA6SCI
Richard R Swinyer
2692 NE Hwy 70 Apt 48

Arcadia FL 34266   Arcadia FL 33821   Arcadia FL 34266

Call Sign: KB8DXC
Ron L Harmon
3550 NE Hwy 70 Lot 161
Arcadia FL 34266

Call Sign: K4UNJ
Harold A Fenstermaker
1315 NE Oak St
Arcadia FL 338215772

Call Sign: K4FTR
Randy D Faul
1254 NW Brownville St
Arcadia FL 34266

Call Sign: KD4UNW
Ronald G Robins
2692 NE Hwy 70 Lot 539
Arcadia FL 34266

Call Sign: K1QV
Sam W Edwards Sr
3278 NE Oltmanns St
Arcadia FL 34266

Call Sign: KF4PMZ
Teresa H Faul
1254 NW Brownville St
Arcadia FL 34266

Call Sign: N1SFW
Albert D Gosselin
2626 NE Hwy 70 Lot 88
Arcadia FL 33821

Call Sign: WB4DZM
Sam W Edwards Sr
3278 NE Oltmanns St
Arcadia FL 34266

Call Sign: AE4KM
Joseph R Mc Kenney
3010 NW CR 661
Arcadia FL 34266

Call Sign: N4ZTB
George W Brown
2692 NE Hwy 70 Lot 98
Arcadia FL 342669761

Call Sign: KG4UTI
Joshua M Erickson
1442 NE Sugar Babe Rd
Arcadia FL 34266

Call Sign: KG4BWD
David P Sams Sr
4576 NW CR 661
Arcadia FL 342665662

Call Sign: W4MIN
Desoto ARC
1593 NE Livingston St
Arcadia FL 34266

Call Sign: KD4JUJ
George P Hagan
2557 NE Theater Rd
Arcadia FL 33821

Call Sign: KG4AIW
Robert A Hudson
4865 NW Dill Rd
Arcadia FL 34266

Call Sign: KN4YT
Douglas R Christ
1593 NE Livingston St
Arcadia FL 34266

Call Sign: K4KMA
George P Hagan
2557 NE Theater Rd
Arcadia FL 34266

Call Sign: KG4AAP
Gary A Mc Donald
2347 NW Garvin Ave
Arcadia FL 342665216

Call Sign: W4HLW
Howard L Ward
3563 NE McIntyre St
Arcadia FL 34266

Call Sign: KD4HJM
Robert D Werner
6048 NE Thomas St
Arcadia FL 33821

Call Sign: N4XQF
Roscoe M Gill Jr
2604 NW Haile Dean Rd
Arcadia FL 34266

Call Sign: KF4SPS
Steve A Bretton
6317 NE Moore Ave
Arcadia FL 34266

Call Sign: KF4GAI
David K Dixon
2552 NE Turner Rd Lot 2
Arcadia FL 34266

Call Sign: KB0UTD
Lelia F Thurmond
3460 NW Hwy 72
Arcadia FL 34266

Call Sign: WD4KDL
Dorothy E Fenstermaker
1315 NE Oak St

Call Sign: KF4GNF
Randy D Faul
1254 NW Brownville St

Call Sign: W0RUY
Richard A Thurmond
3460 NW Hwy 72

Arcadia FL 34266

Arcadia FL 34266

Arcadia FL 33821

Call Sign: KC0HIZ
Andrew Mitchell IV
4810 NW Hwy 72 104
Arcadia FL 34266

Call Sign: K4EYO
Howard J Moore
7672 Pine Island Rd
Arcadia FL 34266

Call Sign: N1AFF
Harold L Wood
1292 SE Granada Dr
Arcadia FL 33281

Call Sign: AD4YT
William H Hopkins
4810 NW Hwy 72 Lot 108
Arcadia FL 34266

Call Sign: N3BMU
John J Herman Jr
138 S Hernando Ave
Arcadia FL 342664603

Call Sign: N4AQF
Paul T Thibodeaux
2371 SE Hwy 31 Lot 33
Arcadia FL 34266

Call Sign: KF4EOB
Betty H Hopkins
4810 NW Hwy 72 Lot 108
Arcadia FL 34266

Call Sign: KC4IZF
Robert L Johnson
17 S Manatee Ave
Arcadia FL 33821

Call Sign: K1DOW
Harvey R Tower
1809 SE Maple Dr
Arcadia FL 34266

Call Sign: KF4YOW
Robert M Benkovich
1438 NW Magnolia Ter
Arcadia FL 34266

Call Sign: K2CEP
Frances B Adrian
1840 SE 18th Ave
Arcadia FL 33821

Call Sign: K4IRK
Lyle Mehl
11412 SE Mehl Ave
Arcadia FL 34266

Call Sign: N4RXT
Claude Thurman
1231 NW Pine Creek Ave
Arcadia FL 34265

Call Sign: KB4JJD
Wayne M Thompson
1448 SE Cherry Dr
Arcadia FL 338217446

Call Sign: KD4SOK
John G Gantzer Sr
1809 SE Peach Dr
Arcadia FL 33821

Call Sign: KI4HXT
Robert V Davies
2402 NW Pinewood Ave
Arcadia FL 34266

Call Sign: KE7YQ
Bob H Singh
5327 SE CR 760
Arcadia FL 34266

Call Sign: KE4QCK
Juanita P Gantzer
1809 SE Peach Dr
Arcadia FL 34266

Call Sign: WB4HYH
Leon G Reckinger
1672 NW Windy Pine Ave
Arcadia FL 33821

Call Sign: K4LAY
Bob H Singh
5327 SE CR 760
Arcadia FL 34266

Call Sign: KF4DXO
Rose M Helser
7672 SE Pine Island Rd
Arcadia FL 34266

Call Sign: WA4ORX
Patricia V Reckinger
1672 NW Windy Pine Ave
Arcadia FL 33821

Call Sign: KD4WYM
Vernon S Langfang
10702 SE CR 763
Arcadia FL 34266

Call Sign: KE4HBX
Mary W Cassada
2443 SE Pointer Ave
Arcadia FL 33821

Call Sign: KF4RCR
Leo P Davis II
64 Park Pl Estates

Call Sign: KC4IVV
Dorothy H Rusnak
2139 SE E & T Cir

Call Sign: K1ILQ
Donald T Cassada
2443 SE Pointer Ave

Arcadia FL 34266

Call Sign: KF4LDZ
Jeanne M Walker
1620 SE Tangelo Dr
Arcadia FL 34266

Call Sign: KJ4JTJ
Travis W Walker
1620 SE Tangelo Dr
Arcadia FL 34266

Call Sign: WD4BYK
Joseph E Walker
1620 SE Tangelo Dr
Arcadia FL 34266

Call Sign: KI4WGN
Roberto R San Luis
5 Stirrup Way
Arcadia FL 34266

Call Sign: KD4GOJ
Earl L Owens
230 SW 20th St
Arcadia FL 33821

Call Sign: KF4VSF
Evelyn J Harrison
1145 SW Anita St
Arcadia FL 34266

Call Sign: K4VSF
Evelyn J Harrison
1145 SW Anita St
Arcadia FL 34266

Call Sign: K4TUU
Robert Harrison
1145 SW Anita St
Arcadia FL 34266

Call Sign: KE4SVV
Walter M Christensen
10210 SW Boggess Ave

Arcadia FL 34269

Call Sign: W1FJS
Andrew N Ring
11241 SW Branson Ave
Arcadia FL 342696658

Call Sign: KA4VDI
Rhoda Skavroneck
2712 SW CR 769
Arcadia FL 34266

Call Sign: KF4MXK
George G Beggs
5943 SW CR 769
Arcadia FL 34266

Call Sign: KE4SBT
Sally A Langfang
10597 SW CR 769
Arcadia FL 342698162

Call Sign: W4AUX
Luther A Goff
7500 SW Cty Hwy 769
Arcadia FL 34269

Call Sign: N8HHC
James H Nichols
12865 SW Hwy 17 Site
263
Arcadia FL 34269

Call Sign: KB8EWT
Joan M Nichols
12865 SW Hwy 17 Site
263
Arcadia FL 34269

Call Sign: K4RNF
Kenneth Cannon
8251 SW Hwy 72
Arcadia FL 34266

Call Sign: N3QBM

Stanley L Hendrzak Sr
11912 SW Lake George Tr
Arcadia FL 34269

Call Sign: WB8AGN
Robert F Cooper
8252 SW Liverpool Rd
Arcadia FL 34266

Call Sign: KG4AQT
Joe T Henley
2357 SW Lois Ave
Arcadia FL 34266

Call Sign: KD4KWI
Francis R Poole
11854 SW Loop Ter
Arcadia FL 342695969

Call Sign: KD4SIF
Ryan N Prescott
7224 SW Ogden Acres Rd
Arcadia FL 34269

Call Sign: KB6ASH
Peter L Barker
10649 SW Park Ave
Arcadia FL 34269

Call Sign: N8COE
William R Woofenden II
10673 SW Park Ave
Arcadia FL 342697011

Call Sign: KA8OLK
Joann Woofenden
10673 SW Park Ave
Arcadia FL 342697011

Call Sign: KA2GJQ
Leon E Pease Jr
12826 SW Pembroke Cir
Arcadia FL 34266

Call Sign: W8ZXP

John Oros
11378 SW Thornton Ave
Arcadia FL 342664180

Call Sign: KI4DVA
William D Walker
10943 SW Walker Rd
Arcadia FL 34269

Call Sign: KA8ZDA
Burton P Baker
9675 SW Yacht Dr
Arcadia FL 33821

Call Sign: WA8VFS
Howard E Thom
12 Texas Ave
Arcadia FL 33821

Call Sign: K4HVX
Terr A Seymour
4898 Tomlin Dr SE
Arcadia FL 34266

Call Sign: KD4YNJ
Cody E Deering
556 Turner Rd
Arcadia FL 33821

Call Sign: KI4ZEW
Desoto Red Cross Radio
Club
207 W Oak St
Arcadia FL 34266

Call Sign: WD4RC
Desoto Red Cross Radio
Club
207 W Oak St
Arcadia FL 34266

Call Sign: K4LU
Harry B Evers
404 W Whidden St
Arcadia FL 34266

Call Sign: K4NOT
Nocatee Amateur Radio
Society
404 W Whidden St
Arcadia FL 34266

Call Sign: W4MEE
Mary E Evers
404 W Whidden St
Arcadia FL 34266

Call Sign: N8TWA
Roy F Bousson
1434 Whispering Pine Rd
Arcadia FL 34266

Call Sign: N4WXN
Bette L Gill
Arcadia FL 33821

Call Sign: N4XKS
Roscoe M Gill III
Arcadia FL 33821

Call Sign: KD4SEP
Todd K Esper
Arcadia FL 33821

Call Sign: KF4GNE
Burnis L Moore
Arcadia FL 33821

Call Sign: KE4QNZ
Eddie Diaz
Arcadia FL 33821

Call Sign: KC4DI
John F Parker
Arcadia FL 33821

Call Sign: KE4SBR
Shannon P Donaldson
Arcadia FL 33821

Call Sign: KG4KAM
Alma L Carr
Arcadia FL 34265

Call Sign: N4ALF
Alma L Carr
Arcadia FL 34265

Call Sign: WD5EDX
Helen L Papke
Arcadia FL 34265

Call Sign: KD4SEQ
John M Gulla
Arcadia FL 34265

Call Sign: WB5MPU
Larry E Papke
Arcadia FL 34265

Call Sign: KA4KPQ
Robert L Carr Sr
Arcadia FL 34265

Call Sign: N4RLC
Robert L Carr Sr
Arcadia FL 34265

Call Sign: KF4GAP
Gregory A Sainsbury
Arcadia FL 342652984

**FCC Amateur Radio
Licenses in Ave Maria**

Call Sign: KK4DEI
Rachel A Smolinski
5178 Italia Ct
Ave Maria FL 34142

Call Sign: N7HUQ
Steven P Schultz
5210 Milano St
Ave Maria FL 341429550

Call Sign: KJ4AKJ
John J Mccann
5882 Plymouth Pl
Ave Maria FL 34142

Call Sign: W9PHO
Floyd E Schilling
304 Bass Ln
Avon Park FL 338258805

Call Sign: KC4BMF
Richard R Howard Sr
2186 Berkley Rd
Avon Park FL 33825

Call Sign: KG4HBA
Robin K Towery
1 Century Blvd
Avon Park FL 33825

Call Sign: KE4VEJ
Charles F Masterman
39 Century Blvd
Avon Park FL 33825

Call Sign: KD4WDZ
Paul Duffey
42 Century Blvd
Avon Park FL 33825

Call Sign: WA4PLM
Tully S Callaway
100 Dallas St
Avon Park FL 33825

Call Sign: KC2LDI
James A Busse
904 Dyal St
Avon Park FL 33825

Call Sign: KG4IVK
David M Oliver

E Adams St
Avon Park FL 33825

Call Sign: KG4MCZ
Danny W Selph
4859 E Butler Rd
Avon Park FL 33825

Call Sign: KG4MLH
Luke A Selp
4859 E Butler Rd
Avon Park FL 33825

Call Sign: KE4HFZ
Madeline M Simmons
127 E Camphor St
Avon Park FL 33825

Call Sign: KB4DFF
Charles G Metcalfe Jr
200 E Charles St
Avon Park FL 33825

Call Sign: KJ4OVT
Bryant R Mccall
4366 E Kinsey Rd
Avon Park FL 33825

Call Sign: WB4CMP
Raymond W Sherertz
810 E Lake Lotela Dr
Avon Park FL 338259729

Call Sign: WA8ZQH
Albert A Sager
2856 E Spinnaker Dr
Avon Park FL 33825

Call Sign: WA4BWO
David B Hale Sr
222 E Walnut St
Avon Park FL 33825

Call Sign: W2UNU
Willard E Cross

1025 Entrance Rd
Avon Park FL 33825

Call Sign: KB4BEV
Dale A Hahn Sr
314 Fondulac Rd
Avon Park FL 33825

Call Sign: KT3T
Paul H Angstadt Jr
3116 Glacier Ave
Avon Park FL 33825

Call Sign: KI4SIK
Scott W Rigby
615 Kimberleigh Rd
Avon Park FL 33825

Call Sign: KG4MLG
Larson M Burgess
277 Lake Damon Dr
Avon Park FL 33825

Call Sign: WB4YRD
Donald B Serdynski
1375 Lake Lotela Dr
Avon Park FL 33826

Call Sign: KK4BFE
William F Latham
1457 Lake Lotela Dr
Avon Park FL 33825

Call Sign: K4WFL
William F Latham
1457 Lake Lotela Dr
Avon Park FL 33825

Call Sign: KA3YUH
Gary A Pendrak
1001 Locke St
Avon Park FL 33825

Call Sign: WA4EAA
Henry W Mc Lendon

2304 N Archer Rd
Avon Park FL 33825

Call Sign: KI4WBC
Randal L Geiger
2095 N Berkley Rd
Avon Park FL 33825

Call Sign: KI4LCI
David C Anderson
2200 N Devco Rd
Avon Park FL 33825

Call Sign: KF4GPY
William J Kuh
3265 N Horseshoe Dr
Avon Park FL 33825

Call Sign: KE4HOL
Angelito C Manahan
2242 N Huntington Rd
Avon Park FL 33825

Call Sign: KE4HOK
Wilfred Jaurigue
2242 N Huntington Rd
Avon Park FL 33825

Call Sign: KG4RHL
Bernabe Gonzalez Crespo
2614 N Lacona Rd
Avon Park FL 33825

Call Sign: WA2RGU
Clifford G Riker
1350 N Lake Ave Lot 74
Avon Park FL 33825

Call Sign: K4ROB
Robert A Jordan
604 N Lake Verona Blvd
Avon Park FL 33825

Call Sign: KD4CZK
Roland H Lee Jr

2871 N Lowell Rd
Avon Park FL 33825

Call Sign: NP3G
Terry A Burkholder
2990 N Millden Rd
Avon Park FL 33825

Call Sign: N4TB
Terry A Burkholder
2990 N Millden Rd
Avon Park FL 33825

Call Sign: NP3F
Karen E Whall
2990 N Millden Rd
Avon Park FL 33825

Call Sign: W4JA
Karen E Whall
2990 N Millden Rd
Avon Park FL 33825

Call Sign: WB4HSA
Robert L Jones
2445 N Orangewood St
Avon Park FL 33825

Call Sign: K4JJZ
Robert A Woodruff
131 N Prospect Ave
Avon Park FL 33825

Call Sign: KF4IZT
John R Bliss
615 N Roberts Rd
Avon Park FL 33825

Call Sign: KI4QHT
Joseph G Sliva
1836 N Taconic Rd
Avon Park FL 33825

Call Sign: KD4DHC
Tilman L Davis

2986 N Tivoli Rd
Avon Park FL 33825

Call Sign: N4QBG
Terry G Johnson
1766 N Torrington Rd
Avon Park FL 33825

Call Sign: KC4RTS
William D Elwell
2719 Nautilus Dr
Avon Park FL 33825

Call Sign: KK4BFF
Paul T Mcginness
3000 Oakhill Dr
Avon Park FL 33825

Call Sign: AA4ME
Frederick A Seely
3039 Oakhill Dr
Avon Park FL 338256507

Call Sign: KA4WBZ
James F W Watson
2827 Palo Verde Dr
Avon Park FL 33825

Call Sign: WA9GVZ
Max N Horton
2829 Palo Verde Dr
Avon Park FL 33825

Call Sign: KA9IYT
Robert J Moyer
2481 Priester Rd
Avon Park FL 33825

Call Sign: KA8DEE
Eugene C Notestine
3236 Red Water Dr
Avon Park FL 33825

Call Sign: WB4GUQ
Angela M Combs

3259 Redwater Dr
Avon Park FL 33825

Call Sign: KK4YL
N John Hooper
3149 S Country Club Dr
Avon Park FL 33825

Call Sign: N4APC
Robert M Reisig
512 S Highlands Ave
Avon Park FL 33825

Call Sign: KA4AVD
Shirley S Reisig
512 S Highlands Ave
Avon Park FL 33825

Call Sign: KG4GNF
Spencer W Whitmire Jr
136 S Kissimmee Blvd
Avon Park FL 33825

Call Sign: WN1J
Ronald D Wilson
2455 S Lake Letta Dr Lot
39
Avon Park FL 33825

Call Sign: KG4PVT
Kara A Whitmire
138 S Riverdale Rd
Avon Park FL 33825

Call Sign: W4ERC
Spencer W Whitmire Jr
138 S Riverdale Rd
Avon Park FL 33825

Call Sign: K4FWG
Frank J Ross
2085 Saginaw Rd
Avon Park FL 338258194

Call Sign: KJ4PIP

Moises Perez
1328 Stratford Rd
Avon Park FL 33825

Call Sign: KD4GF
Charles C Castle
8 Sunshine Ln
Avon Park FL 33825

Call Sign: KB4DFG
Billy J Gallion
2100 US Hwy 27 N 4
Avon Park FL 33825

Call Sign: KC4UIP
Barbara A Butler
3460 W Astor Rd
Avon Park FL 33825

Call Sign: KC4UIM
Charles W Butler
3460 W Astor Rd
Avon Park FL 33825

Call Sign: W8HSB
Maitland L Perkins
401 W Bell St
Avon Park FL 33825

Call Sign: KJ4QWY
Damaris E Ashton
2350 W Camelot Rd
Avon Park FL 33825

Call Sign: W4FNW
Damaris E Ashton
2350 W Camelot Rd
Avon Park FL 33825

Call Sign: KO4CO
Edward C Simon
1214 W Canfield St
Avon Park FL 338253453

Call Sign: WP4FRK

Emilio Mendoza
508 W Circle St
Avon Park FL 33825

Call Sign: KF4YY
Phillip E Nichols
407 W Cornell St
Avon Park FL 33825

Call Sign: NP3G
Abner Gomez
1850 W Foxglove Rd
Avon Park FL 33825

Call Sign: NP3G
Abner Gomez
1850 W Foxglove Rd
Avon Park FL 33825

Call Sign: WP4BGM
Gladys Gomez
1850 W Foxglove Rd
Avon Park FL 33825

Call Sign: KC8CPL
Richard C Smith
1220 W Hall St
Avon Park FL 33825

Call Sign: N4EBE
Thomas B Seifert
200 W Lake Trout Dr
Avon Park FL 33825

Call Sign: KJ4GET
Ramon E Gomez
2680 W Stryker Rd
Avon Park FL 33825

Call Sign: KI4GRE
Ramon E Gomez
2680 W Stryker Rd
Avon Park FL 33825

Call Sign: WB3JZQ

David R Heacock
7 W Thomas St
Avon Park FL 33825

Call Sign: K4GND
Robert C Bartholow
Avon Park FL 33825

Call Sign: N6GLI
Lola A Olsen
Avon Park FL 33826

Call Sign: KE4ADP
Rafael D Del Sol
Avon Park FL 33826

Call Sign: WA4DXD
Stanley H Wells
Avon Park FL 33826

FCC Amateur Radio Licenses in Boca Grande

Call Sign: W8ZES
Charles J Hire
Gasparilla Rd
Boca Grande FL 33921

Call Sign: KG4PVZ
James E Martin
Boca Grande FL 33921

Call Sign: KC4NAG
Maurice B Wood
Boca Grande FL 33921

FCC Amateur Radio Licenses in Bokeelia

Call Sign: K9GZT
Edward H Radke
5543 Ann Arbor Dr
Bokeelia FL 33922

Call Sign: N9AJ

Faustin Prinz
12537 Aubrey Ln
Bokeelia FL 33922

Call Sign: W4UKQ
David R C Rhyne
12877 Aubrey Ln
Bokeelia FL 33904

Call Sign: W4MQC
Alan R Pike
7999 Barrancas Ave
Bokeelia FL 33922

Call Sign: WA8HME
Richard L Morrison
5371 Blue Crab Cir M6
Bokeelia FL 33922

Call Sign: N2WVR
Edward C Anderson
5241 Blue Crab Key Cir
D2
Bokeelia FL 33922

Call Sign: KE4HWW
Jeanine A Kenyon
5923 Bomar Ln
Bokeelia FL 339222903

Call Sign: KD4RYH
Richard D Russell
16136 Bowline St
Bokeelia FL 33922

Call Sign: KD4RYC
Sarah M Russell
16136 Bowline St
Bokeelia FL 339221648

Call Sign: KC0ZK
David R Humme
7656 Caloosa Dr NW
Bokeelia FL 33922

Call Sign: W3AEU
Edward G Asbury
7439 Cares Away Park Cir
Bokeelia FL 33922

Call Sign: KI4ECR
Neil G Walls
12281 Dolphin Rd
Bokeelia FL 33922

Call Sign: AI4IQ
Neil G Walls
12281 Dolphin Rd
Bokeelia FL 33922

Call Sign: KF4QWS
Keith E Baugher
12382 Dolphin Rd
Bokeelia FL 33922

Call Sign: KI6UE
Daniel S Ballou
11481 Flint Ln
Bokeelia FL 33922

Call Sign: N3ZYV
Joseph D Vaughan
5473 Henley St
Bokeelia FL 33922

Call Sign: KI4IUZ
Mirko Popovich
7252 Kreamers Dr
Bokeelia FL 33922

Call Sign: W9PTO
Edward Elrod
15837 Missouri St
Bokeelia FL 339220532

Call Sign: KD4ZJC
E Wayne Reed
13350 Morningstar Dr
Bokeelia FL 33922

Call Sign: N8HJM
Kevin S Weirick
7181 Orange Ave
Bokeelia FL 33922

Call Sign: KB2DVD
John B Nicholson
7364 Pinehurst Dr
Bokeelia FL 33922

Call Sign: N8EEK
David E Morris
7309 Pomegranate Dr
Bokeelia FL 33922

Call Sign: KB1KD
James V Ezekiel Jr
7671 Raymary St
Bokeelia FL 33922

Call Sign: WA1JJA
Lorraine F Ezekiel
7671 Raymary St
Bokeelia FL 33922

Call Sign: N2JDK
Hoyt P Richberg Jr
7811 Raymary St
Bokeelia FL 33922

Call Sign: KE4GUF
Martin C Ellis
5779 Samoa Dr
Bokeelia FL 33922

Call Sign: K2SWC
Robert L Washburn
14295 Sandarae Dr
Bokeelia FL 33922

Call Sign: N0JKH
Dennis P Bradley
15175 Stringfellow
Bokeelia FL 33922

Call Sign: KC4URX
Christopher J Benson
5604 Thomas St
Bokeelia FL 33922

Call Sign: W2VDE
Ralston H Connell
6117 Valeria Rd
Bokeelia FL 33922

Call Sign: K4DCB
David S Penney
14400 Windsong Ln
Bokeelia FL 33922

Call Sign: WA9FRL
Norman B Polley
Bokeelia FL 33922

FCC Amateur Radio Licenses in Bonita Springs

Call Sign: WB8VQU
David L Ducett
226 3rd St Apt 208
Bonita Springs FL 34134

Call Sign: KJ4MFQ
Gary A Lee
165 4th St
Bonita Springs FL 34134

Call Sign: K8YMN
Gary A Lee
165 4th St
Bonita Springs FL 34134

Call Sign: KJ4DUG
Michael Freund
76 4th St App 15 201
Bonita Springs FL 34134

Call Sign: WA1BWT
Gordon F W Eaves

202 6th St W
Bonita Springs FL 33923

Call Sign: N4SQJ
George W Lake
203 6th St W R4
Bonita Springs FL 33923

Call Sign: KE8NA
Merle W Zeek
86 8th St
Bonita Springs FL
341347452

Call Sign: W4MWZ
Merle W Zeek
86 8th St
Bonita Springs FL
341347452

Call Sign: WB9NHL
Harold M Brown
74 9th St
Bonita Springs FL
341347421

Call Sign: N4YKM
Leo J Gross
84 9th St
Bonita Springs FL 34134

Call Sign: N4WEG
Robert C Schwartz
88 9th St
Bonita Springs FL 33923

Call Sign: WA8VKO
John F Stec Jr
9768 Alhambra Ln
Bonita Springs FL 34135

Call Sign: KB4KEV
Chester E Boyce
11771 Amanda Ln
Bonita Springs FL 33923

Call Sign: KI4IKV
Timothy M Prosser
3734 Bailes St
Bonita Springs FL 34134

Call Sign: WA1TIM
Timothy M Prosser
3734 Bailes St
Bonita Springs FL 34134

Call Sign: KI4BRP
Scott E Strickland
266 Barefoot Beach Blvd
204
Bonita Springs FL 34134

Call Sign: W0NUX
Richard J Le Blanc
27099 Belle Rio Dr
Bonita Springs FL 34135

Call Sign: KI4AHN
Anita P Corbin
4801 Bonita Bay Blvd
2203
Bonita Springs FL 34134

Call Sign: N0DC
Daniel E Corbin Jr
4801 Bonita Bay Blvd
2203
Bonita Springs FL 34134

Call Sign: W4ZKE
Joe D Colson
27296 Bourbonniere Dr
Bonita Springs FL 34135

Call Sign: KJ4ZOM
Daniel J Antos
26154 Cabana Rd
Bonita Springs FL 34135

Call Sign: W4ASQ

Charles M Bartlett Sr
24945 Carnoustie Ct SE
Bonita Springs FL
341357626

Call Sign: K1SNZ
William Hill
3481 Cassia Ct
Bonita Springs FL 34134

Call Sign: KB9OED
Eric Pachner
23110 Coconut Shores Dr
Bonita Springs FL 34134

Call Sign: W4DGB
David G Bennett Jr
24065 Dietz Dr
Bonita Springs FL 34135

Call Sign: KI4ZMD
Christopher A Durbin
27698 Dortch Ave
Bonita Springs FL 34135

Call Sign: KB9ABX
Christopher A Durbin
27698 Dortch Ave
Bonita Springs FL 34135

Call Sign: N1SXL
Leonard Dean Whitsett
28070 Dovewood Ct 105
Bonita Springs FL 34135

Call Sign: KF4KGC
Milan E Soklic
28090 Dovewood Ct 106
Bonita Springs FL 34135

Call Sign: KO4EM
Joseph P Vesce
27397 Duvernay Dr
Bonita Springs FL 34135

Call Sign: KC8DUO
Tomas E Sagamang
26174 Earl Rd
Bonita Springs FL 34135

Call Sign: K9PWQ
Robert B Funston
25230 Fairway Dunes Ct
Bonita Springs FL 34135

Call Sign: KC4IRH
Starla M Gibson
27725 Forester Dr
Bonita Springs FL 33923

Call Sign: N3LWB
Myron B Kratzer
25419 Galashields Cir
Bonita Springs FL 34134

Call Sign: KA3EHE
Rocco J Los Calzo
27181 Gasparilla Dr
Bonita Springs FL 33923

Call Sign: K0DME
Joseph M Ness
24911 Goldcrest Dr
Bonita Springs FL 34134

Call Sign: W4LGF
Lawrence G Fehrenbaker
25041 Goldcrest Dr
Bonita Springs FL
341347952

Call Sign: KG4YKP
Robert K Baker
27641 Hacienda Blvd E
Unit 324D
Bonita Springs FL 34135

Call Sign: K2JSU
Robert K Baker

27641 Hacienda Blvd E
Unit 324D
Bonita Springs FL 34135

Call Sign: N4MXI
Adrian S Cherepusko
26603 Hickory Blvd
Bonita Springs FL 33923

Call Sign: W2QNI
Paul J Lindstrom
26659 Hickory Blvd
Bonita Springs FL 34134

Call Sign: W9LPS
Raymond J Kengott Jr
28284 Hidden Lake Dr
Bonita Springs FL 34134

Call Sign: KE4LVL
Martha R Tatum
9300 Highland Woods
Blvd 3202
Bonita Springs FL 34135

Call Sign: KC4WCM
William J Tatum
9300 Highland Woods
Blvd 3202
Bonita Springs FL 34135

Call Sign: W4BN
Alfred D Killian Jr
12751 Hunters Ridge Dr
Bonita Springs FL 34135

Call Sign: N3JTL
Joseph S Hemler
25630 Impatiens Ct
Bonita Springs FL
341359412

Call Sign: KF4AEP
Stanford E Jones
25750 Impatiens Ct

Bonita Springs FL 33923

Call Sign: KI4LUB
Ronald D Barnett
10923 K 9 Dr
Bonita Springs FL 34135

Call Sign: N7LXZ
Lj Knoll
25211 Killdeer Dr
Bonita Springs FL 34135

Call Sign: N3FKD
William P Jackson Jr
26063 Kings Rd
Bonita Springs FL 34135

Call Sign: N2LXV
James M Mohart
15357 Laughing Gull Ln
Bonita Springs FL 34135

Call Sign: N2PCM
Tina M Mohart
15357 Laughing Gull Ln
Bonita Springs FL 34135

Call Sign: W8CPZ
John A Fortier
264 Lely Beach Blvd 604
Bonita Springs FL 34124

Call Sign: K2ZEL
George W Reynolds Jr
26951 Leport St
Bonita Springs FL 33923

Call Sign: KI4AHM
Gerald B Terry
28269 Lisbon Ct Unit
3112
Bonita Springs FL 34135

Call Sign: KI4EPT
Luke S Vadas

26658 Little John Ct Unit
93
Bonita Springs FL 34135

Call Sign: KD4OBE
Harold R Johnston
25 Macke Ibe 3168
Bonita Springs FL 33923

Call Sign: AA7LY
Donna L Machlan
28750 Megan Dr
Bonita Springs FL 34135

Call Sign: AC4LG
William R Allen
26440 Montgomery Dr
Bonita Springs FL 33923

Call Sign: WI9T
Terrance C Mc Nichols
15484 Orlanda Dr
Bonita Springs FL 34135

Call Sign: K4JNB
John H Stuewe
27252 Patrick St SE
Bonita Springs FL 33923

Call Sign: KI4BSK
John G Von Ohlen
4723 Pembrooke Ln
Bonita Springs FL 34134

Call Sign: K4JVO
John G Von Ohlen
4723 Pembrooke Ln
Bonita Springs FL 34134

Call Sign: KI4CFM
Thomas F Von Ohlen
4723 Pembrooke Ln
Bonita Springs FL 34134

Call Sign: K4TVO

Thomas F Von Ohlen
4723 Pembrooke Ln
Bonita Springs FL 34134

Call Sign: KA3CUM
Ralph C Little
935 Pennsylvania Ave Apt
14
Bonita Springs FL 33923

Call Sign: KG4PUP
Brenda L Wall
27812 Pension Pl
Bonita Springs FL 34135

Call Sign: KG4LAD
Lawrence E Wall
27812 Pension Pl
Bonita Springs FL 34135

Call Sign: KJ4KLJ
Christian V Bronton
27031 Pine Ave
Bonita Springs FL 34135

Call Sign: KF4SVG
Lloyd F Brenner Jr
9261 Pitt Rd
Bonita Springs FL 34135

Call Sign: WA3MZF
P Frank Miller Jr
9255 Pitt Rd SE
Bonita Springs FL 33923

Call Sign: N4IIA
Charles S Canning
26050 Princess Ln
Bonita Springs FL 34135

Call Sign: WB8SSN
Walter D Wolbert
24202 Production Cir Lot
35
Bonita Springs FL 34135

Call Sign: W1NYN
James M Clubb
26270 Queen Mary Ln
Bonita Springs FL 34135

Call Sign: KI4LUA
David B Barnett
11541 Red Bud Ln
Bonita Springs FL 34135

Call Sign: K1FUJ
Arthur A Macchi
26035 Reed Ct SE
Bonita Springs FL 33923

Call Sign: W1CKT
Robert E Weissman
9410 Reserve Pointe Ct
Bonita Springs FL 34135

Call Sign: KE4KFW
Aubrey V Martinez
27253 Rio Vista Cir
Bonita Springs FL 34135

Call Sign: N1USZ
Cynthia G Slack
27547 Riverbank Dr
Bonita Springs FL 34134

Call Sign: N1NOO
Walter C Slack
27547 Riverbank Dr
Bonita Springs FL 34134

Call Sign: KG4JRI
Daniel O Pogue
3731 Riviera Cir
Bonita Springs FL 34134

Call Sign: KI4HKQ
Dennis L Hamby
27645 S View Dr
Bonita Springs FL 34135

Call Sign: KJ4QBB
Richard A Farmer
28621 San Lucas Ln 201
Bonita Springs FL 34135

Call Sign: K1HSV
James H Lannan
10313 Sandy Hollow Ln
Bonita Springs FL 34135

Call Sign: N4HYM
Jeffrey G Wilson
2674 Stoken Ct
Bonita Springs FL
341355356

Call Sign: WB9NTC
Boyd E Nelson
26470 Summer Greens Dr
Bonita Springs FL 34135

Call Sign: K4GYM
Robert L Pierce
28358 Tasca Dr
Bonita Springs FL 34135

Call Sign: KD4JEE
Daniel P Robinson
27501 Tierra Del Sol Ln
Bonita Springs FL 33923

Call Sign: KD4JED
Leslie J Robinson
27501 Tierra Del Sol Ln
Bonita Springs FL 33923

Call Sign: WB2TXF
Fred C Von Brook
27658 Tierra Del Sol Ln
Bonita Springs FL 34135

Call Sign: KA1RZ
John C Bill
9856 Treasure Cay Ln

Bonita Springs FL 34135

Call Sign: KB4DEC
Joyce M Blair
27448 Valois Dr
Bonita Springs FL 34135

Call Sign: KD4WXQ
Robert L Merbler
28385 Verde Ln
Bonita Springs FL 33923

Call Sign: K4JH
E Clifford Argue
23650 Via Veneto Unit
101
Bonita Springs FL 34134

Call Sign: KB3HTY
Renard L Biltgen
24851 Wax Myrtle Dr
Bonita Springs FL 34134

Call Sign: KD8CR
Donald K Wareham
23031 Whispering Ridge
Dr
Bonita Springs FL 34135

Call Sign: W4SPF
Donald K Wareham
23031 Whispering Ridge
Dr
Bonita Springs FL 34135

Call Sign: K4SJ
Donald K Wareham
23031 Whispering Ridge
Dr
Bonita Springs FL 34135

Call Sign: KK4GVC
Bruno Sapone Jr
28787 Wild Coffee Ct
Bonita Springs FL 34135

Call Sign: N4KB
Edward Hart Jr
27870 Windsor Rd
Bonita Springs FL 33923

Call Sign: KJ4BEJ
Michael Tiberii
9021 Windswept Dr
Bonita Springs FL 34135

Call Sign: KB9ML
Albro D Daniel
3652 Woodlake Dr
Bonita Springs FL 34134

Call Sign: KA9DYK
James R Steele
Bonita Springs FL 33923

Call Sign: K8JOE
William B King
Bonita Springs FL 33923

Call Sign: W8HXT
Ben F Bissman III
Bonita Springs FL 33959

Call Sign: KB4NIT
George E Nelson
Bonita Springs FL 33959

Call Sign: N4KVT
Timothy W Thompson Sr
Bonita Springs FL 33959

Call Sign: WO4D
Junior Matteson
Bonita Springs FL 33923

Call Sign: N3ASL
Charles R Davidson
Bonita Springs FL 34133

Call Sign: KI4AIL

Jack M Faulks
Bonita Springs FL 34133

Call Sign: WA2BMM
Leonard Coleman
Bonita Springs FL 34133

Call Sign: KI4KGI
Bobby Finney III
Bonita Springs FL 34136

Call Sign: KA1KRU
Roswell F Busby
Bonita Springs FL 34136

Call Sign: K9HB
A H Bott
Bonita Springs FL
341366367

**FCC Amateur Radio
Licenses in Bowling
Green**

Call Sign: KN4NE
Walter R Goulding
Box 105
Bowling Green FL 33834

Call Sign: KG4HJT
Elizabeth A Rice
2908 Country Club Dr
Bowling Green FL 33834

Call Sign: KU4SV
John T Rice
2908 Country Club Dr
Bowling Green FL 33834

Call Sign: KI4YIE
Eugene L Alderman Jr
511 E Main St
Bowling Green FL 33834

Call Sign: K4MBW

Marvin B Walker
5061 Hollis Rd
Bowling Green FL 33834

Call Sign: KI4SPG
Charles C Adler Jr
Bowling Green FL 33834

Call Sign: KI4ZOZ
Eugene L Alderman Sr
Bowling Green FL 33834

Call Sign: KI4ZOY
John G Adler
Bowling Green FL 33834

Call Sign: KB2PZR
Dianne J Sherwood
Bowling Green FL
338341687

Call Sign: N2NGF
Richard B Sherwood
Bowling Green FL
338341687

**FCC Amateur Radio
Licenses in Cape Coral**

Call Sign: KJ4LCO
John S Young
1729 13th Ter
Cape Coral FL 33990

Call Sign: KJ4MBT
Amanda T Hawkins
1301 Andalusia Blvd
Cape Coral FL 33909

Call Sign: KJ4MBS
Eric B Hawkins
1301 Andalusia Blvd
Cape Coral FL 33909

Call Sign: KC4JEE

Edward W Healey
5313 Bay Point Ct
Cape Coral FL 33904

Call Sign: WZ4I
Chester K Heicher
433 Bay Shore Dr
Cape Coral FL 33904

Call Sign: AD4KK
Robert E Peer
1639 Beach Pkwy 201
Cape Coral FL 339047409

Call Sign: N2UFI
Carol L Riggall
1804 Beach Pkwy W
Cape Coral FL 33914

Call Sign: NY2AR
Miles A Riggall
1804 Beach Pkwy W
Cape Coral FL 33914

Call Sign: W1IFO
Hans F Seebo
2209 Cape Coral Pkwy W
Cape Coral FL 33914

Call Sign: KI4RGY
Remy E Morales
1519 Cape Coral Pkwy W
6
Cape Coral FL 33914

Call Sign: KD4LAX
Gordon G Stuermer
5310 Cobalt Ct
Cape Coral FL 339045816

Call Sign: KQ4NV
Patsy B Osborne
5366 Colony Ct
Cape Coral FL 33904

Call Sign: N1BEP
George W Allen
542 Coral Dr
Cape Coral FL 33904

Call Sign: WD8QZW
Dennis K Secrist
2126 Coral Point Dr
Cape Coral FL 339906832

Call Sign: W2FWP
Edward Flowers
1735 Cornwallis Pkwy
Cape Coral FL 339044057

Call Sign: W1RP
Paul S Ramsden
1930 Cornwallis Pkwy
Cape Coral FL 339044065

Call Sign: KD4CWN
Karel Rivadulla
2012 Cornwallis Pky
Cape Coral FL 33904

Call Sign: KJ4MBU
Iris A Whittington
1506 Country Club Blvd
Cape Coral FL 33990

Call Sign: AB9IR
Mark W Smith
4117 Country Club Blvd
Cape Coral FL 33904

Call Sign: K4UAW
Mark W Smith
4117 Country Club Blvd
Cape Coral FL 33904

Call Sign: KN2R
Paul E Aidukas
4233 Country Club Blvd
Cape Coral FL 33904

Call Sign: W4MFD
Carl L Habermann
1416 Country Club Blvd
27
Cape Coral FL 33990

Call Sign: KE4NPC
Elmer G Northrop
3817 Country Club Blvd 8
Cape Coral FL 339045173

Call Sign: KD4QMM
Tom S Zeller
5342 Darby Ct
Cape Coral FL 33904

Call Sign: KD6VUU
John L Jones
5366 Del Monte Ct
Cape Coral FL 33903

Call Sign: KE4PFH
Ralph L Donaldson
Del Prado Blvd 318
Cape Coral FL 33990

Call Sign: KE4PFP
Paul V Scott
5302 Delano Ct
Cape Coral FL 33904

Call Sign: KA2VEC
Robert W Pashley
941 Dolphin Dr
Cape Coral FL 33904

Call Sign: KG6DHF
Alma J Stuermer
5819 Driftwood Pkwy
Cape Coral FL 33904

Call Sign: KD4IVZ
David W Mc Tighe
1217 E Cape Coral Pkwy
227

Cape Coral FL 339049604

Call Sign: K1JZP
John B Mac Donald
4930 Edith Esplanade
Cape Coral FL 33904

Call Sign: W2OLR
William D Miller
127 El Dorado Pkwy W
Cape Coral FL 339147144

Call Sign: KK4HQE
Richard W Hillyer Sr
700 El Dorado Pkwy W
Cape Coral FL 33914

Call Sign: KG4UCD
Thomas H Kreulen
1200 El Dorado Pkwy W
Cape Coral FL 33914

Call Sign: WB8GIT
Jerry L Dutton
1417 El Dorado Pkwy W
Cape Coral FL 33914

Call Sign: KA6QIP
Maria L Lewis
2108 El Dorado Pkwy W
Cape Coral FL 33914

Call Sign: KJ4VDL
Charles R Lawrence
1813 Everest Pkwy
Cape Coral FL 33904

Call Sign: KE1KE
Mark H Wynn
1848 Everest Pkwy
Cape Coral FL 33904

Call Sign: KF4IDY
Eric M Scott
2512 Everest Pkwy

Cape Coral FL 33904

Call Sign: KD4YEG
Sheldon H Ruiz
2424 Everest Pky
Cape Coral FL 33904

Call Sign: WB3GAM
Robert A Benninger
5716 Flamingo Dr
Cape Coral FL 33904

Call Sign: KJ4VDO
Roland P Cournoyer
519 Gleason Pkwy
Cape Coral FL 33914

Call Sign: KC4KYK
Scott A Wilk
1019 Hancock Bd Pky
Cape Coral FL 33990

Call Sign: KI6BUN
Cape Coral ARC
1329 Hancock Bridge
Pkwy
Cape Coral FL 33990

Call Sign: KU0BA
Cape Coral ARC
1329 Hancock Bridge
Pkwy
Cape Coral FL 33990

Call Sign: KG4UIA
Juan C Berberena
1329 Hancock Bridge
Pkwy
Cape Coral FL 339901716

Call Sign: AG4XJ
Juan C Berberena
1329 Hancock Bridge
Pkwy
Cape Coral FL 339901716

Call Sign: KJ4VDP
Briceida Placido
141 Kamal Pkwy
Cape Coral FL 33904

Call Sign: KI4UAR
Brian M Bolen
622 Kismet Pkway E
Cape Coral FL 33909

Call Sign: KI4HEZ
Jeffrey A Bolen
622 Kismet Pkwy E
Cape Coral FL 33909

Call Sign: KC0PN
Leonard G Smith
1113 Lenox Ct
Cape Coral FL 33904

Call Sign: KC4VTB
Sal C Mellon
1133 Lenox Ct
Cape Coral FL 33904

Call Sign: K4FLK
Delmar L Diederich
1136 Lorraine Ct
Cape Coral FL 33904

Call Sign: KM4OS
Curtis D Bullock
1144 Lucerne Ave
Cape Coral FL 33904

Call Sign: WB2RMW
Joseph C Dietlmeier
12308 Matlacha Blvd
Cape Coral FL 33914

Call Sign: KG4VUU
Sebastian Fernandez
2518 Miracle Pkwy
Cape Coral FL 33914

Call Sign: K4BAC
Sebastian Fernandez
2518 Miracle Pkwy
Cape Coral FL 33914

Call Sign: N3UVH
Sharon K Basil
802 Miramar Ct
Cape Coral FL 339045934

Call Sign: WB9OQQ
Paul J Wolf
241 NE 10th Ave
Cape Coral FL 33909

Call Sign: KB2PZL
Sergio C Pais
1914 NE 10th Pl
Cape Coral FL 33909

Call Sign: KJ4MSO
Alexandros Katsaounis
317 NE 10th St
Cape Coral FL 33909

Call Sign: K9SCM
Donnell L Carnes
1205 NE 11th Ter
Cape Coral FL 33909

Call Sign: KV4FJ
Donnell L Carnes
1205 NE 11th Ter
Cape Coral FL 33909

Call Sign: W4LAZ
Lazaro Andino
1035 NE 13th Ave
Cape Coral FL 339091525

Call Sign: KI4BCN
Lazaro Andino
1035 NE 13th Ave
Cape Coral FL 339091525

Call Sign: KG4DYD
Robert J Jason
2017 NE 13th Ave
Cape Coral FL 339094412

Call Sign: KE4CB
Charles T Brown
1315 NE 13th Pl
Cape Coral FL 33909

Call Sign: KC4QHZ
Marilyn J Stevens
226 NE 14th Pl
Cape Coral FL 33909

Call Sign: KC4BRO
Jady A Morris
2209 NE 14th Pl
Cape Coral FL 33909

Call Sign: AG4XK
Lawrence W Zimmer
633 NE 15th Ct
Cape Coral FL 33909

Call Sign: KC2CAR
Coast Guard Auxillary
Throgs Neck Radio
2229 NE 15th St
Cape Coral FL 33909

Call Sign: KB2TDE
Angela E Giovaniello
2229 NE 15th St
Cape Coral FL 33909

Call Sign: N2KGU
Stanislao Giovaniello
2229 NE 15th St
Cape Coral FL 33909

Call Sign: KG4ONW
Robert C Rodenhiser
322 NE 19th Ave

Cape Coral FL 33909

Call Sign: KK4HQA
Laurence A Wolf
1210 NE 19th Ter
Cape Coral FL 33909

Call Sign: KK4DEJ
Juan C Berberena
1408 NE 19th Ter
Cape Coral FL 33909

Call Sign: WJ6C
Juan C Berberena
Gonzalez
1408 NE 19th Ter
Cape Coral FL 339095377

Call Sign: KC4ONO
Carrie M Tibbett
1810 NE 1st St
Cape Coral FL 33909

Call Sign: KA8ZHY
Peter M Kuchling
2730 NE 20 Ct
Cape Coral FL 33909

Call Sign: W4FES
Clarence R Austerman
316 NE 21st St
Cape Coral FL 33909

Call Sign: WA4KGK
Edna J Austerman
316 NE 21st St
Cape Coral FL 33909

Call Sign: KD9EL
Randy K Gartee
2009 NE 23rd Pl
Cape Coral FL 33909

Call Sign: KJ4RVB
Lloyd F Duhon II

2134 NE 26th St
Cape Coral FL 33909

Call Sign: AA4N
Gurdon E Cooper
1708 NE 26th Ter
Cape Coral FL 33909

Call Sign: KB3NGI
Mark C Franz
1511 NE 2nd St
Cape Coral FL 33909

Call Sign: KI4GAF
Adam P Fuller
1815 NE 2nd St
Cape Coral FL 33909

Call Sign: AE5JO
John W Heger
2321 NE 34th Ln
Cape Coral FL 33909

Call Sign: KB8KNK
Joey K Rademaker
2115 NE 4th Pl
Cape Coral FL 33919

Call Sign: KJ4HZS
Leonard G Foster
2221 NE 4th Pl
Cape Coral FL 33909

Call Sign: KI4ZXL
Susan A Sherman
2221 NE 4th Pl
Cape Coral FL 33909

Call Sign: KB2IDX
Christopher T Freundlich
1534 NE 4th Ter
Cape Coral FL 33909

Call Sign: N8EYF
Jack D Harness

2924 NE 5th Pl
Cape Coral FL 33909

Call Sign: KD4QXP
Aldrich R Thomas
125 NE 6th Pl
Cape Coral FL 33909

Call Sign: KE6GOJ
Taiden Brown
1920 NE Van Loon Ter
Cape Coral FL 33909

Call Sign: KG4DVF
William B Herstam
4921 Normandy Ct
Cape Coral FL 33904

Call Sign: KV4DY
William B Herstam
4921 Normandy Ct
Cape Coral FL 33904

Call Sign: KM4P
William B Herstam
4921 Normandy Ct
Cape Coral FL 33904

Call Sign: KC4IIF
Lesley L Peterson
967 Nott Rd
Cape Coral FL 33991

Call Sign: KA4RCN
Walter E Peterson
967 Nott Rd
Cape Coral FL 33991

Call Sign: KG4ZAH
James M Gorgas
1406 NW 13th Ter
Cape Coral FL 339935005

Call Sign: K6GU
Steve W Lanyi

536 NW 14th Ter
Cape Coral FL 33993

236 NW 22nd Pl
Cape Coral FL 33993

2704 NW 2nd Pl
Cape Coral FL 33993

Call Sign: KA3PYO
Virginia M Batchler
2602 NW 15th St
Cape Coral FL 33993

Call Sign: KP4LQ
Andres Caro
501 NW 25th Ave
Cape Coral FL 33993

Call Sign: N9FGU
Rodney W Holler
3306 NW 2nd Ter
Cape Coral FL 33993

Call Sign: NT4TS
Laing T Batchler
2602 NW 15th St
Cape Coral FL 33993

Call Sign: WJ2N
Andres Caro
501 NW 25th Ave
Cape Coral FL 33993

Call Sign: KJ4KGU
David A Gydosh
4336 NW 31st
Cape Coral FL 33993

Call Sign: KI4ICV
John V Stanford
1113 NW 15th Ter
Cape Coral FL 33993

Call Sign: KK4BUR
Samuel D Bradley
1711 NW 25th Ln
Cape Coral FL 33993

Call Sign: KC8GM
Cornelis D Vandenberg
611 NW 32nd St
Cape Coral FL 33993

Call Sign: KI4PET
Cecil D Phillips
1719 NW 21st St
Cape Coral FL 33993

Call Sign: KF4WNI
Renate G Nolting
4235 NW 26th St
Cape Coral FL 33993

Call Sign: KJ4OJA
Don Rizzo
2318 NW 33rd Pl
Cape Coral FL 33993

Call Sign: N4OKS
Cecil D Phillips
1719 NW 21st St
Cape Coral FL 33993

Call Sign: KU4QY
Ralf-Reiner Nolting
4235 NW 26th St
Cape Coral FL 339933402

Call Sign: AG4CQ
Frantisek Slintak
218 NW 37 Pl
Cape Coral FL 33993

Call Sign: KI4VYY
Frances P Zimmer
1719 NW 21st St
Cape Coral FL 33993

Call Sign: AF4YI
Ralf-Reiner Nolting
4235 NW 26th St
Cape Coral FL 339933402

Call Sign: KB4FS
Frantisek Slintak
218 NW 37 Pl
Cape Coral FL 33993

Call Sign: K4FPZ
Frances P Zimmer
1719 NW 21st St
Cape Coral FL 33993

Call Sign: N4DOT
Thomas S Golembeski
1000 NW 28th Ave
Cape Coral FL 33993

Call Sign: KH8AJ
Kathleen C Morrell
225 NW 39th Ave
Cape Coral FL 33993

Call Sign: W4LWZ
Lawrence W Zimmer
1719 NW 21st St
Cape Coral FL 33993

Call Sign: K1VLX
Jeremiah J Williams
1437 NW 29th Pl
Cape Coral FL 33993

Call Sign: AH8M
Robert W Morrell
225 NW 39th Ave
Cape Coral FL 339935505

Call Sign: N0VOM
William G Mayfield

Call Sign: KJ4NKL
Michael J Mcginn

Call Sign: WB4PTC
David C Scott

1220 NW 43rd Ave
Cape Coral FL 339939117

Call Sign: KY3PG
David C Scott
1220 NW 43rd Ave
Cape Coral FL 339939117

Call Sign: W4DC
Denis E Catalano
3028 NW 43rd Pl
Cape Coral FL 33993

Call Sign: W4CIK
Carol I King
3028 NW 43rd Pl
Cape Coral FL 33993

Call Sign: KJ4YNH
Joseph C Evanson
513 NW 4th Ter
Cape Coral FL 33993

Call Sign: KJ4KGW
Penny L Videen
3042 NW 6th Ave
Cape Coral FL 33993

Call Sign: W3DAV
Samuel D Bradley
2721 NW Juanita Pl
Cape Coral FL 33993

Call Sign: KG4VDS
William P Pavela
3317 NW Juanita Pl
Cape Coral FL 33993

Call Sign: KJ4KGV
Dennis J Videen
3042 NW Ln
Cape Coral FL 33993

Call Sign: KA2QCR
Dominick M Giordano

3616 Oasis Blvd
Cape Coral FL 33914

Call Sign: W1RIK
Richard W Williams
1013 Old Burnt Store Rd
Cape Coral FL 33993

Call Sign: N8AQW
Norman L Fleek Jr
3228 Old Burnt Store Rd
Cape Coral FL 339937905

Call Sign: WD8PND
Earl L Lancaster
3032 Old Burnt Store Rd
Cape Coral FL 33993

Call Sign: AB4FC
Walter F Densmore
3244 Old Burnt Store Rd
N
Cape Coral FL 339937905

Call Sign: KF4GEM
William L Todd II
1808 Palaco Grande Pkwy
Cape Coral FL 33904

Call Sign: AA6JI
Ernest J Ibach
1928 Palaco Grande Pkwy
Cape Coral FL 33904

Call Sign: AF6L
Marguerite D Ibach
1928 Palaco Grande Pkwy
Cape Coral FL 33904

Call Sign: KD4FPO
Ryan M Danis
2021 Palaco Grande Pkwy
Cape Coral FL 33904

Call Sign: KN3T

Toni L Zimmer
2028 Palaco Grande Pkwy
Cape Coral FL 33914

Call Sign: KP2AU
William A Harrison
4903 Pelican Blvd
Cape Coral FL 33914

Call Sign: KF4OSX
Bruce R Malo
5237 Pelican Blvd
Cape Coral FL 339146529

Call Sign: KJ4KGM
Terrance D Kelley
1842 Piccadilly Cir
Cape Coral FL 33991

Call Sign: KI4PTZ
Patrick M Meehan
1926 Piccadilly Cir
Cape Coral FL 339913163

Call Sign: KA2WDQ
James Rodriguez
11538 Royal Tee Cir
Cape Coral FL 33991

Call Sign: K4JMD
Theodore L Parker
1333 Santa Barbara Blvd
525
Cape Coral FL 33991

Call Sign: KC4VGN
Frank W Wetmore
3218 Santa Barbara Blvd
N
Cape Coral FL 33993

Call Sign: KF3DZ
William Almeyda Jr
3302 Santa Barbara Blvd
N

Cape Coral FL 33915

Cape Coral FL 339044707

Cape Coral FL 33990

Call Sign: KJ4TP
Richard G Zopp
5150 Santa Rosa Ct
Cape Coral FL 33904

Call Sign: W4MKC
William E Quay
4128 SE 10th Ave
Cape Coral FL 39904

Call Sign: WB2PPV
Donald G Cole
4512 SE 11th Ave
Cape Coral FL 33904

Call Sign: KK4HQF
Stephen D Jackson
2577 Sawgrass Lkae Ct
Cape Coral FL 33909

Call Sign: K9CPY
Donald B Schumacher
2101 SE 10th Ln
Cape Coral FL 33990

Call Sign: WA2JNM
Donald G Cole
4512 SE 11th Ave
Cape Coral FL 33904

Call Sign: KJ4KGR
Daniel J Videen
5058 Saxony Ct
Cape Coral FL 33904

Call Sign: KF4RSE
Valerie E Poleski
1914 SE 10th Pl
Cape Coral FL 33990

Call Sign: KA1SMQ
Hector F Lopez
227 SE 11th Ter
Cape Coral FL 33990

Call Sign: WD4MEF
William G Vent
3517 SE 10 Pl
Cape Coral FL 33904

Call Sign: K2TIU
Donald Mac Kellar
1927 SE 10th Pl
Cape Coral FL 339904545

Call Sign: KB2QJH
William R Perry
1903 SE 11th Ter
Cape Coral FL 33990

Call Sign: KD4HNZ
Louis C Navarra
18 SE 10th Ave
Cape Coral FL 33990

Call Sign: KJ4VDN
Raymond M Vega
2117 SE 10th Pl
Cape Coral FL 33990

Call Sign: KI4ARC
Rafael A Pina
1809 SE 12 Ter
Cape Coral FL 33990

Call Sign: KC4CBT
Stephanie L Clark
406 SE 10th Ave
Cape Coral FL 33990

Call Sign: W8UJ
James L Old
3421 SE 10th Pl
Cape Coral FL 33904

Call Sign: KC1D
Joseph B Dolliver
4002 SE 12th Ave
Cape Coral FL 33904

Call Sign: KD4GRS
Michael P Apicella
409 SE 10th Ave
Cape Coral FL 33990

Call Sign: KE4DLW
Derek J Carnwath
2110 SE 10th Ter
Cape Coral FL 33990

Call Sign: N1CXC
Nancy C M Dolliver
4002 SE 12th Ave
Cape Coral FL 33904

Call Sign: KF2LD
Robert E Strauss
3309 SE 10th Ave
Cape Coral FL 339044714

Call Sign: KC4RSV
Omesh Somaru
1936 SE 11 Ave
Cape Coral FL 33990

Call Sign: KC4LHI
Melyssa A Vutsinas
2115 SE 12th St
Cape Coral FL 33990

Call Sign: W4BI
Rodney L Whitten
3511 SE 10th Ave

Call Sign: KC4KHW
Jason R Farnum
945 SE 11th Ave

Call Sign: KE4KJX
Cory W Helmuth
1711 SE 12th Ter

Cape Coral FL 33990 Cape Coral FL 339906901 Cape Coral FL 33990

Call Sign: K4ENA
Basil J Gray
1723 SE 12th Ter
Cape Coral FL 33990

Call Sign: N4PCH
Edward Kostelak
1211 SE 14th Ter
Cape Coral FL 33904

Call Sign: WA8MTU
William A Vagi
1433 SE 16th St
Cape Coral FL 33990

Call Sign: KB7OBF
James D Cousins
1009 SE 13th Ave
Cape Coral FL 33990

Call Sign: KC4QXJ
Matthew L Clark
1416 SE 14th Ter
Cape Coral FL 33990

Call Sign: K1KHP
John W Phipps
1711 SE 16th St
Cape Coral FL 33990

Call Sign: KJ4LCQ
Dawn C Krakow
306 SE 13th St
Cape Coral FL 33990

Call Sign: N4LIZ
Joseph P Rotino Sr
2228 SE 15th Pl
Cape Coral FL 33990

Call Sign: KF4KIT
Gary H Greene
2044 SE 16th St
Cape Coral FL 33990

Call Sign: KI4BAI
Jeffrey A Fisher
1421 SE 13th St
Cape Coral FL 33990

Call Sign: KD4CQT
Michael T Abbattista
1114 SE 15th St
Cape Coral FL 33990

Call Sign: KD4YVR
Elizabeth A Vitella
219 SE 16th Ter
Cape Coral FL 33990

Call Sign: W4PRL
Donald A Gurney
4523 SE 14th Ave
Cape Coral FL 33904

Call Sign: WB8REJ
Perley O Willett
1431 SE 15th Ter
Cape Coral FL 339906716

Call Sign: KJ4MCB
William A Vitella
219 SE 16th Ter
Cape Coral FL 33990

Call Sign: KD4CWK
Sean T Eaton
1314 SE 14th St
Cape Coral FL 33990

Call Sign: W2GRI
Dale M Springsted
1802 SE 15th Ter
Cape Coral FL 33990

Call Sign: KD4BYZ
Heath L Roody
1210 SE 16th Ter
Cape Coral FL 33990

Call Sign: KB2UMG
Tina M Coates
1439 SE 14th St
Cape Coral FL 33990

Call Sign: KE4UOF
Charles T Brown
2505 SE 16th Pl
Cape Coral FL 33904

Call Sign: KD4QWM
Cheritt L Gingerich
502 SE 17th Ave
Cape Coral FL 33990

Call Sign: KB2UMH
Wayne N Coates Jr
1439 SE 14th St
Cape Coral FL 33990

Call Sign: KD4CWM
Jacob C Wise
3501 SE 16th Pl
Cape Coral FL 33904

Call Sign: KD4QWL
Michael F Mannella
3405 SE 17th Ave
Cape Coral FL 33904

Call Sign: NF6O
Julius H Green Jr
2208 SE 14th St

Call Sign: KJ4TSE
Juan A Santiago
1111 SE 16th St

Call Sign: KS4SS
John J Falduti
3410 SE 17th Ave

Cape Coral FL 339044404

Cape Coral FL 33990

Cape Coral FL 33904

Call Sign: KG4PXV
Earl A Carron Jr
459 SE 17th Pl
Cape Coral FL 33990

Call Sign: N2HWN
Martin F Mulgannon
4312 SE 18 Ave
Cape Coral FL 339046020

Call Sign: KB9TCE
Larry J Peterson
4421 SE 19th Pl
Cape Coral FL 33904

Call Sign: W8LED
Raymond E Kanehl
4703 SE 17th Pl 503
Cape Coral FL 339048789

Call Sign: KB1JII
Joseph E Vierra
1038 SE 18th Ave
Cape Coral FL 339901839

Call Sign: KI4ODE
Gordon H Coffman
4001 SE 19th Pl 7
Cape Coral FL 33904

Call Sign: KE4KJY
Greg P Crist
1512 SE 17th St
Cape Coral FL 33990

Call Sign: AA9TW
Randall W Wagnon
4108 SE 18th Ave Apt 102
Cape Coral FL 33904

Call Sign: KF4IDV
Lyndsey K Fitzgerald
1223 SE 19th St
Cape Coral FL 33990

Call Sign: WA8PDG
James E Stahl
302 SE 17th Ter
Cape Coral FL 33990

Call Sign: KA4YLV
Otto K Musall
3121 SE 18th Pl
Cape Coral FL 33904

Call Sign: N3NAI
Joseph A Ryan Jr
407 SE 19th Ter
Cape Coral FL 33990

Call Sign: KF4MQR
Michael E Maschenik
910 SE 17th Ter
Cape Coral FL 33990

Call Sign: KG4BSI
Ralph D White
3908 SE 18th Pl
Cape Coral FL 33904

Call Sign: K4DYR
Richard M Simmons
4321 SE 1st Ave
Cape Coral FL 33904

Call Sign: KF4BBC
Walter A Clemence
1224 SE 17th Ter
Cape Coral FL 33990

Call Sign: KJ4MUY
Timothy D Bennett
3921 SE 18th Pl
Cape Coral FL 339045010

Call Sign: N3ZX
Denny H Dorton
4417 SE 1st Ave
Cape Coral FL 33904

Call Sign: KF4RSD
Michael E Clemence
1224 SE 17th Ter
Cape Coral FL 33990

Call Sign: N4CRO
William C Stewart
1131 SE 18th St
Cape Coral FL 339904518

Call Sign: K3DDX
Denny H Dorton
4417 SE 1st Ave
Cape Coral FL 33904

Call Sign: KB8RRS
Robert H Browning
1304 SE 17th Ter
Cape Coral FL 33990

Call Sign: KC8GW
Irvin L Heineman
1442 SE 18th Ter
Cape Coral FL 33990

Call Sign: KP4AT
Joseph C Ducros
4008 SE 1st Ct
Cape Coral FL 33904

Call Sign: KF4IDW
Samantha J Nerad
316 SE 18 Ave

Call Sign: KA1HHO
Armand A Laflam
3007 SE 19th Ave

Call Sign: KE4BOH
Jeffrey R Kennedy
3525 SE 1st Pl

Cape Coral FL 33904   Cape Coral FL 33990   Cape Coral FL 33990

Call Sign: KC2DJX   Call Sign: K5BVH   Call Sign: W4IVF
David J Lawrence   William A Riggs   Lawrence C Mennitt
3826 SE 1st Pl   4026 SE 20 Pl C2   4015 SE 20th Pl 202
Cape Coral FL 33904   Cape Coral FL 33904   Cape Coral FL 33904

Call Sign: AI4JU   Call Sign: N4GUI   Call Sign: KD4GRA
David J Lawrence   Maurice J Boren   Amy M Arcaneaux
3826 SE 1st Pl   1029 SE 20th Ave   1315 SE 20th St
Cape Coral FL 33904   Cape Coral FL 339901848   Cape Coral FL 33990

Call Sign: KQ4IQ   Call Sign: KB2UKK   Call Sign: WB2OJQ
Karla A Holmes   Paul Whalen   John H Lambert Jr
3912 SE 1st Pl   4501 SE 20th Ave   1202 SE 21st Ave
Cape Coral FL 33904   Cape Coral FL 33904   Cape Coral FL 33990

Call Sign: KQ4MQ   Call Sign: N8EL   Call Sign: W4PJK
Gerald A Holmes   Egon Loeckel   John C Lester
3912 SE 1st Pl   237 SE 20th Ct   2545 SE 21st Ave
Cape Coral FL 33904   Cape Coral FL 33990   Cape Coral FL 33904

Call Sign: N3LBS   Call Sign: KC4QXL   Call Sign: W4NQJ
Melissa J Fox   Timothy J Skjold   Stephen V Tingley Jr
4008 SE 1st Pl   249 SE 20th Ct   2549 SE 21st Ave
Cape Coral FL 33904   Cape Coral FL 33990   Cape Coral FL 33904

Call Sign: KM3C   Call Sign: KF4CUQ   Call Sign: KB2ECO
Stanley C Fox   Lee G Morrison   Frank J Miletti Jr
4008 SE 1st Pl   502 SE 20th Ct   2624 SE 21st Ave
Cape Coral FL 33904   Cape Coral FL 339901856   Cape Coral FL 33904

Call Sign: W2DSE   Call Sign: KD4YEH   Call Sign: KK4XH
George Wallington   Ian L Morrissey   Thomas B Dowling
4207 SE 1st Pl   603 SE 20th Ct   3705 SE 21st Pl
Cape Coral FL 33904   Cape Coral FL 33990   Cape Coral FL 33904

Call Sign: KT4SN   Call Sign: KI4RGZ   Call Sign: KD6VCB
Lawrence E Prief   John J Schroder   Michael R D Agostino
522 SE 1st Ter   1051 SE 20th Ct   1515 SE 21st St
Cape Coral FL 33990   Cape Coral FL 33990   Cape Coral FL 33990

Call Sign: W4NLV   Call Sign: K3FOZ   Call Sign: N3JNG
Harry J Wiggins   Edward F Drass   John N Piergrossi
1115 SE 1st Ter   310 SE 20th Pl   1118 SE 21st Ter

Cape Coral FL 33990   Cape Coral FL 33990   Cape Coral FL 33990

Call Sign: N4HAS
John C Lewis
3513 SE 22 Ave
Cape Coral FL 33904

Call Sign: KC4KYJ
Gerano B White
1218 SE 23rd Ave
Cape Coral FL 33990

Call Sign: KE4MSI
Brandon M Burke
1305 SE 23rd Ter
Cape Coral FL 33990

Call Sign: KD4RCO
Henry O Sanchey
1439 SE 22 Ter
Cape Coral FL 33990

Call Sign: KC4RVF
Ronald L Cruz
1004 SE 23rd Pl
Cape Coral FL 33990

Call Sign: KC4QXK
Joseph A Carbone
1434 SE 23rd Ter
Cape Coral FL 33990

Call Sign: WB2IDG
Edward V Engel Jr
2522 SE 22nd Pl
Cape Coral FL 33904

Call Sign: KF4QWG
Margaret G Janson
2514 SE 23rd Pl
Cape Coral FL 33904

Call Sign: KD4JTC
Scott J Whitacre
9 SE 24th Ave
Cape Coral FL 33990

Call Sign: N4TGU
James C L Taylor
3320 SE 22nd Pl
Cape Coral FL 339044245

Call Sign: KA3PFI
William A Janson Jr
2514 SE 23rd Pl
Cape Coral FL 33904

Call Sign: KD4SER
Mike A Greene
115 SE 24th Ave
Cape Coral FL 33904

Call Sign: KA4MBN
George P Eckenrode
3335 SE 22nd Pl
Cape Coral FL 339044426

Call Sign: KI4KGG
Robert D Schmidt
609 SE 23rd Ter
Cape Coral FL 33990

Call Sign: N9CJK
Ricardo F Kalybatas
2719 SE 24th Ct
Cape Coral FL 339043313

Call Sign: KI4VLQ
Dorian F Gulledge
628 SE 22nd St
Cape Coral FL 33990

Call Sign: W4KNY
Robert D Schmidt
609 SE 23rd Ter
Cape Coral FL 33990

Call Sign: N8UQO
Cheryl M Strong
209 SE 27th Ter
Cape Coral FL 339042731

Call Sign: KI4FQX
Darryl J Kwasny
1320 SE 22nd Ter
Cape Coral FL 33990

Call Sign: KI4NFR
Leslie E Schmidt
609 SE 23rd Ter
Cape Coral FL 33990

Call Sign: WB6PXO
Carmen Petrone
626 SE 27th Ter
Cape Coral FL 33904

Call Sign: K5WAS
Darryl J Kwasny
1320 SE 22nd Ter
Cape Coral FL 33990

Call Sign: K4PMS
Leslie E Schmidt
609 SE 23rd Ter
Cape Coral FL 33990

Call Sign: WA6RBG
Dorothy A Petrone
626 SE 27th Ter
Cape Coral FL 33904

Call Sign: WB9DRG
Harold E Spankus
119 SE 23rd Ave

Call Sign: WB1FXR
Robert E Day Jr
617 SE 23rd Ter

Call Sign: KD4CFV
Daniel M Davis
1116 SE 29 Ter

Cape Coral FL 33904

Cape Coral FL 33904

Cape Coral FL 33904

Call Sign: WB4OGT
George N Meyers Sr
3625 SE 2nd Ave
Cape Coral FL 33904

Call Sign: N8EOG
Alice L Underwood
619 SE 31st St
Cape Coral FL 339043546

Call Sign: KE4EWB
Lon P Lentz
806 SE 32nd St
Cape Coral FL 33904

Call Sign: KA3MAL
Albert J Paar
3814 SE 2nd Ave
Cape Coral FL 33904

Call Sign: KI4YR
Julius Teres
1417 SE 31st St
Cape Coral FL 33904

Call Sign: KB4YUG
James W Warren
1145 SE 32nd St
Cape Coral FL 33904

Call Sign: N1GOW
Robert G Hyssong
4101 SE 2nd Ave
Cape Coral FL 33904

Call Sign: N0RPL
Ronald E Newquist
1420 SE 31st St
Cape Coral FL 339043983

Call Sign: KB4YUL
Mary P Warren
1145 SE 32nd St
Cape Coral FL 33904

Call Sign: N3MGX
George W Thomas Jr
4105 SE 2nd Ave
Cape Coral FL 339048466

Call Sign: WA2QWO
Ronald F Krzos Sr
119 SE 31st Ter
Cape Coral FL 33904

Call Sign: WB2IWC
William E Warren Sr
1145 SE 32nd St
Cape Coral FL 33904

Call Sign: N2IXP
Anna M De Vito
1846 SE 2nd St
Cape Coral FL 33990

Call Sign: WB2QWO
Suzanne C Krzos
119 SE 31st Ter
Cape Coral FL 33904

Call Sign: KC4HAS
Brenda L Keeley
1518 SE 32nd St
Cape Coral FL 33904

Call Sign: W4OZ
Frank M De Vito
1846 SE 2nd St
Cape Coral FL 33990

Call Sign: WA6LSR
Lewis E Lint
1219 SE 31st Ter
Cape Coral FL 33904

Call Sign: KB4KJM
Thomas D Keeley
1518 SE 32nd St
Cape Coral FL 33904

Call Sign: NP2BN
Dorothy M Scholar
2120 SE 2nd Ter
Cape Coral FL 33990

Call Sign: K4JZY
Robert W Arndt
1401 SE 31st Ter
Cape Coral FL 339043944

Call Sign: W2TLI
Wayne R Beardsley
1923 SE 32nd Ter
Cape Coral FL 33904

Call Sign: KI4GAG
Mathew M Notte
413 SE 31 St
Cape Coral FL 33904

Call Sign: N8SAR
Sharon K Douglas
1438 SE 31st Ter
Cape Coral FL 33904

Call Sign: KD4USW
Jennifer A Moore
1323 SE 33 St
Cape Coral FL 33904

Call Sign: KJ4LCR
John R Reaville
615 SE 31 Ter

Call Sign: KO4RU
Frank H Shorkley
1510 SE 32 St

Call Sign: N8MZH
William H Kolberg
921 SE 33rd St

Cape Coral FL 33904   Cape Coral FL 33904   Cape Coral FL 33990

Call Sign: KE4SMQ
Robert T Sharp
546 SE 33rd Ter
Cape Coral FL 33904

Call Sign: W0CLA
Edward A Kroencke
1918 SE 37th Ter
Cape Coral FL 339045036

Call Sign: W7GXW
Charles S Brightman
527 SE 3rd St
Cape Coral FL 33990

Call Sign: KC8PNR
Jonathan M Steele
706 SE 33rd Ter
Cape Coral FL 33904

Call Sign: WB9ZLA
Kenneth R Moberley
1715 SE 39th Ter
Cape Coral FL 33904

Call Sign: WD8KUN
Danny R Beitelschies
849 SE 3rd Ter
Cape Coral FL 33990

Call Sign: KF4PHB
Donald M Marzonie
1303 SE 34 St
Cape Coral FL 33904

Call Sign: K4KRM
Kenneth R Moberley
1715 SE 39th Ter
Cape Coral FL 33904

Call Sign: WD8KTN
Rhonda K Beitelschies
849 SE 3rd Ter
Cape Coral FL 33990

Call Sign: WA4ADC
Frank J Convertine Jr
316 SE 34th St
Cape Coral FL 33904

Call Sign: KG4VOE
Albert J Da Conceicao
3507 SE 3rd Ave
Cape Coral FL 33904

Call Sign: KK4EM
Donald S Thorburn
1729 SE 40th St
Cape Coral FL 33904

Call Sign: KF4IDZ
Colin E Wood
1219 SE 34th Ter
Cape Coral FL 33904

Call Sign: KI4IRE
Grant A Lipps
2115 SE 3rd St
Cape Coral FL 33990

Call Sign: N4PFX
Eileen M Thorburn
1729 SE 40th St
Cape Coral FL 33904

Call Sign: KD4IB
Kingdon A Davidson
614 SE 35th St
Cape Coral FL 33904

Call Sign: KE4DLX
Christine A Knight
2118 SE 3rd St
Cape Coral FL 33990

Call Sign: KG4FTL
David T O Connor
1731 SE 40th Ter
Cape Coral FL 33904

Call Sign: N2YTT
Peter J Hall
909 SE 35th St
Cape Coral FL 33904

Call Sign: KJ4UDB
Lane Williams
2215 SE 3rd St
Cape Coral FL 33990

Call Sign: W9HUC
David T O Connor
1731 SE 40th Ter
Cape Coral FL 33904

Call Sign: KR4RX
Paul H J Kroppen
1932 SE 35th St
Cape Coral FL 33094

Call Sign: W0LRW
Lane Williams
2215 SE 3rd St
Cape Coral FL 33990

Call Sign: N1OLG
Donald G Anthony
1911 SE 40th Ter Apt 202
Cape Coral FL 33904

Call Sign: KF4WUW
Tara Salomone
1917 SE 36th St

Call Sign: N1OLJ
Charles E Brightman
527 SE 3rd St

Call Sign: KG6NMY
Horst Dieter Kemper
846 SE 41 St

Cape Coral FL 33904

Cape Coral FL 33904

Cape Coral FL 33990

Call Sign: KJ4OYP
Brittany A Mcdonnell
126 SE 41st St
Cape Coral FL 339048321

Call Sign: WD4IHM
David C Coffman Sr
150 SE 44th St
Cape Coral FL 33904

Call Sign: AI4OH
Russell F Moorman
935 SE 4th Pl
Cape Coral FL 33990

Call Sign: W1OLF
Henry A Gowing
1016 SE 41st St
Cape Coral FL 33904

Call Sign: KA2YHG
Susan E Ahrens
1901 SE 44th St
Cape Coral FL 33904

Call Sign: WX4L
Russell F Moorman
935 SE 4th Pl
Cape Coral FL 33990

Call Sign: KG4JRH
Richard E Mylchreest
117 SE 41st Ter
Cape Coral FL 33904

Call Sign: WB2MHY
Charles P Ahrens
1901 SE 44th St
Cape Coral FL 339046036

Call Sign: N4FLE
Richard K Fuson Sr
1906 SE 4th St
Cape Coral FL 339901325

Call Sign: KT4JI
Walter K Bicknese
413 SE 42nd Ter
Cape Coral FL 33904

Call Sign: W4DPS
Owen J Mc Reynolds
201 SE 44th Ter
Cape Coral FL 33904

Call Sign: KJ4WXK
Rodolfo O De Los Santos
1504 SE 5th Ct
Cape Coral FL 33990

Call Sign: WA4LT
Walter K Bicknese
413 SE 42nd Ter
Cape Coral FL 33904

Call Sign: N3WIV
Carl A Turner
1935 SE 45th St
Cape Coral FL 339041249

Call Sign: KJ4VXM
Gregory D Gang
4566 SE 5th Pl 204
Cape Coral FL 33904

Call Sign: W4LRB
Charles W Mc Dormand
1035 SE 43rd St
Cape Coral FL 33904

Call Sign: KI4BAH
Norman J Bille
243 SE 46th Ln
Cape Coral FL 33904

Call Sign: KC4KHY
Mark C Bove
1813 SE 5th Ter
Cape Coral FL 33990

Call Sign: W4KA
Leo C Haijsman
1044 SE 43rd St
Cape Coral FL 33904

Call Sign: KA4SOJ
Donald R Langevin
1739 SE 46th Ln 202
Cape Coral FL 33904

Call Sign: W2TXA
Norman J Krueger
2114 SE 5th Ter
Cape Coral FL 33990

Call Sign: W2ZTO
Jack E Roomy
408 SE 43rd Ter
Cape Coral FL 33904

Call Sign: K8WUG
Frank H Mathias
605 SE 4th Pl
Cape Coral FL 33990

Call Sign: KD4YEF
Rishi A Puran
1109 SE 6 Ter
Cape Coral FL 33990

Call Sign: KK4HW
Julius Lewis
1224 SE 43rd Ter

Call Sign: N8GJG
Patricia J Mathias
605 SE 4th Pl

Call Sign: KF4HWX
Barbara L Howard
4628 SE 6th Ave D

Cape Coral FL 33904   Cape Coral FL 33990   Cape Coral FL 33904

Call Sign: KE4YGP   Call Sign: KJ4LCS   Call Sign: KG4CWP
James M Howard Jr   James B Miller Jr   David M Burnett
4628 SE 6th Ave D   3110 SE 8th Pl   4112 SE 9th Ct
Cape Coral FL 33904   Cape Coral FL 33904   Cape Coral FL 339045316

Call Sign: KJ4DOY   Call Sign: W9TJG   Call Sign: KB4ZNN
Patricia A Westbrook   Kenneth R Fleming   Brian J O Callaghan
4511 SE 6th Pl 103   3648 SE 8th Pl   429 SE 9th Pl
Cape Coral FL 33904   Cape Coral FL 33904   Cape Coral FL 33990

Call Sign: KJ4ZSX   Call Sign: KJ4MCA   Call Sign: KC4HHR
Hartmut Krueger Jr   Deborah A Depont   Marie E O Callaghan
602 SE 6th Ter   114 SE 8th St   429 SE 9th Pl
Cape Coral FL 33990   Cape Coral FL 33990   Cape Coral FL 33990

Call Sign: KD4YEE   Call Sign: WA2AQC   Call Sign: KF4WUX
Nadia F Noor   Jeffrey T Levine   Matthew C Hogencamp
1808 SE 6th Ter   1622 SE 8th St   707 SE 9th Pl
Cape Coral FL 33990   Cape Coral FL 33990   Cape Coral FL 33900

Call Sign: KE4PCN   Call Sign: N2III   Call Sign: KC2CZC
Marc R Hawkins   Jeffrey T Levine   Kathleen B Webb
1300 SE 7th St   1622 SE 8th St   1814 SE 9th Ter
Cape Coral FL 33990   Cape Coral FL 33990   Cape Coral FL 33990

Call Sign: KC4LMH   Call Sign: KC4NSF   Call Sign: KB2EO
Bryan A Munsey   John T Lison   Wayne Webb
1918 SE 7th St   1803 SE 8th St   1814 SE 9th Ter
Cape Coral FL 33990   Cape Coral FL 33990   Cape Coral FL 33990

Call Sign: K3QEG   Call Sign: KD4PLF   Call Sign: KD4NPS
Henry A Kues Jr   Joseph M Henderson   Jason M Alpen
2140 SE 8th Ave   1832 SE 8th Ter   2216 SE 9th Ter
Cape Coral FL 33990   Cape Coral FL 33990   Cape Coral FL 33990

Call Sign: KF4JUH   Call Sign: KJ4WXG   Call Sign: KD4WJI
Jay B Halase   William Mangus Sr   Lynne F Manley
205 SE 8th Pl   727 SE 9th Ave   5227 Seminole Ct
Cape Coral FL 33990   Cape Coral FL 33990   Cape Coral FL 33904

Call Sign: KF4RSO   Call Sign: KG4ISV   Call Sign: K1LYN
Jessica L Evans   Vicki L Burnett   Lynne F Manley
1401 SE 8th Pl   4112 SE 9th Ct   5227 Seminole Ct

Cape Coral FL 33904

Call Sign: W6PCP
Gordon R Meyer
4964 Seville Ct
Cape Coral FL 33904

Call Sign: KA4FZI
Phyllisan West
1410 Shelby Pkwy
Cape Coral FL 33904

Call Sign: KE4ZVJ
Michael E Glazer
2601 Shelby Pkwy
Cape Coral FL 33901

Call Sign: KM6KJ
Leonhard Schmidl
5275 Skylark Ct
Cape Coral FL 33904

Call Sign: WA1YLS
Paul H Harlow
2620 Somerville Loop
Unit 2005
Cape Coral FL 339913085

Call Sign: WR4J
A Harrison Ewing Jr
4956 Sorrento Ct
Cape Coral FL 339049434

Call Sign: KB5SNJ
Robert D Stauffer
5055 Sorrento Ct
Cape Coral FL 33904

Call Sign: N8AVK
Eugene C Mc Carthy
5207 Stratford Ct
Cape Coral FL 33904

Call Sign: KE4EPW
Carolyn M Benson

5242 Stratford Ct
Cape Coral FL 33904

Call Sign: N6WRG
John C Benson
5242 Stratford Ct
Cape Coral FL 33904

Call Sign: KO4SH
William J Donaldson
5246 Stratford Ct
Cape Coral FL 33904

Call Sign: W2VGP
Elmer E White
5121 Sunnybrook Ct
Cape Coral FL 33904

Call Sign: K8JZK
Donald C Clifford Sr
2902 Surfside Bl
Cape Coral FL 33914

Call Sign: N2RSR
Peter A Burt
2520 Surfside Blvd
Cape Coral FL 33914

Call Sign: KE4KJS
Richard H Key
4930 SW 10th Ave
Cape Coral FL 33914

Call Sign: KJ4USZ
Norman W Cherry
505 SW 10th Pl
Cape Coral FL 33991

Call Sign: W1NWC
Norman W Cherry
505 SW 10th Pl
Cape Coral FL 33991

Call Sign: NC3F
Norman W Cherry

505 SW 10th Pl
Cape Coral FL 33991

Call Sign: W9UCR
Robert W Lade
2941 SW 10th Pl
Cape Coral FL 33914

Call Sign: KA4MOP
Andrew S Lade
2941 SW 10th Pl
Cape Coral FL 33914

Call Sign: N9HZT
Nancy J Lade
2941 SW 10th Pl
Cape Coral FL 33914

Call Sign: KE4PVS
Evaldo C Lopez
1113 SW 11th Ave
Cape Coral FL 33991

Call Sign: K4CLD
Clark L Durpo Jr
5301 SW 11th Ave
Cape Coral FL 33914

Call Sign: KY8Y
Peggy H Griffith
1025 SW 11th Ct
Cape Coral FL 33991

Call Sign: W2ZUC
Robert H Griffith
1025 SW 11th Ct
Cape Coral FL 33991

Call Sign: KK4BQP
Robert W Draper
806 SW 11th Pl
Cape Coral FL 33991

Call Sign: AA9U
John L Zimmerman

810 SW 11th Pl
Cape Coral FL 33991

4209 SW 14
Cape Coral FL 33914

3922 SW 1st Ave
Cape Coral FL 33914

Call Sign: WB9OIG
Shirley A Zimmerman
810 SW 11th Pl
Cape Coral FL 339912453

Call Sign: KD4YEI
Karen R Price
2511 SW 15th Ave
Cape Coral FL 33914

Call Sign: WA4MHP
Harry L Sutter
4502 SW 1st Ave
Cape Coral FL 33914

Call Sign: N5OVM
Jack C Thompson
5012 SW 11th Pl
Cape Coral FL 339147079

Call Sign: K3URN
William T Copes
716 SW 15th Ter
Cape Coral FL 339912780

Call Sign: KI4KGH
Michael R Pfaff
5936 SW 1st Ave
Cape Coral FL 33914

Call Sign: KF4ECZ
Kenneth M Baumann
5510 SW 11th Pl
Cape Coral FL 33914

Call Sign: WT4T
Dale A Pavlicek
2003 SW 17th Pl
Cape Coral FL 33991

Call Sign: KF4ZMI
Scott J Eisenmann
3322 SW 1st Pl
Cape Coral FL 33914

Call Sign: KJ4MBV
Craig C Martin
2540 SW 12 Pl
Cape Coral FL 33914

Call Sign: KA4ZUQ
Julie A Previty
856 SW 18th Ter
Cape Coral FL 33991

Call Sign: WB2MDK
Mary Ann E Haycook
2603 SW 1st Ter
Cape Coral FL 33991

Call Sign: KJ4MBZ
Cynthia L Martin
2540 SW 12th Pl
Cape Coral FL 33914

Call Sign: KA4EET
Ronald A Previty
856 SW 18th Ter
Cape Coral FL 33991

Call Sign: WB9MNK
Mark S Schaller
4228 SW 20th Ave
Cape Coral FL 33914

Call Sign: KJ4MBW
Kyle R Martin
2540 SW 12th Pl
Cape Coral FL 33914

Call Sign: KC2BZS
Carlos Porta
435 SW 19th Ter
Cape Coral FL 33991

Call Sign: KJ4EUO
Mark A Shamrock Sr
4516 SW 20th Pl
Cape Coral FL 33914

Call Sign: KJ4MBY
Nathan C Martin
2540 SW 12th Pl
Cape Coral FL 33914

Call Sign: KI4FMJ
Brian E Murray
3745 SW 1st Ave
Cape Coral FL 33914

Call Sign: W9MSS
Mark A Shamrock Sr
4516 SW 20th Pl
Cape Coral FL 33914

Call Sign: KJ4MBX
Travis J Martin
2540 SW 12th Pl
Cape Coral FL 33914

Call Sign: KJ4KGX
Leonard Varcadipane
3752 SW 1st Ave
Cape Coral FL 33914

Call Sign: WR4A
Mark A Shamrock Sr
4516 SW 20th Pl
Cape Coral FL 33914

Call Sign: KG4GZJ
Wm C Wilkinson

Call Sign: K4YSN
Tandy Way

Call Sign: KF2QS
Carl F Sutphin

225 SW 22nd Pl
Cape Coral FL 33991

4105 SW 27 Ave
Cape Coral FL 33914

5402 SW 2nd Pl
Cape Coral FL 33914

Call Sign: AD4CS
Carl F Sutphin
225 SW 22nd Pl
Cape Coral FL 33991

Call Sign: KI4SYN
Julius Morreal
4105 SW 27 Ave
Cape Coral FL 33914

Call Sign: KJ4MMS
Norma J Gafford
231 SW 31st St
Cape Coral FL 33914

Call Sign: KC2IAG
Ethel H Sutphin
225 SW 22nd Pl
Cape Coral FL 33991

Call Sign: N0WL
Joseph P Markowski
4906 SW 27th Pl
Cape Coral FL 339147600

Call Sign: KJ4MMR
Tommie L Gafford
231 SW 31st St
Cape Coral FL 33914

Call Sign: KB4EHS
Ethel H Sutphin
225 SW 22nd Pl
Cape Coral FL 33991

Call Sign: KR4LL
Stephen T Grice
5314 SW 27th Pl
Cape Coral FL 33914

Call Sign: KI4REJ
Matthew D Faust
236 SW 33 St
Cape Coral FL 33614

Call Sign: N0FRS
Mark L Heuer
2900 SW 25th Ave
Cape Coral FL 33914

Call Sign: W4JAB
James W Travis
4102 SW 28th Ave
Cape Coral FL 33914

Call Sign: KA9MRQ
Gary A Binder
209 SW 33rd St
Cape Coral FL 33914

Call Sign: KC4ZVE
Thomas G Phillips
3921 SW 25th Pl
Cape Coral FL 33914

Call Sign: WB4DFM
David G Schlobohm Pe
2576 SW 28th Pl
Cape Coral FL 339143844

Call Sign: KJ4DI
Pablo M Fernandez Sr
114 SW 35th Ter
Cape Coral FL 33914

Call Sign: KE4ZVI
Sigmund M Eisenreich
4006 SW 25th Pl
Cape Coral FL 33914

Call Sign: W8DNO
Timothy L Runion
2629 SW 29th Pl
Cape Coral FL 33914

Call Sign: KB1B
David S Taylor
2808 SW 36th Ter
Cape Coral FL 33914

Call Sign: KI4HST
Lori N Blydenburgh
353 SW 26 Pl
Cape Coral FL 33991

Call Sign: KG4PUL
Randy A Thompson
2617 SW 2nd Ave
Cape Coral FL 33914

Call Sign: WA2EVP
Robert M Pierson Sr
820 SW 37th St
Cape Coral FL 33914

Call Sign: KI4AHO
Mark A Blydenburgh
353 SW 26th Pl
Cape Coral FL 33991

Call Sign: WB8IIX
Richard V Millett
4907 SW 2nd Ave
Cape Coral FL 339147198

Call Sign: N0VBL
George F James
2801 SW 38th Ter
Cape Coral FL 339142808

Call Sign: KI4SYM
Jeanette Morreal

Call Sign: KJ4HEU
Major E Weber

Call Sign: N1XVW
Larry W Vincent

222 SW 39th Ter
Cape Coral FL 33914

Call Sign: KF4IDX
Mary C Pickel
401 SW 39th Ter
Cape Coral FL 33914

Call Sign: WA2GSH
William H Seegmuller
2803 SW 39th Ter
Cape Coral FL 33914

Call Sign: KD9RB
Larry L Smith
803 SW 3rd Ave
Cape Coral FL 339912504

Call Sign: W3ITO
Frederick R Muccino
3222 SW 3rd Ave
Cape Coral FL 339145018

Call Sign: KI4JUF
Guido Husgen
4536 SW 3rd Ave
Cape Coral FL 33914

Call Sign: AI3A
Guido Husgen
4536 SW 3rd Ave
Cape Coral FL 33914

Call Sign: KJ4HFR
Armin Irlacher
4536 SW 3rd Ave
Cape Coral FL 33914

Call Sign: WA9SMN
Steven T Barefoot
5118 SW 3rd Ave
Cape Coral FL 33914

Call Sign: KD3I
Thomas E Hassing

5312 SW 3rd Ave
Cape Coral FL 33914

Call Sign: KK4GBW
Willis G Miller
1140 SW 42nd Ter
Cape Coral FL 33914

Call Sign: KB8LZP
Richard D Staeb
237 SW 43rd St
Cape Coral FL 33914

Call Sign: KJ4ZEU
Raymond Strods Jr
2126 SW 44 Ter
Cape Coral FL 33914

Call Sign: KC4WIH
Thomas F Phillips
1157 SW 44th St
Cape Coral FL 33914

Call Sign: KJ4N
Janice R Scheuerman
413 SW 46th Ter
Cape Coral FL 33914

Call Sign: WA2YL
Janice R Scheuerman
413 SW 46th Ter
Cape Coral FL 33914

Call Sign: KG4MSF
Cape Coral Young Ladies
ARC
413 SW 46th Ter
Cape Coral FL 339146466

Call Sign: WA4YL
Cape Coral Young Ladies
ARC
413 SW 46th Ter
Cape Coral FL 339146466

Call Sign: WB9ZPN
Kenneth R Gustafson
1314 SW 47th St
Cape Coral FL 33914

Call Sign: WA2MZX
Raffaele J Cerbone
303 SW 47th Ter
Cape Coral FL 33914

Call Sign: WB2KTM
David J Hawkins
1016 SW 48th Ter 204
Cape Coral FL 33914

Call Sign: W2AOK
Clarence L Morris
1522 SW 49th St
Cape Coral FL 33914

Call Sign: N3CSP
Roger C Stuart
1404 SW 49th Ter
Cape Coral FL 339146933

Call Sign: KB2WDW
Brian P Mazur
1805 SW 4th Ave
Cape Coral FL 33991

Call Sign: KF4KVW
Jose R Gonzalez
1202 SW 4th Pl
Cape Coral FL 33991

Call Sign: KA4WNP
John J Ruskai
163 SW 51 Ter
Cape Coral FL 33904

Call Sign: KB3HZ
Allen A Orr III
142 SW 51st St
Cape Coral FL 339147126

Call Sign: KB2TD
Jaime Ares
2205 SW 51st St
Cape Coral FL 33914

Call Sign: AD4LX
Raymond S Phelps
1440 SW 53rd Ter
Cape Coral FL 33914

Call Sign: K4BDG
Bruce D Gehrke
608 SW 6th Ave
Cape Coral FL 33991

Call Sign: W1JHZ
Robert P Duff
139 SW 52D Ter
Cape Coral FL 339147114

Call Sign: W2PAC
Sebastian Greif
1209 SW 54th Ln
Cape Coral FL 33914

Call Sign: KG4HGN
David A Strongin
4340 SW 6th Ave
Cape Coral FL 33914

Call Sign: W2QVB
Martin C Durciansky
154 SW 52nd St
Cape Coral FL 339147126

Call Sign: N3JSS
Matthew W Kania
128 SW 54th St
Cape Coral FL 33914

Call Sign: KF4YOX
Samuel A Strongin
4340 SW 6th Ave
Cape Coral FL 33914

Call Sign: KI4LUC
Catherine C Randlett
2613 SW 52nd St
Cape Coral FL 339147601

Call Sign: W3IIE
Joseph T Holland Jr
114 SW 56th Ter
Cape Coral FL 33914

Call Sign: KB8AVN
Cornelis D Vandenberg Jr
4404 SW 6th Ave
Cape Coral FL 33914

Call Sign: KB8GV
Frank W Ade
1416 SW 52nd Ter
Cape Coral FL 33904

Call Sign: WB2IEV
Joseph C Gafa
1507 SW 56th Ter
Cape Coral FL 33914

Call Sign: KI4DYP
Joseph A Elliot
5415 SW 6th Ave
Cape Coral FL 33914

Call Sign: KB0LPM
Don P Lawson
1411 SW 53rd Ln
Cape Coral FL 33914

Call Sign: KD4NZA
Linda Saha
111 SW 59 St
Cape Coral FL 33914

Call Sign: AA1MG
Bernard J Orcutt
1425 SW 6th Pl
Cape Coral FL 339912759

Call Sign: KE4AIU
Cecil R Hazen Jr
1525 SW 53rd Ln
Cape Coral FL 33914

Call Sign: KA1KG
Kevin J Mc Namara
4705 SW 5th Pl
Cape Coral FL 33914

Call Sign: KI4ZDA
Daniel W Barrett
925 SW 7th Ave
Cape Coral FL 33991

Call Sign: KR4MZ
Jacqueline J Kampfert
1533 SW 53rd Ln
Cape Coral FL 33914

Call Sign: N1YLS
Patricia K Orcutt
1425 SW 6 Pl
Cape Coral FL 33991

Call Sign: KE4ZIZ
Kent W Williams
4218 SW 7th Ave
Cape Coral FL 33914

Call Sign: KO4JP
Donald E Costa
1212 SW 53rd St
Cape Coral FL 33914

Call Sign: KI4IUM
Bruce D Gehrke
608 SW 6th Ave
Cape Coral FL 33991

Call Sign: KD4ELK
William C Rigney
5344 SW 8 Pl
Cape Coral FL 33914

Call Sign: KA9VRY
John E Webb
5344 SW 8th Ct
Cape Coral FL 33914

Call Sign: KI4AHP
Sonia M Raymond
4811 SW 8th Pl 102E
Cape Coral FL 33914

Call Sign: K1BDR
Edward W Dahn
4937 SW 9th Pl
Cape Coral FL 33914

Call Sign: W4LSI
Kaye Palmer
5209 SW 9th Pl
Cape Coral FL 339147016

Call Sign: W8ULH
Walter H Struze
5336 SW 9th Pl
Cape Coral FL 33914

Call Sign: N4WTL
Timothy G Wilson
419 SW Pine Island Rd 5 8
Cape Coral FL 33991

Call Sign: KD6VVC
Linda S Pignatano
1242 SW Pine Island Rd
Ste 42 502
Cape Coral FL 33991

Call Sign: KN1P
Neil D Pignatano
1242 SW Pine Island Rd
Ste 42 502
Cape Coral FL 33991

Call Sign: KF4TZP
Louis J Ziakas Sr
1232 SW Santa Barbara Pl

Cape Coral FL 33991

Call Sign: N1UUW
Carmine M D Amore
2720 SW Santa Barbara Pl
Cape Coral FL 33914

Call Sign: KB9CJ
Albert W Hofmann
524 SW Trafalgar Pkwy
Cape Coral FL 33991

Call Sign: KN6WC
Lawrence S Lewis
5925 Tarpon Gardens Cir
101
Cape Coral FL 33914

Call Sign: N4VPN
Agnes M Thornber
5238 Tiffany Ct
Cape Coral FL 33904

Call Sign: KI4FD
Thomas J Whatley
5238 Tiffany Ct
Cape Coral FL 33904

Call Sign: KJ4INU
Dennis P Ukele
1449 Vendome Ct
Cape Coral FL 33904

Call Sign: K4DPU
Dennis P Ukele
1449 Vendome Ct
Cape Coral FL 33904

Call Sign: KD4YLM
Edward C Godfrey
708 Victoria Dr Unit 105
Cape Coral FL 33904

Call Sign: K1CCI
Gerard J De Stefano

1441 Viking Ct
Cape Coral FL 33904

Call Sign: KD4CFW
Mike Ware
4904 Vincennes Ct Apt
204
Cape Coral FL 33904

Call Sign: K8CBA
Hyman Lapirow
4940 Vincennes St 103
Cape Coral FL 33904

Call Sign: K3JXC
Casper Tootgooshian
2325 Viscaya Pky
Cape Coral FL 33990

Call Sign: N0LTS
Robert D Henry
1616 W Cape Coral Pkwy
Ste 226
Cape Coral FL 33914

Call Sign: N4RRH
Susan P Henry
1616 W Cape Coral Pkwy
Ste 226
Cape Coral FL 33914

Call Sign: KG4NBC
Scott B Upton
2051 Willow Branch Dr
Cape Coral FL 33919

Call Sign: AE4BW
John I Murphy
1402 Willshire Ct
Cape Coral FL 33904

Call Sign: KC4ZSO
Forrest L Futral
1417 Windsor Ct
Cape Coral FL 33904

Call Sign: N4FKM
Frank E Rowe
5235 Wisteria Ct
Cape Coral FL 33904

Call Sign: WD6AMH
Jack R Cockrell
5239 Wisteria Ct
Cape Coral FL 33904

Call Sign: WB9UCZ
Everett L Spring
5249 Wisteria Ct
Cape Coral FL 33904

Call Sign: KB0BDL
Beverly C Miller
5141 York Ct
Cape Coral FL 33904

Call Sign: KG4VOD
Yoshifumi Ueda
4920 York St 3
Cape Coral FL 33904

Call Sign: KC4OHI
Lowell A O Grady Jr
Cape Coral FL 33915

Call Sign: K2CEK
Daniel J Goodman
Cape Coral FL 339153003

Call Sign: KC4EHW
Marie Anne J Densmore
Cape Coral FL 33909

Call Sign: KJ4GAW
Margery L Lamb
Cape Coral FL 33910

Call Sign: N1JHC
Christie L Malloy
Cape Coral FL 33915

Call Sign: KI4SYL
Mark R Morreal
Cape Coral FL 33915

Call Sign: W4QY
Michael J Harrington
Cape Coral FL 33915

Call Sign: N1FXP
Patrick J Malloy
Cape Coral FL 33915

Call Sign: N4TGV
Bruce R Bezdek
Cape Coral FL 33990

Call Sign: WB9VVV
Raymond J Schneider
Cape Coral FL 339151622

Call Sign: N2XWQ
Deanna C M Konior
Cape Coral FL 339152317

Call Sign: K4RFK
Robert F Konior
Cape Coral FL 339152317

Call Sign: KB8BTS
Dennis W Malloy
Cape Coral FL 339152922

**FCC Amateur Radio
Licenses in Cape Haze**

Call Sign: KG4RSG
John P Combs
255 Capstan Dr
Cape Haze FL 33946

Call Sign: K9JPC
John P Combs
255 Capstan Dr
Cape Haze FL 33946

Call Sign: W4VMD
John P Combs
255 Capstan Dr
Cape Haze FL 33946

Call Sign: K2YKW
William J Dahms
385 Capstan Dr
Cape Haze FL 33946

Call Sign: KE4YHS
Hank Irvine
255 N Green Dolphin Dr
Cape Haze FL 33946

Call Sign: KJ4ZXB
Ray Ann Antonucci
8409 Placida Rd 406
Cape Haze FL 33946

Call Sign: W1JF
John S Fogle
435 Spaniards Rd
Cape Haze FL 33946

**FCC Amateur Radio
Licenses in Captiva**

Call Sign: KG6PSS
David N Starr
Captiva FL 33924

Call Sign: WA8GGX
Michael D Mc Millan
Captiva FL 33924

**FCC Amateur Radio
Licenses in Charlotte
Harbor**

Call Sign: K0REQ
Wendell C Peterson
120 Danforth Dr
Charlotte Harbor FL 33980

Call Sign: WD4HPJ
Charles J Zimmerman
23425 Harborview Rd 11B
Charlotte Harbor FL 33980

Call Sign: W9QHW
James D Fry
24437 Harborview Rd Site
67
Charlotte Harbor FL
339802345

Call Sign: KD4KWH
James L Harris
4032 Oakview Dr H8
Charlotte Harbor FL 33980

Call Sign: KD3BI
Mark A Hoseley
22300 Vick St
Charlotte Harbor FL 33980

FCC Amateur Radio Licenses in Chokoloskee

Call Sign: KC4NSJ
Arthur L Becton Sr
Chokoloskee FL 33925

Call Sign: KG8HJ
Lawrence O Beck
Chokoloskee FL 34138

FCC Amateur Radio Licenses in Clewiston

Call Sign: WB4TWQ
Francisco Cabrera
542 Ave Del Sur
Clewiston FL 33440

Call Sign: KJ4PMW
William Gonzalez
542 Ave Del Sur

Clewiston FL 33440

Call Sign: KI4BQC
Chen Jian Hu
1056 Bayberry Loop
Clewiston FL 33440

Call Sign: KF4UFD
Ronald E Bock Jr
Box 374
Clewiston FL 33440

Call Sign: KA1EGS
Harvey A Morse
828 E Concordia Ave Apt
1
Clewiston FL 33440

Call Sign: KE4IFA
William E Bailey
315 E El Paso Ave
Clewiston FL 33440

Call Sign: AI4D
Ralph J Marotta
518 E Esperanza
Clewiston FL 33440

Call Sign: KF4VYL
Adelaida E Ramirez
330 E Obispo Ave
Clewiston FL 33440

Call Sign: KF4VYU
Alberto Ramirez
330 E Obispo Ave
Clewiston FL 33440

Call Sign: KF4VYJ
John Herrera
330 E Obispo Ave
Clewiston FL 33440

Call Sign: K4ZND
James W Rider Sr

602 E Osceola Ave
Clewiston FL 33440

Call Sign: W4DCN
James W Rider Sr
602 E Osceola Ave
Clewiston FL 33440

Call Sign: WA4PAM
Frank C Harris
512 E Pasadena Ave
Clewiston FL 33440

Call Sign: KI4AYW
Big Lake ARC
512 E Pasadena Ave
Clewiston FL 33440

Call Sign: KI4YCY
Alex A Abreu
2041 Everhigh Acres Rd
Clewiston FL 33440

Call Sign: KG4JCP
Alisa M Abreu
2041 Everhigh Acres Rd
Clewiston FL 33440

Call Sign: KI4HJG
Nicholas J Simicich
1000 Marco Ave
Clewiston FL 334405674

Call Sign: K9NJS
Nicholas J Simicich
1000 Marco Ave
Clewiston FL 334405674

Call Sign: KG4HHK
Rene C Mondejar
735 N Datil St
Clewiston FL 33440

Call Sign: NP4WT
Carlos I Infante

170 N Lindero St
Clewiston FL 33440

170 S Datil St
Clewiston FL 33440

135 W Crescent Dr
Clewiston FL 334402903

Call Sign: KJ4PMY
Miguel Infante
170 N Lindero St
Clewiston FL 33440

Call Sign: WB4TWA
Marilyn Garcia
170 S Datil St
Clewiston FL 33440

Call Sign: KF4VYI
Epifanio Bovilla
600 W Obispo Ave
Clewiston FL 33440

Call Sign: KF4HXP
Nellie Zayas
170 N Lindero St
Clewiston FL 33440

Call Sign: KJ4GNO
Sherilynn Gonzalez
170 S Datil St
Clewiston FL 33440

Call Sign: KI4GKG
Jose I Juarez
307 W Sugarland Cir
Clewiston FL 33440

Call Sign: KI4X
Anthony Toulis
821 N Lopez St
Clewiston FL 33440

Call Sign: KG4APX
Elena Medina
370 S Fronda St
Clewiston FL 33440

Call Sign: KB5EXH
Dan A Jacobson
324 W Ventura Ave
Clewiston FL 33440

Call Sign: KF4ZQT
Jerry A Rushing
1550 Old US 27 Lot 299
Clewiston FL 33440

Call Sign: W4CD
Luis Medina
370 S Fronda St
Clewiston FL 33440

Call Sign: KG4NNN
Carl D Cardin
Clewiston FL 33440

Call Sign: KG4TQA
Christopher J Norwood
Clewiston FL 33440

Call Sign: KG4NSI
Jessica D De La Cruz
1550 Old US 27 Lot 82
Clewiston FL 33440

Call Sign: AJ4WJ
Ernesto Lopez
245 S Olivo St
Clewiston FL 33440

Call Sign: AF4BI
Gary L Moore
Clewiston FL 33440

Call Sign: KJ4GVO
Juan A Cabrera Batista
100 Palm Ave
Clewiston FL 33440

Call Sign: KA4PRF
Charles F Bolland
355 S Romero St
Clewiston FL 33440

Call Sign: KJ4JLM
Gary L Sapp
Clewiston FL 33440

Call Sign: KJ4GVV
Reina Veamonte Alonso
100 Palm Ave
Clewiston FL 33440

Call Sign: WA8DAF
Gary D Wilson
613 Sabal Ave
Clewiston FL 334405007

Call Sign: WA4SQH
James J Pappas
Clewiston FL 33440

Call Sign: KI4MBA
Roger P Plouffe
718 Poinciana St
Clewiston FL 33440

Call Sign: KJ4SWN
Silvia L Suarez
245 Soliuost
Clewiston FL 33440

Call Sign: KJ4JLL
Margarita O Sapp
Clewiston FL 33440

Call Sign: WB4EPP
Raymond O Reynolds
Clewiston FL 33440

Call Sign: KJ4GNM
Marilyn Garcia

Call Sign: W3ALE
Samuel S Thomas

Call Sign: WB4MQO
William G Perry
Clewiston FL 33440

Call Sign: K2XOX
Cw Operators Club
Clewiston FL 33440

Call Sign: AA4BN
James P Sparks
Clewiston FL 334400924

Call Sign: WR6DX
Winfried E Bender
Clewiston FL 334402384

FCC Amateur Radio Licenses in East Fort Myers

Call Sign: KG4EAF
Thomas B Burnett
6100 Industry Ave
East Fort Myers FL 33905

FCC Amateur Radio Licenses in El Jobean

Call Sign: KJ4YFE
Phyllis A Atha
El Jobean FL 33927

FCC Amateur Radio Licenses in Estero

Call Sign: KG4ZLB
David A Worboys
21066 Butchers Holler
Estero FL 33928

Call Sign: KC4IDC
Patricia S Walton
20280 Carriage Ct
Estero FL 33928

Call Sign: KC4ETD
William H Walton Jr
20280 Carriage Ct
Estero FL 33928

Call Sign: N1INV
Raymond S Falcoa Sr
20331 Castlemaine Ave
Estero FL 33928

Call Sign: N1QQM
Suzanne D Falcoa
20331 Castlemaine Ave
Estero FL 33928

Call Sign: KG4ODY
Andrew M Herold
20576 Charing Cross Cir
Estero FL 33928

Call Sign: WD8JKO
Georgia W Gates
20131 Cobblestone Ct
Estero FL 33928

Call Sign: WD8KFV
Raymond J Gates
20131 Cobblestone Ct
Estero FL 33928

Call Sign: K4VVB
Irvin L Weathers
17550 Corkscrew Rd
Estero FL 33928

Call Sign: KD4JNP
William T Mc Morris
8524 Covewood Dr
Estero FL 33928

Call Sign: KD4JNN
George M Gille
8508 Firwood
Estero FL 33928

Call Sign: KB8ACJ
Douglas J Scofea
22914 Forest Ridge Dr
Estero FL 33928

Call Sign: N3HRW
Richard P Lee
23151 Grassy Pine Dr
Estero FL 339284329

Call Sign: KG4ZKB
Robert W Gosnell
20771 Groveline Ct
Estero FL 339283136

Call Sign: KD8VL
Stanley R Grabiec
20810 Hammock Greens
Ln Unit 302
Estero FL 33928

Call Sign: WA1FJ
Frederick S Jarvis
4218 Jace Ct
Estero FL 33928

Call Sign: KE4PXN
Henry W Kinghorn
4690 Jefferson David Blvd
W
Estero FL 33928

Call Sign: AD4VW
Ralf A Wehr
4561 Jefferson Davis Blvd
E
Estero FL 33928

Call Sign: KC8DH
James R Blake
21450 Knighton Run
Estero FL 33928

Call Sign: AE4JN

William C Dwyer
4571 Lafayette Ln E
Estero FL 33928

Call Sign: KB8DGQ
Keith W Minnick
4721 Lincoln Ln W
Estero FL 33928

Call Sign: KK4HQH
Jeffery T Wolf
4791 Palmetto Ter
Estero FL 33928

Call Sign: N0ILX
Arthur A Habighorst
20841 Persimmon Pl
Estero FL 33928

Call Sign: WA0TXO
Marc C Miller
4558 Pinehurst Greens Ct
Estero FL 33928

Call Sign: WD4PSP
Philip F Pumilia
20537 Port Hole Ct
Estero FL 33928

Call Sign: WA2MLN
Philip F Pumilia
20537 Porthole Ct
Estero FL 33928

Call Sign: K1YZI
Sterling M Nickless
10726 Red Cardinal Cir
Estero FL 33928

Call Sign: K8IJZ
Warren E Geng
10705 Rio Mar Cir
Estero FL 33928

Call Sign: AA7MH

Harwood Shepard Jr
20322 Rookery Dr
Estero FL 33928

Call Sign: K7HS
Spruce Mountain Amateur
Radio Society
20322 Rookery Dr
Estero FL 33928

Call Sign: W9ACF
Jeffrey Stone
10717 San Tropez Cir
Estero FL 33928

Call Sign: KD4PSX
Christopher G Spell
22701 Sandy Bay Dr 201
Estero FL 33928

Call Sign: KE4CFV
William F Schultheis
4530 Sawmill Dr E
Estero FL 33928

Call Sign: AC4TM
James T Muye
22134 Seashire Cir
Estero FL 33928

Call Sign: WA8LRC
Allen F Collver
22049 Seashore Cir
Estero FL 33928

Call Sign: KI4ZXO
James T Muye
22134 Seashore Cir
Estero FL 33928

Call Sign: KA4GVZ
G Edward Church
3 Stork Cir
Estero FL 33928

Call Sign: KG4QXV
Alice A Frigge
10811 Stork Cir
Estero FL 33928

Call Sign: W0MEN
Alice A Frigge
10811 Stork Cir
Estero FL 33928

Call Sign: KG4QXW
James D Tate
10811 Stork Cir
Estero FL 33928

Call Sign: KK4JDT
James D Tate
10811 Stork Cir
Estero FL 33928

Call Sign: KE6TCP
Debbie L Sirois
20463 Torre Del Lago St
Estero FL 33928

Call Sign: KF6IUA
Donna Sirois
20643 Torre Del Lago St
Estero FL 33928

Call Sign: KG4UAA
Marlyn K Kandra
4234 Ute Ct
Estero FL 33928

Call Sign: KD7BUW
Michael S Trueblood
8533 Via Garibaldi Cir 201
Estero FL 33928

Call Sign: KB9SBQ
Franklin A Cirino Jr
9701 Willow Way
Estero FL 33928

Call Sign: KK4FRE
Richard J Korecki Jr
21703 Windham Run
Estero FL 33928

Call Sign: WB3IIM
John Migliore
20063 Wolfel Trl
Estero FL 33928

Call Sign: KF4LJL
Amy A Kolb
Estero FL 33928

Call Sign: KI4UNB
Darlene B Wrona
Estero FL 33928

Call Sign: KC5FQW
James A Finan Jr
Estero FL 33928

Call Sign: KI4UEC
Rodger A Wrona
Estero FL 33928

FCC Amateur Radio Licenses in Everglades City

Call Sign: N4ICY
Robert H Rosen
707 Collier Ave
Everglades City FL 33929

Call Sign: KC4IDA
Jane B Barber
Glades Edge
Everglades City FL 33929

Call Sign: KA4EXC
Harry E Brett
302 Storter Ave
Everglades City FL 33929

Call Sign: KD4IQC
Lincoln J Frost Sr
75 W Flamingo Dr
Everglades City FL 34139

Call Sign: K9HLQ
Thomas W Brandis
Everglades City FL 34139

FCC Amateur Radio Licenses in Felda

Call Sign: KA4ROF
John F Charlton
Felda FL 33930

FCC Amateur Radio Licenses in Fort Myers

Call Sign: KC4EYO
Catherine R Sowa
107 1st St
Fort Myers FL 33907

Call Sign: KK4BQN
Donald A Riegels
2797 1st St 301
Fort Myers FL 33916

Call Sign: KF4IYZ
Ladislav Smid
13256 2nd St
Fort Myers FL 33905

Call Sign: KE4SJE
Clarence H Casto
13844 2nd St SE
Fort Myers FL 33905

Call Sign: KE4SJF
Maewanda N Casto
13844 2nd St SE
Fort Myers FL 33905

Call Sign: NP4LV

Elga Comellas
13833 3rd St
Fort Myers FL 33905

Call Sign: WP4UC
Joel Comellas
13833 3rd St
Fort Myers FL 33905

Call Sign: WP4NBF
Jose L Comellas Torres
13833 3rd St
Fort Myers FL 33905

Call Sign: WP4NBG
Merari Comellas Torres
13833 3rd St
Fort Myers FL 33905

Call Sign: KA4TXB
Vanhenry Rush
19009 Acorn Rd SE Rt 30
Fort Myers FL 33912

Call Sign: KJ4MNB
Ana E Gonzalez
878 Adelphi Ct
Fort Myers FL 33919

Call Sign: KJ4MNC
Rosendo Gonzalez
878 Adelphi Ct
Fort Myers FL 33919

Call Sign: K2ICG
Edward C Wilmot
Aeries Way Dr
Fort Myers FL 33912

Call Sign: KF4UXI
Scott R Wolf
8069 Albatross Rd
Fort Myers FL 33967

Call Sign: KF4UTH

Thomas R Bennett III
2306 Aldridge Ave
Fort Myers FL 339074145

Call Sign: KD4VNY
Christian C Vivet
9892 Almetta Ave
Fort Myers FL 33919

Call Sign: N6BUM
Carl J Reder
8288 Aloha Rd
Fort Myers FL 33912

Call Sign: KJ4KLI
Pamela I Blozis
15671 Anderson Ln
Fort Myers FL 33912

Call Sign: KJ4JOO
Richard Blozis
15671 Anderson Ln
Fort Myers FL 33912

Call Sign: KI4UTF
Philip Martinez
3310 Antica St
Fort Myers FL 33905

Call Sign: W4PJG
Louis E Persons
1013 Aqua Ln
Fort Myers FL 33919

Call Sign: W4EYE
Louis E Persons
1013 Aqua Ln
Fort Myers FL 33919

Call Sign: KK4AHB
Joseph Stratton
2062 Aruba Ave
Fort Myers FL 33905

Call Sign: NS2B

Herbert E Hedlund
16258 Ashboro Ct
Fort Myers FL 33908

Call Sign: N1DBB
Paul J Haasis Sr
16265 Asheboro Ct
Fort Myers FL 33908

Call Sign: KC4GJD
David L Maiyer
631 Astarias Cir
Fort Myers FL 33919

Call Sign: KD4MHN
John S Brough
641 Astarias Cir
Fort Myers FL 33919

Call Sign: K7KQ
Scott M Hower
666 Astarias Cir
Fort Myers FL 33919

Call Sign: KE4UHY
Linda J Jansen
12788 Aston Oaks Dr
Fort Myers FL 33912

Call Sign: AF4VE
Philip R Jansen
12788 Aston Oaks Dr
Fort Myers FL 33912

Call Sign: K4YMR
Willard Kells
20814 Athenian Ln
Fort Myers FL 33917

Call Sign: KI4LBI
Efrain Mercado Mora
5193 Atlanta Ave
Fort Myers FL 33905

Call Sign: N4GCV

Melvin R Rodman
486 Avanti Way Blvd
Fort Myers FL 33917

Call Sign: N1FEU
Ronald E Myrick Sr
9332 Aviano Dr Apt 201
Fort Myers FL 33913

Call Sign: AK4HS
Ronald E Myrick Sr
9332 Aviano Dr Apt 201
Fort Myers FL 33913

Call Sign: AH6HA
Gordon T Armstrong
10589 Avila Cir
Fort Myers FL 339137040

Call Sign: AG0Y
Paul W Edwards
2050 Bahama Ave
Fort Myers FL 33905

Call Sign: N4DRI
Neil C Matzek
8427 Bahama Ct
Fort Myers FL 33907

Call Sign: WA4MTM
Joseph J Warner
5988 Baker Ct
Fort Myers FL 33919

Call Sign: KJ4GQX
Carolyn F Veger
321 Balboa Ave
Fort Myers FL 33905

Call Sign: KJ4GQY
John P Veger
321 Balboa Ave
Fort Myers FL 33905

Call Sign: WD4EQT

Bettie C Sloat
3631 Ballard Dr
Fort Myers FL 33916

Call Sign: K6AAO
James E Robinson
2100 Barkeley Ln C24
Fort Myers FL 33907

Call Sign: KB4TIU
Robert B Doing
36 Barkley Cir 205
Fort Myers FL 33907

Call Sign: K4GWW
Howard W Rieman
36 Barkley Cir 237
Fort Myers FL 33907

Call Sign: KG4BSG
Carl J Ekholm
1655 Bates Cir
Fort Myers FL 33901

Call Sign: KI4RTF
Allan D Bristol
9751 Baughman Ln
Fort Myers FL 33917

Call Sign: K3HXM
Thomas D Castelucci
8961 Beacon St
Fort Myers FL 33907

Call Sign: KK4DQK
Brian C Harris
5813 Beechwood Trl
Fort Myers FL 33919

Call Sign: NE2L
Richard P Kramlich
10515 Bella Vista Dr
Fort Myers FL 339137005

Call Sign: W8BBU

Francis J Starzec
3575 Bennington Dr 25
Fort Myers FL 33919

Call Sign: W1EIM
Abraham Checkoway
1737 Bent Tree Cir SW
Fort Myers FL 33907

Call Sign: KC8SFH
Keith C Ekstrom
17880 Bermuda Dunes Dr
Fort Myers FL 33967

Call Sign: N4KCE
Keith C Ekstrom
17880 Bermuda Dunes Dr
Fort Myers FL 33967

Call Sign: KV4CR
George L Iber
8437 Blackberry Rd
Fort Myers FL 33912

Call Sign: KD4FGI
Robert G Bowser
4568 Bowling Green Blvd
2
Fort Myers FL 33907

Call Sign: K4DFC
Nels G Thor
Box T133
Fort Myers FL 33908

Call Sign: N5ICT
Jerry L Heckerman
1325 Bradford Rd
Fort Myers FL 33901

Call Sign: KD5JMB
Carole D Dillon
11820 Bramble Cove Dr
Fort Myers FL 339056260

Call Sign: WA8VWS
Burl Sizemore
14121 Brant Point Cir Apt
118
Fort Myers FL 33919

Call Sign: KG4FFM
Willy A Wallace
1735 Brantley Rd Apt 709
Fort Myers FL 33907

Call Sign: KL1EC
Sydney A Wells
9279 Breno Dr
Fort Myers FL 339132005

Call Sign: KE8PY
Thomas B Hewton
9310 Breno Dr
Fort Myers FL 33913

Call Sign: KA1ZTD
Teresa E Krass
8144 Breton Cir
Fort Myers FL 33912

Call Sign: KB4SEP
Daniele M J Kellams
15810 Briarcliff Ln
Fort Myers FL 33912

Call Sign: WD9GHS
Keith R Hamlin
3706 Broadway Ave 39
Fort Myers FL 33901

Call Sign: AE4IQ
William L Genevrino
9290 Buckingham Rd
Fort Myers FL 33905

Call Sign: KJ4OIX
William S Genevrino
9290 Buckingham Rd
Fort Myers FL 33905

Call Sign: KF4MYO
Louis W Boudreau
10371 Butterfly Palm Dr
846
Fort Myers FL 33966

Call Sign: KJ4OLM
Grover M Whidden
15567 Caloosa Creek Cir
Fort Myers FL 33908

Call Sign: KA4OFE
Woodrow Pemberton
1118 Cameo Ct
Fort Myers FL 33908

Call Sign: K3MAC
Charles E Mac Peek
7513 Cameron Cir
Fort Myers FL 339125664

Call Sign: KB2OLN
Anibal Rivera
2034 Canal St Apt 206
Fort Myers FL 33901

Call Sign: WA1YLE
Peter F Ashley
11220 Caravel Cir
Fort Myers FL 33908

Call Sign: N1JZI
Carl R Hohenstein
11374 Caravel Cir
Fort Myers FL 33908

Call Sign: WA1FZE
John Randall
11371 Caravel Cir 131
Fort Myers FL 33908

Call Sign: N4FJS
Charles E Chambers
11500 Caravel Cir 4027

Fort Myers FL 33908

Call Sign: KD8TT
Nora J Wdowicki
11500 Caravel Cir SW
4017
Fort Myers FL 33908

Call Sign: N8FZK
Norm D Wdowicki
11500 Caravel Cir SW
4017
Fort Myers FL 33908

Call Sign: AB7BS
Phillip C Landmeier
13482 Caribbean Blvd
Fort Myers FL 33905

Call Sign: KJ4BEI
Joyce H Botchford
6789 Carmelle Dr
Fort Myers FL 33919

Call Sign: KI4GED
Charles Istenes Jr
310 Carol Dr
Fort Myers FL 33905

Call Sign: KB1TO
Richard C Gibson
19833 Casa Verde Way
Fort Myers FL 33967

Call Sign: KA2FPZ
Mike F Conte
19913 Casa Verde Way
Fort Myers FL 33967

Call Sign: KJ4RSE
Thailynn S Powell
19655 Casaverde Way
Fort Myers FL 33967

Call Sign: KF4PEJ

Lee E Carey
14001 Castle Hill Way
Fort Myers FL 33919

Call Sign: K4LEC
Lee E Carey
14001 Castle Hill Way
Fort Myers FL 33919

Call Sign: AH8J
Everett R Walter
205 Center Rd
Fort Myers FL 339071510

Call Sign: KH8BC
Joan C Walter
205 Center Rd
Fort Myers FL 339071510

Call Sign: WA4PIL
Ralph F Hauser Jr
2920 Central Ave
Fort Myers FL 33901

Call Sign: KB4LTT
Sean T Hauser
2920 Central Ave
Fort Myers FL 33901

Call Sign: K2SAL
Salvatore J Lo Piccolo
9251 Central Park Dr Apt
F203
Fort Myers FL 33919

Call Sign: KA8V
L Fred Chaney
32 Channel Ln
Fort Myers FL 33905

Call Sign: KF4NJS
Jeffery H Highsmith
9649 Channelside Way
201
Fort Myers FL 33919

Call Sign: WA4SCW
William A Walker
1445 Charles Rd
Fort Myers FL 339191704

Call Sign: N4PJT
Mark S Fuchs
1477 Charmont Pl
Fort Myers FL 33919

Call Sign: W8JFF
Thomas B Irvine
8256 Charter Club Cir
2502
Fort Myers FL 33919

Call Sign: N4SRK
Clement Concodora
8420 Charter Club Cir 8
Fort Myers FL 33919

Call Sign: KA2KNZ
Ernest R Richards
8607 Chatham St
Fort Myers FL 33907

Call Sign: KJ4MFU
Emerson Burris
8625 Chatham St
Fort Myers FL 33907

Call Sign: W4SFX
George T Alderman
8625 Chatham St
Fort Myers FL 33907

Call Sign: NP2DB
James R Allen
6931 Cherokee Ave
Fort Myers FL 33905

Call Sign: W2TXH
James W Haerer
6980 Cherokee Ave

Fort Myers FL 33905

Call Sign: KD4RX
Terry C Davis
9230 Chestnut Tree Loop
Fort Myers FL 33912

Call Sign: KJ4EWB
Frank L Jannelli
954 Clarellen Dr
Fort Myers FL 33919

Call Sign: K4IHB
Robert M Lewis
977 Clarellen Dr
Fort Myers FL 33901

Call Sign: KG4ASJ
Lee County Chapter
American Red Cross
2516 Colonial Blvd
Fort Myers FL 33907

Call Sign: KK4HUQ
Danielle M Hardre
2723 Colonial Blvd 101
Fort Myers FL 33907

Call Sign: N4NCG
James C Ward
2747 Colonial Blvd 104
Fort Myers FL 33907

Call Sign: KB4QFC
Anne C Kniskern
11211 Compass Point Dr
Fort Myers FL 339084940

Call Sign: N4DFJ
Philip N Kniskern
11211 Compass Point Dr
Fort Myers FL 339084940

Call Sign: KA1TMS
Vincent P Brennan Sr

243 Connecticut Ave
Fort Myers FL 339052640

Call Sign: WA3MGL
John A Mac Donald
7292 Coolidge Rd
Fort Myers FL 33912

Call Sign: KI4ZW
Lucille C Gainer
7269 Coon Rd
Fort Myers FL 339173217

Call Sign: WB5EJJ
David H Greenlee
649 Coquina Ct
Fort Myers FL 339081621

Call Sign: WB5ERS
J Harold Greenlee
649 Coquina Ct
Fort Myers FL 339081621

Call Sign: KD4HML
Jason M Perretta
9336 Coral Dr
Fort Myers FL 33967

Call Sign: KF4QWC
William B Floyd Jr
13280 Corbel Cir 1917
Fort Myers FL 33907

Call Sign: N4OHL
Robert L Wood
5809 Cordwood Ln
Fort Myers FL 33919

Call Sign: WA2IOF
Edward J Madonna
16626 Coriander Ln SW
Fort Myers FL 33908

Call Sign: KA4HLT
James R Coleman

1459 Cornell Pl
Fort Myers FL 33919

Call Sign: KE4DCM
Orlyn W Fowler
3 Coves End Dr
Fort Myers FL 33908

Call Sign: KJ4CVT
John T Mcgee II
1589 Covington Cir E
Fort Myers FL 33919

Call Sign: KD4VRZ
Gary L Randall
18461 Creek Dr
Fort Myers FL 33908

Call Sign: W4EEP
Michele A Perez
3628 Crestwood Lake Ave
301
Fort Myers FL 33901

Call Sign: KB4MG
Henry M Crichton
1478 Cumberland Ct
Fort Myers FL 33919

Call Sign: K4BNG
Jane C Mc Intyre
10100 Cypress Cove Dr
Fort Myers FL 33908

Call Sign: K4BNI
Richard Mc Intyre
10100 Cypress Cove Dr
159
Fort Myers FL 33908

Call Sign: W0OZ
Douglas L Eckhardt
10100 Cypress Cove Dr
Apt 226
Fort Myers FL 339087653

Call Sign: N4WCP
Edwin C Williams
10100 Cypress Cove Dr
Apt 464
Fort Myers FL 33908

Call Sign: KD8DQ
Bruce A Pendleton
8120 Cypress Dr N
Fort Myers FL 33967

Call Sign: KJ4UTB
Karl D Drews
8261 Cypress Dr S
Fort Myers FL 33967

Call Sign: KC4UDK
John C Stahl Jr
12121 Cypress Dr SW
Fort Myers FL 339082479

Call Sign: W4KOB
George Williams
4355 Cypress Ln
Fort Myers FL 33905

Call Sign: W4KOI
George D Williams
4355 Cypress Ln
Fort Myers FL 33905

Call Sign: W4FUM
John D Cody
4363 Cypress Ln
Fort Myers FL 33905

Call Sign: N4SRG
Robert E Barden
5680 Dana Rd
Fort Myers FL 33905

Call Sign: KB4AME
Susan V Greene
6800 Danah Ct

Fort Myers FL 33908

Call Sign: WB4WGH
James J Kleis
8624 Dartmouth St
Fort Myers FL 33907

Call Sign: N0DOY
James R Faughn
2127 Davis Blvd
Fort Myers FL 33905

Call Sign: KR4UO
John F Sabiston
12401 Davis Blvd
Fort Myers FL 33905

Call Sign: N3JFN
Frederick D Broszeit
1448 Davis Dr
Fort Myers FL 33919

Call Sign: KJ4GQZ
Thomas A Lee Jr
11410 Deal Rd
Fort Myers FL 33917

Call Sign: KI4UDM
Mark S Cookman
4615 Deleon St 245G
Fort Myers FL 33907

Call Sign: KI4WEW
Mark S Cookman
4615 Deleon St 245G
Fort Myers FL 33907

Call Sign: WD4AWN
Janet F Jones
4628 Deleon St E220
Fort Myers FL 33907

Call Sign: WA2PTG
Seymour M Banks
14292 Devington Way

Fort Myers FL 33912

Call Sign: W9LBY
Don W Kilpatrick
12854 Devonshire Lakes
Cir
Fort Myers FL 339137967

Call Sign: N9ATU
Iris J Kilpatrick
12854 Devonshire Lakes
Cir
Fort Myers FL 339137967

Call Sign: WA2MHZ
Walter B Goldenberg
12878 Devonshire Lakes
Cir
Fort Myers FL 33913

Call Sign: WD8DVE
Roger A Benson
19375 Devonwood Cir
Fort Myers FL 33912

Call Sign: KD4VSE
Irwin M Yarmo
4850 Dockside Dr
Fort Myers FL 33919

Call Sign: WD9AEP
Louis W Bal
2249 Dora St
Fort Myers FL 33901

Call Sign: KG4JHJ
Adam M Curry
1457 Dubonet Ct
Fort Myers FL 33919

Call Sign: KJ4MCG
Corrinna L Klebs
17368 Duquesne Rd
Fort Myers FL 33967

Call Sign: K8XYL
Corrinna L Klebs
17368 Duquesne Rd
Fort Myers FL 33967

Call Sign: KJ4MCH
Tobey D Klebs
17368 Duquesne Rd
Fort Myers FL 33967

Call Sign: KJ4MCI
Weston L Klebs
17368 Duquesne Rd
Fort Myers FL 33967

Call Sign: K3CQ
William P Hall Jr
2525 E 1st St Apt 2013
Fort Myers FL 33901

Call Sign: K3RAB
Winifred V Miller
2525 E 1st St Ste 1605
Fort Myers FL 33901

Call Sign: KA4AZH
Howard L Holt
E Gardenia
Fort Myers FL 33908

Call Sign: KC4SFC
Howard B Lee
4427 E Mainmast Ct
Fort Myers FL 33919

Call Sign: W3SRU
Howard C Gilpin
42 E Palm Dr
Fort Myers FL 33908

Call Sign: WB4SGT
Eric D Nielsen
4081 E River Dr
Fort Myers FL 33901

Call Sign: KO4HB
Stephen B Smith
4840 E Riverside Dr
Fort Myers FL 33905

Call Sign: KC8GVT
Clayton H Lautzenhiser Jr
13555 Eagle Ridge Dr Apt
918
Fort Myers FL 33912

Call Sign: KG4AOP
Louis Sansregret
13850 Eagle Ridge Lakes
Dr 203
Fort Myers FL 33912

Call Sign: KR4PI
Richard G Schnieders
6865 Eagle St
Fort Myers FL 33912

Call Sign: KJ4RFA
Eugene P Sipe Jr
14020 Eagleridge Lakes
Dr Apt 203
Fort Myers FL 339120708

Call Sign: W0VOM
Drexel H Turner
7670 Eaglet Ct
Fort Myers FL 33912

Call Sign: W4DHT
Drexel H Turner
7670 Eaglet Ct
Fort Myers FL 33912

Call Sign: KF4HWY
Herbert H Warren
2424 Edwards Dr 1103
Fort Myers FL 33901

Call Sign: KA4YIR
Arthur E Giertsen

5682 Eichen Cir
Fort Myers FL 33919

Call Sign: KI4CPR
Steven M Goldfarb
8620 El Mirasol Ct
Fort Myers FL 33967

Call Sign: W4KET
Herbert B Reaves
1445 El Prado
Fort Myers FL 33901

Call Sign: KJ4KGS
Beverly A Holtz
7171 Emily Dr
Fort Myers FL 33908

Call Sign: KJ4KGT
Thomas E Holtz
7171 Emily Dr
Fort Myers FL 33908

Call Sign: KK4GBX
Michael Ingenito
406 Endoven St
Fort Myers FL 33903

Call Sign: WA9AGC
Larry E Ford
906 Entrada Dr
Fort Myers FL 33919

Call Sign: KC4UCN
Addison R Lawrence
763 Entrada Dr SW
Fort Myers FL 33919

Call Sign: KG4KQV
Addison R Lawrence
763 Entrada Dr SW
Fort Myers FL 33919

Call Sign: KF4JUJ
Maxine C Tunnis

2325 Ephraim Ave
Fort Myers FL 33907

Call Sign: KK6FK
Nathan Efries
12560 Equestrian Cir 1308
Fort Myers FL 33907

Call Sign: KI4MOS
Richard E Lupo
12571 Equestrian Cir Apt
903
Fort Myers FL 33907

Call Sign: KF4SQH
Richard S Royle
13 Esper Ct
Fort Myers FL 33912

Call Sign: WB4EVJ
John J Erasmus
5022 Fairfield Dr
Fort Myers FL 33919

Call Sign: W4BOO
Theodore M Fleck
447 Fairview Ave
Fort Myers FL 33905

Call Sign: KK4CQL
James M Mcgregor Jr
18261 Fern Rd
Fort Myers FL 33967

Call Sign: KJ4UA
Frank P Rollins
5144 Fiddleleaf Dr
Fort Myers FL 33905

Call Sign: KE4KRY
Tonie L Sutton
19050 Flamingo Rd
Fort Myers FL 33912

Call Sign: KD7KTN

John W Mann
2061 Flower Dr
Fort Myers FL 33907

Call Sign: KD7SUD
Brenda G Mann
2061 Flowers Dr
Fort Myers FL 33907

Call Sign: N3AII
Gregory R Hoy
16845 Fox Den
Fort Myers FL 33908

Call Sign: WA4GYA
Robert J Propp
13551 Freshman Ln
Fort Myers FL 33912

Call Sign: WN4TKC
Jack A Mc Clure
4231 Fulton Cir
Fort Myers FL 33905

Call Sign: KA4YHP
Alvin J Cathey Sr
4804 Garcia Ave
Fort Myers FL 33905

Call Sign: AE4DP
William S Hartman
4940 Garcia Ave
Fort Myers FL 33905

Call Sign: K9DNN
Melvin C Stuart
26 Garden Dr
Fort Myers FL 33908

Call Sign: WA9RFN
Robert P Saunders
9241 Garden Pointe
Fort Myers FL 33908

Call Sign: KI4GAI

Frank D Hayes
16608 Gardenia Dr
Fort Myers FL 33908

Call Sign: KD4OGV
Charles E Mayhugh Sr
6656 Garland St
Fort Myers FL 33912

Call Sign: WA4JLD
Lawrence D Askins
216 Gazelle Dr
Fort Myers FL 33917

Call Sign: WB4WAQ
Ronald J Miller
8750 Gladilous Dr
Fort Myers FL 33908

Call Sign: N2TTL
Jay A Elliott
9722 Gladiolus Bulb Loop
Fort Myers FL 33908

Call Sign: KI4UQF
Lawrence S Henninger
9540 Gladious Preserve
Cir
Fort Myers FL 33908

Call Sign: KI4IRD
Debra J Almeida
15910 Gleneagle Ct
Fort Myers FL 33908

Call Sign: W9DDB
Steve Rukavina
7111 Golden Eagle Ct 524
Fort Myers FL 339121743

Call Sign: W0UGM
Jerome F Riley Sr
7379 Golf Villa Dr
Fort Myers FL 33912

Call Sign: K0GPW
Mary M Riley
7379 Golf Villa Dr
Fort Myers FL 33912

Call Sign: KF4WBN
Ivan L Davies Sr
2243 Gorham Ave
Fort Myers FL 339074227

Call Sign: WA4YYT
Robert V Senseman
19801 Gottarde Rd
Fort Myers FL 339174505

Call Sign: AB9Z
Paul W Mc Creery
118 Granada
Fort Myers FL 33905

Call Sign: KF4WNG
Gary W Maisel
5521 Granada Rd
Fort Myers FL 33919

Call Sign: N4QCT
Harry N Carr
Green Cypress Ln
Fort Myers FL 33905

Call Sign: KC3K
Stewart J Ehrreich
15640 Greenock Ln SE
Fort Myers FL 33912

Call Sign: W0AEP
Leon T Berandt
13257 Greywood Cir
Fort Myers FL 339127510

Call Sign: N4NYS
James A Cockburn
1542 Grove Ave
Fort Myers FL 33901

Call Sign: KB6ECH
Felicia Deininger
1915 Halgrim Ave Apt
1106
Fort Myers FL 339017996

Call Sign: WB9NOJ
David P Moss
Halyards Ct
Fort Myers FL 33919

Call Sign: WD4ERA
Donald E Redd
13236 Hampton Park Ct
Fort Myers FL 33913

Call Sign: K4FQU
Earl R Spencer
1735 Hanson St
Fort Myers FL 33901

Call Sign: KB4IXY
William R Bess Jr
1231 Hanton Ave
Fort Myers FL 33901

Call Sign: WB2SUP
Robert L Sanford
3502 Harbor Ct
Fort Myers FL 33908

Call Sign: WA0PJV
Stanley H Anonsen
4505 Harbor Ct
Fort Myers FL 33908

Call Sign: KP4DPQ
Dario Ruiz
4733 Harbortown Ln
Fort Myers FL 33919

Call Sign: KJ3A
James M Myers III
5480 Harbour Castle Dr
Fort Myers FL 33907

Call Sign: WA8WFL
Raymond F Shetrone
2313 Harvard Ave
Fort Myers FL 33907

Call Sign: KF4OHP
David T Childress III
18206 Hepatica Rd
Fort Myers FL 33967

Call Sign: N4WXJ
Philip J Hooks
17468 Ingram Rd
Fort Myers FL 33912

Call Sign: KF4CMB
Paul W Jahnig
2225 Havana Ave
Fort Myers FL 33905

Call Sign: W2ABB
William A Roett
12155 Hibiscus Dr SW
Fort Myers FL 33908

Call Sign: N4LRP
Claus P Schilsky
13380 Island Rd SE
Fort Myers FL 33905

Call Sign: K4PWJ
Paul W Jahnig
2225 Havana Ave
Fort Myers FL 33905

Call Sign: KK4ECG
Steven Bingham
13081 Hickory Grove Ct
Fort Myers FL 33905

Call Sign: KE4BWI
Gene A Hopper
13515 Island Rd SE
Fort Myers FL 33905

Call Sign: N1UKZ
Nancy P Jahnig
2225 Havana Ave
Fort Myers FL 33905

Call Sign: KI4ICS
Jimmy L Sanders
12098 Hidden Links Dr
Fort Myers FL 33913

Call Sign: KE4BWH
Marilyn M Hopper
13515 Island Rd SE
Fort Myers FL 33905

Call Sign: NS1F
Warren C Boles
2242 Havana Ave SE
Fort Myers FL 33905

Call Sign: KA1DBC
Lucien J Gagne
18136 Hilda Dr SE Rt 39
Fort Myers FL 33912

Call Sign: K9OJI
Stevan W Speheger
12698 Ivory Stone Loop
Fort Myers FL 33913

Call Sign: KF4QAZ
Linda L Keene
3005 Hazel Ave S
Fort Myers FL 33906

Call Sign: KA9EKT
Robert M Sipe
1932 Hill Ave
Fort Myers FL 33901

Call Sign: KI4UPZ
Hubert G Gomez
16811 Jacaranda Dr
Fort Myers FL 33908

Call Sign: K9TVP
James D Price
14571 Headwater Bay Ln
Fort Myers FL 33908

Call Sign: KJ4IDS
Sarah E Coon
17501 Holly Oak Ave
Fort Myers FL 33967

Call Sign: KF4HCE
Harold A Imhoff
2828 Jackson St
Fort Myers FL 33901

Call Sign: KE1IC
George W Wood
13190 Heather Ridge Loop
Fort Myers FL 339661553

Call Sign: KC4HLI
Vivian M Kerr
196 Imbert Ct
Fort Myers FL 339126314

Call Sign: KC4LVE
Nancy E Schiller
2300 Jasper Ave
Fort Myers FL 33907

Call Sign: WA8ADJ
William M Spikowski
1617 Hendry St 416
Fort Myers FL 33901

Call Sign: N2HKE
Bernard J Hart Jr
199 Imbert Ct
Fort Myers FL 33912

Call Sign: KC4LVD
Thomas M Schiller
2300 Jasper Ave
Fort Myers FL 33907

Call Sign: KD4JNO
Robert M Holzbaur
2448 Jasper Ave
Fort Myers FL 33907

Call Sign: WB4FOW
Clark Barrow
2469 Jasper Ave
Fort Myers FL 33907

Call Sign: KB4UNN
Rosemary E Scheetz
4386 Jib Boom Ct 2E
Fort Myers FL 33907

Call Sign: K4KH
George J Faatz
3713 Junonia Ct
Fort Myers FL 33908

Call Sign: W2VBH
Leland W Wight
5701 Junonia Ct
Fort Myers FL 33908

Call Sign: N3BZ
Jack Farrance
51 Kala Ct
Fort Myers FL 33912

Call Sign: W8DDQ
Raleigh W Wise
12982 Kedleston Cir
Fort Myers FL 33912

Call Sign: W4DDQ
Raleigh W Wise
12982 Kedleston Cir
Fort Myers FL 33912

Call Sign: N4VZ
Raleigh W Wise
12982 Kedleston Cir
Fort Myers FL 33912

Call Sign: KB4LPL
Carol L Griffith
476 Keenan Ave
Fort Myers FL 33919

Call Sign: KA0GYF
Douglas G Deininger
480 Keenan Ave
Fort Myers FL 33919

Call Sign: KA0RUL
Marilyn I Rock
480 Keenan Ave
Fort Myers FL 33919

Call Sign: WA4YYJ
Wilbur Wein
585 Keenan Ave
Fort Myers FL 33907

Call Sign: N4GGQ
Marcello A Ebelini
465 Keenan Ct
Fort Myers FL 33919

Call Sign: KI4SYO
Lester E Brenkman
12870 Kelly Greens Blvd
Fort Myers FL 33908

Call Sign: N3AWX
Donald M Smith
12520 Kelly Greens Blvd
351
Fort Myers FL 33908

Call Sign: KQ4TR
Colleen G Sammons
3667 Kelly St
Fort Myers FL 33901

Call Sign: WA4JOF
Grove R Sammons
3667 Kelly St

Fort Myers FL 33901

Call Sign: KE4ZYD
Lee International ARS
3667 Kelly St
Fort Myers FL 33901

Call Sign: WA4DQE
Grove E Sammons
3667 Kelly St
Fort Myers FL 339017942

Call Sign: KK4ECD
Michael G Bracci
Kenwood Ln
Fort Myers FL 33907

Call Sign: K4NUK
Michael G Bracci
Kenwood Ln
Fort Myers FL 33907

Call Sign: KC4ZZN
Marc D Forman
15822 Keygrass Ln SE
Fort Myers FL 33905

Call Sign: KI4UQB
Judith A Earle
6962 Kimberly Ter
Fort Myers FL 33919

Call Sign: KK4CQM
Kimberly D Barselou
2474 King Arthurs Ct
Fort Myers FL 33912

Call Sign: KB4KIM
Kimberly D Barselou
2474 King Arthurs Ct
Fort Myers FL 33912

Call Sign: KJ4USY
Lee H Pavel
8490 Kingbird Loop 911

Fort Myers FL 33967

Call Sign: K4LHP
Lee H Pavel
8490 Kingbird Loop 911
Fort Myers FL 33967

Call Sign: KG4UID
Keeling H Sisson
209 Kingston
Fort Myers FL 33905

Call Sign: KG4FFG
Earlene R Crespo
362 Kingston Dr E
Fort Myers FL 33905

Call Sign: W8LPP
Donald D Albert
222 Kittery Ct
Fort Myers FL 339126317

Call Sign: WA4YYK
Sharon J Senseman
1202 La Faunce Way
Fort Myers FL 33907

Call Sign: WB4YYI
Vercil F Senseman
1202 La Faunce Way
Fort Myers FL 33907

Call Sign: N4TFX
Donald L Fair
15680 Lake Candlewood
Dr
Fort Myers FL 339081720

Call Sign: KJ4JPO
Kenneth E Silver
16645 Lake Cir Dr Apt
711
Fort Myers FL 33908

Call Sign: KK4EUI

David R Kelley
10081 Lake Cove Dr Apt
302
Fort Myers FL 33908

Call Sign: WA4VEI
John C Kagan
6981 Lake Devonwood Dr
Fort Myers FL 33908

Call Sign: KC4BF
Floyd L Huffman
3739 Lake St
Fort Myers FL 33901

Call Sign: WU8C
Thomas C Mathison
15031 Lakeside View Dr
2202
Fort Myers FL 33919

Call Sign: N2XYZ
Joseph R Cramer
12507 Lakewood Ct
Fort Myers FL 33908

Call Sign: WB8MXB
James I Marsh
10680 Lakewood Shores
Cir
Fort Myers FL 339036626

Call Sign: KG4ZCD
Anthony A Balog
17397 Lebanon Rd
Fort Myers FL 33912

Call Sign: KJ4RSF
John C Udart
17512 Lebanon Rd
Fort Myers FL 33967

Call Sign: KC9ANK
Sandra S Stergulz
8428 Lemon Rd

Fort Myers FL 33967

Call Sign: WB9CWH
Richard A Stergulz
8428 Lemon Rd
Fort Myers FL 33967

Call Sign: WD4PSP
Philip F Pumilia
7319 Louise Ct SE
Fort Myers FL 33912

Call Sign: WA2MLN
Philip F Pumilia
7319 Louise Ct SE
Fort Myers FL 33912

Call Sign: KI4HAD
Mark R Cannedy
18259 Lowe Dr
Fort Myers FL 33912

Call Sign: N8INQ
James J Hooper
3910 Lucina Ct
Fort Myers FL 33908

Call Sign: W8DWS
Charles B Basinger
4900 Lucina Ct
Fort Myers FL 33908

Call Sign: W1QP
Frederic J Albert Jr
Lucina Ct
Fort Myers FL 339081673

Call Sign: KK4HQC
Howard D Fritcher
3902 Luverne St
Fort Myers FL 33901

Call Sign: KK4HQD
Patrick D Fritcher
3902 Luverne St

Fort Myers FL 33901

Call Sign: KC4GYI
George W Krause
3936 Luzon St
Fort Myers FL 33901

Call Sign: KG4MKV
Daniel Aponte
1825 Lynhart Ave 39A
Fort Myers FL 33901

Call Sign: WB4BON
Penny R Bonnema
135 Macoma Ct
Fort Myers FL 33908

Call Sign: W1OMP
Robert R Silva
Macoma Ct
Fort Myers FL 33908

Call Sign: KJ4NKI
Nickolas N Goranov
13708 Magnolia Lake Ct
Fort Myers FL 33907

Call Sign: KB0KCY
James D Ryan
1711 Main St
Fort Myers FL 33931

Call Sign: KI4FQY
George M Foliart Jr
14552 Majestic Eagle Ct
Fort Myers FL 33912

Call Sign: KT4NC
Anthony N Barton
Malt Dr Parkwoods
Fort Myers FL 33907

Call Sign: W9LXR
Kevin C Ehringer
5200 Manatee Bay Ln

Fort Myers FL 33905

Call Sign: KJ4LCP
Jolene M Bergman
5370 Manatee Bay Ln
Fort Myers FL 33905

Call Sign: W4STA
Alva R Jones Jr
4136 Mandarin Ct
Fort Myers FL 33916

Call Sign: K4NXZ
Carolyn J Jones
4136 Mandarin Ct
Fort Myers FL 33916

Call Sign: KG4WSD
Leonard S Deibert
4018 Manning Ave
Fort Myers FL 33916

Call Sign: KJ4YVO
James H Fuller Sr
1420 Manuels Dr
Fort Myers FL 339015824

Call Sign: N3LA
James H Fuller Sr
1420 Manuels Dr
Fort Myers FL 339015824

Call Sign: KF4AL
Howard L Ritchie
1849 Maravilla Ave Apt
A9
Fort Myers FL 339017113

Call Sign: NP3JK
Mario J Martinez Gonzalez
1849 Maravilla Ave Apt D
1
Fort Myers FL 33901

Call Sign: KA4ZIR

Joseph J Frasketi Jr
2019 Maravilla Cir
Fort Myers FL 33901

Call Sign: W3JI
James M Hall
2025 Maravilla Cir
Fort Myers FL 33901

Call Sign: N4JYZ
Joseph Frasketi
2043 Maravilla Cir
Fort Myers FL 33901

Call Sign: KI4VLO
Crystal J Mansell
10631 Marie St
Fort Myers FL 33905

Call Sign: KG4JRM
Sean G Reilly
4289 Mariner Way 111
Fort Myers FL 33919

Call Sign: KE4KJT
Carol S Sutton
4289 Mariner Way 309
Fort Myers FL 33919

Call Sign: WZ1Z
John A Wolff
4309 Mariner Way A101
Fort Myers FL 33919

Call Sign: W8SZU
Gene C Baber
13301 Marquette Blvd
Fort Myers FL 33905

Call Sign: K4GUE
Kenneth G Lewis
13347 Marquette Blvd
Fort Myers FL 33905

Call Sign: KP4HN

Jose L Comellas
13600 Marquette Blvd
Fort Myers FL 33905

Call Sign: WP4CMH
Rosa M Torres Hernandez
136000 Marquette Blvd
Fort Myers FL 33905

Call Sign: W4MUY
Doris S Lewis
13347 Marquette Blvd SE
Fort Myers FL 339051836

Call Sign: N9GBD
Denis E Richardson
8465 Matahzas Rd
Fort Myers FL 33912

Call Sign: WA4ZD
William E Smith
13906 Matanzas Dr
Fort Myers FL 33905

Call Sign: N4XRQ
William E Smith
13906 Matanzas Dr
Fort Myers FL 339052125

Call Sign: N2NXQ
John A Carbona
2424 McGregor Blvd
Fort Myers FL 33901

Call Sign: WB4LPX
John R O Connor
10700 McGregor Blvd
Fort Myers FL 33919

Call Sign: KI4KQM
Asha Ramsarran
16950 McSpadden Rd
Fort Myers FL 33917

Call Sign: KC4RCB

Joseph P Randall
15520 Meadow Cir
Fort Myers FL 33908

Call Sign: WB4HYB
David L Callaway
3625 Meadowbrook Ln
Fort Myers FL 33901

Call Sign: KY0T
John E Stamps
1329 Melaleuca Ln
Fort Myers FL 339018852

Call Sign: W4AHE
Mike Perry
9672 Mendocino Dr
Fort Myers FL 33919

Call Sign: KG4BZD
Denise A Purcell
135 Meta St
Fort Myers FL 33905

Call Sign: W3UBQ
Karl H Muller
14157 Montauk Ln
Fort Myers FL 33919

Call Sign: KI4QDX
Everett A Eyre
1899 Monte Vista St
Fort Myers FL 33901

Call Sign: W4TXY
Everett A Eyre
1899 Monte Vista St
Fort Myers FL 33901

Call Sign: WA4TXY
Everett A Eyre
1899 Monte Vista St
Fort Myers FL 33901

Call Sign: K4HNW

Joseph H Burgess
6292 Morgan La Fee Ln
Fort Myers FL 33912

Call Sign: WA1ONV
Scott E Bates
315 Morse Plaza
Fort Myers FL 33905

Call Sign: W2UMC
Christopher K Rasmussen
463 Muskegon Ave
Fort Myers FL 339053314

Call Sign: AA1SG
Eugene S Slota
14081 Mystic Seaport Way
Fort Myers FL 339197700

Call Sign: KQ4OR
James M Niccum
4408 N Atlantic Cir
Fort Myers FL 33903

Call Sign: AF4YH
James M Niccum
4408 N Atlantic Cir
Fort Myers FL 33903

Call Sign: W2PZF
Frederick W Winters
462 Nathan Hale Ln
Fort Myers FL 339174012

Call Sign: KF4SQI
Deborah M Dinsmore
1645 Newport Ct
Fort Myers FL 33907

Call Sign: KE4REK
Steven J Stehl
5099 Northampton Dr
Fort Myers FL 33919

Call Sign: KC4GWE

James E Mosier
671 Nuna Ave
Fort Myers FL 33905

Call Sign: K4XK
Donnie B Wright
1516 Oak Dr
Fort Myers FL 33907

Call Sign: WB4LND
Robert J Mc Cleary
1351 Oaklawn Ct
Fort Myers FL 33907

Call Sign: W9HNI
James F Novak
11309 Oakmont Ct
Fort Myers FL 33908

Call Sign: WB9BFU
Gerald E Warner
11506 Oakmont Ct
Fort Myers FL 33908

Call Sign: W0QX
Charles R Durrell
11810 Oakmont Ct
Fort Myers FL 339082826

Call Sign: W4TKS
Claude L Jones
1240 Old Bridge Rd
Fort Myers FL 33917

Call Sign: KA4USU
Harry H Halonen
14183 Old Olga Rd
Fort Myers FL 33905

Call Sign: N0WWY
Jeff A Marsh
18513 Olive Rd
Fort Myers FL 33912

Call Sign: KG4USQ

Gregory A Bramlett Sr
7630 Omni Ln Apt 305
Fort Myers FL 33905

Call Sign: KN4ET
Jerry J Touche
16038 On Par Blvd
Fort Myers FL 33908

Call Sign: KR4QC
Marion R Touche
16038 On Par Blvd
Fort Myers FL 33908

Call Sign: AG4K
Davis F Gates
1255 Osceola Dr
Fort Myers FL 33901

Call Sign: KD4FB
Charles W Brundage
13710 Osprey Dr
Fort Myers FL 339085809

Call Sign: K9ALX
Harry F Arnold
41 Otley Ct
Fort Myers FL 33912

Call Sign: W4IR
James L Waller
7060 Overlook Dr
Fort Myers FL 33907

Call Sign: W9NWD
Russell C Ashby
5749 Palm Beach Blvd 23
Fort Myers FL 33905

Call Sign: W1QNM
Warren C Chase
5749 Palm Beach Blvd Lot
282
Fort Myers FL 33905

Call Sign: WA2BHW
Edward A Wilgress
12041 Palm Dr
Fort Myers FL 33908

Call Sign: KI4OUM
Oisin F Dolley
15137 Palm Isle Dr
Fort Myers FL 33919

Call Sign: WB4YTO
Ralph D Benedict
1517 Palmwoode Dr
Fort Myers FL 33919

Call Sign: K4IAU
Edward C Mc Elligatt Sr
6771 Panther Ln U3
Fort Myers FL 33919

Call Sign: N8ZXU
Gary M Close
Park Meadows Dr
Fort Myers FL 33907

Call Sign: KI4UQE
Sandra A Larsen
6261 Park Rd
Fort Myers FL 33908

Call Sign: KJ4SAL
Sandra A Larsen
6261 Park Rd
Fort Myers FL 33908

Call Sign: W2MOR
William Kovacs
15166 Parkside Dr 3
Fort Myers FL 33908

Call Sign: N3HOQ
Gregory E Parsons
9090 Paseo De Valencia St
Fort Myers FL 33908

Call Sign: W4SMK
Kenneth D Stewart
1917 Passaic Ave
Fort Myers FL 33901

Call Sign: KA8AQA
William B Mc Bride
1781 Pebble Beach Dr 401
Fort Myers FL 339075789

Call Sign: KE4PUR
Ernest F Heyl
1781 Pebble Beach Dr Apt
206
Fort Myers FL 339078080

Call Sign: KI4ZXN
Steven D Goldstein
13091 Pebblebrook Point
Cir 101
Fort Myers FL 33905

Call Sign: KF4RSC
Matthew E Medvecky
569 Peck Ave
Fort Myers FL 33919

Call Sign: KF4HPC
Edward W Moran
7225 Pelas Cir
Fort Myers FL 33917

Call Sign: KB1DAG
Kent A Askin
13064 Pennington Pl 201
Fort Myers FL 33913

Call Sign: KB1CFR
Joseph L Carastro
537 Periwinkle Ct
Fort Myers FL 33908

Call Sign: WA3ZRC
Leroy S Yerkes
11471 Persimmon Ct

Fort Myers FL 33913

Call Sign: KB4VU
Frank C Richards
6946 Pickadilly Ct
Fort Myers FL 33919

Call Sign: WB0MUC
Donald R Mc Mullen
1828 Pine Valley Dr
Fort Myers FL 33907

Call Sign: W4NMF
Lawrence J Hassel
1580 Pine Valley Dr 416
Fort Myers FL 33907

Call Sign: KF4AEQ
Samuel Y Barbakoff
1828 Pinevalley Dr
Fort Myers FL 33907

Call Sign: KJ4WKS
Nathalie L Burlingame
7100 Pinnacle Dr Apt B23
Fort Myers FL 33907

Call Sign: K3IBH
Catherine M Panner
119 Placid Dr
Fort Myers FL 33919

Call Sign: AF4EL
Karl Friedrich Bettinger
6539 Planatation Preserve
Cir
Fort Myers FL 33912

Call Sign: K2CBM
James E Hamann
6542 Plantation Pines Blvd
Fort Myers FL 339661321

Call Sign: KA0STM
Kevin S Taylor

6556 Plantation Pines Blvd
Fort Myers FL 33912

Call Sign: KC4RQA
Earl S Van Atta III
6555 Plantation Pines Blvd
SE
Fort Myers FL 33966

Call Sign: KP3O
William T Genter
11598 Plantation Preserve
Cir S
Fort Myers FL 339668371

Call Sign: WA4HDH
Abbott Kagan
1362 Plumosa Dr
Fort Myers FL 33901

Call Sign: W9LPV
Norbert N Engelman
63 Plymouth Bend
Fort Myers FL 33917

Call Sign: N9LUL
Peter J Syczka
40 Poinsettia Dr
Fort Myers FL 33905

Call Sign: WA8LVR
Waldo L Gray
111 Poinsettia Dr
Fort Myers FL 33905

Call Sign: WD9AQG
Donald G Humphrey
241 Poinsettia Dr
Fort Myers FL 33905

Call Sign: WP4HNG
Juan S Vila Calderon
10861 Pond Ridge Dr
Fort Myers FL 33913

Call Sign: N8BOJ
Ralph F Janas
1500 Popham Dr B 15
Fort Myers FL 33919

Call Sign: KF4FRZ
Leon Knickerbocker
17807 Port Boca Cir
Fort Myers FL 33908

Call Sign: WA4HXU
George L Dissette
105 Powell Creek Cir
Fort Myers FL 33917

Call Sign: N4FTD
Paul A Schwan
376 Prather Dr
Fort Myers FL 33919

Call Sign: KJ4VDK
James A Luccisano
6325 Presidential Ct 1A
Fort Myers FL 33919

Call Sign: WA2UCW
Jack S Keifer
Principia
Fort Myers FL 33919

Call Sign: W4JAH
Jack A Hurst Jr
15031 Punta Rassa Rd Ste 104
Fort Myers FL 33908

Call Sign: W8CFS
Jack A Hurst Jr
15031 Punta Rassa Rd Ste 104
Fort Myers FL 33908

Call Sign: K4JAH
Jack A Hurst Jr

15031 Punta Rassa Rd Ste 104
Fort Myers FL 33908

Call Sign: KE4SMM
Malcolm S Britton
7077 Quail Run Ct
Fort Myers FL 33908

Call Sign: KC9CXE
Jon E Scharbrough
4060 Rainbow Dr
Fort Myers FL 339162830

Call Sign: N4SCH
Brian D O Callaghan
14813 Randolph Ct
Fort Myers FL 33905

Call Sign: KD4IBN
J Frederick Lasby
1515 Ransom St
Fort Myers FL 33901

Call Sign: KI4AHR
Dante Ciolfi
1765 Red Cedar Dr 18
Fort Myers FL 339077658

Call Sign: KI4WDS
Edward J Osis
1761 Red Cedar Dr 7
Fort Myers FL 33907

Call Sign: N3DMA
Rhoda E Ehrreich
15640 Reenock Ln SE
Fort Myers FL 33912

Call Sign: KE4DUN
Jerry W Nix
2974 Ribbon Ct
Fort Myers FL 33905

Call Sign: KI4UQH

Guillermo A Barrios
1019 Ridgeway Dr
Fort Myers FL 33903

Call Sign: KB9NQQ
David J Benjamin
9296 River Otter Dr
Fort Myers FL 33912

Call Sign: KB4FOA
Lee Mc Michen
13751 River Rd
Fort Myers FL 33905

Call Sign: WB4IXZ
Marion T Saunders
15416 Riverby Rd
Fort Myers FL 33908

Call Sign: KB4GGX
Virginia L Rollick
14556 Riverside Dr
Fort Myers FL 33905

Call Sign: W4IGE
Walter D Rollick
14556 Riverside Dr
Fort Myers FL 33905

Call Sign: W4EDL
Robert L Barnett
13726 Rivesr Forest Dr SE
Fort Myers FL 339051820

Call Sign: K0JPN
W Frank Simms Jr
6641 Rolland Ct
Fort Myers FL 33908

Call Sign: W8WSW
Burron G Piatt
47 Rollo Ct
Fort Myers FL 33912

Call Sign: WA9DKE

Lawrence R Gavin
11651 Rosemount Dr
Fort Myers FL 33913

Call Sign: WB3BMW
John F Grove Jr
12051 Rosemount Dr
Fort Myers FL 33913

Call Sign: W9NOL
Thomas S Teetor
14220 Royal Harbour Ct
610
Fort Myers FL 33908

Call Sign: KJ4HEV
Gene V Marshall Sr
14200 Royal Harbour Ct
805
Fort Myers FL 33908

Call Sign: KG4ZFK
Mark W Keohane
14841 Royal Oak Ct
Fort Myers FL 33919

Call Sign: KD4UTC
Walter G Horn
6483 Royal Woods Dr
Fort Myers FL 33908

Call Sign: KG4ACH
Barry L Draper
6519 Royal Woods Dr
Fort Myers FL 33908

Call Sign: KE6ZLK
Thomas E Walter
6445 Royal Woods Dr SW
Fort Myers FL 33908

Call Sign: KG4LHT
Thomas E Walter
6445 Royal Woods Dr SW
Fort Myers FL 33908

Call Sign: KG4WSF
Jordan L Kilpatrick
1666 Rudy Ct
Fort Myers FL 33901

Call Sign: KG4WSE
Tammy S Kilpatrick
1666 Rudy Ct
Fort Myers FL 33901

Call Sign: K3GL
John L Alline
1304 S Brandywine Cir 4
Fort Myers FL 33919

Call Sign: KA1GQ
Walter J Tucker
1499 S Brandywine Cir
Apt 453
Fort Myers FL 33919

Call Sign: N5QPZ
Douglas H Morrison Sr
12860 S Cleveland Ave
219
Fort Myers FL 339073800

Call Sign: N3DOB
James G Riley
4944 S Cleveland Ave Lot
D4
Fort Myers FL 33907

Call Sign: KB7GAT
Lorna R Brown
1688 S Hermitage Rd
Fort Myers FL 33919

Call Sign: KJ4DKJ
Mervin D Hart II
4666 S Landings Dr
Fort Myers FL 33919

Call Sign: KI4BAD

Michael J Angel
4681 S Landings Dr
Fort Myers FL 33919

Call Sign: N6SAI
Lynne P Birdt
5260 S Landings Dr 702
Fort Myers FL 339194676

Call Sign: KI6BO
Marvin S Birdt
5260 S Landings Dr 702
Fort Myers FL 339194676

Call Sign: WB1AIM
Philip M George
1466 S Larkwood Sq
Fort Myers FL 33919

Call Sign: KJ4VXO
Michael D Burlingame
15701 S Pebble Ln
Fort Myers FL 33912

Call Sign: N0FOS
Donald D Church
16900 S Tamiami Trl
Fort Myers FL 33908

Call Sign: KE4AQR
Raymond Wells
19370 S Tamiami Trl
Fort Myers FL 33908

Call Sign: NV2S
Earl E Williams
19370 S Tamiami Trl
Fort Myers FL 33908

Call Sign: KJ4UTA
Scot Klingenmeier
16520 S Tamiami Trl 138
Fort Myers FL 33908

Call Sign: K6DE

Scot Klingenmeier
16520 S Tamiami Trl 138
Fort Myers FL 33908

Call Sign: KF4DNK
Ronald R Cipriano
18050 S Tamiami Trl Lot
117
Fort Myers FL 33908

Call Sign: W7LVW
Lewis C Midlam
17595 S Tamiami Trl Ste
300
Fort Myers FL 33908

Call Sign: WB2ZHD
Lee J Grills
14600 Sagamore Ct
Fort Myers FL 33908

Call Sign: KJ4MBR
Jack J Lombard
7525 San Carlos Blvd
Fort Myers FL 33967

Call Sign: W1JJL
Jack J Lombard
7525 San Carlos Blvd
Fort Myers FL 33967

Call Sign: WB4PNY
Joyce A Dolby
16299 San Carlos Blvd
Fort Myers FL 33908

Call Sign: WA4EQW
Patrick W Dolby
16299 San Carlos Blvd
Fort Myers FL 33908

Call Sign: KK4DQI
Thomas G Patterson
16299 San Carlos Blvd
Fort Myers FL 33908

Call Sign: W2BFB
Trygve W Olsen Jr
16299 San Carlos Blvd
Fort Myers FL 33908

Call Sign: KE4GSE
Sanford E Black
16410 San Carlos Blvd
Box 363
Fort Myers FL 33908

Call Sign: N3XGL
Artis W Kitchens
8045 San Rd
Fort Myers FL 33912

Call Sign: W2RKL
Frederick W Werner
941 Sand Dollar Shell
Point Village
Fort Myers FL 33908

Call Sign: KG4WCE
Durell B Phillips
1466 Sandra Dr
Fort Myers FL 33901

Call Sign: KE4JPQ
William P Wood
552 Sanford Dr
Fort Myers FL 33919

Call Sign: KB4AXE
Bruce C Goeller
18573 Sebring Rd
Fort Myers FL 33967

Call Sign: N2EUP
Eleanor D Burgmaster
8431 Sedonia Cir
Fort Myers FL 339120546

Call Sign: K2BGJ
John J Burgmaster

8431 Sedonia Cir
Fort Myers FL 339120546

Call Sign: KF4VHE
Charles D Mc Bride
6750 Seminole Ave
Fort Myers FL 33905

Call Sign: KC4LLB
Gordon P Mc Hughen
1040 Shaddelee Ln
Fort Myers FL 33919

Call Sign: WA2EVE
Irwin Rappaport
9133 Shadow Glen Way
Fort Myers FL 33913

Call Sign: KC4GOB
Bethene G Deibert
139 Shaw Blvd Morse
Shores
Fort Myers FL 33905

Call Sign: KC4GOA
Leonard G Deibert
145 Shaw Blvd Morse
Shores
Fort Myers FL 33905

Call Sign: KD9ZM
Richard H Peterson
1394 Sheffield Way
Fort Myers FL 33919

Call Sign: K2DXN
William E Moore
327 Shoreland Dr
Fort Myers FL 33905

Call Sign: KB3DLV
Samuel B Selby
359 Shoreland Dr
Fort Myers FL 33905

Call Sign: W4LFG
Albert F Surmont
16121 Siesta Dr
Fort Myers FL 33908

Call Sign: NQ6U
Warren E Anthony
7391 Sika Deer Way
Fort Myers FL 339665716

Call Sign: KF4LJK
Gary M Albritton
13060 Silver Sands Dr
Fort Myers FL 33913

Call Sign: KG4FFH
Mary L Brunson
2185 Simon Ct
Fort Myers FL 33916

Call Sign: NP2EH
Wellington M Bertolet II
13831 Sleepy Hollow Ln
Fort Myers FL 33905

Call Sign: N2IWL
Joseph M Fanelli
13849 Sleepy Hollow Ln
Fort Myers FL 33905

Call Sign: KI4SYP
Robert E Beals
13867 Sleepy Hollow Ln
Fort Myers FL 33905

Call Sign: AA8RL
Donna J Bentley
38 Solcedo Ct
Fort Myers FL 33912

Call Sign: AA8NS
Jack C Bentley
38 Solcedo Ct
Fort Myers FL 33912

Call Sign: K1DOT
Dorothy J Mc Arthur
9807 Solera Cove Pointe
Unit 105
Fort Myers FL 33908

Call Sign: K1QT
Robert J Mc Arthur
9807 Solera Cove Pointe
Unit 105
Fort Myers FL 33908

Call Sign: W9PEH
Everett B Foust
5616 Solera Ct SW
Fort Myers FL 33919

Call Sign: KE4FTV
Elizabeth J Schelper
2120 South St
Fort Myers FL 33901

Call Sign: WA4LLC
Robert C Flynn Sr
2349 South St
Fort Myers FL 33901

Call Sign: W2IPL
Constance Bottinelli
9080 Spring Mountain
Way
Fort Myers FL 33908

Call Sign: K3QGY
Constance Bottinelli
9080 Spring Mountain
Way
Fort Myers FL 33908

Call Sign: KE6BKT
William N Colgrove
9765 Spyglass Ct
Fort Myers FL 33903

Call Sign: KI4LTX

John R Hendricks
6234 St Andrews Cir
Fort Myers FL 33919

Call Sign: AA4TX
John R Hendricks
6234 St Andrews Cir
Fort Myers FL 33919

Call Sign: KI4ODD
Luke D Hendricks
6234 St Andrews Cir
Fort Myers FL 33919

Call Sign: KI4YQF
Bonnie T Hendricks
6234 St Andrews Cir
Fort Myers FL 33919

Call Sign: K4JGP
Walter L Gustavson
6241 St Andrews Cir
Fort Myers FL 33907

Call Sign: KF4BBU
Paul J Holsen II
6791 St Edmunds Loop
Fort Myers FL 33912

Call Sign: K4PJH
Paul J Holsen II
6791 St Edmunds Loop
Fort Myers FL 33966

Call Sign: KB2HAA
Paul Kampa Sr
6911 St Edmunds Loop
Fort Myers FL 33912

Call Sign: KC4ZGD
Robert C Hannon II
6721 St Ives Ct
Fort Myers FL 33912

Call Sign: KI4QE

Gerald M Jones
17410 Sterling Lake Dr
Fort Myers FL 33912

Call Sign: KJ4SMA
Timothy J Mace
12881 Stone Tower Loop
Fort Myers FL 33913

Call Sign: KA1IFX
Ronald A Jurek
9845 Sugarberry Way
Fort Myers FL 33905

Call Sign: KI4HEW
Luna E Smith
12161 Summergate Cir
104
Fort Myers FL 33913

Call Sign: KI4DBI
Rodney J Smith
12161 Summergate Cir
104
Fort Myers FL 339138069

Call Sign: KD4SPY
Annette Monet
19333 Summerlin Rd
Fort Myers FL 33908

Call Sign: KE4CFZ
Harry M Halvorsen Sr
19681 Summerlin Rd
144H
Fort Myers FL 33908

Call Sign: KB3AMF
Barbara J Miller
15880 Summerlin Rd 300
Fort Myers FL 33908

Call Sign: K4YKA
Edward V Sexton

19681 Summerlin Rd Lot
116
Fort Myers FL 33908

Call Sign: N1RYY
Bernard V Martin
11386 Summerwinds Ct
Fort Myers FL 33908

Call Sign: W4FF
Frank L Fugle Jr
12553 Summerwood Dr
SW
Fort Myers FL 33908

Call Sign: KE0TG
John W Anderson Jr
206 Suncircle
Fort Myers FL 33905

Call Sign: KA4MQQ
Gerald P Kynett Jr
2404 Sundial Ct
Fort Myers FL 339081623

Call Sign: N4CYP
Virginia S Kynett
2404 Sundial Ct
Fort Myers FL 339081623

Call Sign: KI4ICR
Richard W Arnold
633 Sunnyside Ct
Fort Myers FL 33919

Call Sign: KF4YAU
Lorenzo O Moore
1826 Sunset Pl
Fort Myers FL 33901

Call Sign: WD4DEE
Michael S Ford
15291 Tahitian Dr
Fort Myers FL 33908

Call Sign: WA8NQU
James H Huff
13207 Tall Pine Cir
Fort Myers FL 339075941

Call Sign: KG4RVY
James H Huff
13207 Tall Pine Cir
Fort Myers FL 339075941

Call Sign: WA4SBK
Marcia H Guest
1351 Tanglewood Pkwy
Fort Myers FL 339191934

Call Sign: WB4BDQ
John E Warren
1343 Tanglewood Pky
Fort Myers FL 33919

Call Sign: WA4SBE
Edward W Guest
1351 Tanglewood Pky
Fort Myers FL 33919

Call Sign: WA4WNF
Joseph W Dunnett
206 Tellidora Ct
Fort Myers FL 33908

Call Sign: KB4ANA
Mary E Dunnett
206 Tellidora Ct
Fort Myers FL 33908

Call Sign: KE4PUN
Norman H Wood
232 Tellidora Ct
Fort Myers FL 33908

Call Sign: KK4CQK
Joseph L Banfield
9096 Temple Rd W
Fort Myers FL 33967

Call Sign: KC4GT
James C Campbell
7991 Tiger Palm Way
Fort Myers FL 33966

Call Sign: WB2PMU
Lawrence R Hause
8911 Timber Run Ct
Fort Myers FL 339087614

Call Sign: W4LRH
Lawrence R Hause
8911 Timber Run Ct
Fort Myers FL 339087614

Call Sign: W9HBZ
Allen J Davis
16985 Timberlakes Dr SW
Fort Myers FL 33908

Call Sign: N8QVA
Pamela J Owens
5650 Trailwinds Dr 123
Fort Myers FL 339078326

Call Sign: K8UIE
Dudley P Damon
2197 Treehaven Cir
Fort Myers FL 33907

Call Sign: W3RIH
Russell I Sellers
14364 Trinidad St
Fort Myers FL 339052315

Call Sign: KC4HWH
Charles A Bedell
33 Tropic Dr
Fort Myers FL 33908

Call Sign: KI4RHC
William P Schaffner
17133 Tropical Rd
Fort Myers FL 33912

Call Sign: N4PSU
Marion M Cornwell Jr
4342 Tufts Ave
Fort Myers FL 33901

Call Sign: N4PSV
Nell S Cornwell
4342 Tufts Ave
Fort Myers FL 33901

Call Sign: N2FWA
Edward R Budd
4810 Turban Ct
Fort Myers FL 339081605

Call Sign: W2GPR
Winfield E Fromm
Turban Ct
Fort Myers FL 33908

Call Sign: NA0M
Virginia S Cunningham
73 Ultimo Ct
Fort Myers FL 33912

Call Sign: KC4FBH
Max Van Keeken
13499 US 41 SE 133
Fort Myers FL 33907

Call Sign: KG4QFE
Michael Hedden
12930 Valdosta Pl
Fort Myers FL 33913

Call Sign: KE4VUM
John Cronmiller
431 Van Buren E1
Fort Myers FL 33916

Call Sign: KF4NWW
David L Sloan
7132 Vassar Dr
Fort Myers FL 33908

Call Sign: K9ZMQ
Emmett R Bubb
67 Verlo Ct
Fort Myers FL 33912

Call Sign: KE4UPY
Eric J D India
1250 Vesper Dr
Fort Myers FL 33901

Call Sign: K9GMJ
Richard G Kelly
9367 Via Murano Ct
Fort Myers FL 33905

Call Sign: W9OKL
Christine S Kerr
16098 Via Solera Cir Unit
104
Fort Myers FL 33908

Call Sign: AB4VS
Selmer M Salvesen III
8384 Villaire Ct
Fort Myers FL 33919

Call Sign: W4PAP
Russel W Haggstrom
60 Vinales Ct
Fort Myers FL 33912

Call Sign: WA3QHF
Rose K Hobson
16 Vinata Ct
Fort Myers FL 33912

Call Sign: K3KPA
John F Hobson
16 Vinata Ct
Fort Myers FL 339126389

Call Sign: N1HYQ
Donald W Sciarretta
1925 Virginia Ave
Fort Myers FL 33901

Call Sign: K3QC
John T Burik
2235 Virginia Ave
Fort Myers FL 33905

Call Sign: W8OWS
Octagon Wildlife
Sanctuary
2235 Virginia Ave
Fort Myers FL 33905

Call Sign: W4FMY
Lee County Fm
Association
2235 Virginia Ave
Fort Myers FL 339054713

Call Sign: KC0OD
Charles D Ehinger
1910 Virginia Ave 1403B
Fort Myers FL 33901

Call Sign: K4JTB
Olga Radio Club
2235 Virginia Ave SE
Fort Myers FL 33905

Call Sign: K4QCW
Qcwa Edison Chapter 196
2235 Virginia Ave SE
Fort Myers FL 33905

Call Sign: WA8PXL
John T Burik
2235 Virginia Ave SE
Fort Myers FL 339054713

Call Sign: WA8PXL
Qcwa Edison Chapter 196
2235 Virginia Ave SE
Fort Myers FL 339054713

Call Sign: KG4STZ
Qcwa Edison Chapter 196

2235 Virginia Ave SE
Fort Myers FL 339054713

Call Sign: K4CAH
Robert E Hendry
2065 W 1st St
Fort Myers FL 33901

Call Sign: KI4RHA
Joseph W Savage
2104 W 1st St 3203
Fort Myers FL 33901

Call Sign: NB2Z
Martin R Small
14011 W Hyde Park Dr
Apt 204
Fort Myers FL 33912

Call Sign: W4AAA
Henry R Propst
8619 W Park
Fort Myers FL 33907

Call Sign: K8WYC
Harold M Espenschied
1335 Walden Dr
Fort Myers FL 33901

Call Sign: W8ATZ
S Jean E Espenschied
1335 Walden Dr
Fort Myers FL 33901

Call Sign: KD4EER
Allan A Kunze
12820 Waterford Cir
Fort Myers FL 33919

Call Sign: W6JUP
Neal J Greenberg
12831 Waterford Cir
Fort Myers FL 33919

Call Sign: KI4CE

George J Bates
12973 Waterford Cir
Fort Myers FL 33919

Call Sign: KC4PBR
M Joanne Linderoth
12770 Waterford Cir Apt
304
Fort Myers FL 33919

Call Sign: WB4FQX
Helen V Scott
12820 Waterford Cir Apt
309
Fort Myers FL 33919

Call Sign: K4SJP
Charles C Harper
12903 Waterford Cir
Waterford Pl
Fort Myers FL 33919

Call Sign: WJ3X
Clinton C Cottrell
11485 Waterford Village
Dr
Fort Myers FL 33913

Call Sign: KK4BQO
Anthony G Pietroniro
9865 Weather Stone Pl
Fort Myers FL 33913

Call Sign: KB8LLE
Arthur G Boyds
232 Wecuwa Ave
Fort Myers FL 33912

Call Sign: KB8LLD
Beverly J Boyds
232 Wecuwa Ave
Fort Myers FL 33912

Call Sign: W4SEM
Hugh Pulliam

106 Wecuwa Dr
Fort Myers FL 33912

Call Sign: KI4HFB
Charles H Clement
11980 Wedge Dr
Fort Myers FL 33913

Call Sign: KD4NYZ
Robert W Williams Jr
14754 Westport Dr
Fort Myers FL 33908

Call Sign: WA4MOE
Carl C Hampton
6920 Westwood Acres Rd
Fort Myers FL 33905

Call Sign: KD4ZYF
John V Geyer
1471 Whiskey Creek Dr
Fort Myers FL 33919

Call Sign: W9ITI
Thomas W Gleason
1685 Whiskey Creek Dr
Fort Myers FL 33919

Call Sign: KI4RHB
Barry H Axelrod
1744 Whiskey Creek Dr
Fort Myers FL 33919

Call Sign: WA4EAS
Harold R Dunlap
8331 Whiskey Preserve
Cir Apt 447
Fort Myers FL 339198786

Call Sign: K3JTD
Billie G Key
13262 White Haven Ln
608
Fort Myers FL 33912

Call Sign: WB5OST
Norbert E Auer
1660 White Plains Ter
Fort Myers FL 339033459

Call Sign: N5DTQ
Caroline M Auer
1660 White Plains Ter
Fort Myers FL 339034659

Call Sign: N2RPL
Barry D Pearse
2850 Wildwood Ln
Fort Myers FL 339055600

Call Sign: KG4FFF
Lawnce E Mollison
3109 Willard St Unit 32
Fort Myers FL 33916

Call Sign: W4JMC
David L Kemp
7450 Willems Dr Rr 24
Fort Myers FL 33908

Call Sign: KI4HSS
Barbara A Richards
17501 Williamsburg Dr
Fort Myers FL 33917

Call Sign: KI4HSR
William G Mawhinney
17501 Williamsburg Dr
Fort Myers FL 33917

Call Sign: N1SAE
Adore H Cloutier
5595 Williamson Way
Fort Myers FL 33919

Call Sign: W4CBV
Peter A Kwasney
6562 Willow Lake Cir
Fort Myers FL 33966

Call Sign: KB2EYE
Richard A Tauson
4496 Windjammer Ln Unit
2A
Fort Myers FL 33919

Call Sign: WA2JZE
Elio P Corini
9614 Windsor Club Cir SE
Fort Myers FL 33905

Call Sign: KG4FFJ
Georgia R Thomas
8381 Winged Ft Dr
Fort Myers FL 33912

Call Sign: W4EOB
George X Sand
1412 Winkler Ave
Fort Myers FL 33901

Call Sign: KA4YAB
Lou B Sand
1412 Winkler Ave
Fort Myers FL 33901

Call Sign: KF4GTT
Harry Sombor
2674 Winkler Ave 404
Fort Myers FL 33901

Call Sign: KA8DGM
Gunnard R Lundgren
2674 Winkler Ave Apt 221
Fort Myers FL 33901

Call Sign: KD4OVD
Angelo A Catalano
2674 Winkler Ave Unit
421
Fort Myers FL 33901

Call Sign: KF4JUI
David J Moore
6730 Winkler Rd H4

Fort Myers FL 33919

Call Sign: KJ4RSD
Samantha L O Garro
18528 Winterhaven Rd
Fort Myers FL 33967

Call Sign: WD4PPA
Carl E Bergner Jr
1603 Woodford Ave
Fort Myers FL 339012425

Call Sign: KG4ERM
Wayne B Blythe
7793 Woodland Bend Cir
Fort Myers FL 33912

Call Sign: K4CD
Mike Loria
2413 Woodland Blvd
Fort Myers FL 33907

Call Sign: WD8JUM
David L Cottrell
2461 Woodland Cir
Fort Myers FL 33907

Call Sign: W4ZEY
Joseph S Dutka
2472 Woodland Cir
Fort Myers FL 33907

Call Sign: K9WHE
Ruel F Burns Jr
3655 Woodstork Ct
Fort Myers FL 33908

Call Sign: WA9URD
Dwight E Smith
277 Yorkshire Ave SW
Fort Myers FL 33908

Call Sign: WD4NZN
Benjamin C James
Yukon Cir SW

Fort Myers FL 33907

Call Sign: KC4AXO
Charles E Clay
Fort Myers FL 33902

Call Sign: KD4OJJ
Margrit K Skolfield
Fort Myers FL 33902

Call Sign: W4CYU
Robert Hecksher
Fort Myers FL 33902

Call Sign: KB4UFP
Robert G Bruce Sr
Fort Myers FL 33902

Call Sign: K4VGN
Robert W Sloat
Fort Myers FL 33902

Call Sign: K4GVI
John H Marshall
Fort Myers FL 33906

Call Sign: WK4P
Edward E Matheny
Fort Myers FL 33911

Call Sign: KC2ADM
Scott A Jackowski
Fort Myers FL 33092

Call Sign: KS4XF
Glenn K Cary
Fort Myers FL 33902

Call Sign: N9NFT
Kevin M Lange
Fort Myers FL 33902

Call Sign: KE4LPS
Larry M Bradshaw
Fort Myers FL 33902

Call Sign: KF4BBW
Robbi R Cary
Fort Myers FL 33902

Call Sign: AB4DY
James A Brennan
Fort Myers FL 33902

Call Sign: KF4QWD
Gary A Keene
Fort Myers FL 33906

Call Sign: N4RNW
Harold J Leyes
Fort Myers FL 33906

Call Sign: K4ZAP
James A Midgley
Fort Myers FL 33906

Call Sign: KI4GAH
James A Myers
Fort Myers FL 33906

Call Sign: KJ4VDJ
James R Fellabaum
Fort Myers FL 33906

Call Sign: AE4QH
William S Amore
Fort Myers FL 33906

Call Sign: W4LX
Fort Myers ARC
Fort Myers FL 33906

Call Sign: KG4CBU
Joshua R Lewis
Fort Myers FL 33911

Call Sign: KG4CBT
Samuel S Lewis
Fort Myers FL 33911

Call Sign: KG4FFI
Terry J Foshee
Fort Myers FL 33911

Call Sign: WB4OYV
Ronald E Pierce
Fort Myers FL 33919

Call Sign: KF4FDJ
Michael J Gilchrist
Fort Myers FL 339020763

Call Sign: KA4MBM
Vivian J Hauser
Fort Myers FL 339021478

Call Sign: KG4BSF
David J Beauchesne
Fort Myers FL 339021909

Call Sign: KE4HXP
Howard A Bartels Sr
Fort Myers FL 339060472

**FCC Amateur Radio
Licenses in Fort Myers
Beach**

Call Sign: NG9K
Lewis V Heck
127 Albatross St
Fort Myers Beach FL
33931

Call Sign: WD4AFF
Frank J Fuleky
190 Anchorage St
Fort Myers Beach FL
33931

Call Sign: KJ4SGD
Edward A Milde Jr
Anchorage St
Fort Myers Beach FL
33931

Call Sign: N4STO
Donald Peacock
4451 Bay Beach Ln 423
Fort Myers Beach FL
339314909

Call Sign: N4TEI
Helene M Peacock
4451 Bay Beach Ln Unit
423
Fort Myers Beach FL
339314909

Call Sign: KO6LM
Joseph A Strillchuk
107 Bay Mar Dr
Fort Myers Beach FL
339313807

Call Sign: N4VCC
Jack G Ramp
21470 Bay Village Dr Apt
241
Fort Myers Beach FL
33931

Call Sign: KF0ID
Scot D Gronewold
11300 Bayside Blvd
Fort Myers Beach FL
339313130

Call Sign: W8BMA
Jack R Rinker
94 Blackbeard Way
Fort Myers Beach FL
33931

Call Sign: W3CNO
George C Hengen
25 Bougainvillea Ln
Fort Myers Beach FL
33931

Call Sign: W3URU
Sarah L Hengen
25 Bougainvillea Ln
Fort Myers Beach FL
33931

Call Sign: KB2ROL
Carl W Huntley
8016 Buccaneer Dr
Fort Myers Beach FL
33931

Call Sign: NF4Q
George W Mangus
17650 Canal Cove Ct
Fort Myers Beach FL
33931

Call Sign: N4GRO
Lois W Mangus
17650 Canal Cove Ct
Fort Myers Beach FL
33931

Call Sign: KE1CG
David B Wallace
265 Carolina Ave
Fort Myers Beach FL
339312811

Call Sign: KU4XH
H Dieter Decker
290 Carolina Ave
Fort Myers Beach FL
33931

Call Sign: KJ4LCM
Dale R Clift
166 Chapel St
Fort Myers Beach FL
33931

Call Sign: KG4UAG
Andrew G Dolak
18212 Cutlass Dr

Fort Myers Beach FL
33931

Call Sign: W8QUO
William A Hillebrand
18371 Cutlass Dr
Fort Myers Beach FL
33931

Call Sign: AH2AH
John J Boucher
18532 Deep Passage Ln
Fort Myers Beach FL
33931

Call Sign: KG6JBB
Judith E Boucher
18532 Deep Passage Ln
Fort Myers Beach FL
33931

Call Sign: KC4DP
Eugene W Warnock
240 Driftwood Ln
Fort Myers Beach FL
33931

Call Sign: KD4LLJ
Manfred Boldt
16 Emily Ln
Fort Myers Beach FL
33931

Call Sign: KD4LLK
Rosemarie Boldt
16 Emily Ln
Fort Myers Beach FL
33931

Call Sign: KB4RWP
Richard T Miniear
18 Emily Ln
Fort Myers Beach FL
33931

Call Sign: KJ4VDQ
Mark C Duncan
4109 Estero Blvd
Fort Myers Beach FL
33931

Call Sign: WB9GGT
Allen H Phillips
6655 Estero Blvd
Fort Myers Beach FL
33931

Call Sign: KD4LIG
Francis J Gebo
7330 Estero Blvd
Fort Myers Beach FL
33931

Call Sign: NZ3D
Eugene J Kordowski
2949 Estero Blvd Unit 11
Fort Myers Beach FL
33931

Call Sign: KH6JCZ
Patrick J Fitzmaurice
124 Falkirk St
Fort Myers Beach FL
33931

Call Sign: K9VDL
Raymond C Owens
30 Iroquois D N
Fort Myers Beach FL
339312404

Call Sign: K1WXU
Roger H Poirier
19 Iroquois Dr S
Fort Myers Beach FL
33931

Call Sign: KA2GIV
Maria T Belcher

22736 Island Pines Way
Apt 302
Fort Myers Beach FL
33931

Call Sign: KM4RG
William Belcher
22736 Island Pines Way
Apt 302
Fort Myers Beach FL
33931

Call Sign: K8ZNB
Charles C Hefling
18 Kiowa Dr
Fort Myers Beach FL
33931

Call Sign: WA6OCJ
William B Paulus
55 N Kiowa Dr
Fort Myers Beach FL
33931

Call Sign: W1EUU
Howard G Robinson Jr
66 Nancy Ln
Fort Myers Beach FL
33931

Call Sign: KA4TXX
William A Doubleday
171 Osage Trl
Fort Myers Beach FL
33931

Call Sign: WN4J
Robert L Abbey
17871 Peppard Dr
Fort Myers Beach FL
33931

Call Sign: KB4JCS
Ila B M Strife
291 Peppard Dr SW

Fort Myers Beach FL
33931

Call Sign: KG4WCF
Anthony D Angelini
260 Primo Dr
Fort Myers Beach FL
33931

Call Sign: KU4LZ
Phillip O Babcock
320 Randy Ln
Fort Myers Beach FL
339314012

Call Sign: W3ZR
David F Kosh
17881 Rebecca Ave
Fort Myers Beach FL
339313002

Call Sign: WA2MRL
Ferrin T Sullivan
17279 San Carlos Blvd
Fort Myers Beach FL
339313957

Call Sign: KG4WBQ
Donald Atkins
18032 San Carlos Blvd
100
Fort Myers Beach FL
33931

Call Sign: KF4OLY
Daniel L Galvin
17105 San Carlos Blvd A
6178
Fort Myers Beach FL
33931

Call Sign: KC4IXS
Derek G Bunker
17340 San Carlos Bvd 804

Fort Myers Beach FL
33931

Call Sign: K8RDF
Jack L Ulrich
587 Sioux Trl
Fort Myers Beach FL
33931

Call Sign: WA4TAY
J Glenn Loveless
120 Voorhis St
Fort Myers Beach FL
33931

Call Sign: KB3DHF
Brady L Brown
6110 Whiskey Ck Dr Unit
207
Fort Myers Beach FL
33932

Call Sign: KI4HKP
Linda W Card
Fort Myers Beach FL
33932

Call Sign: KI4CPS
Patricia A Castle
Fort Myers Beach FL
33932

Call Sign: KC4OZH
Robert R Pijanowski Jr
Fort Myers Beach FL
33932

Call Sign: KI4NFS
Philip M Ratliff
Fort Myers Beach FL
33932

**FCC Amateur Radio
Licenses in Fort Ogden**

Call Sign: KD4DNN
Olive L Kramer
Fort Ogden FL 33842

Call Sign: KK4AMU
Edward Diaz
Fort Ogden FL 34267

Call Sign: KK4APN
Edward Diaz
Fort Ogden FL 34267

Call Sign: KF4THH
Lori A Biagioli
Fort Ogden FL 34267

Call Sign: KF4RFE
Mark L Biagioli
Fort Ogden FL 34267

**FCC Amateur Radio
Licenses in Golden Gate**

Call Sign: KF4AER
Jack B Randolf
5020 32nd Ave SW
Golden Gate FL 34116

Call Sign: KF4MCM
William A Silva
210 Weber Blvd SW
Golden Gate FL 34117

**FCC Amateur Radio
Licenses in Goodland**

Call Sign: KJ4NKK
Ronald Whitten
385 Angler Dr C 14
Goodland FL 34140

Call Sign: KB4IXM
Alf S Fischer
667 Palm Ave W
Goodland FL 34140

Call Sign: KC4DIY
William F Barclay Jr
401 Papaya St
Goodland FL 33933

Call Sign: WD0EBG
John A Cartwright Sr
311 Pettit Dr
Goodland FL 34140

Call Sign: KA4JLG
Paul D Cartwright
323 Pettit Dr Box 234
Goodland FL 33933

FCC Amateur Radio Licenses in Grove City

Call Sign: NT9K
Dennis G Babcock
1960 Mississippi Ave
Grove City FL 342245527

Call Sign: N9TFU
Linda L Greene
1960 Mississippi Ave
Grove City FL 342245527

Call Sign: N4SYP
George S Wheelock
York St
Grove City FL 34224

Call Sign: N4ZCR
Jerald A De Long
Grove City FL 34224

FCC Amateur Radio Licenses in Harbour Heights

Call Sign: W1GMI
Arthur W Sevigny
3315 N San Marino Dr

Harbour Heights FL 33983

Call Sign: KC4GUR
Rita G Collins
3209 Wheeler Ct
Harbour Heights FL 33983

FCC Amateur Radio Licenses in Immokalee

Call Sign: W4VGE
James T Lester
1709 Carson Rd
Immokalee FL 33934

Call Sign: KD4IFQ
Eduardo Martinez
505 Hope Cir
Immokalee FL 33934

Call Sign: KD4IFR
Margarita Serrano
505 Hope Cir
Immokalee FL 33934

Call Sign: KG4HIG
Carol L German
6001 Lake Trafford Rd
Immokalee FL 34142

Call Sign: W4SXD
Paul Martin
6001 Lake Trafford Rd
Immokalee FL 34142

Call Sign: KD5TVZ
Jayson W Street
709 N 11th St
Immokalee FL 34142

Call Sign: N5KFR
Thomas W Street
709 N 11th St
Immokalee FL 34142

Call Sign: KE4FGJ
Vickie L Street
709 N 11th St
Immokalee FL 34142

Call Sign: KJ4INT
William B Armbrester Jr
Immokalee FL 34143

Call Sign: KF4MCL
Richard R Soltow Jr
Immokalee FL 341430497

Call Sign: KG4QXU
Ismael Perez
Immokalee FL 341435113

FCC Amateur Radio Licenses in LaBelle

Call Sign: WD4SJR
Anna M Mitchell
998 Avalon St
LaBelle FL 33935

Call Sign: AG3X
Harry W Claypool
240 Belmont St
LaBelle FL 33935

Call Sign: WB4ZIA
Nadine P Trickel
Box 186
LaBelle FL 33935

Call Sign: KJ4QLS
Richard E Smith
620 Broward Ave
LaBelle FL 33935

Call Sign: WA4CWG
Alfred C Fox
151 Caloosa Est Dr
LaBelle FL 33935

Call Sign: KE4PFG
Ronald R Zimmerly
193 Cottage Ave
LaBelle FL 33935

Call Sign: KE4PFF
Silas R Zimmerly
193 Cottage Ave
LaBelle FL 33935

Call Sign: KI4MAZ
Kristen L Abreu
4061 Edgewater Cir
LaBelle FL 33935

Call Sign: KI4HKR
David J Radford
800 Ft Thompson
LaBelle FL 33935

Call Sign: K3ZJN
Gene Taraborrelli
900 Hickpoochee Aqua
Isles M16
LaBelle FL 33935

Call Sign: KR4YD
David H Burroughs
2475 Howard Rd
LaBelle FL 33935

Call Sign: KC4WEI
John T Krystyniak Jr
104 Howe Ave
LaBelle FL 33935

Call Sign: KB8FVU
Robert W Kyle
16630 Jay Ter
LaBelle FL 33935

Call Sign: AD4JD
Nancy L Bidwell
490 Kathryn St
LaBelle FL 33935

Call Sign: N7BSM
Kathleen E Walsh
150 Live Oak Ln
LaBelle FL 33935

Call Sign: N8FSL
Andrew L Toth Jr
371 Mahogany Ct
LaBelle FL 33935

Call Sign: KG4LAF
Joe H Crunk
2010 Mainstay St
LaBelle FL 33935

Call Sign: KD1IM
Lawrence N Boyd
413 Maple Dr SW
LaBelle FL 33935

Call Sign: K4GMO
James E Hurtt
333 Missouri Ave
LaBelle FL 33975

Call Sign: W9FFP
Charles W Wilson
499 Noble Pine Dr
LaBelle FL 33935

Call Sign: KI4ONY
Narciso Flores
168 Orange St
LaBelle FL 33935

Call Sign: KF4VAK
Mary M Tyner
100 Oxbow Dr Unit A 202
LaBelle FL 33935

Call Sign: K4ACU
Leo F Maness
4460 Pollywog Dr SW
LaBelle FL 33935

Call Sign: K8UIW
James S Eden
450 Pollywog Point
LaBelle FL 33935

Call Sign: W9VDS
Peter F Sutton
4015 Rainbow Cir
LaBelle FL 339355416

Call Sign: KT4GA
Warren L Grant
4020 Rainbow Cir
LaBelle FL 33935

Call Sign: K8YT
Robert O Baker
4036 Rainbow Cir
LaBelle FL 33935

Call Sign: N0OYE
Linda S Mc Vey
200 Riverview Dr
LaBelle FL 33935

Call Sign: N0OYD
Michael T Mc Vey
200 Riverview Dr
LaBelle FL 33935

Call Sign: N0JCC
Norman G Dillman
344 Riviera Vista Blvd
LaBelle FL 33935

Call Sign: N0MJB
Phyllis A Dillman
344 Riviera Vista Blvd
LaBelle FL 33935

Call Sign: KG4SJH
Kara H Dillman
344 Riviera Vista Blvd
LaBelle FL 33935

Call Sign: KA1OKG
Ronald S Novak
4008 Rye Ct
LaBelle FL 33935

Call Sign: NE1SW
Ronald S Novak
4008 Rye Ct
LaBelle FL 33935

Call Sign: KN4VU
Christine C Novak
4008 Rye Ct
LaBelle FL 33935

Call Sign: N2ARS
Thomas G Phillips
3022 S Balsam Cir
LaBelle FL 33935

Call Sign: KF4GAA
Derrek J Abreu
4061 S Edgewater Cir
LaBelle FL 33935

Call Sign: W4CER
Robert L Roper
620 S Main St
LaBelle FL 33935

Call Sign: K3FTE
Harry W Schoene Jr
4035 School Cir
LaBelle FL 339355503

Call Sign: KQ4YM
Don Brown
4513 Springview Cir
LaBelle FL 33935

Call Sign: KF4HCG
Sarah R Miller
5540 SR 80
LaBelle FL 33975

Call Sign: KJ4CIR
Francis E Smith
2099 Summeral Rd
LaBelle FL 33935

Call Sign: W4WRX
Paul F Fletcher
4010 Teak Ln
LaBelle FL 33935

Call Sign: KI4ZYT
Lynne E Kilcoyne
1715 Tom Coker Rd
LaBelle FL 33935

Call Sign: KF4UXT
James C Tyner
1033 Villa Dr Apt A 202
LaBelle FL 33935

Call Sign: K2BQ
Paul W Haczela
1005 Western Way NW
LaBelle FL 33935

Call Sign: KD4ZIX
Janice R Miller
LaBelle FL 33935

Call Sign: KD4VTL
Robert A Miller
LaBelle FL 33935

Call Sign: AD4RD
Frank R Miller
LaBelle FL 33975

Call Sign: KS4HB
Thomas B Millican Jr
LaBelle FL 339350254

Call Sign: KI4EYI
George W Barnette
LaBelle FL 33975

Call Sign: KF4MVE
Joseph F Kotvas
LaBelle FL 33975

Call Sign: KF4RSL
Michelle D Runyon
LaBelle FL 33975

Call Sign: KF4HCF
Peter J Miller
LaBelle FL 33975

Call Sign: KF4RSM
Timothy J Miller
LaBelle FL 33975

Call Sign: KI4QVD
Debora T Simicich
LaBelle FL 33975

Call Sign: KF4NJU
Lisa M Kotvas
LaBelle FL 33975

Call Sign: KF4QWE
Dean D Runyon
LaBelle FL 339751155

Call Sign: KF4YXM
Antonia M Rafalsky
LaBelle FL 339751816

Call Sign: KF4RSK
Patty E Runyon
LaBelle FL 339751155

**FCC Amateur Radio
Licenses in Lake Placid**

Call Sign: KB4YUB
Gilbert S Griffiths
66 2nd St
Lake Placid FL 33852

Call Sign: KF4VQU
Carol A Thorp
1614 5th St
Lake Placid FL 33852

Call Sign: KJ4SWT
Raul Rodriguez
137 Bimini St NE
Lake Placid FL 33852

Call Sign: NR8P
George I Pearl
403 Buddy Ave
Lake Placid FL 33852

Call Sign: KC4EQF
Donald W Hofferth
5th St
Lake Placid FL 33852

Call Sign: KG4IVL
Alvin G Powell
3053 Birch Rd
Lake Placid FL 33852

Call Sign: N4XZL
Herbert J Phelan
1009 Burnett St
Lake Placid FL 33852

Call Sign: WV4F
Robert D Strathy
30 Acacia Ct S
Lake Placid FL 33852

Call Sign: W9KFY
Alvin G Powell
3053 Birch Rd
Lake Placid FL 33852

Call Sign: K4FAB
Frederick A Bowen
104 Captiva Ct NE
Lake Placid FL 33852

Call Sign: KB4VOF
Alice C Rasmussen
347 Adams Ave
Lake Placid FL 338528829

Call Sign: KD4CQG
Phyllis J Dibble
3053 Birch Rd
Lake Placid FL 33852

Call Sign: K4VLE
B Stephen Johnson
355 Catfish Creek Rd
Lake Placid FL 33852

Call Sign: N3BAC
Nancy C Reaney
3008 Ash St
Lake Placid FL 338528465

Call Sign: KE4WU
William B Dibble
3053 Birch Rd
Lake Placid FL 338528422

Call Sign: N8XBR
Richard J Ganski
720 Catfish Creek Rd
Lake Placid FL 33852

Call Sign: N3BAB
Richard B Reaney
3008 Ash St
Lake Placid FL 338528465

Call Sign: KI4XM
Ernest T Rasmussen
347 Bottlebrush Ave
Lake Placid FL 338528829

Call Sign: WB8ZBL
George V Cook
1612 Cedar St
Lake Placid FL 33852

Call Sign: KI4TID
Jack Sangalli
24 Beachfront Ln
Lake Placid FL 33852

Call Sign: KF4VQT
David H Alden
3 Brachs St
Lake Placid FL 33852

Call Sign: AF4UC
George V Cook
1612 Cedar St
Lake Placid FL 33852

Call Sign: KF4BXB
Richard C Ferguson
3006 Beech
Lake Placid FL 33852

Call Sign: WA4LOM
Barbara A Welch
749 Bryce St
Lake Placid FL 338527990

Call Sign: K5VHK
John A Curtice
1616 Churchill St
Lake Placid FL 33852

Call Sign: WB4YQZ
Ronald L Adams
617 Bell Pl
Lake Placid FL 33852

Call Sign: W9NMX
Gene A Welch
749 Bryce St
Lake Placid FL 338527990

Call Sign: N4GGM
Robert C Rowe
1736 Citadel St
Lake Placid FL 33852

Call Sign: KU4YU
Emma E Pearl
403 Clark Ave
Lake Placid FL 33852

Call Sign: WB4NSS
Robert G Hargrove
109 Daphne Ave NW
Lake Placid FL 33852

Call Sign: AC4XR
Elliott M Moses
1082 Flamingo Dr
Lake Placid FL 33852

Call Sign: WA4PAF
James Kamis
108 Club Rd NW
Lake Placid FL 33852

Call Sign: KK4CYH
Brian E Conklin
12 Diamond Bay Dr
Lake Placid FL 33852

Call Sign: KK4CYG
Jared S Chaput
3254 Forrest View Ave
Lake Placid FL 33852

Call Sign: N4ESY
Therese R Kamis
108 Club Rd NW
Lake Placid FL 33852

Call Sign: W3AVI
Dennis V Faulkner
217 E Washington St
Lake Placid FL 338526254

Call Sign: KK4LI
John R Chaput
3254 Forrest View Ave
Lake Placid FL 33852

Call Sign: KF4TKB
Gregory F Gustin
97 Cole Danley Dr
Lake Placid FL 33852

Call Sign: W4FOC
Highlands Foc
61 Eden Ln
Lake Placid FL 33852

Call Sign: WA4AB
Ralph H Austin
110 Fox Ridge Rd
Lake Placid FL 338528502

Call Sign: KB9TCP
James G Lagrone
33 Connie Dr
Lake Placid FL 33852

Call Sign: WB4OSN
Joseph L Picior
61 Eden Ln
Lake Placid FL 33852

Call Sign: K2CP
Roger W Warrick
125 Fox Ridge Rd
Lake Placid FL 33852

Call Sign: W4IHW
Irving H Vosbrink
40 Copperhead Dr
Lake Placid FL 33852

Call Sign: W4IR
Joseph L Picior
61 Eden Ln
Lake Placid FL 33852

Call Sign: AA5IV
Donald G Bitz
243 Fox Ridge Rd
Lake Placid FL 33852

Call Sign: W9LNA
Jonathan F Schoemann
17 Cubby Ln Comp 3
Lake Placid FL 33852

Call Sign: KG4ERZ
Gary P Mcgrady
114 Ellison Ave
Lake Placid FL 338524291

Call Sign: WB1DHA
Bernice A Lambert
126 Gates Ave
Lake Placid FL 33852

Call Sign: WA8GAK
Ralph R Metheny
280 Cumquat Rd NW
Lake Placid FL 33852

Call Sign: KG4EWD
Lois A Mcgrady
114 Ellison Ave
Lake Placid FL 338524291

Call Sign: WA1URB
Paul A Lambert
126 Gates Ave
Lake Placid FL 33852

Call Sign: KB4VLW
John W Hopkins
719 Cumquat Rd NW
Lake Placid FL 33852

Call Sign: KJ4FJB
Donald R Rodrigue
13 Fishermans Cove
Lake Placid FL 33852

Call Sign: KA4HAX
Duane J Rigge
44 Grandview Blvd
Lake Placid FL 33852

Call Sign: KD4QFA
M Ruth Dove
123 Grape Rd NW
Lake Placid FL 33852

Call Sign: W9CIY
Paul M Dove
123 Grape Rd NW
Lake Placid FL 33852

Call Sign: K4RBR
F Norman Ward
254 Grissom Rd NW
Lake Placid FL 338526829

Call Sign: KG4OLS
Highlands County ARC
254 Grissom Rd NW
Lake Placid FL 338526829

Call Sign: KD4UZV
Jo Anne H Catlett
214 Guymon Ave NW
Lake Placid FL 32907

Call Sign: N3HC
Hugh W Catlett
214 Guymon Ave NW
Lake Placid FL 33852

Call Sign: KP4BQM
Henry G Hayes
131 Highlands Lake Dr
Lake Placid FL 33852

Call Sign: K4GAF
Millard H Vanderford
131 Highlands Lake Dr
Lake Placid FL 33852

Call Sign: KE4IEA
Gary B Veldhuis
171 Hillside Dr
Lake Placid FL 33852

Call Sign: W4ZPO
Richard W Mc Coy
211 Hoover Ave NE
Lake Placid FL 33852

Call Sign: KB4SBC
Esther C Perez
748 Jefferson Ave
Lake Placid FL 33852

Call Sign: KB4HGJ
Manuel N Perez
748 Jefferson Ave
Lake Placid FL 33852

Call Sign: K4ZNB
Harry H Mottinger
20 Keith Ave NW
Lake Placid FL 33852

Call Sign: W4VSM
Ruth E Mottinger
230 Keith Ave NW
Lake Placid FL 33852

Call Sign: KD4APE
Garland G Warren Jr
1712 Lake Clay Dr
Lake Placid FL 33852

Call Sign: N4ANY
Gerald Entel
1718 Lake Clay Dr
Lake Placid FL 33852

Call Sign: AD4VJ
Beverly M Kenniston
1719 Lake Clay Dr
Lake Placid FL 33852

Call Sign: KA4PHP
Edgar A Green
482 Lake Francis
Lake Placid FL 33852

Call Sign: KE4VEI
William T Overhulser
275 Lake Francis Rd
Lake Placid FL 33852

Call Sign: KA4FVF
Albert W Truax
41 Lake Gardens Dr
Lake Placid FL 33852

Call Sign: KK4DXX
Allen C Altvater
49 Lake Henry Dr
Lake Placid FL 33852

Call Sign: K4LQ
Frederick M Perkins Jr
3437 Lake Josephine Dr
Lake Placid FL 33852

Call Sign: K4FCG
Florida Contest Group
3437 Lake Josephine Dr
Lake Placid FL 33852

Call Sign: KI4LCP
Raymond A Meyers
828 Lake June Rd
Lake Placid FL 33852

Call Sign: WD4REM
Herbert B Lee
105 Lake Ridge Dr
Lake Placid FL 33852

Call Sign: W8FJU
Dorothy M Urband
119 Lincoln Rd NE
Lake Placid FL 33852

Call Sign: W8OKW
Selwyn M Urband
119 Lincoln Rd NE
Lake Placid FL 33852

Call Sign: W4MXX
George F Mc Cartha
600 Lonesome Island Rd
Lake Placid FL 33852

Call Sign: KC4LPR
Gordon E Hadley
118 Murray Ct NW
Lake Placid FL 33852

Call Sign: KD4QDD
Michael W Maxwell
111 Pine Tree Dr
Lake Placid FL 33852

Call Sign: KE4FDL
Steve Mc Cartha
600 Lonesome Island Rd
Lake Placid FL 33852

Call Sign: KG4KZE
Richard J Ottaviano
1610 Noble Fir St
Lake Placid FL 33852

Call Sign: KE4HDP
Larry D Carmody
132 Pine Tree Dr
Lake Placid FL 33852

Call Sign: WA3DTL
John G Ayers
6 Maplewood Ct
Lake Placid FL 33852

Call Sign: KC4OC
Keith C Johnson
1565 Oak Ave
Lake Placid FL 33852

Call Sign: KF4WUB
Debbie Smedley
153 Pine Tree Dr
Lake Placid FL 33852

Call Sign: KF4YIB
Helen F Dayton
183 McCoy Dr
Lake Placid FL 33852

Call Sign: WA2ZHM
Alfred J Stipo
119 Oak Grove St
Lake Placid FL 338529338

Call Sign: KE4GZV
Mark A Smedley Sr
153 Pine Tree Dr
Lake Placid FL 33852

Call Sign: WA1MRT
R James Dayton
183 McCoy Dr
Lake Placid FL 33852

Call Sign: K2AJS
Alfred J Stipo
119 Oak Grove St
Lake Placid FL 338529338

Call Sign: KA8IPT
Raymond L Yoder Sr
25 Pinecrest St
Lake Placid FL 338528119

Call Sign: KG4AQD
Paul J Smith Sr
34 Meadow Lake Cir S
Lake Placid FL 33852

Call Sign: KG4INS
Andrew M Welden
1224 Orange Dr
Lake Placid FL 33852

Call Sign: NU4P
Robert N Rader
4042 Placid Lakes Blvd
Lake Placid FL 33852

Call Sign: KK4CYC
Jerald L Higginbotham
12 Mia Casa Ln
Lake Placid FL 33852

Call Sign: KG4INT
Karen H Welden
1224 Orange Dr
Lake Placid FL 33852

Call Sign: W4CXH
Richard M Mc Garry
324 Roosevelt Ave NE
Lake Placid FL 33852

Call Sign: AC4MO
Robert E Monroe
32 Miami Dr
Lake Placid FL 338525228

Call Sign: KF4EV
Luke W Seignious Jr
1228 Orange Dr
Lake Placid FL 33852

Call Sign: KC4VNE
Edward L Rose
342 Royal Palm Ave
Lake Placid FL 33852

Call Sign: WA4VZC
James A Engle
100 Murray Ct NW
Lake Placid FL 33852

Call Sign: N4RKB
Russell V Seignious
1228 Orange Dr
Lake Placid FL 33852

Call Sign: KG4MXG
Donald L Kesterson Jr
13600 S Jefferson Ave
Lake Placid FL 33852

Call Sign: KJ4AVU
Richard E Gurnitz
719 S Sun N Lakes Blvd
Lake Placid FL 33852

Call Sign: KD4UQO
George L Forsyth
1411 S Washington Blvd
NW
Lake Placid FL 33852

Call Sign: WB4PWC
Darrell D Mc Kinley
1422 S Washington Blvd
NW
Lake Placid FL 33852

Call Sign: WB4JPZ
Robert L Heaton
318 Sirena Dr
Lake Placid FL 33852

Call Sign: KD4TVZ
Daniel A Green
149 St Lucie St
Lake Placid FL 338527457

Call Sign: K4LZN
Robert O Love
650 Summit St
Lake Placid FL 33852

Call Sign: W1JBG
Robert E Barrett
1138 Sycamore St
Lake Placid FL 33852

Call Sign: WD4IPW
Dan H Bishop Sr
24 Tall Oaks Trl
Lake Placid FL 33852

Call Sign: KF4JDP
Scott A Terry
120 Tangerine Rd

Lake Placid FL 33852

Call Sign: W5YNF
Scott A Terry
120 Tangerine Rd
Lake Placid FL 33852

Call Sign: W8NBU
Anthony J Buchheit
255 Tangerine Rd NW
Lake Placid FL 338526551

Call Sign: KK4CYE
Addie L Owens
1801 Tayloe Ln
Lake Placid FL 33852

Call Sign: KC4ZHF
Robert M Bowden
3012 Timberline Ave
Lake Placid FL 33852

Call Sign: AC4LR
Darwin C Gittens Sr
211 Twilight Dr
Lake Placid FL 33852

Call Sign: KD4GMK
Norman W Shiver
1208 Van Buren St
Lake Placid FL 33852

Call Sign: KI4TIE
Rosemarie Shiver
1208 Van Buren St
Lake Placid FL 33852

Call Sign: KF4NNO
Walter Grabowski
106 Vanguard Ave NW
Lake Placid FL 33852

Call Sign: AB4RT
Richard H Hunter
25 Victoria Ln

Lake Placid FL 33852

Call Sign: K2HP
Herman W Pfeiffer
103 Villa Av
Lake Placid FL 33852

Call Sign: K2LEQ
Marian Pfeiffer
103 Villa Ave
Lake Placid FL 33852

Call Sign: WA4SNI
Richard J Ruttan
402 W Waterway Ave NW
Lake Placid FL 33852

Call Sign: W5OG
William E Fells
402 W Waterway Ave NW
Lake Placid FL 33852

Call Sign: KF4VSE
Grady E Billingsley
331 Washington Blvd
Lake Placid FL 33852

Call Sign: KC4ZUO
Edith C Yaciw
1756 Washington Blvd
NW
Lake Placid FL 33852

Call Sign: KK4HBB
James R Reinhardt
1764 Washington Blvd
NW
Lake Placid FL 33852

Call Sign: KG4HBG
Donna Weeks
76 Weeks Rd
Lake Placid FL 33852

Call Sign: KF4EYQ

Todd Weeks
76 Weeks Rd
Lake Placid FL 33852

Call Sign: N4WPU
Carl V Guest
8 Wesley Way
Lake Placid FL 33852

Call Sign: N4MFS
Fredrick L Semon Sr
1050 Western Blvd
Lake Placid FL 33852

Call Sign: N4NAT
Sharron E Semon
1050 Western Blvd
Lake Placid FL 33852

Call Sign: KC4LZJ
Edwin Rivera Jr
323 Willow Ave
Lake Placid FL 33852

Call Sign: KN4VR
Jan J Schauff
Lake Placid FL 33852

Call Sign: W4KMM
Olga S Bond
Lake Placid FL 33852

Call Sign: W4WDK
Gerald Eichhorn
Lake Placid FL 338620993

Call Sign: WB4EDV
Charles D Stidham
Lake Placid FL 33852

Call Sign: KD6OND
Elias E Gregory
Lake Placid FL 33852

Call Sign: KE4RY

Melvin Page
Lake Placid FL 33852

Call Sign: KE4ZCI
Edward A Corby
Lake Placid FL 33862

Call Sign: KA8CJI
Edward F Stanley
Lake Placid FL 33862

Call Sign: KP4ELI
Eliseo R Martinez
Lake Placid FL 33862

Call Sign: KF4RSQ
Jose L Santos
Lake Placid FL 33862

Call Sign: KE4ZCH
Louisa E J Corby Torlish
Lake Placid FL 33862

Call Sign: KF4JTL
Robert L Spiegel
Lake Placid FL 33862

Call Sign: W4ZD
Beverley B Cavender
Lake Placid FL 338620088

Call Sign: KD4DZT
Frank Aquilino
Lake Placid FL 338621260

Call Sign: KG4ZHI
Juan C Rivero
Lake Placid FL 338621802

Call Sign: K4RTC
Juan C Rivero
Lake Placid FL 338621802

Call Sign: AB4NY
Thomas F Mc Donald

Lake Placid FL 338622587

Call Sign: KD4VQN
Gail T Pelley
12215 Kingsway Cir
Lake Suzy FL 33821

Call Sign: KD4VQL
Paul W Pelley
12215 Kingsway Cir
Lake Suzy FL 33821

Call Sign: K2IOX
Charles J Asea
11648 SW Ctly Manor
Lake Suzy FL 342697030

Call Sign: KF9M
Dennis A Duffy
11437 SW Ctney Dr
Lake Suzy FL 34269

Call Sign: KD8LV
Harold H Bolt
11644 SW Egret Cir 1803
Lake Suzy FL 34269

Call Sign: K4EEP
George J Zins
12274 SW Egret Cir Apt
2901
Lake Suzy FL 34266

Call Sign: N4FQP
Gerald F Downs
11970 SW Kingsway Cir
Lake Suzy FL 34269

Call Sign: WD4NKZ
Kenneth L Gifford
12243 SW Kingsway Cir
Lake Suzy FL 34269

FCC Amateur Radio Licenses in Lakeport

Call Sign: KG4BFT
Jeanne Berry
765 E Sr 78 56
Lakeport FL 334718836

Call Sign: KF4YWF
George F Berry
765 E State Rd 78 56
Lakeport FL 334718836

Call Sign: KG4BHB
Judy C Currie
9925 Jerdik Dr
Lakeport FL 33471

Call Sign: KG4BHC
R Dan Currie
9925 Jerdik Dr NW
Lakeport FL 334718660

FCC Amateur Radio Licenses in Lee

Call Sign: WA8NAZ
Lowell P Rieger
Box 1154
Lee FL 32059

Call Sign: N4ZED
Pauline W Melay
Box 2355
Lee FL 32059

Call Sign: K4VNZ
Edgar O Yates
Box 2685
Lee FL 32059

Call Sign: K4WOI
Albert E Norris
Box 515

Lee FL 32059

Call Sign: KC2EPP
Rodger D Jones Jr
5957 E US Hwy 10
Lee FL 32059

Call Sign: KK4HYA
Sarah M Anderson
123 NE Calabazila Trl
Lee FL 32059

Call Sign: W4FAO
Jimmie D Anderson Sr
123 NE Calabazilla Tr
Lee FL 32059

Call Sign: W4MYF
Basil V Edmondson
543 NE Catnip Way
Lee FL 32059

Call Sign: AC4DF
Gerald F Moses
2293 NE CR 255
Lee FL 32059

Call Sign: W2GFM
Gerald F Moses
2293 NE CR 255
Lee FL 32059

Call Sign: KC4VPJ
Sevier P Odom Jr
2826 NE Old Blue Springs
Rd
Lee FL 32059

Call Sign: KA4BEF
William H Yeager
161 NE Peachtree Dr
Lee FL 32059

Call Sign: KJ4NHW
Bonnie K Keen

1490 SE Midway Church
Rd
Lee FL 32059

Call Sign: KI4IFD
Jacob W Keen
1490 SE Midway Church
Rd
Lee FL 320596244

Call Sign: KD4EKR
Timothy L De Motsis
8378 US Hwy 90 E
Lee FL 320596023

Call Sign: KG4VFL
Carolyn T Blair
Lee FL 32059

Call Sign: KC4IYC
Robert W Blair
Lee FL 32059

Call Sign: KG4VIN
Robert W Blair
Lee FL 32059

Call Sign: KG4YXJ
Troy E Wright
Lee FL 32059

FCC Amateur Radio Licenses in Lehigh Acres

Call Sign: KJ4WXH
Anthony D Angelo
3718 11th St W
Lehigh Acres FL 33971

Call Sign: N9KSE
Warren C K Yamanishi
3730 11th St W
Lehigh Acres FL
339715114

Call Sign: KF4SQJ
Floyd J Petitte
2002 14 St E
Lehigh Acres FL 33936

Call Sign: KC4QAY
Richard C Johnstone
3902 16th St W
Lehigh Acres FL 33971

Call Sign: KI4ODC
Thomas S Marsh
3104 21st St W
Lehigh Acres FL 33971

Call Sign: AI4VQ
Gary R Hall
4547 25th St SW
Lehigh Acres FL 33973

Call Sign: KB9VXL
Linda A Bell
5214 25th St SW
Lehigh Acres FL 33973

Call Sign: W9BEL
William V Bell
5214 25th St SW
Lehigh Acres FL 33973

Call Sign: KC4HAQ
David W Kaschak
4117 2nd St W
Lehigh Acres FL 33971

Call Sign: W4POC
William S Hoffer
1209 3rd St E
Lehigh Acres FL 33936

Call Sign: KA2SEY
Philip Casey Jr
3213 41st St W
Lehigh Acres FL 33971

Call Sign: KJ4PMX
Ramon A Alvarez
3407 52nd St W
Lehigh Acres FL 33971

Call Sign: AE4ES
Ramon A Alvarez
3407 52nd St W
Lehigh Acres FL 33971

Call Sign: KB4PXY
Guillermo Garcia Barbon
3102 54 St W
Lehigh Acres FL 33971

Call Sign: WI4E
Guillermo Garcia Barbon
3102 54 St W
Lehigh Acres FL 33971

Call Sign: WA4FBH
Barry O Mc Donnell
4313 5H St W
Lehigh Acres FL
334711210

Call Sign: K4FD
Barry O Mc Donnell
4313 5H St W
Lehigh Acres FL
334711210

Call Sign: KJ4JOP
James B Yelvington
4017 6th St W
Lehigh Acres FL 33971

Call Sign: KE4ABG
James B Yelvington
4017 6th St W
Lehigh Acres FL 33971

Call Sign: KG4WCP
Douglas E Harmon
4318 6th St W

Lehigh Acres FL 33971

Call Sign: KB2WUE
William M Zerillo
2906 7th St W
Lehigh Acres FL 33971

Call Sign: KC4WQD
Robert J Craddock
3204 9th St W
Lehigh Acres FL 33971

Call Sign: KE4FTW
Judith Tuller
15 Abbott Ave
Lehigh Acres FL 33936

Call Sign: KE4EWC
Christopher E Tuller Sr
15 Abbott Ave
Lehigh Acres FL
339362216

Call Sign: KG4ACO
Christopher E Tuller
15 Abbott Ave
Lehigh Acres FL
339392216

Call Sign: KG4FFK
Joseph J Elyard
917 Abbott Ave
Lehigh Acres FL 33972

Call Sign: KD4NYX
Michael J Walsh
114 Airview Ave
Lehigh Acres FL 33936

Call Sign: WB9TFK
Richard G Reece
1429 Archer St
Lehigh Acres FL 33972

Call Sign: WD4IFC

Stephen S Reaves
2405 Atlantic Cir
Lehigh Acres FL 33972

Call Sign: KC8FJU
Sean R Mellor
730 Barcia St E
Lehigh Acres FL 33974

Call Sign: KB2OHU
James A Breckenridge
1218 Barnsdale St
Lehigh Acres FL
339364839

Call Sign: WD4IFB
Alvin S Reaves
2405 Bay Plaza
Lehigh Acres FL 33936

Call Sign: KF4RHD
Paul F Fletcher
5016 Beecher St
Lehigh Acres FL 33971

Call Sign: N2QOP
Kenneth W Wright
2137 Berkley Way
Lehigh Acres FL 33973

Call Sign: WX4W
Curtis W Wright
1200 Broad St W Apt
602B
Lehigh Acres FL 33936

Call Sign: WA4OEA
Terence H Wolfley
1506 Broadway Ave
Lehigh Acres FL
339722223

Call Sign: N4ZAW
Sean M Ware
103 Bruce Ave N

Lehigh Acres FL 33971

Call Sign: N8KK
John J Radigan
2259 Carnaby Ct
Lehigh Acres FL 33971

Call Sign: KA9YDJ
Larry W Bergeson
2261 Carnaby Ct
Lehigh Acres FL 33973

Call Sign: NA4LB
Larry W Bergeson
2261 Carnaby Ct
Lehigh Acres FL 33973

Call Sign: KI4DQA
Carl Aust
505 Causeway Dr
Lehigh Acres FL 33936

Call Sign: N1GTO
Peter J Bronson
26 Charwood Cir
Lehigh Acres FL 33936

Call Sign: N1JXU
Rose M Bronson
26 Charwood Cir
Lehigh Acres FL 33936

Call Sign: N2MQI
Charles E Starr
1020 Columbus Ave
Lehigh Acres FL 33972

Call Sign: N2MXQ
Joan H Starr
1020 Columbus Ave
Lehigh Acres FL
339723538

Call Sign: KI4GLA
Diane M Dinan

140 Coolidge Ave
Lehigh Acres FL
339366266

Call Sign: KI4GKZ
Joseph H Dinan Jr
140 Coolidge Ave
Lehigh Acres FL
339366266

Call Sign: W4PKP
Edgar H Peters
204 Coolidge Ave
Lehigh Acres FL 33936

Call Sign: AI2B
Raymond Metzger
501 Coolidge Ave
Lehigh Acres FL 33936

Call Sign: KA2HES
James D Harrison
714 Cortez Ave
Lehigh Acres FL 33972

Call Sign: KI4KQJ
Susanne Stiles
1628 Covington Meadows
Cir
Lehigh Acres FL 33936

Call Sign: AI4HD
Frederick L Stiles
1628 Covington Meadows
Cir
Lehigh Acres FL
339367721

Call Sign: WF4LS
Frederick L Stiles
1628 Covington Meadows
Cir
Lehigh Acres FL
339367721

Call Sign: N2FSU
Michael J Gonzalez
653 Crabtree Ct
Lehigh Acres FL 33974

Call Sign: W4FVU
Carl Seese
201 Danby Rd
Lehigh Acres FL 33936

Call Sign: KB4DVC
John J Fitz Gerald Jr
128 Dania Cir
Lehigh Acres FL 33936

Call Sign: KD4CVA
Kurt Vega
1008 Dayton Ave
Lehigh Acres FL 33972

Call Sign: KE4UHL
Nancy C Vega
1008 Dayton Ave
Lehigh Acres FL 33972

Call Sign: WB4ILO
Donald S Ullock
339 Dellwood Ave
Lehigh Acres FL 33936

Call Sign: K4QV
Donald A Nolde Sr
2803 E 3rd St
Lehigh Acres FL 33936

Call Sign: K4DRB
Shirlene E Nolde
2803 E 3rd St
Lehigh Acres FL 33972

Call Sign: KA4NAI
Richard A Nascak
503 E 6th St
Lehigh Acres FL
339723962

Call Sign: KA2ZSS
Michel A Prosperi Sr
905 E Bougainvillea Rd
Lehigh Acres FL 33936

Call Sign: KD4WXI
Patrick R Deisch
803 E Jersey Rd
Lehigh Acres FL 33936

Call Sign: KB0MQ
Marion T Cagle
905 E Penn Rd
Lehigh Acres FL
339366440

Call Sign: KD6NEP
David W Reeve
320 Edward Ave
Lehigh Acres FL 33972

Call Sign: KG4DIY
Joseph J Raday
4692 Fairloop Run
Lehigh Acres FL 33971

Call Sign: KG4ZTY
Charles P Robbins
2409 Fisher Ct
Lehigh Acres FL 33936

Call Sign: KJ4WXI
Erik T Mitchell
310 Fitch Ave
Lehigh Acres FL
339362225

Call Sign: KF4YXL
James Johnstone
343 Fleetwood Ave
Lehigh Acres FL
339364827

Call Sign: KB4DEX

Richard E Davies Sr
1426 Ford Cir
Lehigh Acres FL 33936

Call Sign: KG4RAF
Bonnie F Dones
727 Gaylord Ave S
Lehigh Acres FL 33974

Call Sign: N4AOE
Bruce H Dones
727 Gaylord Ave S
Lehigh Acres FL 33974

Call Sign: KJ4DOX
Jennifer A Dickinson
704 Gilbert Ave N
Lehigh Acres FL 33971

Call Sign: KB4KQB
Phillip M Sandahl
744 Goodrich Ave S
Lehigh Acres FL 33974

Call Sign: N2ZKK
Charles A Kazakwic
213 Greenwood Ave
Lehigh Acres FL
339725152

Call Sign: KI4FHH
Charles A Kazakwic
213 Greenwood Ave
Lehigh Acres FL
339725152

Call Sign: N2FSU
Michael J Gonzalez
1121 Hamilton Ave
Lehigh Acres FL 33936

Call Sign: N4FSU
Michael J Gonzalez
1121 Hamilton Ave
Lehigh Acres FL 33972

Call Sign: N9FSU
Michael J Gonzalez
1121 Hamilton Ave
Lehigh Acres FL 33972

Call Sign: K9VKZ
Lehigh Acres ARC
1121 Hamilton Ave
Lehigh Acres FL 33972

Call Sign: W4LHI
Lehigh Acres ARC
1121 Hamilton Ave
Lehigh Acres FL 33972

Call Sign: K3LBM
Edward C Helmetag
56 Hamlin Ct
Lehigh Acres FL 33936

Call Sign: K1VQP
Michael W Doane
760 Hargrove Ave S
Lehigh Acres FL 33974

Call Sign: KA2DKJ
Everett N Rice
38 Heath Aster Ln
Lehigh Acres FL 33936

Call Sign: KA2DKK
Pauline B Rice
38 Heath Aster Ln
Lehigh Acres FL 33936

Call Sign: N7PYM
Jeffrey C King
1112 Henry Ave
Lehigh Acres FL 33972

Call Sign: KE4VVJ
Joe K Whitman
604 Hibiscus Ave
Lehigh Acres FL 33936

Call Sign: KF4OHR
Christopher R Tice
1611 Highland Ave
Lehigh Acres FL 33972

Call Sign: KJ4WJ
Carroll W Huff
119 Highview Ave
Lehigh Acres FL 33936

Call Sign: KK4AWG
Scott M Mcdill
206 Homer Ave N
Lehigh Acres FL 33971

Call Sign: KS4JZ
James T Beatty
1509 Honor Ct
Lehigh Acres FL 33971

Call Sign: KO4V
Dale F Voss
15 Iowa Rd
Lehigh Acres FL 33936

Call Sign: WB1EWI
Edward E Seal
10658 Jacatree Ct
Lehigh Acres FL 33936

Call Sign: WA4GUK
David Penezic
616 Jackson Ave
Lehigh Acres FL 33972

Call Sign: WG4K
David Penezic
616 Jackson Ave
Lehigh Acres FL 33972

Call Sign: KK4HGC
Jose M Nieves
441 Jaguar Blvd
Lehigh Acres FL 33974

Call Sign: WD4SDE
Jose M Nieves
441 Jaguar Blvd
Lehigh Acres FL 33974

Call Sign: WA4AIZ
John J Cable
218 Jefferson Ave
Lehigh Acres FL 33936

Call Sign: WD4GXF
Rhonda S Cable
218 Jefferson Ave
Lehigh Acres FL 33936

Call Sign: N4TUR
Roy S Yawn
1010 Jefferson Ave
Lehigh Acres FL 33936

Call Sign: KF4MCN
Terence W Weaver
719 Joel Blvd A
Lehigh Acres FL 33972

Call Sign: KE4GBH
David R Goodrich
1709 John S Ave
Lehigh Acres FL 33972

Call Sign: K0ART
Arthur T Nickel
1518 Junior Ct
Lehigh Acres FL
339712044

Call Sign: N6XMI
David S Dillman
178 Karlow Ave
Lehigh Acres FL
339361120

Call Sign: WA2CSL
Robert G Hewitt

410 Lake Ave
Lehigh Acres FL
339724040

Call Sign: KJ4REZ
Floyd J Petitte
520 Lake Ave
Lehigh Acres FL 33972

Call Sign: W4IPR
William F Norris
1416 Lake Ave SE
Lehigh Acres FL 33936

Call Sign: KG4GZL
John E Libby Sr
10450 Lake Port Ct
Lehigh Acres FL 33936

Call Sign: KF4MCQ
Richard A Barget
10 Lincoln Ave
Lehigh Acres FL 33936

Call Sign: WB8AZM
Quentin W Morgan
210 Lincoln Ave
Lehigh Acres FL
339365155

Call Sign: KG4EAH
Robert K Dutka
1516 Lindale Cir
Lehigh Acres FL 33936

Call Sign: N4OIA
Lewis F Fish
1544 Lindale Cir
Lehigh Acres FL 33936

Call Sign: N4WXU
Rachel M Ottinger
1544 Lindale Cir
Lehigh Acres FL 33936

Call Sign: WB2UTA
Joseph H Beale Jr
208 Lowry Ave
Lehigh Acres FL 33936

Call Sign: K2UGH
Michael C Gurka
610 Maple Ave N
Lehigh Acres FL
339724005

Call Sign: WB2FAU
Stella J Gurka
610 Maple Ave N
Lehigh Acres FL
339724005

Call Sign: KI4LJA
K2Ugh Kilowatt Club
610 Maple Ave N
Lehigh Acres FL
339724005

Call Sign: K2UGH
K2Ugh Kilowatt Club
610 Maple Ave N
Lehigh Acres FL
339724005

Call Sign: KG4SGI
Lehigh Psk-31 Club
610 Maple Ave N
Lehigh Acres FL
339724005

Call Sign: W2UXL
Lehigh Psk 31 Club
610 Maple Ave N
Lehigh Acres FL
339724005

Call Sign: W2YXE
L Paul De Long
1700 Margate Blvd
Lehigh Acres FL 33936

Call Sign: KJ4GRB
Nelson E Kinsey III
21 Maryland Rd
Lehigh Acres FL 33936

Call Sign: KC4PSI
Kenneth M Newton
115 N Maple Ave
Lehigh Acres FL 33936

Call Sign: K3KEN
Kenneth M Newton
115 N Maple Ave
Lehigh Acres FL 33936

Call Sign: KJ4UDA
Linda S Newton
115 N Maple Ave
Lehigh Acres FL 33936

Call Sign: KF4DNJ
James R Burkhart
101 N Oregon Rd
Lehigh Acres FL 33936

Call Sign: AC4XX
James A Rudolph Sr
818 N Richmond Ave
Lehigh Acres FL 33936

Call Sign: KB7VGO
Sherilan D Lane
508 Noridge Dr
Lehigh Acres FL
339367504

Call Sign: WA4UCZ
William R Sutton
204 Oakmont Pkwy
Lehigh Acres FL 33936

Call Sign: KC8FOD
Angela K Harps
315 Ohio Rd

Lehigh Acres FL 33936

Lehigh Acres FL 33936

Lehigh Acres FL 33936

Call Sign: K8NZ
Ronald Harps
315 Ohio Rd
Lehigh Acres FL 33936

Call Sign: KB3BAD
Jodi M Payne
2304 Queen Dr
Lehigh Acres FL 33971

Call Sign: KG4PCJ
Larry M Burgess
245 S Lake Dr
Lehigh Acres FL 33936

Call Sign: KE4TEK
Robert L Boyce
18454 Orangecrest Ct
Lehigh Acres FL 33936

Call Sign: N8AZV
Mike L Nussman
19 Richmond Ave N
Lehigh Acres FL 33936

Call Sign: KJ4KGO
Vincent M Sciacca
117 S Richmond Ave
Lehigh Acres FL 33936

Call Sign: KC4AEM
Riddell R Calderon
19393 Orchidtree Ct
Lehigh Acres FL 33936

Call Sign: WU4V
Mike L Nussman
19 Richmond Ave N
Lehigh Acres FL 33936

Call Sign: KF4RSN
Thomas P Miller
309 Schoolside Dr
Lehigh Acres FL 33936

Call Sign: N5XNS
James P Sharp
307 Oregon Rd W
Lehigh Acres FL 33936

Call Sign: KD4KIS
Amy S Acosta
275 Richmond Ave S
Lehigh Acres FL 33936

Call Sign: WA2RIR
Donald E Fletcher
216 Seaton Ave
Lehigh Acres FL
339365851

Call Sign: KI4ERB
Bernd Bracher
1108 Palmetto Ave
Lehigh Acres FL 33936

Call Sign: KD4NDW
Rogelio Acosta
275 Richmond Ave S
Lehigh Acres FL 33936

Call Sign: KE4SJG
Nils G Lindroth
843 Sentinela Blvd
Lehigh Acres FL 33936

Call Sign: KM3Z
Bernd Bracher
1108 Palmetto Ave
Lehigh Acres FL 33936

Call Sign: WA8PGN
William A Holland
1216 Robert Ave
Lehigh Acres FL 33936

Call Sign: KG4MMR
Shane J Welborn
5017 SW 24th St
Lehigh Acres FL 33971

Call Sign: KJ4KGP
Mario A Sciacca
16 Parkwood Villas Ct
Lehigh Acres FL 33936

Call Sign: KI4KQI
Douglas P Breland Jr
10589 Roxbury Ct
Lehigh Acres FL 33936

Call Sign: KD4NZC
Tina M Devore
3809 SW 4th St
Lehigh Acres FL 33971

Call Sign: WD9EMF
Victor B Maue Jr
929 Portland Ave S
Lehigh Acres FL 33974

Call Sign: KC4RVN
Daniel J Rash
409 Rushmore Ave S
Lehigh Acres FL 33936

Call Sign: KD4OGM
Michael T Miller
104 Texas Rd
Lehigh Acres FL 33936

Call Sign: KR4DB
Thomas B Mast
211 Purdue St

Call Sign: N4WF
Rebecca D Rash
409 Rushmore Ave S

Call Sign: KE4ZMI
Henry C Avery

1900 Titus Ct
Lehigh Acres FL 33972

Call Sign: K4SN
Terry G Pfeiffer
735 Troy Ave
Lehigh Acres FL 33936

Call Sign: N2PGQ
Richard D Cordasco
1236 Village Lakes Blvd
Apt 103
Lehigh Acres FL
339727567

Call Sign: AE4UH
Harold G Breckenridge
1234 Village Lakes Blvd
Apt 312
Lehigh Acres FL 33936

Call Sign: KC4VXU
Ray W P Williamson
1121 Vine Yard St
Lehigh Acres FL 33936

Call Sign: KF4GAW
Austin V Moss
704 W Cleveland Ln
Lehigh Acres FL 33936

Call Sign: KI4BOO
Dustin J Maggard
506 W Leeland Hghts Blvd
Lehigh Acres FL 33936

Call Sign: K8RF
Daniel J Flaig
1910 Wellington Ave
Lehigh Acres FL 33972

Call Sign: KE4UHK
Wilson F Munz
1200 Williams Ave
Lehigh Acres FL 33936

Call Sign: W1KWA
Walter J Kochanek
708 Willow Dr
Lehigh Acres FL 33936

Call Sign: W2RTD
Roger C Berry
18 Willow St
Lehigh Acres FL 33936

Call Sign: KE4IUY
Lawrence F Ritchie
1300 Woodward Ct 38
Lehigh Acres FL
339366516

Call Sign: KJ4GRA
Myrta P Feldman
Lehigh Acres FL 33970

Call Sign: KG4AVW
Kenneth M Croy II
Lehigh Acres FL
339700305

Call Sign: KB8ODF
Carol K Hadd
Lehigh Acres FL
339700306

Call Sign: KB8ODG
Dennis L Hadd
Lehigh Acres FL
339700306

Call Sign: WD4RCC
Andrew Frame
Lehigh Acres FL
339702051

**FCC Amateur Radio
Licenses in Lorida**

Call Sign: KD4YWU

Robert E Bonville Sr
2501 2nd Ave
Lorida FL 33857

Call Sign: W4NUT
George M Hunt Sr
Box 508 94 Ft Rd
Lorida FL 33857

Call Sign: KD4MEF
Ronald E Garceau
964 CR 721 Lot 107
Lorida FL 33857

Call Sign: W4BFN
Edgar L Kindell Sr
964 CR 721 Lot 90
Lorida FL 33857

Call Sign: N4ZGN
Richard C Nelson
3316 Elaine
Lorida FL 33857

Call Sign: KE4HYV
Gregory P Watts
2716 Hacienda Dr
Lorida FL 33857

Call Sign: KI4LNW
Rolland B Huddleston
3301 Pamala Dr
Lorida FL 33897

Call Sign: W4IBD
Theodore R Crawford Jr
1865 US Hwy 98
Lorida FL 33857

Call Sign: N4WRN
John F Smith
1857 Willow Ln
Lorida FL 33857

Call Sign: KI4LXU

Bruce Wade Helms
Roberts
Lorida FL 33857

Call Sign: KG4KMX
Hugh F Mac Gregor
1012 Anglers Cove 204
Marco Island FL 34145

Call Sign: WB9YRY
Jerry J Stought
740 Austin Ct
Marco Island FL 33937

Call Sign: KG4KMW
Peter J Fleming
1085 Bald Eagle Dr Apt
A503
Marco Island FL 34145

Call Sign: KJ4QBI
Joseph L Rola
879 Banyan Ct
Marco Island FL 34145

Call Sign: KQ4OD
Leonard P Bryan
190 Bermuda Rd
Marco Island FL 34145

Call Sign: KG4WCG
Christopher J Sparacino
514 Bradford Ct
Marco Island FL 34145

Call Sign: WK2F
Andrew Singer
836 Buttonwood Ct
Marco Island FL 34145

Call Sign: KF2YQ
Harold W Baum Dr

930 Cape Marco Dr 501
Marco Island FL
341456347

Call Sign: N1UL
Ulrich L Rohde Phd
990 Cape Marco Dr
Merida Penthouse 2
Marco Island FL 34145

Call Sign: KE9OE
Alexander J Schwarz
990 Cape Marco Dr Ph 2
Marco Island FL 34145

Call Sign: KI4VLP
Erhard A Salow
990 Cape Marco Dr Ph 2
Marco Island FL 34145

Call Sign: N4EAS
Erhard A Salow
990 Cape Marco Dr Ph 2
Marco Island FL 34145

Call Sign: N2OFY
Christina S Rohde
990 Cape Marco Dr Ph2
Marco Island FL 34145

Call Sign: K5MI
Marco Island Radio Club
990 Cape Maroo Dr Ph 2
Marco Island FL 34145

Call Sign: WD4AYX
Charles H Slagle
805 Caribbean Crt
Marco Island FL 33937

Call Sign: WD4AYW
Nancy K Slagle
805 Caribbean Ct
Marco Island FL
341453400

Call Sign: KC4VAS
Gordon L Smiley
1884 Cascade Ct
Marco Island FL 33937

Call Sign: KA2CDT
Ronald G De Angelis
217 Castaways St
Marco Island FL 34145

Call Sign: K8ZTE
Robert E Kimble
1580 Caxambas Ct
Marco Island FL 34145

Call Sign: KJ4IBN
James J Carroll Sr
908 Collier Ct 401
Marco Island FL 34145

Call Sign: KJ4NPW
Robert V Prestyly Sr
90 Copperfield Ct
Marco Island FL 34145

Call Sign: W8HZI
Harry A Lake
849 Dandelion Ct
Marco Island FL 33937

Call Sign: N1EQQ
Lewis R Bowe
909 Joy Cir
Marco Island FL 34145

Call Sign: KF4FLG
Helen C Gleason
355 Kendall Dr
Marco Island FL 33937

Call Sign: W1RED
Patrick D Gleason
355 Kendall Dr
Marco Island FL 33937

Call Sign: WA2YAB
Donna A Kahn
561 Kendall Dr
Marco Island FL 34145

Call Sign: K4MIF
Donna A Kahn
561 Kendall Dr
Marco Island FL 34145

Call Sign: KB2LD
Stephen A Kahn
561 Kendall Dr
Marco Island FL 34145

Call Sign: K5MIF
Stephen A Kahn
561 Kendall Dr
Marco Island FL 34145

Call Sign: N1NAX
Robert F Stoico Jr
1395 Leland Way
Marco Island FL 34145

Call Sign: N8JNU
John W Sponaugle
1119 Lighthouse Ct
Marco Island FL 34145

Call Sign: K1PQY
John D Abbiuso
1151 Ludlam Ct
Marco Island FL
341455805

Call Sign: K1SUE
Rose M Abbiuso
1151 Ludlam Ct
Marco Island FL
341455865

Call Sign: WA8FRX
Richard W Prior

1590 Ludlow Rd
Marco Island FL 33937

Call Sign: KI4SZH
Patrick J Walsh
874 Magnolia Ct
Marco Island FL 34145

Call Sign: K4CPT
Patrick J Walsh
874 Magnolia Ct
Marco Island FL 34145

Call Sign: W4PFS
George C Perkins
1230 Martinique Ct
Marco Island FL
341452322

Call Sign: N3OMN
William B Hammond
241 Meadowlark Ct
Marco Island FL 34145

Call Sign: KB9UIN
Victor A Martiny
775 Milan Ct
Marco Island FL
341453465

Call Sign: KI4NE
Lee E Oldershaw
1271 Mulberry Ct
Marco Island FL
341452323

Call Sign: N2DZJ
Robert B Witte
560 N Barfield Dr
Marco Island FL 34146

Call Sign: N2CGA
Robert B Witte
560 N Barfield Dr
Marco Island FL 34146

Call Sign: WI1P
Greg A Sheard
905 N Barfield Dr
Marco Island FL 34145

Call Sign: WA4PJZ
Morris D Rosenberg
936 N Barfield Dr
Marco Island FL 34145

Call Sign: KJ4QBF
Barbara A Prigge
1369 N Collier Blvd
Marco Island FL 34145

Call Sign: KJ4QBG
Louis W Prigge
1369 N Collier Blvd
Marco Island FL 34145

Call Sign: KG4KMY
William R Gaston Sr
58 N Collier Blvd 110
Marco Island FL 34145

Call Sign: KJ4AKH
Arjie L Doerhoefer
1083 N Collier Blvd 193
Marco Island FL 34145

Call Sign: W4AYL
Arjie L Doerhoefer
1083 N Collier Blvd 193
Marco Island FL 34145

Call Sign: KM4MI
K Michael Doerhoefer
1083 N Collier Blvd 193
Marco Island FL 34145

Call Sign: WB4AJZ
K Michael Doerhoefer
1083 N Collier Blvd 193

Marco Island FL
341452539

Call Sign: N8JOJ
Kurt W Mikat
1083 N Collier Blvd 304
Marco Island FL 34145

Call Sign: AG4HB
Kurt W Mikat
1083 N Collier Blvd 304
Marco Island FL 34145

Call Sign: KJ4AKM
David R Hershberger
1083 N Collier Blvd 315
Marco Island FL 34145

Call Sign: KJ4AKI
Kathleen C Hershberger
1083 N Collier Blvd 315
Marco Island FL 34145

Call Sign: KK4GLC
William R Doyle
61 Peach Ct
Marco Island FL 34145

Call Sign: KJ4IDF
David C Dumas
756 Pelican Ct
Marco Island FL 34145

Call Sign: KC6OQR
Diana S Glover
1792 Piedmont Ct
Marco Island FL
341453823

Call Sign: KK6PW
William L Glover
1792 Piedmont Ct
Marco Island FL
341453823

Call Sign: K5MIR
Curtis J Henry Jr
1795 Piedmont Ct
Marco Island FL 34145

Call Sign: N1LAN
Herman G Diebler
761 Plantation Ct
Marco Island FL 34145

Call Sign: N4GOV
Jack J Shulman
767 Plantation Ct
Marco Island FL 33937

Call Sign: W1IZT
Robert F Stoico Sr
907 Raymond Ct
Marco Island FL 34145

Call Sign: W4ARG
Robert D Pease
422 Richards Ct
Marco Island FL 34145

Call Sign: W4LFK
George P Baron Sr
4000 Royal Marco Way
Unit 828
Marco Island FL 34145

Call Sign: KJ4QBE
Shawn D Hurtley
121 S Bahama Ave
Marco Island FL 34145

Call Sign: KB0LSP
Loyd J Carrender
600 S Barfield Dr
Marco Island FL 34145

Call Sign: KJ4BMX
Sabrina B Carrender
600 S Barfield Dr
Marco Island FL 34145

Call Sign: K3AVR
Loyd J Carrender
600 S Barfield Dr
Marco Island FL
341455923

Call Sign: KK9TT
Joseph J Grant
1090 S Collier Blvd 314
Marco Island FL 34145

Call Sign: KK9TTL
Lisa M Grant
1090 S Collier Blvd 314
Marco Island FL 34145

Call Sign: K4IM
Stephen A Wheelock
900 S Collier Blvd Apt
405
Marco Island FL
341456316

Call Sign: N4XIC
J Thomas Menaker
220 S Collier Blvd Unit
805
Marco Island FL
341454852

Call Sign: WA9AAA
Douglas W Weber Sr
980 San Marco Rd
Marco Island FL 34145

Call Sign: WA8DIP
Glenn A Loy
1090 San Marco Rd
Marco Island FL 33937

Call Sign: KJ4QBK
Diane L Wruk
1970 San Marco Rd
Marco Island FL 34145

Call Sign: KG5QD
Dale B Huguley
100 Sandhill St
Marco Island FL 34145

Call Sign: KJ4AKO
Jim B Heidings
807 Sea Ct
Marco Island FL 34145

Call Sign: KY4JOE
Joseph E Wilkins
800 Seagrape Dr
Marco Island FL 34145

Call Sign: KG4ODZ
Martin H Reeb
205 Seminole Ct
Marco Island FL 34145

Call Sign: W4YUC
Jack D Patterson
251 Shadowridge Ct
Marco Island FL 33937

Call Sign: WB2FTZ
George J Gueterbock
159 Shorecrest Ct
Marco Island FL
341454140

Call Sign: KI4BGW
Curtis J Henry Jr
197 Stillwater Ct
Marco Island FL 34145

Call Sign: KG6NKT
Linda B Spell
916 Sundrop Ct
Marco Island FL 34145

Call Sign: KG6NKR
Raymond H Rosenberg
916 Sundrop Ct

Marco Island FL 34145

Call Sign: KG4CNB
David P Satterfield
928 Sundrop Ct
Marco Island FL 34145

Call Sign: KD4LUU
Leonard L Moore Sr
921 Sycamore Ct
Marco Island FL 33937

Call Sign: KJ4REK
Lee H Henderson
686 Thrush Ct
Marco Island FL 34145

Call Sign: KK4GLD
Debra A Johnson
1139 Vernon Pl
Marco Island FL 34145

Call Sign: KK4GQE
Morley A Johnson
1139 Vernon Pl
Marco Island FL 34145

Call Sign: KA4TRC
Thomas W Singleton
133 Vintage Bay Dr A 12
Marco Island FL 34145

Call Sign: KI4HFA
Monte Lazarus
222 Waterway Ct 202
Marco Island FL 34145

Call Sign: K0LAW
Monte Lazarus
222 Waterway Ct 202
Marco Island FL 34145

Call Sign: N3EVH
Martin T Roddy
1860 Watson Rd

Marco Island FL 34145

Call Sign: WA3DAV
William E Gerlach
816 Wintergreen Ct
Marco Island FL 34145

Call Sign: K4MGS
Jack L Barnes
829 Wintergreen Ct
Marco Island FL
341453463

Call Sign: KJ4CUE
Ernest Martinez
1873 Woodbine Ct
Marco Island FL 34145

Call Sign: N9ADT
Ralph E Krisher Jr
Marco Island FL
341461909

FCC Amateur Radio Licenses in Matlacha

Call Sign: KA0NHT
Robert C Barton
2569 Bridgeview St
Matlacha FL 33993

Call Sign: WA4REC
Ronald C Ott
2643 Clyde St
Matlacha FL 33993

Call Sign: KE4NPD
Ronald L Schlegel
2775 Geary Dr
Matlacha FL 33909

Call Sign: KF2XD
Pamela A Bristol
2680 Geary St
Matlacha FL 33993

Call Sign: KF2WY
Robert W Bristol
2680 Geary St
Matlacha FL 33993

Call Sign: K4GFF
Herbert C Wagner
2863 Janet St NW
Matlacha FL 33909

FCC Amateur Radio Licenses in Moore Haven

Call Sign: KM4HV
Bud J Compton
18 2nd St
Moore Haven FL 33471

Call Sign: KE4IIT
Virginia M West
12355 Anchor Ln
Moore Haven FL 33471

Call Sign: KS4BC
Norman E West
12355 Anchor Ln SW
Moore Haven FL 33471

Call Sign: N4AZZ
Helmut G W Heine
12635 Aqua Ln
Moore Haven FL 33471

Call Sign: KF4TIO
Ernest I Putman
456 Ave O
Moore Haven FL 33471

Call Sign: KF4FLI
Edwin R Purcell
Box 27
Moore Haven FL 33471

Call Sign: N4PZG

John B Sabine
Box 34 3rd St
Moore Haven FL 33471

Call Sign: KE4IFF
John D Stanton
Box 451
Moore Haven FL 33471

Call Sign: W4TAW
Thomas A Wunsch
7770 Coffey Rd NW
Moore Haven FL 33471

Call Sign: N4TAZ
James A Greene
1046 Dolphin Ln
Moore Haven FL 33471

Call Sign: KA4IVZ
Aubry J Mc Callum
12085 Dolphin Ln SW
Moore Haven FL
334718077

Call Sign: KA9KIE
Fleming M Sandersen
12160 Dolphin Ln SW
Moore Haven FL 33471

Call Sign: KB4VFE
Paul A Dicke
12175 Dolphin Ln SW
Moore Haven FL
334718079

Call Sign: KG4LAE
Marlin D Jenkins
12220 Dolphin Ln SW
Moore Haven FL 33471

Call Sign: KJ4SAK
Chad O Thomas
12447 E Sr 78
Moore Haven FL 33471

Call Sign: KB1JCZ
Raymond A Michaelis
1207 Friendship Dr
Moore Haven FL 33471

Call Sign: KJ4IXP
Elizabeth W Ottino
1183 Martin Blvd
Moore Haven FL 33471

Call Sign: WA4YNU
John P Ottino Jr
1183 Martin Blvd
Moore Haven FL 33471

Call Sign: KE4IQT
Charles A Gillette
1820 River Rd SW
Moore Haven FL
334719601

Call Sign: NW4R
James R Schneider
901 Riverside Dr
Moore Haven FL 33471

Call Sign: KE4JPW
George G Nicola
12145 Schooner Ln
Moore Haven FL 33471

Call Sign: KG4EAI
Christa E Nicola
12145 Schooner Ln SW
Moore Haven FL 33471

Call Sign: N0IQO
Louise A Harman
12200 Schooner Ln SW
Moore Haven FL 33471

Call Sign: N0ILI
Randall W Harman
12200 Schooner Ln SW

Moore Haven FL 33471

Call Sign: WZ4U
Anita Martinec
12240 Schooner Ln SW
Moore Haven FL
334719691

Call Sign: KJ4FJD
Austin E Moorhouse
916 Thatcher Blvd SW
Moore Haven FL 33471

Call Sign: KJ4FJC
Teresa M Moorhouse
916 Thatcher Blvd SW
Moore Haven FL 33471

Call Sign: KJ4IXS
David W Evans
1116 W Anchor Ln
Moore Haven FL 33471

Call Sign: KJ4SAN
Robert F Williams
1173 Wagontrail
Moore Haven FL 33471

Call Sign: KB4NJW
Morriss L Holliday
857 Yacht Club Way
Moore Haven FL
334710988

Call Sign: KE4LWG
Ernest W Hilliard Jr
Moore Haven FL 33471

Call Sign: N4OYQ
Howard Marvin
Moore Haven FL 33471

Call Sign: KD4UWR
James F Jackson
Moore Haven FL 33471

Call Sign: KJ4SAO
Joseph Hernandez
Moore Haven FL 33471

Call Sign: KF4NIK
Sam C Caliendo
Moore Haven FL 33471

Call Sign: KJ4CIQ
Tony D Bevis
Moore Haven FL 33471

Call Sign: KI4NUP
John V Caola
Moore Haven FL
334710341

Call Sign: KF4TSS
Rino L Malizia
Moore Haven FL 33471

FCC Amateur Radio Licenses in Murdock

Call Sign: KG4GFT
Dan A Kerrigan
Murdock FL 33938

FCC Amateur Radio Licenses in Naples

Call Sign: KA3YLN
John G Hutnick
15210 1
Naples FL 34110

Call Sign: W4YOE
Yoel Reinoso
430 18
Naples FL 34120

Call Sign: K2SZU
Anthony J Picorale
668 100th Ave

Naples FL 33940

Call Sign: K1DPG
Philip J Haigis
600 100th Ave N
Naples FL 33940

Call Sign: KD4VOT
Eric L Standridge
764 102nd
Naples FL 33963

Call Sign: N4ZZH
George M Suydam
632 104th Ave N
Naples FL 33963

Call Sign: KC4EKZ
Robert B Grill
727 104th Ave N
Naples FL 33963

Call Sign: W4MLZ
George W Stevens
763 104th Ave N
Naples FL 33963

Call Sign: AA4RX
Howard S Roux
789 105th Ave N
Naples FL 34108

Call Sign: N4VDI
Jeffrey J Skubick
791 106th Ave
Naples FL 33963

Call Sign: K8JS
John P Skubick
791 106th Ave N
Naples FL 341081849

Call Sign: KA6CHL
Brian K Lacy
696 10th Ave NE

Naples FL 34120   Naples FL 34120   Naples FL 34116

Call Sign: KD4KES   Call Sign: KE4VNU   Call Sign: KI4DBJ
Manuel J Frometa   Stanley J Viva   Jean Chonoles
4025 10th Ave NE   405 12th Ave NW   391 14th St SE
Naples FL 34120   Naples FL 33964   Naples FL 341173690

Call Sign: WA9FNY   Call Sign: N4YNP   Call Sign: KI4BOM
Jerry A Goldberg   Michael O Brigham Sr   Benjamin B Storey
6030 10th Ave NW   6185 12th Ave NW   505 15th Ave S
Naples FL 34119   Naples FL 33999   Naples FL 34102

Call Sign: KB4OJR   Call Sign: WA1VUQ   Call Sign: KC4VFK
Juan J Gonzalez   Donald N Iorio   Miatta S Massaquoi
3585 10th Ave SE   500 12th Ave S   3675 15th Ave SW
Naples FL 33117   Naples FL 34102   Naples FL 33964

Call Sign: KC4MZD   Call Sign: KG4QPD   Call Sign: KI4HEY
Diane C Day   Mark L Kennedy   Eric D Rice
569 110th Ave N   1241 12th St N   821 15th St SW
Naples FL 33963   Naples FL 34102   Naples FL 34117

Call Sign: N4VMU   Call Sign: K4SWF   Call Sign: KI4LUD
Eddie S Day   Mark L Kennedy   Robert A Quinn
569 110th Ave N   1241 12th St N   921 15th St SW
Naples FL 33963   Naples FL 34102   Naples FL 34117

Call Sign: KC4NQC   Call Sign: WA4MK   Call Sign: KI4NWU
James T Smith   Mark L Kennedy   Cindy L Quinn
592 110th Ave N   1241 12th St N   921 15th St SW
Naples FL 33963   Naples FL 34102   Naples FL 341174403

Call Sign: N4VUM   Call Sign: AF4LH   Call Sign: KD4GTG
John W Tiger Sr   Larry M Davis   Michael A Carufe
269 11th Ave S   1030 13St SW   5991 16th Ave NW
Naples FL 33940   Naples FL 34117   Naples FL 33999

Call Sign: KC4FYH   Call Sign: KF4MCO   Call Sign: KD4LXX
David G Bennett Sr   Barry Liebowitz   Nelida Carufe
1243 11th Ct N   2765 14th Ave NE   5991 16th Ave NW
Naples FL 341025223   Naples FL 34120   Naples FL 33999

Call Sign: KK4PG   Call Sign: KK6GM   Call Sign: W1YG
Peter P Gaddy   Michael J Silva   Parker Heinemann
370 12th Ave NW   5370 14th Ave SW   745 16th Ave S

Naples FL 33940

Naples FL 34120

Naples FL 34119

Call Sign: WA6YGX
Robert G Gross
190 16th Ave S
Naples FL 34102

Call Sign: KI5TV
Diane E Landreth
4220 18th St NE
Naples FL 374126408

Call Sign: WB7UON
E J Knoll
4160 1st Ave Ws
Naples FL 34119

Call Sign: NH6GR
Sharron M Miner
1921 16th Ave SW
Naples FL 34117

Call Sign: KD4NPO
John L Norman
3520 19th Ave SW
Naples FL 33964

Call Sign: KS4UC
Charles B Barnes
2880 20th Ave NE
Naples FL 34120

Call Sign: KI4KQK
Conrad S Braun
241 16th St SE
Naples FL 34117

Call Sign: KC4OKB
Charles N Eveleno
4417 19th Ave SW
Naples FL 33999

Call Sign: N4DJJ
David J Johnson
2785 20th Ave SE
Naples FL 34117

Call Sign: KJ4IBT
Jorge R Puente
930 16th St SE
Naples FL 34117

Call Sign: N7HBZ
William J Richard
4417 19th Ave SW
Naples FL 33999

Call Sign: KA3FYP
Norman A Skinner
4166 20th Ave SW
Naples FL 341166006

Call Sign: KB1OMN
David J Johnson
4265 18th Ave NE
Naples FL 34120

Call Sign: KD4QML
Matthew S Zaleznik
771 19th St SW
Naples FL 34117

Call Sign: KG4HVD
Norman A Skinner
4166 20th Ave SW
Naples FL 341166006

Call Sign: WA0AWA
John Pudans
589 18th Ave NW
Naples FL 34120

Call Sign: KD9N
James D Mayberry
2410 19th St SW
Naples FL 34117

Call Sign: AD4MS
Ernest H Schmidt
5721 20th Ave SW
Naples FL 33999

Call Sign: KA4YSL
Robert K Wardwell
4318 18th Pl SW
Naples FL 33999

Call Sign: WB4FUS
George W Henderson
150 1st Avc N
Naples FL 33940

Call Sign: KE6RTQ
Lawrence J Ohleyer
4935 20th St NE
Naples FL 34120

Call Sign: KJ4NKJ
David L Sheppard
591 18th St NE
Naples FL 34120

Call Sign: KB7GEQ
Linette R Knoll
4160 1st Ave SW
Naples FL 34119

Call Sign: KI4HQP
Elio E Hernandez
590 20th St SE
Naples FL 34117

Call Sign: W9STW
Odus A Landreth
4220 18th St NE

Call Sign: W8AKB
Morton H Hueston
4445 1st Ave SW

Call Sign: KC4SJN
Waldimiro Soler Jr
881 20th St SE

Naples FL 34117

Call Sign: KJ4QBC
Richard L Gossard Jr
3690 21st Ave SW
Naples FL 34117

Call Sign: WA8SOF
Christine A Bartlett
881 21st St SW
Naples FL 34117

Call Sign: KE4WAC
Thomas C Pistone
881 22nd Ave NW
Naples FL 33964

Call Sign: KC4CNT
Arthur A Krause
4401 22nd Pl SW
Naples FL 34116

Call Sign: KI4AIN
Carolyn S Conklin
4233 23rd Ave SW
Naples FL 34116

Call Sign: AI4CZ
Carolyn S Conklin
4233 23rd Ave SW
Naples FL 34116

Call Sign: KI4AIM
Richard N Conklin
4233 23rd Ave SW
Naples FL 341167007

Call Sign: KD4OZW
Raymond T Heffernan III
120 23rd St SW
Naples FL 34117

Call Sign: KC4DYT
Bill E Muston Sr
4700 25th Ave SW

Naples FL 34116

Call Sign: N3LBY
James A Mc Nichol
4420 27th Ave NE
Naples FL 341208945

Call Sign: KA4WES
Bonnie L Buchholz
3841 27th Ave SW
Naples FL 34117

Call Sign: WD4BCC
James L Buchholz
3841 27th Ave SW
Naples FL 34117

Call Sign: KE4UOE
Dale I Hunt
5096 27th Pl SW
Naples FL 33999

Call Sign: KD4OZV
Robert G Pence Jr
5496 27th Pl SW
Naples FL 33999

Call Sign: WB1FJA
James G Macquarrie III
190 27th St SW
Naples FL 34117

Call Sign: WB1FHJ
Susan S Macquarrie
190 27th St SW
Naples FL 34117

Call Sign: N4VMT
Philip W Potter
1555 27th St SW
Naples FL 34117

Call Sign: KC4RPP
Harry A Romano
5072 28th Pl SW

Naples FL 34116

Call Sign: KJ4MCD
Lionel S Pereira
3340 29th Ave SW
Naples FL 34117

Call Sign: KC4IWL
Karen S Foster
110 29th St SW
Naples FL 33964

Call Sign: WA4UKB
Kenneth A Ransom
371 29th St SW
Naples FL 34117

Call Sign: WA4UJK
Shirley N Ransom
371 29th St SW
Naples FL 34117

Call Sign: KD4SZP
Jeffrey S Pehlke
1540 29th St SW
Naples FL 33964

Call Sign: AD4YE
William H Hicks
280 2nd Ave S
Naples FL 33940

Call Sign: K2HNY
Jack B Harvey
2331 2nd Ave SE
Naples FL 341173713

Call Sign: KA2QWS
Lewis K Day
4270 2nd Ave SE
Naples FL 341179017

Call Sign: N3POQ
Joyce E Stuckey
145 2nd St

Naples FL 34113

Naples FL 34117

Naples FL 34120

Call Sign: KA4PNT
Ronald K Stuckey
145 2nd St
Naples FL 34113

Call Sign: N4DMD
Douglas M Dunfee
3561 3rd Ave SW
Naples FL 34117

Call Sign: K4LLW
Linda M Wallen
111 3rd St NW
Naples FL 34120

Call Sign: KB2SFA
Joseph A Rowtie
120 2nd St N E
Naples FL 34120

Call Sign: KI4GJT
Taylor K Dunfee
3561 3rd Ave SW
Naples FL 34117

Call Sign: KJ4MCE
William H Robinson
361 3rd St NW
Naples FL 34120

Call Sign: KB2TRD
Dana A Rowtie
120 2nd St NE
Naples FL 34120

Call Sign: K4TKD
Taylor K Dunfee
3561 3rd Ave SW
Naples FL 34117

Call Sign: KI4GIE
Yoel Reinoso
1736 41st Ter SW
Naples FL 34116

Call Sign: N3YDS
Jennifer A Stuckey
145 2nd St Trl Acres
Naples FL 34113

Call Sign: KI4RHD
Siva R Krishna
3631 3rd Ave SW
Naples FL 34117

Call Sign: WB2QLP
Jordan E Mash
2033 42nd St SW
Naples FL 34116

Call Sign: KG4VFT
Julie-Ann Morales
2891 30th Ave SE
Naples FL 34117

Call Sign: K1SUN
Siva R Krishna
3631 3rd Ave SW
Naples FL 34117

Call Sign: KJ4MCC
Michael K Casady
2174 42nd St SW
Naples FL 34116

Call Sign: K4CAB
Bobbie G Smith
5172 32nd Ave SW
Naples FL 34116

Call Sign: KG4LTG
Carter E Bryan
26 3rd St N
Naples FL 34102

Call Sign: AD4MF
Donald R Peterson
2996 44th Ter SW
Naples FL 341168270

Call Sign: KE4KLM
Donald J Fowler
5196 32nd Ave SW
Naples FL 33999

Call Sign: KI4HEU
Jesse W Wallen
111 3rd St NW
Naples FL 34120

Call Sign: N1QZQ
Thomas F Humes Jr
1757 45th Ter SW
Naples FL 34116

Call Sign: KJ4USX
Jason G Kurek
2765 35th Ave NE
Naples FL 34120

Call Sign: KC4SSD
Timothy J Wallen
111 3rd St NW
Naples FL 34120

Call Sign: KE4KJQ
Dale A Bergenback
2131 46th St SW
Naples FL 34116

Call Sign: KI4DYN
Douglas M Dunfee
3561 3rd Ave SW

Call Sign: KJ4QBJ
Linda M Wallen
111 3rd St NW

Call Sign: KC6VQE
Israel L Cano
2897 47th St SW

Naples FL 34116

Naples FL 34120

Naples FL 33964

Call Sign: KD0LHV
Jeffrey R Hartwell
2831 48th Ave NE
Naples FL 34120

Call Sign: N1TP
Thomas C Palmer
3065 50th Ln SW
Naples FL 34116

Call Sign: NP2LC
John E Wolff
300 5th Ave S 410
Naples FL 34102

Call Sign: KJ4ZRV
Jeffrey R Hartwell
2831 48th Ave NE
Naples FL 34120

Call Sign: KM4MB
John E Sulouff
2311 52nd Ave NE
Naples FL 341201457

Call Sign: KA2EYL
Beverly Buerger
4236 5th Ave SW
Naples FL 34119

Call Sign: KK4EHL
Jeffrey R Hartwell
2831 48th Ave NE
Naples FL 34120

Call Sign: WD8BEZ
Thomas H Delany
2969 54th Ln SW
Naples FL 34116

Call Sign: WB2WIH
Jeffrey I Buerger
4236 5th Ave SW
Naples FL 34119

Call Sign: KE4JZT
Alex D Randolph
1951 48th St SW
Naples FL 33999

Call Sign: KC4NOG
Christina L Blasser
2671 55th St SW
Naples FL 33999

Call Sign: NJ2F
Jeffrey I Buerger
4236 5th Ave SW
Naples FL 34119

Call Sign: KD4LVC
Paul C Schlaupitz
2000 48th St SW
Naples FL 33999

Call Sign: KC4NON
Rebecca S Blasser
2671 55th St SW
Naples FL 33999

Call Sign: KG4WSJ
Robert J Biggs
4410 5th Ave SW
Naples FL 34119

Call Sign: KI4QBM
Jhony Desinor
3985 4th Ave NE
Naples FL 34120

Call Sign: KE4JBT
Paula D Fleishman
3245 5th Ave NW
Naples FL 34120

Call Sign: WA1QDP
Mark V Fadden
660 5th St NW
Naples FL 34120

Call Sign: AE4QN
Chris C Gentile
491 4th St NE
Naples FL 341205070

Call Sign: KD4VRY
Steve H Fleishman
3245 5th Ave NW
Naples FL 34120

Call Sign: WA1IVN
Julia C Jordan
3483 60th Ave NE
Naples FL 341202689

Call Sign: KA2JAS
Carlos B Morales
2861 4th St NW
Naples FL 34120

Call Sign: KB9GAW
Diana C Nelson
3340 5th Ave NW
Naples FL 33964

Call Sign: K1PJ
Peter D Jordan
3483 60th Ave NE
Naples FL 341202689

Call Sign: KI4BAJ
Sylvia R Iturburu
2880 50th Ave NE

Call Sign: KB9ETQ
Dwayne E Nelson
3340 5th Ave NW

Call Sign: N6ZFY
Hugh S Freebairn
3430 66th Ave NE

Naples FL 34120

Call Sign: K4ZFA
Ronald G Bender
2660 66th St SW
Naples FL 34105

Call Sign: N9JHC
Jean Chonoles
3920 6th Ave NE
Naples FL 341209010

Call Sign: K4OML
Ronald E Irons
330 6th St S
Naples FL 341026349

Call Sign: KK7EQ
Jon C Fiori
610 7St SW
Naples FL 34117

Call Sign: AB4HE
Frank F White
1325 7th Ave S
Naples FL 34102

Call Sign: N4ZOP
Timothy J Denton
640 7th St NW
Naples FL 34120

Call Sign: K9RRV
Herbert J Teders
900 8th Ave S
Naples FL 33940

Call Sign: KE4CFO
Alvin C Oppenheim
1100 8th Ave S
Naples FL 33940

Call Sign: N1CGW
Joseph Agresti
4665 8th Ave SE

Naples FL 34117

Call Sign: K1EOJ
Joseph Agresti
4665 8th Ave SE
Naples FL 34117

Call Sign: WA1JOE
Joseph Agresti
4665 8th Ave SE
Naples FL 34117

Call Sign: KE4KTZ
Glenn S Niesen
2707 8th St NW
Naples FL 341080108

Call Sign: KD4HEN
Philip J Teders
806 8th St S
Naples FL 34102

Call Sign: KI4JFQ
David H Schaare
331 8th St SE
Naples FL 34117

Call Sign: W4SFR
David H Schaare
331 8th St SE
Naples FL 34117

Call Sign: KJ4USW
Adam F Garrity
765 8th St SE
Naples FL 34117

Call Sign: KF4MQP
Steven J Donovan
890 8th St SE
Naples FL 34117

Call Sign: W4GC
Eugene W Klein
717 91st Ave N

Naples FL 34108

Call Sign: WD9HGW
Douglas L Mc Gilvra
600 94th Ave N
Naples FL 33963

Call Sign: KG4ONV
Roger D Wahl
811 96th Ave N
Naples FL 34108

Call Sign: KD4LXZ
Peter F Pye
621 97th Ave N
Naples FL 34108

Call Sign: W9KEV
Kevin J Lombardo
733 97th Ave N
Naples FL 34108

Call Sign: KB8DTN
Kenneth E Williams
746 97th Ave N
Naples FL 34108

Call Sign: W9DRT
Wayne F Lovely
512 98th Ave N
Naples FL 33963

Call Sign: WA1ETK
Walter F Wolf
586 98th Ave N
Naples FL 33940

Call Sign: KE4UZM
Mark C Cleary
504 99th Ave N
Naples FL 33963

Call Sign: KE4VUJ
Mark P F Cleary
504 99th Ave N

Naples FL 33963

Call Sign: WD4AQY
Arthur R Lee
1250 9th Ave N
Naples FL 34102

Call Sign: WD4AQU
Lynn G Lee
1250 9th Ave N
Naples FL 34102

Call Sign: KE4AKF
Kevin P Smith
510 9th St NW
Naples FL 33964

Call Sign: KD4YQ
Lee M Brown
2860 Aintree Ln 101
Naples FL 34112

Call Sign: KB4RQD
William M Daniels
2839 Aintree Ln 104
Naples FL 341129302

Call Sign: N1OKP
Glenn Hamilton
8519 Alessandria Ct
Naples FL 34114

Call Sign: KI4HEV
Maurice M Steiner
2116 Amargo Way
Naples FL 341193369

Call Sign: N3FRI
William M Champion
1001 Arbor Lake Dr Unit
406
Naples FL 34110

Call Sign: KK4IBL
Roberto A Payero

2289 Arbour Walk Cir 324
Naples FL 34109

Call Sign: K8KFT
Wilfred H Jaeger Jr
139 Arctic Way
Naples FL 341044104

Call Sign: WB2WPA
Gary S Arnold
3200 Areca Ave
Naples FL 341125912

Call Sign: KA4YWC
Karen D Arnold
3200 Areca Ave
Naples FL 341125912

Call Sign: KJ4KGN
Jonathan R Rivers
3657 Artic Cir
Naples FL 34112

Call Sign: W6TLL
Gerald B Seiff
6073 Ashford Ln 801
Naples FL 341102423

Call Sign: W8PYQ
John O Galloup
4760 Aston Gardens Way
Unit 212
Naples FL 341093591

Call Sign: KC4WQQ
Gerald L Gross
118 Audubon Rd
Naples FL 33961

Call Sign: K8YGN
Jerry L Walrath
590 Augusta Blvd
Naples FL 34113

Call Sign: N3ARC

Edward A Sager
1083 Augusta Falls Way
Naples FL 341191361

Call Sign: KI4EXZ
Jose L Escobedo
950 Auto Ranch Rd 20
Naples FL 34114

Call Sign: WD4FLZ
Michael A Gideon Sr
4930 Aztec Cir
Naples FL 34112

Call Sign: W0ICI
Richard A Matheis
203 Bahia Pt
Naples FL 34103

Call Sign: AI4FM
Theodore C Brew
3150 Barratt Ave
Naples FL 34112

Call Sign: KJ4RHZ
Mark C Tullis
7050 Barrington Cir 202
Naples FL 34108

Call Sign: N6MT
Mark C Tullis
7050 Barrington Cir 202
Naples FL 34108

Call Sign: KI4TUO
Carol B Kepen
8171 Bay Colony Dr 1604
Naples FL 34108

Call Sign: N6XPK
Patrick M Kepen
8171 Bay Colony Dr 1604
Naples FL 34108

Call Sign: W2ETR

Garry G Pettegrove
8930 Bay Colony Dr Unit
1803
Naples FL 34108

Call Sign: KJ4IBR
Carola Koenig
2375 Bayou Ln 6
Naples FL 34112

Call Sign: W4NVS
Vernon E Avant
4260 Bayshore Dr 10
Naples FL 33962

Call Sign: N1NEQ
Susan Krauss
8049 Bayshore Dr Apt B
Naples FL 34112

Call Sign: N1MMQ
William A Krauss
8049 Bayshore Dr Unit B
Naples FL 34112

Call Sign: N3IGB
Sharon L Johnson
3050 Beck Blvd N10
Naples FL 34114

Call Sign: WX4U
Robert L Ferguson Sr
4420 Beechwood Lake Dr
Naples FL 33962

Call Sign: N4QNC
John E Ritchey
4521 Beechwood Lake Dr
N
Naples FL 33962

Call Sign: K2JWH
John W Hann
4126 Belair Ln Apt B10
Naples FL 34103

Call Sign: WD8CUD
Guy M Stevenson
356 Belina Dr Apt 2
Naples FL 34104

Call Sign: N7OFL
David B Obenauf
15 Bennington Dr 5
Naples FL 34104

Call Sign: KE6YXI
Dennis P Trovato
9779 Bent Grass Bend
Naples FL 34108

Call Sign: N1CFG
Claude E Vautin
712 Bentley Dr
Naples FL 341108604

Call Sign: N1CFF
Helen M Vautin
712 Bentley Dr
Naples FL 341108604

Call Sign: KC4FXE
Mark S Cohn
805 Bentwood Dr
Naples FL 33963

Call Sign: KC4FXF
Martin A Cohn
805 Bentwood Dr
Naples FL 33963

Call Sign: W8HHL
Joseph E Crehan
827 Bentwood Dr
Naples FL 33963

Call Sign: W3MHQ
Charles A Schuler
5985 Bermuda Ln
Naples FL 34119

Call Sign: KI4VLN
Alysha B M O Leary
8310 Big Acorn Cir Apt
1004
Naples FL 34179

Call Sign: KR4YX
Kevin J Rambosk
616 Binnacle Dr
Naples FL 34103

Call Sign: W4BJN
Darell E Mc Cloud
6427 Birchwood Ct
Naples FL 34109

Call Sign: KI4UQC
Andrew T Ehrich
1705 Birdie Dr
Naples FL 34120

Call Sign: KB3AGF
Harry D Hanbury
4416 Bittern Ct
Naples FL 34119

Call Sign: KG4ZSL
Robert W Hanbury
4416 Bittern Ct
Naples FL 34119

Call Sign: K5SKP
Robert W Hanbury
4416 Bittern Ct
Naples FL 34119

Call Sign: KG4GNT
Clifford E Argue
11 Bluebill Ave 1004
Naples FL 34108

Call Sign: KJ4JBP
Florida Farm
294 Brady Ln

Naples FL 34114

Call Sign: WD4EBC
Frank P Lualdi
8 Bramblewood Pt
Naples FL 34105

Call Sign: K9KNW
Joseph O Goggin
294 Brandy Ln
Naples FL 34114

Call Sign: KJ4JBQ
Florida Farm
294 Brandy Ln
Naples FL 34114

Call Sign: WA3QHD
Vernon R Smith II
789 Brentwood Pt
Naples FL 34110

Call Sign: WD4FLY
Donald G Mielke
777 Broad Ave S
Naples FL 34102

Call Sign: W2YLP
Jules Allen
2717 Buckthorn Way
Naples FL 34105

Call Sign: K8VJV
Robert T Conway
802 Bunker Hill Dr
Naples FL 33963

Call Sign: WA8QYJ
Robert H Brady Sr
6155 Bur Oaks Ln
Naples FL 34119

Call Sign: N4PAN
David H Sanford Jr
208 Burning Tree Dr

Naples FL 33942

Call Sign: KC4LED
Haines V Reichel
118 Cabbage Palm Ln
Naples FL 33961

Call Sign: WD8EEU
Robert J Durr
119 Calais Ct
Naples FL 34112

Call Sign: KJ4AKG
Torben C Christensen
9270 Campanile Cir 204
Naples FL 34114

Call Sign: W4TJH
Louis S Clark
9573 Campbell Cir
Naples FL 34109

Call Sign: KI4YQG
Marc S Galli Jr
125 Cape Sable Dr
Naples FL 34104

Call Sign: N4DNV
Helga I Scholze
312 Caravelle Ct
Naples FL 34108

Call Sign: KA8IVV
Billie L Silvio
7304 Carducci Ct
Naples FL 34114

Call Sign: KE8S
John F Silvio
7304 Carducci Ct
Naples FL 34114

Call Sign: N1UVY
Richard L Frank
137 Caribbean Rd

Naples FL 34108

Call Sign: N4XSE
Dennis M Spencer
461 Carica Rd
Naples FL 34108

Call Sign: KA4PBU
Barbara A Mischung
5477 Carlton St
Naples FL 33942

Call Sign: WB4ZEI
John J Mischung
5477 Carlton St
Naples FL 341138773

Call Sign: KI4JNO
Paul J Cardella
784 Carrick Bend Cir Unit
103
Naples FL 34110

Call Sign: KA1VY
Ernest D Guimares Jr
13055 Castle Harbor Dr
Apt K 6
Naples FL 341108199

Call Sign: WA1AGK
Alan N Selin
13093 Castle Harbour Dr
Unit L5
Naples FL 33942

Call Sign: KD4YDH
Barry J Steil
275 Cays Dr Unit
Naples FL 34114

Call Sign: WD8BJT
Lorenzo W Wartena
113 Cedar Ln
Naples FL 33961

Call Sign: WX1SVR
Christopher D Nowak
8165 Celeste Dr 2125
Naples FL 34113

Call Sign: KJ4BMY
Richard F Escoffery
5015 Cerromar Dr
Naples FL 34112

Call Sign: KE4KCT
Charles L Frost
523 Chalemagne
Naples FL 34112

Call Sign: KE4MXB
Bonnie J Frost
523 Chalemagne Blvd
Naples FL 34112

Call Sign: KF4DNL
Alan J Boll
129 Channel Dr
Naples FL 34108

Call Sign: N4ALN
Alan J Boll
129 Channel Dr
Naples FL 34108

Call Sign: KG4NBB
Gerry R Wheeler
230 Channing Ct
Naples FL 34110

Call Sign: K1NBC
Fred E Hartford
4530 Chantelle Dr 102K
Naples FL 34112

Call Sign: KJ4FSD
George H Danz
813 Charlemagne Blvd
Naples FL 34112

Call Sign: K8AJG
Jerry C Smith
4638 Chippendale Dr
Naples FL 341125351

Call Sign: W8HQ
Craig A Black
7713 Classics Dr
Naples FL 34113

Call Sign: WB2GGE
Minot R Yeaton
1222 Cobia Ct
Naples FL 33962

Call Sign: N4KXF
Robert L Ralph
1244 Cobia Ct
Naples FL 34102

Call Sign: AB4NE
Henry J Keinanen
208 Cocohatchee Blvd
Naples FL 341101149

Call Sign: KD4JYX
Norman E Cox Jr
911 Coconut Cir E
Naples FL 34104

Call Sign: KI4AIK
Phillip M Mcclellan Sr
4131 Coconut Cir N
Naples FL 34104

Call Sign: K8SRH
Laurence J Bollinger
14960 Collier Blvd 3078
Naples FL 34119

Call Sign: KJ4PFK
Angela E Nelson
6911 Compton Ln S
Naples FL 34104

Call Sign: KJ4PFL
Randall T Nelson
6911 Comton Ln S
Naples FL 34104

Call Sign: WA2WLV
Richard A Hockemeyer
6445 Conning Tower Cir
A3
Naples FL 341122974

Call Sign: W8YPW
Joseph L Goodof
1177 Cooper Dr
Naples FL 34103

Call Sign: KG4KDF
Howard S Roux
152 Coral Vine Dr
Naples FL 34110

Call Sign: KD4SZQ
Mario S Trupiano
7585 Cordoba Cir
Naples FL 33942

Call Sign: WA9SSH
Wayne L Jinske
446 Country Hollow Ct
G103
Naples FL 34104

Call Sign: KI4HEX
Thomas A Shuster
530 Countryside Dr
Naples FL 34104

Call Sign: KC0ZER
Robert D Neal
1765 Courtyard Way 201
Naples FL 34112

Call Sign: KF4CQK
Lyddall W Bowles
445 Cove Towers Dr 1501

Naples FL 34110

Call Sign: KB4OQR
Volney T De Remer
1815 Crayton Rd
Naples FL 33940

Call Sign: N1OIC
Edward F Valenti
2030 Crayton Rd
Naples FL 341025025

Call Sign: KB8TG
Jerry B Tasker
3157 Crayton Rd
Naples FL 33940

Call Sign: KB1IZV
Richard J Ellwanger
4228 Crayton Rd
Naples FL 34103

Call Sign: WA4RZN
James O Bailes
3 Creek Cir
Naples FL 34114

Call Sign: N2OIB
Joseph E Garcia
9629 Crescent Garden Dr
101
Naples FL 34109

Call Sign: KC4OZC
Olga Soler
207 Cricket Lk Dr
Naples FL 34112

Call Sign: KB4TYC
Quay F Austin
9111 Crystal Ct
Naples FL 341204373

Call Sign: KE4VAJ
Mara J Wolski

21 Cypress Point Dr
Naples FL 34105

Call Sign: KA4PYV
Alton B Caldwell
414 Cypress Way E
Naples FL 341101108

Call Sign: KJ4KGQ
Miguel Silva
140 Cypress Way E 2
Naples FL 34110

Call Sign: KD4LYA
Sandra M Santos
146 Cypress Way E 808
Naples FL 33942

Call Sign: KB9MVD
Robert H Chalhoub
180 Cypress Way E B 105
Naples FL 34110

Call Sign: KB2TJX
Toby L Buerger
151 Cypress Way E C105
Naples FL 34110

Call Sign: KF4SHK
Maria L Tabraue
1440 Daffodil Ct
Naples FL 34120

Call Sign: K3OXB
Walter H Denny
5733 Deauville Cir G 202
Naples FL 34112

Call Sign: WB4SRK
Lester A Butler
105 Debron Dr
Naples FL 33962

Call Sign: KA1LO
Arnold H Klau

4970 Deerfield Way 101
Naples FL 34110

Call Sign: KB8MSL
Bernard E Wickham
239 Deerwood Cir
Naples FL 34113

Call Sign: NA4US
Mark R Hoffman
6890 Del Mar Ter
Naples FL 34105

Call Sign: WD4AQV
John H Mason
14 Derhenson Dr
Naples FL 34114

Call Sign: KG4BVT
Don G Polly
980 Diana Ave
Naples FL 34103

Call Sign: KC4JCN
Emmy A Earl
1700 Dolphin Ct
Naples FL 33962

Call Sign: KC4JCO
Harold B Oldak
1700 Dolphin Ct
Naples FL 33962

Call Sign: KA3NAC
Marion J Bauer
3429 Donoso Crt
Naples FL 34109

Call Sign: KX3G
Albert W Bauer
3429 Donoso Ct
Naples FL 33999

Call Sign: KA1PRI
Kenneth R Neenan

139 Drift Wood
Naples FL 34112

Call Sign: KE4VKX
Ciro De Flora
2125 E Crown Point Blvd
Naples FL 34112

Call Sign: KD4LYB
Joseph A Trupiano
2067 E Imperial Dr
Naples FL 33942

Call Sign: WC4AAH
Collier County Emergency
Management
3301 E Tamiami Trl
Naples FL 34112

Call Sign: K9VGA
C Thomas Haste
14100 E Tamiami Trl 53
Naples FL 341148449

Call Sign: W1SWG
Edgar C Smith
14100 E Tamiami Trl Lot
289
Naples FL 33961

Call Sign: WB2UZQ
Sandra E Perrotta
169 Edgemere Way S
Naples FL 34105

Call Sign: W2SEN
Roy A Duffus Jr
197 Edgemere Way S
Naples FL 34105

Call Sign: W2JQ
Siegfried R Boernert
452 Egret Ave
Naples FL 33963

Call Sign: N4SKT
Berta H Boernert
452 Egret Ave
Naples FL 34108

Call Sign: KI4AIJ
Corey E Mugaas
7784 Emerald Cir 104
Naples FL 34109

Call Sign: KC4TRR
Bruce C Chynoweth
3410 Enterprise Ave
Naples FL 33942

Call Sign: KC7PBT
James H Pells
7794 Esmeralda Way 102
Naples FL 34109

Call Sign: WD4ITI
Pat C Cappiello
130 Estelle Dr
Naples FL 34112

Call Sign: KF4EEK
Georga E Williams
1943 Estey Ave
Naples FL 33942

Call Sign: WB1FXB
Ronald F Anderson
154 Eveningstar Cay
Naples FL 34114

Call Sign: KI4JNM
Stephen P Hayes
1060 Everglades Blvd N
Naples FL 34120

Call Sign: KD4NLJ
Diana L Trupiano
104 Flame Vine Dr
Naples FL 33942

Call Sign: KD4FRA
Vito Trupiano IV
104 Flame Vine Dr
Naples FL 33942

Call Sign: KJ4IBQ
Frank Halas
405 Flamingo Ave
Naples FL 34108

Call Sign: W4RBW
Frank Halas
405 Flamingo Ave
Naples FL 34108

Call Sign: NS0I
John A Simander
101 Forest Lakes Blvd 105
Naples FL 34105

Call Sign: KB1KB
Benjamin M Harris
1045 Forest Lakes Dr
Naples FL 34105

Call Sign: KD4JEZ
David C Weigel
656 Fountainhead Way
Naples FL 341032735

Call Sign: W1KEC
Lawrence F Macaluso
5274 Fox Hollow Dr
Naples FL 33942

Call Sign: KJ4ZIV
Naples Contest Crew
208 Foxtail Ct
Naples FL 34104

Call Sign: AA4PP
Naples Contest Crew
208 Foxtail Ct
Naples FL 34104

Call Sign: W9KB
Kenneth J Bills
208 Foxtail Ct
Naples FL 341044909

Call Sign: N4TGP
James Taylor
208 Foxwood Ln
Naples FL 341127211

Call Sign: KD4JMV
Harry H Sevush
2996 Francis Ave 2
Naples FL 341123829

Call Sign: WA1IGL
John S Mac Leod
3430 Frosty Way 3
Naples FL 33962

Call Sign: K5ZF
John C Giberson
192 Furse Lakes Cir H 12
Naples FL 34104

Call Sign: KC4NQB
Gail Duesselmann
379 Gabriel Cir 2301
Naples FL 34104

Call Sign: K5HLS
Millard Carnrick
1100 Galleon Dr
Naples FL 34102

Call Sign: KO4YS
Everett J Hall
1415 Galleon Dr
Naples FL 33940

Call Sign: KS4VO
Harold E Osborn
7541 Garibaldi Ct
Naples FL 34114

Call Sign: K0EPQ
Andrew E Caldwell
6604 George Washington
Way
Naples FL 33963

Call Sign: N4QNE
Charles E Cortright
426 Glades Blvd
Naples FL 34112

Call Sign: KJ4CCK
Jeremy M Costin
232 Glen Eagle Cir
Naples FL 34106

Call Sign: KI4UAU
Kory S Gruenbaum
240 Glen Eagle Cir
Naples FL 34104

Call Sign: KA1JVX
Gersha Z Bayer
5813 Glencove Dr Apt
1105
Naples FL 33963

Call Sign: KA1JVY
Victor Bayer
5813 Glencove Dr Apt
1105
Naples FL 33963

Call Sign: W9WZ
Melvin Bernstein
100 Glenview Pl Apt 605
Naples FL 34108

Call Sign: W2DV
Kenneth V Hardman
100 Glenview Pl Apt 612
Naples FL 33963

Call Sign: K4ADR
Alex D Randolph

3790 Golden Gate Blvd E
Naples FL 34120

Call Sign: KE4VSM
Billy D Anderson
1721 Golden Gate Blvd W
Naples FL 33964

Call Sign: KC4DHE
Lynn K Whitlock
2770 Golden Gate Blvd W
Naples FL 33964

Call Sign: K2VMD
Jean P Gunther Mohr
600 Gordonia Rd
Naples FL 341082615

Call Sign: W2YEW
William R Gripenburg
645 Gordonia Rd
Naples FL 341082633

Call Sign: N1DL
Karl H Geng
285 Grande Way 1803
Naples FL 341106492

Call Sign: KJ4QBA
Karin L Eppard
10350 Greenway Rd
Naples FL 34114

Call Sign: NU8W
Donald G Sang
6825 Grenadier Blvd Ph 3
Naples FL 341087215

Call Sign: KI4JNN
Allen L Baxa
1059 Grove Dr
Naples FL 34120

Call Sign: KK4DQJ
Francis H Raab

1413 Gulf Coast Dr
Naples FL 34110

Call Sign: KA1ESJ
Andrew A Wuhrer
893 Gulf Pavillion Dr
Naples FL 34108

Call Sign: KB4PP
John G Reed
1950 Gulf Shore Blvd
Ap108
Naples FL 341024608

Call Sign: KD4SSZ
Shahn M Nadeau
4041 Gulf Shore Blvd Apt
715
Naples FL 33940

Call Sign: KC4JAQ
Robert R De Long
3333 Gulf Shore Blvd N
Naples FL 33940

Call Sign: KG4FTN
Ralph Arwood
1717 Gulf Shore Blvd N
501
Naples FL 34102

Call Sign: W0VYY
Paul C Hedberg
4400 Gulf Shore Blvd N
605
Naples FL 34103

Call Sign: KP2CA
Jay Goldfarb
4041 Gulf Shore Blvd N
811
Naples FL 34103

Call Sign: W8UVN
Elizabeth O Owen

2777 Gulf Shore Blvd N
Apt 4W
Naples FL 33940

Call Sign: WD4RLW
Bruce S Shannon
1790 Gulf Shore Blvd S
Naples FL 33940

Call Sign: W2FOQ
John C Gorman
10691 Gulf Shore Dr
Naples FL 34108

Call Sign: W0SOJ
John E Hyde
9415 Gulf Shore Dr 302
Naples FL 33963

Call Sign: KA3JRL
Edward H Ten Eyck Jr
2600 Gulfshore Blvd N
Apt 34
Naples FL 34103

Call Sign: W0KGR
William C Ackard
3333 Gulfshore Blvd N
Apt 401
Naples FL 33940

Call Sign: KE4FBE
Steven J Purcell
4651 Gulfshore Blvd N
Apt Ph4
Naples FL 33940

Call Sign: KU4XD
Edward E Johanson
3400 Gulfshore Blvd N
Bldg O Apt 4
Naples FL 34103

Call Sign: N4MXO
Craig S Jones

4051 Gulfshore Blvd N Ph
205 Lamer
Naples FL 33940

Call Sign: WD4DCN
Willard A Gortner
4601 Gulfshore Blvd N
Ph1
Naples FL 33940

Call Sign: N6CVW
Susan E Boucek
10279 Gulfshore Dr
Naples FL 33963

Call Sign: KB3HTS
Yvette N Cendes
1300 Gulfstar Dr S
Naples FL 34112

Call Sign: KJ4NT
Edward H Evans
1747 Harbor Ln
Naples FL 34104

Call Sign: N4SWG
Connie J Mazzacane
1798 Harbor Ln
Naples FL 33942

Call Sign: KC1AR
Louis P Mazzacane
1798 Harbor Ln
Naples FL 33942

Call Sign: K4GAS
Gulfcoast Amateur Society
1798 Harbor Ln
Naples FL 34104

Call Sign: N9DZF
William H Lazear
222 Harbour Dr 218
Naples FL 341034071

Call Sign: W4AVZ
James D Russell
222 Harbour Dr Apt 409
Naples FL 33940

Call Sign: KD4KUM
Ernest G Sanders
5102 Harrogate Ct
Naples FL 33962

Call Sign: KK4GLA
Daniel L Christner
4970 Hawthorn Woods
Way
Naples FL 34116

Call Sign: KA4EGP
John E Kelley
2930 Hawthorne Ct
Naples FL 33942

Call Sign: K1KLH
John H Doherty
900 Henderson Creek
Village 112
Naples FL 33942

Call Sign: KB4ALZ
William W Coolman
43 Henderson Dr
Naples FL 33961

Call Sign: KA2BEQ
John R Nickel
397 Henley Dr
Naples FL 34104

Call Sign: N3MOR
George J Claupein Jr
2329 Hidden Lake Dr Apt
10
Naples FL 34112

Call Sign: N0DEM
Kurt J Glogau

8757 Hideaway Harbor Ct
Naples FL 34120

Call Sign: KC4ABC
John A Wrafter
21 High Point Cir Apt 302
Naples FL 34103

Call Sign: KB4ETT
Corey E Mugaas
1046 Highlands Dr
Naples FL 34103

Call Sign: KA4CCD
Philip P Simon
5 Highpoint Cir W Apt
302
Naples FL 33940

Call Sign: N7EG
Robert A Epstein
6078 Highwood Park Ct
Naples FL 34110

Call Sign: NE4IE
Robert A Epstein
6078 Highwood Park Ct
Naples FL 34110

Call Sign: WA9ZIF
Carl W Foust
260 Huntington Dr
Naples FL 34109

Call Sign: K2DQI
Mark E Uncapher
1823 Hurricane Harbor Ln
Naples FL 33940

Call Sign: KI4BAK
William T Silvester
8265 Ibis Club Dr 605
Naples FL 34104

Call Sign: N8AQV

James B Austin
6562 Ilex Cir
Naples FL 34109

Call Sign: K1OHL
Michael Kyritsis
6626 Ilex Cir
Naples FL 341096809

Call Sign: KG4GZK
James R Smith
6660 Ilex Cir 5 A
Naples FL 34109

Call Sign: KG4PWN
Marilyn J Smith
6660 Ilex Cir Apt 5A
Naples FL 34109

Call Sign: N4IMJ
Marilyn J Smith
6660 Ilex Cir Apt 5A
Naples FL 34109

Call Sign: KE6TCQ
Ronnie R Seese
2338 Immokalee Rd 344
Naples FL 34110

Call Sign: W9VXE
Donald M Ivener
2145 Imperial Cir
Naples FL 341101038

Call Sign: K4GVH
James B Boorstin
1901 Imperial Golf Course
Blvd
Naples FL 33942

Call Sign: WA3JGC
Robert G Roberson
1963 Imperial Golf Course
Blvd
Naples FL 34110

Call Sign: KM3Y
Dale M Shafer
2236 Imperial Golf Course
Blvd
Naples FL 341101098

Call Sign: WA2WJQ
Allan M Karp
5183 Inagua Way
Naples FL 34119

Call Sign: N1NQU
Laurence H Nossen
14506 Indigo Lakes Cir
Naples FL 34119

Call Sign: KJ4QAX
Rolf C Anthony
1862 Ivory Cane Point
Naples FL 34119

Call Sign: W8ICO
Edgar H Parsley
106 Jan Dr
Naples FL 34104

Call Sign: W0MIA
Richard E Pettijohn
1160 Jarden Dr
Naples FL 34104

Call Sign: KI4RSP
Stephan Verhaaren
1042 Jardin Dr
Naples FL 34104

Call Sign: N3ISH
George R Tomlinson
103 Jasmine Ln
Naples FL 341148721

Call Sign: KI4ROD
Ted Brousseau Jr
1450 Jewel Box Ave

Naples FL 34102

Call Sign: KG4MKW
Douglas T Dover
180 Johnycake Dr
Naples FL 34110

Call Sign: AG4OE
Norman I Freedman
8563 Julia Ln
Naples FL 34114

Call Sign: KJ4WXJ
Jesse L Baker
4161 Kathy Ave
Naples FL 34104

Call Sign: N8ZYR
Joe N Clark
3570 Kent Dr
Naples FL 34112

Call Sign: KB9KJC
Robert E Hignite
3672 Kent Dr
Naples FL 34112

Call Sign: KB9LEV
Angela D Hignite
3672 Kent Dr
Naples FL 34112

Call Sign: KJ4IBO
Robert J Gibbons
8294 Key Royal Cir 1636
Naples FL 34119

Call Sign: KI4UAT
Timothy D Gibbons
8294 Key Royal Cir 1636
Naples FL 34119

Call Sign: N4PIX
Timothy D Gibbons
8294 Key Royal Cir 1636

Naples FL 34119

Call Sign: KJ4IBP
Ursula W Gibbons
8294 Key Royal Cir 1636
Naples FL 34119

Call Sign: KA0NBU
John M Coates
2211 Kingfish Rd
Naples FL 341021542

Call Sign: KD4DZU
Charles H Barboni
2369 Kings Lake Blvd
Naples FL 341125307

Call Sign: WA8LPQ
Robert J Koffron Sr
2420 Kings Lake Blvd
Naples FL 34112

Call Sign: K4UES
Dayton E Vaughter
1810 Kings Lake Blvd 104
Naples FL 341125357

Call Sign: KM4IT
James T Cerar
5074 Kingston Way
Naples FL 34119

Call Sign: W4KAT
James T Cerar
5074 Kingston Way
Naples FL 34119

Call Sign: KC4HEU
Nancy D Cerar
5074 Kingston Way
Naples FL 34119

Call Sign: WA4CAT
Nancy D Cerar
5074 Kingston Way

Naples FL 34119

Call Sign: W4GIZ
Jackson E Gissendaner
176 Kirtland Dr
Naples FL 34110

Call Sign: KC4BJT
Mae M Davis
1720 Krape Rd
Naples FL 33964

Call Sign: KE4KUJ
George P Carse
202 La Peninsula Blvd
Naples FL 33962

Call Sign: WB4CEJ
Richard W Jaklitch
447 Lagoon Ave
Naples FL 33940

Call Sign: KE4UCX
James R Comings
144 Lake Point Ln
Naples FL 341127073

Call Sign: W1KWV
Thomas Cianciolo Sr
14980 Lakehouse Ln H1
Naples FL 33963

Call Sign: KC4OGT
Marlena J Brackebusch
2759 Lakeview Dr
Naples FL 33962

Call Sign: N0CRW
Elisabeth G Bailey
3340 Lakeview Dr
Naples FL 34112

Call Sign: W9AKI
Clifford M Rigsbee
4430 Lakewood Blvd

Naples FL 33962

Call Sign: WD4RLM
Louis A Evans
4577 Lakewood Blvd
Naples FL 33942

Call Sign: N9HTW
Terrance P Dolan
720 Lambton Ln
Naples FL 34104

Call Sign: KJ4KGZ
Alexander M Ihrig
8371 Laurel Lakes Blvd
Naples FL 34119

Call Sign: KJ4KGY
Donald M Ihrig
8371 Laurel Lakes Blvd
Naples FL 34119

Call Sign: WB8TNH
Errol J Queen
4863 Least Tern Ct
Naples FL 33999

Call Sign: KJ4MBO
Calvin D Williams
130 Leawood Cir
Naples FL 34104

Call Sign: NY4FL
Richard A Hockemeyer
517 Leawood Cir
Naples FL 341044165

Call Sign: WB2WPA
Collier Emergency Radio
Association
8075 Lely Cultural Pkwy
Ste 445
Naples FL 34113

Call Sign: KJ4AKK

Gerald B Branham
8906 Lely Island Cir
Naples FL 34113

Call Sign: K2IDY
Louis H Gubitosi
8932 Lely Island Cir
Naples FL 34113

Call Sign: AA4GT
George R Tomlinson
1000 Lely Palms Apt E324
Naples FL 34113

Call Sign: NV4Z
Mary L Tomlinson
1000 Lely Palms Apt E324
Naples FL 34113

Call Sign: KG4L
John G Beckley
1000 Lely Palms Dr
Naples FL 33962

Call Sign: W1CHR
Henry B Sprague
1000 Lely Palms Dr Apt E
321
Naples FL 34113

Call Sign: KI4AII
Carl J Pacini
1840 Les Chateaux Blvd
Apt 4 101
Naples FL 34109

Call Sign: WA1UEZ
Richard L Edson
4253 Lighthouse Ln
Naples FL 34112

Call Sign: N4SRQ
Leo V Nothstine
9512 Litchfield Ln
Naples FL 33942

Call Sign: W4IJR
James R Smith
9572 Litchfield Ln
Naples FL 34109

Call Sign: KC4GSM
Cheryll Ann Partridge
2376 Long Boat Dr
Naples FL 33942

Call Sign: KM4RI
Clive A Partridge
2376 Longboat Dr
Naples FL 33942

Call Sign: KI4NFQ
Rodger E Hough
2472 Longboat Dr
Naples FL 34104

Call Sign: K1HH
Rodger E Hough
2472 Longboat Dr
Naples FL 34104

Call Sign: W1GCL
William R Holland
11136 Longshore Way W
Naples FL 33999

Call Sign: KF4WYA
Peter G Casale
8143 Lowbank Dr
Naples FL 341090777

Call Sign: KN4YW
Richard F Oneill
1500 Mainsail Dr Apt 2
Naples FL 341148812

Call Sign: K6HFE
William V Reece
1510 Mainsail Dr Apt 4
Naples FL 341148829

Call Sign: AI4UG
William V Reece
1510 Mainsail Dr Apt 4
Naples FL 341148829

Call Sign: N4KNP
Louis G Ouillette
3520 Malaga Way
Naples FL 33942

Call Sign: KI4QBS
Matthew D Creeger
2175 Malibu Lake Cir
1312
Naples FL 341198705

Call Sign: KA2GUY
Edward A Torre
14290 Manchester Dr
Naples FL 34114

Call Sign: K9OLE
Paul D Johnson
207 Marie Ln
Naples FL 34104

Call Sign: WD8RFL
Michael A Welsh
2211 Marina Dr
Naples FL 34102

Call Sign: WD8RFM
Holly J Welsh
2211 Marina Dr
Naples FL 341027629

Call Sign: W0SE
Perry T Taylor
176 Marseille Dr
Naples FL 34112

Call Sign: KK4QT
Donald B Miner
2352 Mayfield Ct

Naples FL 341052534

Call Sign: KC4ZQH
Marisa Q Maguran
7660 Meadow Lakes Dr
Unit 1
Naples FL 34104

Call Sign: KG4PMY
Yijjaj M Rios
40 Mentor Dr
Naples FL 34110

Call Sign: W4OWF
John H Stockton
233 Mermaids Bight
Naples FL 33940

Call Sign: KJ4MBQ
Jeremy J Belmonte
7103 Mill Pond Cir
Naples FL 34109

Call Sign: KJ4MBP
Richard A Belmonte
7103 Mill Pond Cir
Naples FL 34109

Call Sign: KD4ZIY
Phyllis N Grootemaat
272 Monterey Dr
Naples FL 34119

Call Sign: N4YFQ
Thomas B Grootemaat
272 Monterey Dr
Naples FL 34119

Call Sign: WB9YNL
Martha A Rysner
6615 Monterey Point
Naples FL 34105

Call Sign: KC9OS
Robert F Rysner

6615 Monterey Point
Naples FL 34105

Call Sign: KO4MD
Robert A Smith
1819 Monticello Dr
Naples FL 341108448

Call Sign: KJ4QBH
Russell D Rainey II
3725 Montreux Ln 104
Naples FL 34144

Call Sign: W0MR
Richard J St Amant
11 Moonstone Cir
Naples FL 34112

Call Sign: WA8BBS
Arthur L Ward
33 Moorhead Manor
Naples FL 33962

Call Sign: N8LWR
Helmut Poehlmann
750 Mooring Line 111
Naples FL 34102

Call Sign: KI4PZP
Wilford R Hecox
114 Moorings Park Dr 402
Naples FL 34105

Call Sign: WB5KQN
James C Alexander Jr
150 Moorings Park Dr 502
Naples FL 34105

Call Sign: K4EME
John H Deal
122 Moorings Park Dr 709
Naples FL 33942

Call Sign: N4VWA
John S Stewart

122 Moorings Park Dr Apt
101G
Naples FL 33942

Call Sign: K4ZH
Nathan L Goetz
160 Moorings Park Dr Apt
302
Naples FL 34105

Call Sign: KE4HTG
Bentley C Wilkinson
122 Moorings Park Dr Apt
512
Naples FL 33942

Call Sign: K4FZ
Robert F Weinig
122 Moorings Park Dr Apt
611
Naples FL 33942

Call Sign: W8DR
Albert P Parker
122 Moorings Park Dr Apt
G208
Naples FL 341052169

Call Sign: WB8DAL
Rita C English
122 Moorings Park Dr
G105
Naples FL 34105

Call Sign: NH7AR
Donald A Schneider II
2027 Morning Sun Ln
Naples FL 341193326

Call Sign: KJ4FRM
Lynn P Skabo
4312 Mourning Dove Dr
Naples FL 34119

Call Sign: W1LYN

Lynn P Skabo
4312 Mourning Dove Dr
Naples FL 34119

Call Sign: AI2K
Walter Farrell
182 Muirfield Cir
Naples FL 33962

Call Sign: N8RUN
Charlynn D Krout
8574 Mustang
Naples FL 34113

Call Sign: KD4HKU
Adolf J Chan
3325 N Airport Rd L7
Naples FL 33942

Call Sign: N1NPR
Michael D Provost
2614 N Tamiami Trl 501
Naples FL 34103

Call Sign: W3UWV
Bruce E Packham
7826 Naples Heritage Dr
Naples FL 341122740

Call Sign: N3QLM
Sallie M Packham
7826 Naples Heritage Dr
Naples FL 341122740

Call Sign: KD4MGY
Edward W Hopkins
37 Navajo Trl
Naples FL 33962

Call Sign: W9FBV
Charles J Renard
511 Nettlewood Ln
Naples FL 33962

Call Sign: KA3VUL

Scott A Sweet
6624 New Haven Cir
Naples FL 34109

Call Sign: W1GOG
George G Slade
830 New Waterford Dr
101
Naples FL 339428319

Call Sign: KJ4KHA
John A Hawkins
6620 Newhaven Cir
Naples FL 34109

Call Sign: WB9AJI
Jack E Treadman
3100 North Rd
Naples FL 34104

Call Sign: KC4DUZ
Paul G Kierstein
3789 North Rd
Naples FL 341044034

Call Sign: K4UGE
John N Mc Clung
3800 North Rd
Naples FL 34104

Call Sign: KI5OU
Robert D Bartunek
4386 Novato Ct
Naples FL 34109

Call Sign: KK4GBV
Himala O Udalamatha
Gamage
1022 Oak Forest Dr
Naples FL 34104

Call Sign: KC4JTM
Jo Ann La Fortune
43 Oceans Blvd
Naples FL 34102

Call Sign: KM4RA
Peter B Lafortune
43 Oceans Blvd
Naples FL 34104

Call Sign: W1TN
John E Mc Keen
211 Oceans Blvd
Naples FL 341044135

Call Sign: KG4FNY
Paul Martin
37 Ocho Rios St
Naples FL 34114

Call Sign: KJ4YEL
Calvin W Myer
6815 Old Banyan Way
Naples FL 34109

Call Sign: AK4QP
Calvin W Myer
6815 Old Banyan Way
Naples FL 34109

Call Sign: N4HTA
Robert A Smith
2575 Old Groves Rd 203
Naples FL 34109

Call Sign: KJ4QBD
Charles E Harper
7780 Orvieto Ct
Naples FL 34114

Call Sign: W4CEH
Charles E Harper
7780 Orvieto Ct
Naples FL 34114

Call Sign: KJ4AKN
Jesse S Booth
7846 Orvieto Ct
Naples FL 34114

Call Sign: W3JSB
Jesse S Booth
7846 Orvieto Ct
Naples FL 34114

Call Sign: KI4PHF
John C Daenzer
330 Ospreys Lndg Apt
2004
Naples FL 341046648

Call Sign: N8WGR
Roger G Hartel
4675 Ossabaw Way
Naples FL 34119

Call Sign: KC4KXJ
Anthony J Bunkers
2586 Outrigger Ln
Naples FL 33942

Call Sign: KK4AGT
Reagan M Henry
1228 Oxford Ln
Naples FL 34105

Call Sign: W4TVQ
Arthur M Hale
92 Pacific Way
Naples FL 34104

Call Sign: W2LCC
Shephard S Litt
248 Palm Dr 5
Naples FL 33962

Call Sign: KF4IXD
Peter T Noble
135 Palmetto Dunes Cir
Naples FL 33962

Call Sign: KA2GKC
Perry L Switzen
1929 Par Dr

Naples FL 34120

Call Sign: KA2OCO
Rosalie S Switzen
1929 Par Dr
Naples FL 34120

Call Sign: KF4ME
William V P Sitterley
742 Park Shore Ct
Naples FL 33940

Call Sign: N3FLC
Patrick C Fahey
788 Park Shore Dr Apt
E31
Naples FL 33940

Call Sign: KE8JB
Robert J Storch
16071 Parque Ln
Naples FL 34110

Call Sign: W8IGX
Norman Charns
4625 Pasadena Ct
Naples FL 341093330

Call Sign: N2YHS
Gerald J Dynda
164 Pebble Beach Blvd
Naples FL 33962

Call Sign: KE9KV
Charles W Pearson
6361 Pelican Bay Blvd
1503
Naples FL 34108

Call Sign: AA3A
Derek R Scorer
24 Peridot Ave
Naples FL 341148260

Call Sign: KC4IWJ

Fred T Phelps Jr
318 Pier C
Naples FL 33962

Call Sign: N2EMN
Nevin E Schlichting
203 Pier E
Naples FL 341128125

Call Sign: KJ4BBG
Eric P Davis
681 Pine Cone Ln
Naples FL 34104

Call Sign: WB8IOU
Marilyn T Galloup
545 Pine Grove Ln
Naples FL 34103

Call Sign: W1RDF
Hugh W Hamill
281 Pine Key Ln
Naples FL 33961

Call Sign: KF4SQK
Jacqueline E Daniel
1228 Pine Ridge Rd
Naples FL 34108

Call Sign: KF4MJJ
Frederick C Edwards
6017 Pine Ridge Rd Ste
264
Naples FL 34119

Call Sign: KF4WMC
Luis E Urbina
2697 Pine St
Naples FL 34112

Call Sign: KJ4HZQ
Adrian P Fahringer
674 Pine Vale Dr
Naples FL 34104

Call Sign: KN4WV
Charles E Greene
2433 Poinciana Dr
Naples FL 34105

Call Sign: KC8RRO
Mark J Harms
3152 Poinciana Dr
Naples FL 34105

Call Sign: W1FGX
Albert E Cookson
4301 Pond Apple Dr S
Naples FL 34119

Call Sign: KJ4KGL
Robert W Hooper
13681 Pondview Cir
Naples FL 34119

Call Sign: W1RWH
Robert W Hooper
13681 Pondview Cir
Naples FL 34119

Call Sign: KG4WOE
Brendan M Carroll
750 Portside Dr
Naples FL 34103

Call Sign: WA4AK
Alexander L Kaplan
4487 Prescott Ln
Naples FL 34119

Call Sign: N4RJN
Kenneth S Perry
2248 Prince Ln
Naples FL 34112

Call Sign: N2OBU
Albert T De Quinzio Jr
7360 Province Way 4202
Naples FL 34104

Call Sign: W4PJN
Bernard A Biedenharn
400 Putter Point Dr
Naples FL 34103

Call Sign: WA2BMQ
Norman T Connelly
441 Quail Forest Blvd
A401
Naples FL 341055504

Call Sign: WW2NC
Norman T Connelly
441 Quail Forest Blvd
A401
Naples FL 341055504

Call Sign: KA1TMU
Chanel G Dufour
43 Queen Palm Dr
Naples FL 34114

Call Sign: N8ANW
Nadine M Thomas
1188 Rainbow Dr
Naples FL 33942

Call Sign: N8ANV
Robert E Thomas
1188 Rainbow Dr
Naples FL 34104

Call Sign: AK4MN
James R Farlow
2020 Randall Blvd
Naples FL 34120

Call Sign: K9JPB
Daniel Kamm
8870 Ravello Ct
Naples FL 34114

Call Sign: N4CSH
Steven W Perkins
804 Reef Point Cir

Naples FL 34108

Call Sign: KI4HQQ
John D Cane
6105 Reserve Cir 2104
Naples FL 34119

Call Sign: KJ4QBL
Eileen F Zeidler
1272 Rialto Way 102
Naples FL 34114

Call Sign: N7ZYI
Paul Lejeune
4696 Rio Poco Ct
Naples FL 34109

Call Sign: WB8UUT
Kraig P Krick Sr
2274 River Reach Dr
Naples FL 341046923

Call Sign: KE4QNH
John L Haywood
2025 River Reach Dr 349
Naples FL 34104

Call Sign: W9PVT
John A Van Loon
807 Riverpoint Dr Apt
401D
Naples FL 33942

Call Sign: W1VEM
George W Gallipeau
473 Riviera Blvd W
Naples FL 341129107

Call Sign: WA2ZSH
Lorraine Ostrin
420 Robin Hood Cir 102
Naples FL 34104

Call Sign: WB2TGY
Robert C Ostrin

420 Robin Hood Cir 102
Naples FL 34104

Call Sign: KJ4OIZ
Stewart R Connell
337 Robin Hood Cir 103
Naples FL 34104

Call Sign: KG4TLO
Thomas E Siverson II
510 Robinhood Cir 201
Naples FL 34104

Call Sign: WA4YGP
Parvin H Winchell
1960 Rock Rd
Naples FL 33964

Call Sign: KB4YWR
Donald B Kersey
1326 Rordon Ave
Naples FL 33940

Call Sign: KB8HC
Charles W Browning
144 Rose Ln
Naples FL 34114

Call Sign: N4YZH
Roy K Lundeen
107 Round Key Cir
Naples FL 34112

Call Sign: KI4FMI
William B Jones
2540 Royal Palm Ct
Naples FL 34103

Call Sign: WA2GID
Garfield H A Ricketts Sr
4010 Royal Wood Blvd
Naples FL 33962

Call Sign: KD4RSZ
Robert E Lundquist

4206 Royal Wood Blvd
Naples FL 33962

Call Sign: KD1JD
Richard M Silven
7025 Rue De Marquis
Naples FL 34108

Call Sign: K4MZL
Robert P Lashenka
4912 Rustic Oaks Cir
Naples FL 34105

Call Sign: KJ4IBM
Ulrich Altvater
4916 Rustic Oaks Cir
Naples FL 34105

Call Sign: AG0X
Ulrich Altvater
4916 Rustic Oaks Cir
Naples FL 34105

Call Sign: K9OK
Thomas D Hartman
610 S Golf Dr
Naples FL 34102

Call Sign: WB4SYT
Ernest F Ruth
2155 S Winds Dr
Naples FL 33940

Call Sign: KC8TSE
Charlotte J Harrison
14 San Lu Rue Ave
Naples FL 34104

Call Sign: N8RCQ
Dean R Harrison
14 San Lu Rue Ave
Naples FL 34104

Call Sign: KI4UAS
Jerry L Clark

1243 San Marcos Blvd
Naples FL 34104

Call Sign: WB2RHB
Eric S Frankel
1720 Sanctuary Pointe Ct
Naples FL 34110

Call Sign: N8UCX
Walter K Mc Pherson
1765 Sanctuary Pointe Ct
Naples FL 341104158

Call Sign: W0BKB
George E Phelps Jr
158 Sand Dr
Naples FL 33942

Call Sign: K9KKY
Robert J Cook
3012 Sandpiper Bay Cir
D301
Naples FL 34112

Call Sign: KC4YUL
Mary L Murphy
3061 Sandpiper Bay Cir
J306
Naples FL 33962

Call Sign: KC4YUM
William F Murphy
3061 Sandpiper Bay Cir
J306
Naples FL 33962

Call Sign: N9CLK
Richard A Spindler
2040 Sandpiper St
Naples FL 34102

Call Sign: K1IVX
Victor J Farmer
2727 Sandpiper St
Naples FL 34102

Call Sign: KJ4LPD
Atillio Roberto Piol
3407 Sandpiper Way
Naples FL 34109

Call Sign: AE4AG
Michael E Read
2081 Santa Barbara Blvd
Naples FL 34116

Call Sign: N1XBR
Renato Donadio
124 Santa Clara Dr 2
Naples FL 34104

Call Sign: N1JZJ
Richard L Giampietro
3198 Santorini Ct
Naples FL 34119

Call Sign: K8BBS
Daniel W Dietrich
6863 Satinleaf Rd S 101
Naples FL 341096131

Call Sign: KK4EUH
Robert D Roddy Jr
4059 Sea Oats Ln
Naples FL 34112

Call Sign: KC4UPN
Albert F Read
6478 Seawolf Ct B3
Naples FL 33962

Call Sign: N6MBR
Ronald D Seese
1810 Senegal Date Dr
Naples FL 34119

Call Sign: KC6URZ
Christine L Seese
1810 Senegal Date Dr
Naples FL 34119

Call Sign: W4NEW
Robert D Graf
2085 Sevilla Way
Naples FL 341097113

Call Sign: W2HI
Robert D Graf
2085 Sevilla Way
Naples FL 341097113

Call Sign: N4DHN
Wayne A Le Cureux
2165 Shad Ct
Naples FL 339625525

Call Sign: KF4CQA
Gerard A Preiser
2132 Shadowlawn Dr
Naples FL 33962

Call Sign: WF4C
Larkin C Rogers Jr
5730 Shady Oaks Ln
Naples FL 341191252

Call Sign: W2FH
Larkin C Rogers Jr
5730 Shady Oaks Ln
Naples FL 341191252

Call Sign: WF4C
Larkin C Rogers Jr
5730 Shady Oaks Ln
Naples FL 341191252

Call Sign: KE4VUL
Doris A Nurenberg
4896 Shearwater Ln
Naples FL 33999

Call Sign: KC5GOX
Bradley W Keehn
265 Shellstone Ct
Naples FL 34119

Call Sign: KC4ZPJ
John E Witkowski
33 Shores Ave
Naples FL 34110

Call Sign: KJ4QAY
John D Culter
1231 Silver Lakes Blvd
Naples FL 341149232

Call Sign: N1BCC
Thomas B Garrison
1120 Silver Sands Ave
Naples FL 34109

Call Sign: KF4RQX
Neil T Quick
101 Smugglers Cove
Naples FL 34112

Call Sign: KJ4IBU
John M Weston
2145 Snook Dr
Naples FL 34102

Call Sign: KA4YSM
Michael A Day
4462 Snowy Egret Dr
Naples FL 341198808

Call Sign: KD7PRR
Aaron K Moulton
8043 Sorrento Ln
Naples FL 34114

Call Sign: W9OAO
Bernard H Baldridge
329 Southwind Village
Naples FL 33942

Call Sign: N4REA
Thornton F Turner
2501 Spicebush Ln
Naples FL 34105

Call Sign: W8HKX
Richard L Terrell
1330 Spyglass Ln
Naples FL 33940

Call Sign: N2FNM
Clayton W Ezell
411 St Andrews Blvd
Naples FL 33962

Call Sign: WD4SJS
Karl A Herrmann
414 St Andrews Blvd
Naples FL 34113

Call Sign: W4KAH
Karl A Herrmann
414 St Andrews Blvd
Naples FL 34113

Call Sign: K4FA
Murat M Baker
870 St Andrews Blvd
Naples FL 34113

Call Sign: KJ4REY
Nicholas Finn
4720 St Croix Ln 132
Naples FL 34109

Call Sign: WA5ULS
Marion R Fleming
201 St James Way
Naples FL 33942

Call Sign: KB1OMR
Ruth Wahl
5 St Raphael Dr
Naples FL 34112

Call Sign: KB4JBB
Lawrence A Nelson
5239 Starfish Ave
Naples FL 33940

Call Sign: KI4JUG
Theodore R Bissell
286 Stella Maris Dr
Naples FL 34114

Call Sign: WA4UAK
Gary D Young
7829 Stratford Dr
Naples FL 34104

Call Sign: WD4AGD
Sandra F Young
7829 Stratford Dr
Naples FL 34104

Call Sign: WB2JSB
Robert A Sprague
251 Sugar Loaf Ln
Naples FL 341148433

Call Sign: KB8EMG
Robert D Clay
180 Sugarloaf Ln
Naples FL 34114

Call Sign: KA4PBT
Charlie D Williams
2895 Sunset Blvd
Naples FL 34112

Call Sign: K1UQE
Edward S Esborn
837 Tall Oaks Rd
Naples FL 34113

Call Sign: WA1RON
John A Hooper
100 Tall Pine Ln 2101
Naples FL 341052600

Call Sign: WA4SND
Herbert S Gates Jr
2540 Talon Ct 501
Naples FL 34105

Call Sign: KD4NYW
Robert A Schmitz
14100 Tamiami Tr E Lot
119
Naples FL 33961

Call Sign: N3CNH
Arnold B Irvine Sr
14100 Tamiami Tr E Lot
51
Naples FL 33961

Call Sign: KG4OMD
Collier Emergency Radio
Association
3301 Tamiami Trl E
Turner Bldg F
Naples FL 34112

Call Sign: W8NOE
James M Jolly
107 Tanglewood Ct
Naples FL 34113

Call Sign: KA5YRV
Dan A Spencer
2168 Tarpen Rd
Naples FL 34102

Call Sign: KJ4QAZ
Jordan Da Silva
1697 Tarpon Bay Dr S
Naples FL 34119

Call Sign: KJ7LL
William T Schick
2175 Tarpon Rd
Naples FL 341021563

Call Sign: WB2TMM
Nic P Neumann
503 Terracina Way
Naples FL 341191817

Call Sign: N4NGW
Dennis Carroll
240 Timber Lake Cir 204
Naples FL 33942

Call Sign: K4FX
Kenneth S Vogt
7088 Timberland Cir
Naples FL 341097836

Call Sign: K1DGY
Lawrence R O Hearn
991 Tivoli Ln
Naples FL 341040831

Call Sign: K4LRO
Lawrence R O Hearn
991 Tivoli Ln
Naples FL 341040831

Call Sign: KI4AIH
Kristi J Perrow
418 Tradewinds Ave
Naples FL 34108

Call Sign: KA2RUM
Fara B Singer
1626 Triangle Palm Ter
Naples FL 34119

Call Sign: KJ4AKL
Adam C Brown
147 Trinidad St
Naples FL 34113

Call Sign: W4LZV
Robert A Kobzina Sr
197 Tupelo Rd
Naples FL 34108

Call Sign: WU1G
Joseph D Zaks
4749 Turnstone Ct
Naples FL 34119

Call Sign: W1JDZ
Joseph D Zaks
4749 Turnstone Ct
Naples FL 34119

Call Sign: KE4FUZ
Ernest Spinelli
106 Tuscana Ct 703
Naples FL 33999

Call Sign: WA4TUH
Robert I Pickering
976 Valley Forge Ln
Naples FL 33963

Call Sign: KE4MGM
Edward O Henderson Jr
395 Valley Stream Cir
Naples FL 34113

Call Sign: KD4GOQ
Jeffrey L Dalzell
9740 Vanderbilt Dr
Naples FL 33963

Call Sign: KG4OWL
Myron L Pederson
853 Vanderbilt Dr 203
Naples FL 34108

Call Sign: N4EZA
John R Baer
1284 Venetian Way
Naples FL 34110

Call Sign: WF4E
John R Baer
1284 Venetian Way
Naples FL 34110

Call Sign: KF4RA
Hiram D Driggs
8034 Vera Cruz Way
Naples FL 34109

Call Sign: K4LE
Sam C Hunt
492 Veranda Way E103
Naples FL 341046008

Call Sign: WB1ASX
Peter A Noll
109 Versailles Cir
Naples FL 33962

Call Sign: KF4YOY
Cynthia A Tolbert
9580 Victoria Ln 303
Naples FL 34109

Call Sign: K2LAF
Elmer W Schwittek
2231 Viewpoint Dr
Naples FL 34110

Call Sign: N2DVO
Daniel F O Donovan
7084 Villa Lantana Way
Naples FL 34108

Call Sign: W4VQE
Myron T Kelley
1814 Village Ln
Naples FL 341107917

Call Sign: WD8KYK
Joseph M Klausner
662 Vintage Reserve Cir
8B
Naples FL 34119

Call Sign: KF4BBV
Charles W Grant
188 Vista Ln
Naples FL 34119

Call Sign: KF4BVV
Georgia C Grant
188 Vista Ln
Naples FL 34119

Call Sign: KF4YEN
Mc Gregor Amateur Radio
Society
188 Vista Ln
Naples FL 34119

Call Sign: KE4TEL
Gary R Whitmer
124 W Hilo Dr
Naples FL 34113

Call Sign: W9LRY
Richard L Whitmer
124 W Hilo Dr
Naples FL 34113

Call Sign: KA3JXI
Thomas J Barr
793 Walkerbilt Rd Unit F8
Naples FL 34110

Call Sign: WB2DWN
Michael F Dennis
11819 Warbler Crt
Naples FL 33999

Call Sign: KD4DZR
Gilbert Bartlett
550 Wedge Dr
Naples FL 34103

Call Sign: KI4A
James W Elkins
666 Wedge Dr
Naples FL 33940

Call Sign: N1ACO
Frank P Callahan
4741 West Blvd
Naples FL 33940

Call Sign: KA3RDG
Robert R Stone
6079 Westbourgh Dr

Naples FL 34112

Call Sign: KG4ZCE
Milton Martins
5721 Westport Ln
Naples FL 34116

Call Sign: KB2RST
Bojan M Stricevic
3709 Whidbey Way
Naples FL 34119

Call Sign: KE4JEQ
Dean R Eisenberg
3714 Whidbey Way
Naples FL 34119

Call Sign: KF4MWO
Julie Martinez
2761 White Blvd
Naples FL 34117

Call Sign: KA9ASW
Jeffrey R Brody
2360 White Blvd
Naples FL 34117

Call Sign: N4WCW
Lee P Tippett
13001 White Violet Dr
Naples FL 33999

Call Sign: K4PNJ
James W Ackerson Sr
5425 Whitten Dr
Naples FL 34104

Call Sign: K4HIS
James W Ackerson Sr
5425 Whitten Dr
Naples FL 34104

Call Sign: WA0HPW
Nazarene Amateur Radio
Fellowship

5425 Whitten Dr
Naples FL 34104

Call Sign: K4GP
Robert L Caron
790 Wiggins Bay Dr
Naples FL 341106023

Call Sign: KW4G
Roy G Jackson
1000 Wiggins Pass Rd
Naples FL 341106300

Call Sign: N9RG
Roy G Jackson
1000 Wiggins Pass Rd 241
Naples FL 341106300

Call Sign: KI4DQB
Francis S Mckeen
1000 Wiggins Pass Rd L
10
Naples FL 34110

Call Sign: WA1NBY
Francis S Mckeen
1000 Wiggins Pass Rd L
10
Naples FL 34110

Call Sign: KB4IGP
Alfonso J Tavarez
2770 Wild Pines Ln Apt
1020
Naples FL 34112

Call Sign: N7OMC
Dewey D Cook
128 Wilderness Cay
Naples FL 34114

Call Sign: NU3O
Charles E Brookes
108 Wilderness Dr
Naples FL 34105

Call Sign: KK4GLB
Nathan A Christner
1351 Wildwood Lakes
Blvd 2
Naples FL 34104

Call Sign: KI4AIG
Jerome N Sapp Jr
46 Willoughby Dr
Naples FL 34110

Call Sign: AF3K
John S Howell Jr
723 Willowwood Ln
Naples FL 34108

Call Sign: KJ4JTL
Gerardo A Reyes
2581 Wilson Blvd N
Naples FL 34120

Call Sign: KC2AF
Hugh T Riley
15335 Wimborne Ln
Naples FL 34110

Call Sign: KD4DSN
Caroline J Champion
9675 Winchester Wood
Naples FL 33942

Call Sign: NM5TL
Thomas A Laeser
3090 Windsong Ct 102
Naples FL 34109

Call Sign: KI4IKW
David L Debres
7755 Woodbrook Cir 3803
Naples FL 34104

Call Sign: W9LXC
Robert H Ebenreiter
200 Wyndemere Way

Naples FL 34105

Call Sign: KG2CE
Kevin M Carroll
450 Yucca Rd
Naples FL 34102

Call Sign: KD4LUT
Terry J O Pray
Naples FL 33939

Call Sign: N4JVI
James E Boula
Naples FL 33939

Call Sign: N0ETP
Deborah L Pastian
Naples FL 33941

Call Sign: KB0AF
Ruben A Pastian Jr
Naples FL 33941

Call Sign: W1AYR
Alfred B Nelson
Naples FL 34101

Call Sign: K4FOM
Armon E Morgan
Naples FL 34101

Call Sign: KL1SS
Gregg R Hayford
Naples FL 34101

Call Sign: KF4AIW
Joseph W Andreasen
Naples FL 34101

Call Sign: KB0WDP
Jo Ann C Montbriand
Naples FL 34101

Call Sign: W0OB
Robert M Montbriand

Naples FL 34101

Call Sign: N4GUN
William K Kelly
Naples FL 34102

Call Sign: W4RAZ
Donn E Brown
Naples FL 34106

Call Sign: KI4YRD
Dorothy L Thompson
Naples FL 34106

Call Sign: KB1BCY
Michele B Durkin
Naples FL 34106

Call Sign: AI4ZF
Donald J Ruhl
Naples FL 34107

Call Sign: N6FI
Donald J Ruhl
Naples FL 34107

Call Sign: N0ACA
Donald J Ruhl
Naples FL 34107

Call Sign: KB2AJV
Kevin A Schmidt
Naples FL 34107

Call Sign: KI4NNZ
Kevin A Schmidt
Naples FL 34107

Call Sign: W6SWW
Kevin A Schmidt
Naples FL 34107

Call Sign: KF4IXA
Jackson E Gissendaner
Naples FL 34108

Call Sign: WB2QLP
ARA Of Southwest F
Naples FL 34108

Call Sign: KJ4FAN
Amateur Radio Assn Of
Southwest Florida
Naples FL 34108

Call Sign: K4YHB
Amateur Radio Assn Of
Southwest Florida
Naples FL 34108

Call Sign: K4YHB
ARA Of Southwest F
Naples FL 34108

Call Sign: KO4PK
Rowe C Hudson
Naples FL 34108

Call Sign: KF4CND
George R Fowlkes
Naples FL 341013005

Call Sign: WA3TIH
John A Simander
Naples FL 341018833

Call Sign: KQ0Q
John A Simander
Naples FL 341018833

Call Sign: KG4SYC
Jennifer-Helyne (Bj)
Victor
Naples FL 341060836

FCC Amateur Radio Licenses in North Fort Myers

Call Sign: KI4JFN

Norma C Remson
3382 9 Iron Ct
North Fort Myers FL
33917

Call Sign: K0EOX
William H Starr
17867 Acacia Dr
North Fort Myers FL
339172024

Call Sign: KA3AMQ
Robert W Forster Sr
17903 Acacia Dr
North Fort Myers FL
339172024

Call Sign: KI4DPZ
Werner G Schweikert
802 Adam Dr
North Fort Myers FL
339174095

Call Sign: WA6JUQ
Robert D Dunham
5505 Adam Dr
North Fort Myers FL
33917

Call Sign: KJ4LCN
Merideth Moscato
3385 Amelia Run Way
North Fort Myers FL
33917

Call Sign: WB0R
Robert S Reylek
518 Avanti Way Blvd
North Fort Myers FL
33917

Call Sign: KJ4MFV
Ralph A Stallsworth Jr
10025 Bardmoor Ct

North Fort Myers FL
33903

Call Sign: K4IHS
Ralph A Stallsworth Jr
10025 Bardmoor Ct
North Fort Myers FL
33903

Call Sign: N3GAX
David D Nadalin
18708 Baseleg Ave
North Fort Myers FL
33917

Call Sign: N3GAZ
Patricia L Nadalin
18708 Baseleg Ave
North Fort Myers FL
33917

Call Sign: N9ZJF
Elmer W Strohschine
5519 Ben Franklin Ln
North Fort Myers FL
33917

Call Sign: KI4KQO
Fredrick G Marengo Jr
1351 Betmar Blvd 7
North Fort Myers FL
33903

Call Sign: NP2BB
Jack Gene Kauffman
158 Blue Beard Dr
North Fort Myers FL
33917

Call Sign: W2RPS
Robert B Umberger
15819 Blue Skies Dr
North Fort Myers FL
33917

Call Sign: KI4PFA
Shirley G Bradford
15998 Blue Skies Dr
North Fort Myers FL
33917

Call Sign: KI4PEZ
Jack W Bradford
15998 Blue Skies Dr
North Fort Myers FL
339175497

Call Sign: WA8GGP
Charles R Lawrence
152 Boxmeer Dr
North Fort Myers FL
33903

Call Sign: K4KKP
Charles O Smith Sr
723 Brigantine Blvd
North Fort Myers FL
33917

Call Sign: KF4CX
William J Ackerman
10071 Broken Wood Ct
North Fort Myers FL
339039017

Call Sign: KI4PFB
Donald W Maass
1244 Buena Vista Dr
North Fort Myers FL
33903

Call Sign: K4KKW
Walter E Scholz
5570 Burnham Ct
North Fort Myers FL
33903

Call Sign: KD4JIN
Florence James
9240 Caloosa Dr

North Fort Myers FL
33903

Call Sign: KI4CS
Stephen K James
9240 Caloosa Dr
North Fort Myers FL
33903

Call Sign: KI4GIF
Brandon D Gage
20030 Campbell Rd
North Fort Myers FL
33917

Call Sign: KI4GEC
Leslie A Gage
20030 Campbell Rd
North Fort Myers FL
33917

Call Sign: WA2KZY
John W Ward
102 Carriage Ln
North Fort Myers FL
33917

Call Sign: WB4FYD
Margaret L Ward
102 Carriage Ln
North Fort Myers FL
33917

Call Sign: KP2BU
John P Cobb
1748 Cascade Way
North Fort Myers FL
339172510

Call Sign: NP2DT
Mary E Cobb
1748 Cascade Way
North Fort Myers FL
339172510

Call Sign: WD8DGH
George W Rowe
189 Caviller Ct
North Fort Myers FL
33917

Call Sign: W0CMW
William P Walden
243 Caviller Ct
North Fort Myers FL
33917

Call Sign: KE5DYO
Randy Rickard
2205 Channel Way
North Fort Myers FL
33917

Call Sign: KA4AGI
Elmer H Combs
19703 Charleston Cir
North Fort Myers FL
33917

Call Sign: KB3U
Albert J Romanosky
10391 Circle Pine Rd
North Fort Myers FL
33903

Call Sign: KF4CAP
Charlotte Amateur Radio
Society Inc
10391 Circle Pine Rd
North Fort Myers FL
33903

Call Sign: KA4PJW
Joseph R Combs
8140 Cleaves Rd
North Fort Myers FL
339034326

Call Sign: KD4WEF
Fred D Sundstrom Jr

2826 Cloister St
North Fort Myers FL
33917

Call Sign: KA8RLH
Carl S Lorman
3419 Clubview Dr
North Fort Myers FL
339172009

Call Sign: K1OYI
Maurice R Collins
103 Coachlight Ave
North Fort Myers FL
33917

Call Sign: KI4GID
Klaus Rathnow
1712 Cobia Way
North Fort Myers FL
33917

Call Sign: WA3NTY
Richard J Caldwell
683 Concord Dr
North Fort Myers FL
33917

Call Sign: K9CGC
William H Staley
138 Conestoga Trl
North Fort Myers FL
33917

Call Sign: WB1DZG
Charles W Hayden
19232 Congressional Ct
North Fort Myers FL
33903

Call Sign: KA1FGF
June F Hayden
19232 Congressional Ct
North Fort Myers FL
33903

Call Sign: W4ZGF
Edwin D Bruns
360 Constitution Way Old
Bridge Pk
North Fort Myers FL
33917

Call Sign: KK4HQG
Jane A Rediske
7096 Coon Rd
North Fort Myers FL
33917

Call Sign: KB4KAW
Franklin S Gainer
7269 Coon Rd
North Fort Myers FL
33917

Call Sign: W8KKM
Kathleen J Callanan
473 Copenhagen St
North Fort Myers FL
339032125

Call Sign: KI4WRD
Scott D Maddux
292 Copenhagen St
North Fort Myers FL
33903

Call Sign: K3NMR
Mario C Baratta
1718 Coral Way
North Fort Myers FL
33917

Call Sign: WB8AQA
Donald J Miller
201 Crescent Lake Dr
North Fort Myers FL
33917

Call Sign: WB8SIN

Florence L Miller
201 Crescent Lake Dr
North Fort Myers FL
33917

Call Sign: KF4HWW
Christopher M Sullivan
Crystal Lake Dr
North Fort Myers FL
33917

Call Sign: KI4JFO
John R Sholtis
3858 Cypress Run Rd
North Fort Myers FL
33917

Call Sign: KG4BQR
Ralph A Tarantino
51 Cypress St
North Fort Myers FL
33903

Call Sign: N3BTI
Vincent E Principe
19755 Cypress Wood Ct
North Fort Myers FL
33903

Call Sign: WB2LXT
Robert A Ohlhorst
19879 Cypress Wood Ct
North Fort Myers FL
339039041

Call Sign: KE4FIO
John B Nelson
7464 Dana Lin Cir
North Fort Myers FL
33917

Call Sign: N8BGJ
Larry B Newton
7821 Deni Dr

North Fort Myers FL
33917

Call Sign: KA1EAP
David W Rotthoff
19875 Diamond Hill Ct
North Fort Myers FL
33903

Call Sign: KI4PEU
Ken J Basak
345 Doubloow
North Fort Myers FL
33917

Call Sign: WA2EXI
Eugene A Herrmann Jr
17724 Dracena Cir
North Fort Myers FL
33917

Call Sign: KF4IML
Daniel J Sonke
17430 Durrance Rd
North Fort Myers FL
33917

Call Sign: KF4KZQ
Robert T Morikawa
17430 Durrance Rd
North Fort Myers FL
33917

Call Sign: KE4FI
Henry B Crowley
369 E North Shore Dr
North Fort Myers FL
33917

Call Sign: WB4HC
Henry B Crowley
369 E North Shore Dr
North Fort Myers FL
33917

Call Sign: KI4LFB
Tyler J Cheslosky
409 E North Shore Dr
North Fort Myers FL
33917

Call Sign: KB9CIR
Arnold A Willis
19666 Eagle Trace Ct
North Fort Myers FL
33903

Call Sign: KG4JHL
Michael L Dennee
7837 Ebson Dr
North Fort Myers FL
33917

Call Sign: KG4LTI
Sandra A Dennee
7837 Ebson Dr
North Fort Myers FL
339176612

Call Sign: KD4KIT
Todd N Fogle Sr
8260 Ebson Dr NE
North Fort Myers FL
33917

Call Sign: KE4RUW
Sara L Fogle
8260 Ebson Dr NE
North Fort Myers FL
339176234

Call Sign: WD8LFO
Thomas J Greenfield
50 Eland Dr
North Fort Myers FL
33917

Call Sign: N4RJL
Dale T Holmes
167 Eland Dr

North Fort Myers FL
33917

Call Sign: KF4WWE
Phillip J Melton
361 Eland Dr
North Fort Myers FL
33917

Call Sign: WD8JFR
Arthur F Reiff
1831 Embarcadero Way
North Fort Myers FL
33917

Call Sign: WB9JJU
Marylyn P Kotas
549 Evergreen Rd
North Fort Myers FL
33903

Call Sign: W9IIH
Ronald R Kotas
549 Evergreen Rd
North Fort Myers FL
33903

Call Sign: WD4EQU
Anthony Bober
1516 Flynn Rd
North Fort Myers FL
339035544

Call Sign: W4MXR
Thaddeus Lott
5101 Forest Park Dr
North Fort Myers FL
33917

Call Sign: KA2RRU
Donald R Morell
5421 Forest Park Dr
North Fort Myers FL
33917

Call Sign: K3KT
Horace F Carter
5634 Fox Lake Dr
North Fort Myers FL
33917

Call Sign: KB8GBE
Phillip R Newhart
5725 Fox Lake Dr Apt 6
North Fort Myers FL
33917

Call Sign: WA8TOO
John C Fisher
Foxlake Dr
North Fort Myers FL
33917

Call Sign: N2KSN
Francis G Walsh
19777 Frenchmans Ct
North Fort Myers FL
339039000

Call Sign: N0UJK
Thomas J Stein
7837 Gage Way
North Fort Myers FL
33917

Call Sign: W2YIJ
Kenneth J Ross
4225 Glasgow Ct
North Fort Myers FL
33903

Call Sign: KA2HUY
Walter J Wieland
3531 Gloxinia Dr
North Fort Myers FL
33917

Call Sign: KB2GKW
Donna L Wieland
3531 Gloxinia Dr

North Fort Myers FL
33917

Call Sign: KI4ZXM
Sharon M Wray
3384 Golda Cir
North Fort Myers FL
33917

Call Sign: N8TVL
Donald S Kazuk
3611 Golf Cart Dr
North Fort Myers FL
339177200

Call Sign: N8TUJ
June C Kazuk
3611 Golf Cart Dr
North Fort Myers FL
339177200

Call Sign: KK4ECC
Gary L Blashill
2025 Gray Ct
North Fort Myers FL
33903

Call Sign: KC4FUU
Conrad D Stevens
19321 Green Valley Ct
NW
North Fort Myers FL
33903

Call Sign: N5BPW
Elmer E Shirk Jr
19109 Grenelefe Ct NW
North Fort Myers FL
33903

Call Sign: KJ4JOQ
Linda A Buckmaster
443 Grenier Dr
North Fort Myers FL
33903

Call Sign: KF4CVT
Linda A Buckmaster
443 Grenier Dr
North Fort Myers FL
33903

Call Sign: KF4GAT
William L Buckmaster
443 Grenier Dr
North Fort Myers FL
33903

Call Sign: KB4YCM
John W Boyette
1262 Hall Rd
North Fort Myers FL
33903

Call Sign: KG4ZPU
Paul H Singer
4085 Hancock Bridge
Pkwy 111 360
North Fort Myers FL
33903

Call Sign: KC4KHX
David T Hodges
4352 Harbor Ter
North Fort Myers FL
33903

Call Sign: W1UCI
Boyd E Cooley
4290 Harbour Ln
North Fort Myers FL
33903

Call Sign: KJ4MCF
Mark D Dorothy
8550 Hart Dr
North Fort Myers FL
33917

Call Sign: KB4MXL

Robert M Dillinger
7637 Hart Dr NE
North Fort Myers FL
33917

Call Sign: KE4HFO
Robert E Stintzi
8199 Hart Dr NE
North Fort Myers FL
33917

Call Sign: KE4YFN
David V Martin
8350 Henderson Grade
North Fort Myers FL
33917

Call Sign: KF4MCP
Renee J Boyette
8551 Henderson Grade
North Fort Myers FL
33917

Call Sign: WB4WMJ
James R La Fountain
3921 Hidden Acres Cir
North Fort Myers FL
33903

Call Sign: K4OVC
Paul N Horton
4111 Hidden Acres Cir
North Fort Myers FL
339037108

Call Sign: KF4JA
Elsie B Horton
4111 Hidden Acres Cir
North Fort Myers FL
339037108

Call Sign: WA2EKK
Phillip R Brown
389 Hidden Cove Rd

North Fort Myers FL
33917

Call Sign: W4SY
Phillip R Brown
389 Hidden Cove Rd
North Fort Myers FL
33917

Call Sign: WA2KDR
Martha M Brown
389 Hidden Cove Rd
North Fort Myers FL
339172930

Call Sign: WB1BWO
James F Carroll
77 Holly Berry Ct
North Fort Myers FL
33917

Call Sign: WB1DYJ
Marilyn O Carroll
77 Hollyberry Ct
North Fort Myers FL
33917

Call Sign: K7QY
Don W Chambers
401 Horizon Dr
North Fort Myers FL
33903

Call Sign: W4RDI
Don P Carlson
16307 Horizon Rd
North Fort Myers FL
33917

Call Sign: KJ4KHB
Barbara A Devine
701 Hutto Rd
North Fort Myers FL
33903

Call Sign: KJ4KHC
Joseph R Devine Jr
701 Hutto Rd
North Fort Myers FL
33903

Call Sign: K4HIT
Yale E Vaughn
1714 Inlet Dr
North Fort Myers FL
33903

Call Sign: WA4CDA
Donald B Reeves
19188 Innis Brook Ct
North Fort Myers FL
33903

Call Sign: KC4LMI
Adrian M Lewis
5722 Inverness Cr
North Fort Myers FL
33903

Call Sign: AB4UI
Alison L Ball
490 Jacklin Ln
North Fort Myers FL
33903

Call Sign: AA4YN
David H Howe
941 Jolly Rd
North Fort Myers FL
33903

Call Sign: KD4QVJ
Deanna G Louchart
15850 Jones Rd
North Fort Myers FL
33917

Call Sign: KD4QVK
Ronald L Louchart Jr
15850 Jones Rd

North Fort Myers FL
33917

Call Sign: KB4SUN
Valerie D La Plante
15850 Jones Rd
North Fort Myers FL
33917

Call Sign: W1ENZ
Henry F Sperl
19859 Kara Cir
North Fort Myers FL
33917

Call Sign: KE4FMW
Peter Mayer
47 Knotty Pine Cir
North Fort Myers FL
33917

Call Sign: KE4APY
John A Schum
1084 La Palma Blvd
North Fort Myers FL
33903

Call Sign: KA4FQB
Sonya K Schulte
68 Lagoon Dr
North Fort Myers FL
33903

Call Sign: KK4GK
Robert J Peace
136 Lakeside Cir
North Fort Myers FL
33903

Call Sign: KJ4RSB
Dominic M Skinner
1704 Lakeview Ter
North Fort Myers FL
33903

Call Sign: KJ4RSC
Joshua R Skinner
1704 Lakeview Ter
North Fort Myers FL
33903

Call Sign: KK4ECB
Steve M Lee
1271 Lansdale Dr
North Fort Myers FL
33903

Call Sign: NP2OR
Jack D Dunigan
168 Las Palmas Blvd
North Fort Myers FL
33903

Call Sign: KE1DH
Richard R Margey
158 Las Palmas Blvd
North Fort Myers FL
33903

Call Sign: KE4AT
Richard R Margey
158 Las Palmas Blvd
North Fort Myers FL
33903

Call Sign: WA4AX
Richard R Margey
158 Las Palmas Blvd
North Fort Myers FL
33903

Call Sign: KI4KQN
Stephen J Gdovin
3044 Longview Ln
North Fort Myers FL
339171542

Call Sign: K8IAF
Frank A Zeik
3000 Longview Ln NE

North Fort Myers FL
339171542

Call Sign: KE4LKV
Heather K Mc Dowell
1635 Mansville Ter
North Fort Myers FL
33903

Call Sign: KE4GUG
Reinald F Mc Dowell Jr
1635 Mansville Ter
North Fort Myers FL
33903

Call Sign: N4FGG
Robert R Desfosses
1669 Mansville Ter
North Fort Myers FL
33903

Call Sign: KC4VAP
Michael P Mc Curry
1668 Many Rd
North Fort Myers FL
33916

Call Sign: KI4LBH
Robert J Peters
3446 Marinatown Ln
North Fort Myers FL
33903

Call Sign: KB9LYT
Kristopher A Scheppe
3446 Marinatown Ln
North Fort Myers FL
33903

Call Sign: N2VMX
Arthur S Dunn
7710 Marx Dr
North Fort Myers FL
33917

Call Sign: KJ4JOM
Richard L Hawkins
950 Moody Rd 125
North Fort Myers FL
33903

Call Sign: KE4NLV
John Scott
62 Moonwind Dr
North Fort Myers FL
33903

Call Sign: KJ4MUX
Howard D Tucker
278 Moonwind Dr
North Fort Myers FL
33903

Call Sign: KB4UB
Carl E Asbury
4418 N Bay Cir
North Fort Myers FL
33903

Call Sign: KC8LL
Marvin I Vallad
16549 N Cleveland Ave
Lot 126
North Fort Myers FL
33903

Call Sign: N3EGM
Carol J Elliott
3371 N Key Dr 102
North Fort Myers FL
33903

Call Sign: KE3JO
William T Elliott Jr
3371 N Key Dr 102
North Fort Myers FL
34230

Call Sign: KG4GNR
James S Bane Jr

4510 N Key Dr 106
North Fort Myers FL
33903

Call Sign: KG4PUO
Diane M Zabell
3371 N Key Dr 204
North Fort Myers FL
33903

Call Sign: KG4PUN
John A Zabell
3371 N Key Dr 204
North Fort Myers FL
33903

Call Sign: N9KPI
Lewis H Fairbairn
3490 N Key Dr 519
North Fort Myers FL
339037036

Call Sign: KE2SS
Betty J Harrison
3350 N Key Dr A 202
North Fort Myers FL
33903

Call Sign: KD4SAY
Michael A Futchkar
3460 N Key Dr Apt 306E
North Fort Myers FL
33903

Call Sign: W4NTT
Michael A Futchkar
3460 N Key Dr Apt 306E
North Fort Myers FL
33903

Call Sign: KE4NPB
Conrad W Kress
1209 N Tamiami Trl
North Fort Myers FL
33903

Call Sign: N4XLD
Dale S Neace
1064 N Tamiami Trl 18
North Fort Myers FL
33903

Call Sign: KI4FIB
Russell A Johnson
1895 N Tamiami Trl A 39
North Fort Myers FL
33903

Call Sign: KK4TH
William J Houtler
1895 N Tamiami Trl B54
North Fort Myers FL
33903

Call Sign: WA9LSD
Robert B Boughner
1895 N Tamiami Trl C35
North Fort Myers FL
33903

Call Sign: N2ZAS
James F Sorenson Sr
19250 N Tamiami Trl Site
P7
North Fort Myers FL
33903

Call Sign: KA4AZJ
Rhoda G Graybill
N Twig Ct
North Fort Myers FL
33903

Call Sign: KD4QMN
Homer M Maynard Jr
6541 Nalle Grade Rd
North Fort Myers FL
33917

Call Sign: KF4CPZ

Diane M Honas
18801 Nalle Rd
North Fort Myers FL
33917

Call Sign: AE4IG
Gary L Honas
18801 Nalle Rd
North Fort Myers FL
33917

Call Sign: KI4PEY
Barbara A Eadie
14709 Nantucket Rd
North Fort Myers FL
33917

Call Sign: W8EAX
Fred M Jacob
8250 Nault Rd
North Fort Myers FL
339178701

Call Sign: KE4ECF
Klaus L Hueppe
27 Nicklaus Blvd
North Fort Myers FL
33903

Call Sign: KG4PUM
John R Delargy
17620 Old Bayshore Rd
North Fort Myers FL
33917

Call Sign: KC4RQS
John M Varner
1260 Old Bridge Rd
North Fort Myers FL
33917

Call Sign: WA2VQG
William H Helmetag
19425 Omega Rd

North Fort Myers FL
33917

Call Sign: WA9ZDI
William M Bayley
19435 Omega Rd
North Fort Myers FL
339176045

Call Sign: WB9WLM
Beverly A Bayley
19435 Omega Rd
North Fort Myers FL
33917

Call Sign: KA4SQD
Charles E Vogelsong
928 Orange Blossom Ln
North Fort Myers FL
33903

Call Sign: KE4SJI
Alice C Shearer
4701 Orange Grove Blvd
North Fort Myers FL
339034554

Call Sign: KD4IBV
David G Quick
3161 Orchard Dr
North Fort Myers FL
33917

Call Sign: WB4YMK
Jon E Inbody
950 Palm Ave
North Fort Myers FL
33901

Call Sign: N4HCK
Alan D Fogerson
1721 Palo Duro Blvd
North Fort Myers FL
33917

Call Sign: N4TYY
Wayne D Smith
1721 Palo Duro Blvd
North Fort Myers FL
33917

Call Sign: AC8C
Raymond F Lydon
1951 Palo Duro Blvd
North Fort Myers FL
33917

Call Sign: NE1LL
William J Neill
506 Pangola Dr
North Fort Myers FL
339035289

Call Sign: WA4EIC
Blaine Caudill
217 Park Ln Dr
North Fort Myers FL
339173430

Call Sign: KN4ZW
James V League
7644 Peyraud Ct
North Fort Myers FL
33917

Call Sign: N5MNS
Richard C Nally
3160 Pluto Cir
North Fort Myers FL
33903

Call Sign: KC2ANL
Chris M Welcher
263 Poe Ave
North Fort Myers FL
33903

Call Sign: W4ZVK
George A Lingle Sr
118 Powell Creek Cir

North Fort Myers FL
33917

Call Sign: W4OEY
Fernando Callegari
19466 Ravines Ct
North Fort Myers FL
33903

Call Sign: W9SCM
Donnell L Carnes
103 Rhine Dr
North Fort Myers FL
33903

Call Sign: WB9QZL
Shirley J Carnes
103 Rhine Dr
North Fort Myers FL
33903

Call Sign: KI4JFP
Laura Wesserling
6701 Rich Rd
North Fort Myers FL
33917

Call Sign: WB9RYK
Dale H Wakeley
3780 Richard Rd NE
North Fort Myers FL
33903

Call Sign: K2LU
Edgar A Humphreys
2220 Rio Nuevo Dr
North Fort Myers FL
339176773

Call Sign: W4ASC
Adrian S Cherepusko
1146 River Rd
North Fort Myers FL
339034407

Call Sign: WD8MNO
Edward A Verbanas
1319 River Rd A15
North Fort Myers FL
339033823

Call Sign: KK4I
Raimundo Romeu
4318 S Atlantic Cir
North Fort Myers FL
33903

Call Sign: KG4YNQ
Verlyn S Rogers
4353 S Gulf Cir
North Fort Myers FL
339035020

Call Sign: K4AXA
Verlyn S Rogers
4353 S Gulf Cir
North Fort Myers FL
339035020

Call Sign: K1MOO
Robert E St John
57 S Twig Ct
North Fort Myers FL
33917

Call Sign: WA4MMX
Walter A Neubauer
17850 Sabal Palm Dr
North Fort Myers FL
33917

Call Sign: WA1DIC
Patricia A Sanders
554 Sacramento St
North Fort Myers FL
33903

Call Sign: KI4KQP
Ruth A Mcgleish
258 San Bernadino St

North Fort Myers FL
33703

Call Sign: KI4KQQ
Terrance A Mcgleish
258 San Bernardino St
North Fort Myers FL
33903

Call Sign: KC4TM
Terrance A Mcgleish
258 San Bernardino St
North Fort Myers FL
33903

Call Sign: KI4PRD
Remote Amateur Radio
Stations Group
258 San Bernardino St
North Fort Myers FL
33903

Call Sign: K4RAR
Remote Amateur Radio
Stations Group
258 San Bernardino St
North Fort Myers FL
33903

Call Sign: KD4KIU
Steven M Leffers
335 San Bernardino St
North Fort Myers FL
33903

Call Sign: KI4PEX
David P Jacobs
5519 San Luis Dr
North Fort Myers FL
33903

Call Sign: KW1X
John A Wilson
305 San Remo Ln

North Fort Myers FL
33903

Call Sign: KR4ST
Jeffrey C Graham
5867 Sandburg Dr
North Fort Myers FL
339035838

Call Sign: KK4EUG
Billy J Lee
5912 Sandburg Dr
North Fort Myers FL
33903

Call Sign: KK4ECH
Suzanne Lee
5912 Sandburg Dr
North Fort Myers FL
33903

Call Sign: KD4JIQ
Lloyd F Grace
13091 Sandy Key Bend
Unit 2
North Fort Myers FL
33903

Call Sign: KD4FUY
Estelle F Harrington
232 Santa Fe Trl
North Fort Myers FL
33917

Call Sign: KF9O
Donald D Harrington
232 Santa Fe Trl
North Fort Myers FL
33917

Call Sign: KG4LTH
Edward Sappah Jr
1288 Sappah Dr
North Fort Myers FL
33903

Call Sign: KG4KDG
Darla J Strange-Holbrook
9311 Sedgefield Rd
North Fort Myers FL
33917

Call Sign: KG4KDH
John W Holbrook
9311 Sedgefield Rd
North Fort Myers FL
33917

Call Sign: KU4EH
Philip R Jansen
9451 Sedgefield Rd
North Fort Myers FL
33917

Call Sign: AA4QK
Raymond L Pike
8336 Sevigny Rd
North Fort Myers FL
33917

Call Sign: KC9EKG
Terry L Rood
9560 Shadow Oak Ln
North Fort Myers FL
33917

Call Sign: KG4CPC
Gregory A Rex
16263 Shadow Pine Rd
North Fort Myers FL
33917

Call Sign: W2GAL
James J Mc Cormac
15837 Shellcrest Dr
North Fort Myers FL
33917

Call Sign: K8VDE
Catherine A Hullinger

35 Shrub Ln S
North Fort Myers FL
33917

Call Sign: KG3D
Jerry L Agudio
3050 Skyvilla Ln
North Fort Myers FL
33903

Call Sign: WD4ERH
Glenn B Hays
18300 Slater Rd
North Fort Myers FL
33917

Call Sign: KB9AYG
Denny L Mitchell
16781 Slater Rd
North Fort Myers FL
33917

Call Sign: KA9BMH
Denny L Mitchell
16781 Slater Rd
North Fort Myers FL
33917

Call Sign: KG4WSH
Patrick Von Ahn
5888 Spicer Ct
North Fort Myers FL
33903

Call Sign: K1OXJ
George Dykstra
135 Standish Cir
North Fort Myers FL
33903

Call Sign: KI4JFM
Charles R Poveromo
2749 Steamboat Loop
North Fort Myers FL
33917

Call Sign: KB5DEP
Maria E Leggett
1252 Sunrise Dr
North Fort Myers FL
33917

Call Sign: KF4GAU
Thomas J Harrell
1386 Sunrise Dr
North Fort Myers FL
33917

Call Sign: KG4UEW
Casimir J Zajdel
62 Sunset Cir
North Fort Myers FL
33903

Call Sign: KK4BQQ
Fred W Puhlfuerst
2837 Tara Lakes Cir
North Fort Myers FL
33917

Call Sign: WN4R
David L Wood
19426 Tarpon Woods Ct
North Fort Myers FL
33903

Call Sign: W8JOQ
James J Rudolph
2793 Teakwood Blvd
North Fort Myers FL
339171877

Call Sign: KD4CWL
John C Conroy
1646 Temple Ter
North Fort Myers FL
33917

Call Sign: W0OHZ
Charles W Flynn

14621 Thomas Jefferson
Ln
North Fort Myers FL
33917

Call Sign: KB9LSH
Ronald L Kerlin
1307 Thompson St
North Fort Myers FL
33903

Call Sign: KI4NQM
Roger L Diekema
224 Tiel Ave
North Fort Myers FL
33903

Call Sign: KE4UGJ
Paula J Paszke
6051 Tierra Entrada
North Fort Myers FL
339031335

Call Sign: W8ARW
Carl B Snyder
Timberlane Forest Pk
North Fort Myers FL
33917

Call Sign: KF4PHD
Bobbie O Dixon
1397 Torreay Cir
North Fort Myers FL
33917

Call Sign: KB4VHS
George P Cappos
1332 Torreya Cir NE
North Fort Myers FL
339173406

Call Sign: KB9YDV
Ryan W Kingsbury
6730 Tortoise Run Ct

North Fort Myers FL
33917

Call Sign: KG4ZOV
Ryan W Kingsbury
6730 Tortoise Run Ct
North Fort Myers FL
33917

Call Sign: N4NZJ
Ralph E Clothier
644 Tortugas Dr
North Fort Myers FL
33917

Call Sign: W4JJA
Webb Johnson
54 Twig Ct S
North Fort Myers FL
33917

Call Sign: KB3CZV
Chris P Snyder
2181 Twin Brooks Rd
North Fort Myers FL
33917

Call Sign: K2DPT
Thaddeus A Glenn
17021 Upriver Dr
North Fort Myers FL
33917

Call Sign: WA3BAA
Viola C Ward
17021 Upriver Dr 24
North Fort Myers FL
339173827

Call Sign: KC8EOA
Bruce F Porter
2111 Valparaiso Blvd
North Fort Myers FL
339176789

Call Sign: W0SNX
Frank J Moser
708 Via Del Sol
North Fort Myers FL
33903

Call Sign: WB4GZG
Bryan Walters
720 Via Del Sol
North Fort Myers FL
33903

Call Sign: KJ4EUP
Edwina H Reid
730 Via Del Sol
North Fort Myers FL
33903

Call Sign: KJ4EUR
Robert D Reid
730 Via Del Sol
North Fort Myers FL
33903

Call Sign: KY4LQ
Alexander J Lozano
1792 Whitecap Cir
North Fort Myers FL
33903

Call Sign: KC6ETQ
William E Thompson
20100 Williams Dr
North Fort Myers FL
33917

Call Sign: KC6UZX
Sharron K Thompson
20100 Williams Dr
North Fort Myers FL
33917

Call Sign: KG4WSG
Richard A Zyvoloski Jr
19921 Woodbridge Ln

North Fort Myers FL
339174515

Call Sign: W8RTU
Peter K Cencer
19701 Woodfield Cir
North Fort Myers FL
339176122

Call Sign: N4SUL
Donald R Meachum
North Fort Myers FL
33918

Call Sign: KB4ZCB
Rosalyn B Piehl
North Fort Myers FL
33918

Call Sign: WD9ENO
Darrell W Phillips
North Fort Myers FL
33918

Call Sign: KJ4LCT
Christopher P Owens
North Fort Myers FL
33918

Call Sign: KI4IKU
James R Kelley
North Fort Myers FL
33918

Call Sign: AG4CU
Michael J Harrington
North Fort Myers FL
33918

Call Sign: W4JVZ
Frank T Bodine
North Fort Myers FL
33918

Call Sign: KG4GDE

Robert E Perry
North Fort Myers FL
39918

Call Sign: WD4CHP
Willis K Smith
North Fort Myers FL
339183327

Call Sign: WA2IEV
Albert A Franklin
829 107th Ave
North Naples FL 33940

Call Sign: N1UHG
Kevin T Donnell
Box 51
Ochopee FL 34141

Call Sign: KI4NWT
Paul C Miller
18400 Burns Rd
Ochopee FL 34141

Call Sign: KA4MXQ
Vincent D Doerr
Cypress Tower Rd
Ochopee FL 34141

Call Sign: WD4KBV
Robert A Jones
Box 72
Ona FL 33865

Call Sign: KE4GYX
David J Blalock

575 Roy Moore Rd
Ona FL 33865

Call Sign: KC4ZD
Albert D Mountain III
9505 Main Ave NW 51
Palmdale FL 33944

Call Sign: W4ANR
Albert D Mountain III
9505 Main Ave NW 51
Palmdale FL 33944

Call Sign: KR4ZA
Kevin M West
9820 Main St
Palmdale FL 33944

Call Sign: KE4JCS
Tammy S West
Palmdale FL 33944

Call Sign: WA9BLF
W E Davis
7231 Orange Ave
Pineland FL 33945

Call Sign: KG4JHK
Thomas J Carroll
Pineland FL 339450252

Call Sign: K9BLF
W E Davis
Pineland FL 339450305

Call Sign: N4IRG
Kathleen L Moyer
Pineland FL 339450353

FCC Amateur Radio Licenses in Placida

Call Sign: KJ4DVX
Charles A Lombardi
10 Buccaneer Bend
Placida FL 33946

Call Sign: AJ4IO
Charles A Lombardi
10 Buccaneer Bend
Placida FL 33946

Call Sign: WU4Q
Charles A Lombardi
10 Buccaneer Bend
Placida FL 33946

Call Sign: KE4NVF
John T Lovo
23 Bunker Ln
Placida FL 33947

Call Sign: N4DHQ
Erven I Maki
430 Coral Creek Dr
Placida FL 33946

Call Sign: KE4NZU
Thomas E Blanding
26 Golfview Ct
Placida FL 339472229

Call Sign: KC2ZV
William J Dolan
13121 Placida Point Ct
Placida FL 339462112

Call Sign: W2CWL
William J Dolan
13121 Placida Point Ct
Placida FL 339462112

Call Sign: W2FTL
Lawrence F Luccio

11000 Placida Rd Unit 104
Placida FL 33946

Call Sign: W2RNV
Ralph W Ludy
4728 Pompano St
Placida FL 33946

Call Sign: N3IEF
Peggy A Gainey
30 Windward Ct
Placida FL 33946

Call Sign: KF4YX
Judi J Mattson
Placida FL 33946

Call Sign: AC4BF
Charles T Nesmith
Placida FL 33946

Call Sign: KB2WVY
John Stewart Jr
Placida FL 33946

Call Sign: KC5AS
Keith Kelly
Placida FL 33946

Call Sign: KF6YEA
Carol P Peterson
Placida FL 33946

Call Sign: KF6YEB
William H Peterson Jr
Placida FL 33946

Call Sign: AK4KU
William H Peterson Jr
Placida FL 33946

FCC Amateur Radio Licenses in Port Charlotte

Call Sign: AB4HK
James F Weir
847 2100
Port Charlotte FL 33980

Call Sign: N4SMJ
Margie V Johnson
2500 Aaron St 206
Port Charlotte FL 33952

Call Sign: WA4LHO
Guice W Johnson
2500 Aaron St Apt 206
Port Charlotte FL 33952

Call Sign: KC4EYM
David W Mc Nutt
1500 Abel St
Port Charlotte FL 33952

Call Sign: KK4ON
Francis B Howard
23248 Aberdeen Ave
Port Charlotte FL 33952

Call Sign: W1SWV
Ronald W Bissett
19217 Abhenry Cir
Port Charlotte FL 33948

Call Sign: KG4ERH
Ronald W Bissett
19217 Abherny Cir
Port Charlotte FL 33948

Call Sign: N2DAN
Steve S Nurkiewicz
1385 Abner St
Port Charlotte FL 33980

Call Sign: N4VIW
Michael S Harrell
23367 Abrade Ave
Port Charlotte FL 33980

Call Sign: KD5SML
Alice M Spier
2277 Achilles St
Port Charlotte FL 33980

Call Sign: K5RDS
Roger D Spier
2277 Achilles St
Port Charlotte FL 33980

Call Sign: WA2OGU
Thomas E Kelley
7333 Adana Ave
Port Charlotte FL 33981

Call Sign: K9ZKS
Reginald L Knarzer
4407 Albacore Cir
Port Charlotte FL
339488902

Call Sign: WA4ZEZ
Fritz J Faciane Jr
22266 Albany Ave
Port Charlotte FL
339527242

Call Sign: WB1CYM
Selwyn E Kerrigan
13478 Alberta Ave SW
Port Charlotte FL 33981

Call Sign: K0TBV
Ann C Mc Donough
1374 Allison St NW
Port Charlotte FL 33952

Call Sign: K0UTC
Chester N Mc Donough
1374 Allison St NW
Port Charlotte FL 33952

Call Sign: KF4WHL
Daniel Keene
19199 Almadyde Ct

Port Charlotte FL 33948

Call Sign: KF4WHM
George E Keene
19199 Almadyde Ct
Port Charlotte FL 33948

Call Sign: W4BNS
J Blaine Bennett Jr
10598 Alpaca Cir
Port Charlotte FL 33981

Call Sign: KB4TVI
Jeanna K Bennett
10598 Alpaca Cir
Port Charlotte FL 33981

Call Sign: KI7WH
Myer P Moses
18430 Alphonse Cir
Port Charlotte FL 33948

Call Sign: AE4OK
Harold A Youngblood
21085 Alpine Ave
Port Charlotte FL 33952

Call Sign: KB3MY
Harold L Light Jr
1225 Alton Rd
Port Charlotte FL 33952

Call Sign: K1GLX
Jacintho Fernandes Jr
1289 Alton Rd
Port Charlotte FL
339522877

Call Sign: KM4VA
James C Letzelter
18270 Arapahoe Cir
Port Charlotte FL 33948

Call Sign: K9DPU
Murray E Bassett

343 Arbor St
Port Charlotte FL 33953

Call Sign: W2ORP
Joseph A Riccio
343 Arbor St
Port Charlotte FL 33953

Call Sign: KJ4MJX
Patrick W Muthler
21199 Argyle Ave
Port Charlotte FL 33954

Call Sign: KG4JLI
Donald E Rodgers
9364 Arnaz Cir
Port Charlotte FL 33981

Call Sign: AC5XP
Loek J D Hont
9588 Arnaz Cir
Port Charlotte FL
339814005

Call Sign: W4MEY
Clarence B Diersing Jr
23055 August Ave
Port Charlotte FL
339543514

Call Sign: W0RPM
William F Proetz
21689 Augusta Ave
Port Charlotte FL 33952

Call Sign: K4UAY
Robert C Hogue
21690 Augusta Ave
Port Charlotte FL 33952

Call Sign: K1GVN
David E King
21330 Austin Ave
Port Charlotte FL 33952

Call Sign: W4GVN
David E King
21330 Austin Ave
Port Charlotte FL 33952

Call Sign: K1GVN
David E King
21330 Austin Ave
Port Charlotte FL 33952

Call Sign: KA9YRT
Lori G Larson
18770 Ayrshire Cir
Port Charlotte FL
339489679

Call Sign: KD6PPN
James P Doran
950 Baer Ave
Port Charlotte FL 33948

Call Sign: K6JPD
James P Doran
950 Baer Ave
Port Charlotte FL 33948

Call Sign: ND6M
James P Doran
950 Baer Ave
Port Charlotte FL 33948

Call Sign: K1JAY
Herbert Roshkind
265 Bangsberg Rd
Port Charlotte FL 33952

Call Sign: KB2TLK
Anthony A Mc Leod
254 Barcelona St
Port Charlotte FL 33983

Call Sign: KE4TKT
Kenneth R Couch
2073 Basin St
Port Charlotte FL 33952

Call Sign: N4ZOG
George E Crowther Jr
21184 Bassett Ave
Port Charlotte FL 33952

Call Sign: W9CFZ
Robert L Vore
21201 Bassett Ave
Port Charlotte FL 33952

Call Sign: KD0KG
Douglas C Kewer
4232 Beach View Ct
Port Charlotte FL 33948

Call Sign: K8TMX
Nathan D Vance
1291 Beacon Dr
Port Charlotte FL 33952

Call Sign: WA4ODO
Kenneth D Sanders
3130 Beacon Dr
Port Charlotte FL 33952

Call Sign: W8GPK
Raymond T Pio
7383 Beckley St SW
Port Charlotte FL 33981

Call Sign: KX7I
John T Temples
22178 Belinda Ave
Port Charlotte FL 33952

Call Sign: KJ4HLU
Charles D Sellars
22211 Belinda Ave
Port Charlotte FL 33952

Call Sign: KA8NIF
Roland A Musser
1010 Belmar Ave
Port Charlotte FL 33948

Call Sign: N4FYK
William A Bedford
1116 Belmar Ave
Port Charlotte FL 33948

Call Sign: KA4DQG
Robert R Peterson
2351 Bendway Dr
Port Charlotte FL 33948

Call Sign: KF4YEI
John T Troxell Jr
22208 Beverly Ave
Port Charlotte FL 33950

Call Sign: KF4NCZ
David A Watts
23200 Billings Ave
Port Charlotte FL 33954

Call Sign: KF4MQS
Frederick R Watts
23200 Billings Ave
Port Charlotte FL 33954

Call Sign: KF4NCY
John M Watts
23200 Billings Ave
Port Charlotte FL 33954

Call Sign: WP4XY
Jose F Gonzalez
1177 Birchcrest Blvd
Port Charlotte FL
339521649

Call Sign: WA9NLA
Lloyd L Smith
1350 Birchcrest Blvd
Port Charlotte FL 33952

Call Sign: WD4MBW
Richard L Reese
190 Bishop St

Port Charlotte FL
339544136

Call Sign: WX4E
Joseph H Stevens
20207 Blaine Ave
Port Charlotte FL 33952

Call Sign: KB8HS
Donald R Sorensen
1593 Blue Lake Cir
Port Charlotte FL 33983

Call Sign: N8JGO
Gay M Sorensen
1593 Blue Lake Cir
Port Charlotte FL 33983

Call Sign: KF4GRH
Linda H Bloom
22269 Breezeswept Ave
Port Charlotte FL 33952

Call Sign: KF4BVU
Russell B Richey III
18563 Briggs Cir
Port Charlotte FL 33948

Call Sign: KD4MZE
Paul E Keagle
21320 Brinson Ave 108
Port Charlotte FL 33952

Call Sign: KC4OZK
Charles F Steck III
2148 Broad Ranch Dr
Port Charlotte FL 33948

Call Sign: W9OCC
Howard M Mc Donald
2356 Broad Ranch Dr
Port Charlotte FL 33948

Call Sign: K1ZFK
Willard D Jemson

2538 Broadranch
Port Charlotte FL 33948

Call Sign: KC4FKM
Eddie S Nuguit
144 Brooklyn Ave
Port Charlotte FL 33952

Call Sign: N4TMK
Lee T Nuguit
144 Brooklyn Ave
Port Charlotte FL 33952

Call Sign: KI4REI
John F Schoenthaler
13292 Buckett Cir
Port Charlotte FL 33981

Call Sign: N4XBJ
Peter A Chiccino
21252 Burkhart Dr
Port Charlotte FL 33952

Call Sign: K1OBT
Raymond E Hunkins
18326 Burkholder Cir
Port Charlotte FL 33948

Call Sign: KB0MMX
Ronald F Reeves
2789 Cabaret St
Port Charlotte FL 33948

Call Sign: W6SVQ
Hudson B Gillis
14461 Cannell Ln
Port Charlotte FL 33953

Call Sign: N1ZOZ
Ralph W Trynor
5182 Cannon St
Port Charlotte FL
339811706

Call Sign: N4FOB

Thomas E Ferer
21479 Carleton Ave
Port Charlotte FL 33952

Call Sign: WB4TEX
Alexander F Zaboronak Sr
353 Casale G Dr
Port Charlotte FL 33983

Call Sign: KI4UAX
Russell L Bryan
21945 Catherine Ave
Port Charlotte FL 33952

Call Sign: KG4BWL
Dan G Chilcoat
2126 Cedarwood St
Port Charlotte FL 33948

Call Sign: N6ABQ
David C Weaver
197 Center Ave NW
Port Charlotte FL
339526604

Call Sign: KI4GLU
Adam E Hogan
13611 Chancellor
Port Charlotte FL 33951

Call Sign: KI4GLS
Eve L Hogan
13611 Chancellor Ave
Port Charlotte FL 33591

Call Sign: KI4GLT
William T Hogan
13611 Chancellor Blvd
Port Charlotte FL 33951

Call Sign: KG4EDE
Bryce C Eggleton
6251 Chariot St
Port Charlotte FL 33981

Call Sign: KG4EDG
Colin J Eggleton
6251 Chariot St
Port Charlotte FL 33981

Call Sign: KG4EDF
Pamela J Reil-Eggleton
6251 Chariot St
Port Charlotte FL 33981

Call Sign: K1UEG
Pamela J Reil-Eggleton
6251 Chariot St
Port Charlotte FL 33981

Call Sign: KB2GMY
Carl K Miller
21209 Chatburn Ave
Port Charlotte FL 33952

Call Sign: KG4ODI
Carl K Miller
21209 Chatburn Ave
Port Charlotte FL 33952

Call Sign: W9OR
Richard D Lashbrook
2295 Chilcote Ter
Port Charlotte FL 33981

Call Sign: WA1QCQ
Vicky L Tuttle
18055 Clanton Ave
Port Charlotte FL 33948

Call Sign: K1UTI
Robert E Tuttle
18055 Clanton Ave
Port Charlotte FL 33948

Call Sign: KD4DSM
Douglas J Lawrence
926 Claude Ct
Port Charlotte FL 33952

Call Sign: KF4VHY
Cecila C Sours
2223 Claude Ct
Port Charlotte FL 33952

Call Sign: WA3PRC
Thomas J Hawes
676 Clearview Dr
Port Charlotte FL 33953

Call Sign: K1LXQ
Earl R Fairhurst
701 Clearview Dr
Port Charlotte FL 33953

Call Sign: WB5PLR
George E Moore
855 Clearview Dr
Port Charlotte FL 33953

Call Sign: KE4JRU
Pedro Cintron
17465 Clover Ave
Port Charlotte FL 33948

Call Sign: KF4OPE
Richard T Witt
6534 Coliseum Blvd
Port Charlotte FL 33981

Call Sign: W1EVX
Joseph F Christiano
134 Colonial St SW
Port Charlotte FL 33952

Call Sign: WB8MTR
James D King
15091 Community Ave
Port Charlotte FL 33953

Call Sign: W0RRB
Jon C Wollerman
356 Comstock St
Port Charlotte FL 33954

Call Sign: W4HWM
Jon C Wollerman
356 Comstock St
Port Charlotte FL 33954

Call Sign: KO4MG
Kenneth M Wynne
4379 Concert St
Port Charlotte FL 33948

Call Sign: KA9MZX
John A Cihlar
1066 Congress St
Port Charlotte FL 33952

Call Sign: KJ4CU
Wallace R Stroud
1082 Congress St
Port Charlotte FL 33952

Call Sign: KB0EVM
David K Hanson
1089 Congress St
Port Charlotte FL 33952

Call Sign: WB3HXM
Joseph J Kane
6447 Coniston St
Port Charlotte FL 33981

Call Sign: KA1EFN
Lawrence W Cochrane Jr
2298 Conway Blvd
Port Charlotte FL
339525609

Call Sign: KE4PRU
Christian C Andersen
2462 Conway Blvd
Port Charlotte FL 33952

Call Sign: KJ4YBU
Gregory D Hanlon
2591 Conway Blvd
Port Charlotte FL 33952

Call Sign: WD4NDM
Marvin K Cook
3309 Conway Blvd
Port Charlotte FL 33952

Call Sign: KB2YAP
William S Black
2575 Conway Blvd
Port Charlotte FL 33952

Call Sign: KU4LS
Arthur C Grimes
1236 Corktree Cir
Port Charlotte FL 33952

Call Sign: W3HCD
Harry C Dahlin
12184 Corporal Cir
Port Charlotte FL
339532238

Call Sign: KE4OHC
Anthony J Torres
18386 Cortland Ave
Port Charlotte FL
339483314

Call Sign: WA2RQY
Richard B Lucchesi
21215 Cottonwood Ave
Port Charlotte FL 33952

Call Sign: N4HTP
John P Derr
148 Cousley Dr
Port Charlotte FL 33952

Call Sign: KF4LHR
Robert E Carr
21221 Covington Ave
Port Charlotte FL 33952

Call Sign: KJ4BEK
Stanley A Johnson

136 Creek Dr SE
Port Charlotte FL 33952

Call Sign: K4SAJ
Stanley A Johnson
136 Creek Dr SE
Port Charlotte FL 33952

Call Sign: N1UVN
Sean D Viara
6387 Cutler Ter
Port Charlotte FL 33981

Call Sign: KJ4LMT
Thomas A Lamble Jr
310 Dalton Blvd
Port Charlotte FL 33952

Call Sign: W4LIY
Harvey S Ardel
305 Danley St
Port Charlotte FL 33954

Call Sign: KJ4JCJ
Randy L Mallette
13505 Darnell Ave
Port Charlotte FL 33981

Call Sign: N1LRS
Anthony R Araujo
13578 Darnell Ave
Port Charlotte FL 33981

Call Sign: KG4NKO
Donald Hartlein Sr
141 Dartmouth Dr
Port Charlotte FL 33952

Call Sign: N4NOD
Donald Hartlein Sr
141 Dartmouth Dr
Port Charlotte FL 33952

Call Sign: N4MLJ
Howard B Kuhlman

5738 David Blvd
Port Charlotte FL 33981

Call Sign: N3JWP
Vernon Beck Jr
23514 Dawn Ave
Port Charlotte FL 33954

Call Sign: AF4US
Vernon Beck Jr
23514 Dawn Ave
Port Charlotte FL 33954

Call Sign: KC4HIH
Donald L Lyerly Sr
21452 Dawson Ave
Port Charlotte FL 33952

Call Sign: KC4HLJ
Donald L Lyerly Jr
21452 Dawson Ave
Port Charlotte FL 33952

Call Sign: KG4PZS
Larry A Kraus
1017 Decatur St
Port Charlotte FL 33952

Call Sign: WH6CXT
Richard B Carey
23275 Delavan Ave
Port Charlotte FL 33954

Call Sign: N6OUE
Dewey E Peters
3512 Depew Cir
Port Charlotte FL 33952

Call Sign: W9BSM
Melvin R Rathbun
13525 Dibella Ave
Port Charlotte FL 33981

Call Sign: K3WST
Edmund F Lewis

736 Dobell Ter NW
Port Charlotte FL
339483713

Call Sign: KA9WLH
Paul M Carlson
862 Dolphin Ave
Port Charlotte FL 33948

Call Sign: KE4ZCN
William D Sink
405 Dorchester St
Port Charlotte FL 33954

Call Sign: N1XAO
Charles E Rackette
321 Dover Ave
Port Charlotte FL 33952

Call Sign: KE4MGQ
Betty J Walters
107 Dowling Ave
Port Charlotte FL 33952

Call Sign: W4XBE
John D Easey
18235 Driggers Ave
Port Charlotte FL 33948

Call Sign: N4GFY
Julian W Orr
18235 Driggers Ave
Port Charlotte FL 33948

Call Sign: KG4FFL
Anthony P Flynn
18450 Driggers Ave
Port Charlotte FL 33948

Call Sign: W3NID
William F Brenner
6420 Drucker Cir
Port Charlotte FL 33981

Call Sign: KA4HAT

Anne P Webb
180 Duxbury Ave
Port Charlotte FL 33952

Call Sign: K9HBJ
Robert K Webb
180 Duxbury Ave
Port Charlotte FL 33952

Call Sign: KC4HRD
Robert A Greenberg
217 E Tarpon Blvd
Port Charlotte FL 33952

Call Sign: KC4UVF
Barry A Blume
225 E Tarpon Blvd
Port Charlotte FL 33952

Call Sign: AF4ZA
Patricia G Bagby
498 E Tarpon Blvd
Port Charlotte FL
339526535

Call Sign: KG4SBG
Dennis R Leach
3183 Easy St
Port Charlotte FL 33952

Call Sign: KC4LKQ
Jeffrey A Wright
3342 Easy St
Port Charlotte FL 33952

Call Sign: WB4TEP
Charles E Rochester
3486 Easy St
Port Charlotte FL 33952

Call Sign: WA8VBC
Betty R Hiteman
13273 Ebony Ave
Port Charlotte FL 33981

Call Sign: N4VOH
William C Terza
21113 Edgewater Dr
Port Charlotte FL 33952

Call Sign: WB3DGH
Arlene Smith
21333 Edgewater Dr
Port Charlotte FL 33952

Call Sign: K3AVU
Robert R Smith Jr
21333 Edgewater Dr
Port Charlotte FL 33952

Call Sign: WA9JVB
Thomas V Klier
21762 Edgewater Dr
Port Charlotte FL 33952

Call Sign: KE4ZCJ
Troy B Daniels
21805 Edgewater Dr
Port Charlotte FL 33952

Call Sign: KA4ICI
Hans J Labor
788 Ednor St NW
Port Charlotte FL 33952

Call Sign: KA4ICN
Linda A Labor
788 Ednor St NW
Port Charlotte FL 33952

Call Sign: KK4CDO
Seavey D Morse Jr
3737 El Jobean Rd
Port Charlotte FL 33953

Call Sign: W0WSN
Jerry K Knight
3737 El Jobean Rd K7
Port Charlotte FL 33953

Call Sign: K4KIM
Kimberly A Paez
2576 Elkcam Blvd
Port Charlotte FL 33952

Call Sign: K4SOB
Tom W Collins
2576 Elkcam Blvd
Port Charlotte FL 33952

Call Sign: N4OSK
Freda J Begeal
2120 Ellery St
Port Charlotte FL 33952

Call Sign: KK2L
William F Miller
2120 Ellery St
Port Charlotte FL 33952

Call Sign: K1RXF
Paul A Price
967 Elmira Blvd
Port Charlotte FL 33952

Call Sign: N9DUG
Douglas H Herrold
21041 Evanston Ave
Port Charlotte FL 33952

Call Sign: W4NBE
Melvin R Williams
813 Fairfax Ter
Port Charlotte FL
339483718

Call Sign: WB2IYT
Daniel D Keyser
5354 Farley St
Port Charlotte FL 33981

Call Sign: N2EXE
Lillian M Keyser
5354 Farley St
Port Charlotte FL 33981

Call Sign: KS4AY
Robert J Johnson
286 Fields Ter
Port Charlotte FL 33952

Call Sign: KB9ABM
Barbara W Johnson
286 Fields Ter SE
Port Charlotte FL 33952

Call Sign: KQ4IN
Robert E Harris
1237 Fleetwood Dr
Port Charlotte FL 33948

Call Sign: KI4FJJ
Eugene V Reilly
5266 Forbes Ter
Port Charlotte FL 33981

Call Sign: K2EEL
Lionel E Riley Jr
259 Fortaleza St
Port Charlotte FL 33983

Call Sign: K8WVP
Theodore J Weller Sr
13280 Fowler Ave
Port Charlotte FL
339815521

Call Sign: KF7OHP
Nopadol Temkamolratana
102 Free Ct SE
Port Charlotte FL 33952

Call Sign: KG4ACM
Bill L Bryson II
23227 Freedom Ave 17
Port Charlotte FL 33980

Call Sign: WA9OLA
Steven A Brown
226 Fry Ter

Port Charlotte FL 33952

Call Sign: KD4WUZ
Phil H Hobbes
4511 Gillen St
Port Charlotte FL 33948

Call Sign: W3VM
William R Morgan Jr
5753 Gillott Blvd
Port Charlotte FL 33981

Call Sign: WB8HKJ
Mary L Pillinger
4184 Gingold
Port Charlotte FL 33948

Call Sign: WB8GKE
Norman J Pillinger
4184 Gingold
Port Charlotte FL 33948

Call Sign: KD4KFA
Julia R Plumeri
4207 Gingold St
Port Charlotte FL 33948

Call Sign: KD4CMO
Scott A Rhoades
329 Glendale Ave NE
Port Charlotte FL 33952

Call Sign: W2WZQ
Ralph W Mifflin
23176 Glory Ave
Port Charlotte FL 33952

Call Sign: KF4RST
Brian K Condrey
23183 Glory Ave
Port Charlotte FL 33952

Call Sign: KI4NTC
Harlin D Allen
110 Graham St SW

Port Charlotte FL 33952

Call Sign: KC7MTQ
Randolph S Pratt
23087 Gray Ave
Port Charlotte FL 33980

Call Sign: KG4ERG
John E Koehler
3481 Great Neck St
Port Charlotte FL 33952

Call Sign: WA4YYZ
Peggy A Cox
150 Guava St
Port Charlotte FL 33980

Call Sign: KE4SNP
Norman J Fernandez
57 Hannah St
Port Charlotte FL 33954

Call Sign: N6QAY
Woody E Erwin
65 Hannah St
Port Charlotte FL
339542527

Call Sign: KC4DJI
James J Kolenda
1150 Harbor Blvd
Port Charlotte FL 33952

Call Sign: KG4RNS
Robert F Rogers
3314 Harbor Blvd
Port Charlotte FL 33952

Call Sign: KD4MFV
Peter S Scarpulla Sr
3410 Harbor Blvd
Port Charlotte FL 33952

Call Sign: K3OTY
John B Parsons

3495 Harbor Blvd
Port Charlotte FL
339528005

Call Sign: KS4ST
Reinhold J Zweig
4080 Harbor Blvd
Port Charlotte FL
339529009

Call Sign: KG4DAH
Randal T Barber
4376 Harbor Blvd
Port Charlotte FL 33952

Call Sign: KC4LKM
John T Montagna
1493 Harmony Dr
Port Charlotte FL 33952

Call Sign: KF4UHA
Dewey W Ogle Jr
23342 Hartley Ave
Port Charlotte FL 33954

Call Sign: KI4WGV
David C Crockwell
1403 Hayworth Rd
Port Charlotte FL 33952

Call Sign: KJ4JCI
Eric W Sihr
21955 Hernando Ave
Port Charlotte FL 33952

Call Sign: N2ASY
Lorraine Forshner
2418 Herron Ter
Port Charlotte FL 33981

Call Sign: N2ASZ
Marvin Forshner
2418 Herron Ter
Port Charlotte FL 33981

Call Sign: KF4SGR
Paul E King
2290 Highlands Rd
Port Charlotte FL 33983

Call Sign: N1TOJ
William D Minogue
17181 Hillsborough Blvd
Port Charlotte FL
339541551

Call Sign: N4SLN
Thomas W Ponder
23068 Hillsdale Ave
Port Charlotte FL 33954

Call Sign: WE4N
Thomas W Ponder
23068 Hillsdale Ave
Port Charlotte FL 33954

Call Sign: N4YHX
Daniel K Richards
18329 Hottelet Cir
Port Charlotte FL 33948

Call Sign: KD4ICC
Harry E Rector
2095 Hyatt Dr
Port Charlotte FL
339482064

Call Sign: KD4ZQV
Deborah C Mc Cormick
17466 Inglewood Ave
Port Charlotte FL 33954

Call Sign: KE4HWH
Randy G Mc Cormick
17466 Inglewood Ave
Port Charlotte FL 33954

Call Sign: KD4PCS
Jon R Schriver
441 Ivanhoe St

Port Charlotte FL 33952

Call Sign: K1VLV
Alice N Meehan
874 Ivanhoe St
Port Charlotte FL 33952

Call Sign: N4KNF
Rhonda G Livingston
2160 Ivy St
Port Charlotte FL 33952

Call Sign: N4ZGH
Roger E Livingston
2160 Ivy St
Port Charlotte FL 33952

Call Sign: KC4DJG
Michele A Weaver
2784 Jacobs St
Port Charlotte FL 33953

Call Sign: KA1ZFO
Michael E Fox
3500 Jennings Blvd
Port Charlotte FL 33981

Call Sign: KG4CNL
Ron W Jones
5226 Johnson Ter
Port Charlotte FL 33981

Call Sign: KE6YFW
Bruce J Pierce
23213 Jules Ave
Port Charlotte FL 33980

Call Sign: KI4FIH
Carla A Barnes
17180 Kellog Ave
Port Charlotte FL 33954

Call Sign: KE4GEO
Robert G Wilson
5541 Kempson Ln

Port Charlotte FL 33981

Call Sign: N3FBW
Robert E Mc Cormack
1361 Kenmore St
Port Charlotte FL 33949

Call Sign: KE4TJO
Gino J Ferranti
391 Kenova St
Port Charlotte FL 33954

Call Sign: WB4GDX
Miguel A Jimenez
1106 Kensington St
Port Charlotte FL
339521522

Call Sign: KC8WGC
Christopher D Stapp
21421 Kenyon Ave
Port Charlotte FL 33952

Call Sign: N4KIZ
Richard M Bueche
18550 Kerrville Cir
Port Charlotte FL 33948

Call Sign: W0EFM
Everett S Frank
20262 Kinderkemac Ave
Port Charlotte FL 33952

Call Sign: WA0AOU
Kathleen L Frank
20262 Kinderkemac Ave
Port Charlotte FL 33952

Call Sign: KB4EBN
Anthony Arroyo
2100 King Hwy 864
Port Charlotte FL 33980

Call Sign: N4VOT
Bruce A Hiscoe

73355 Kings Hwy
Port Charlotte FL 33980

Call Sign: KB4SZP
Leo A Brule
Kings Hwy
Port Charlotte FL 33980

Call Sign: KN4HG
Robert G Wood
Kings Hwy
Port Charlotte FL 33980

Call Sign: KC4DST
Eleanor G Chase
Kings Hwy
Port Charlotte FL 33980

Call Sign: WA8AIU
Earl L Snyder
1000 Kings Hwy 129
Port Charlotte FL 33980

Call Sign: WA4VHW
George M Hemingway
1999 Kings Hwy 12B
Port Charlotte FL
339804288

Call Sign: KF4IQE
Robert G Ruff
1000 Kings Hwy 192
Port Charlotte FL 33980

Call Sign: W4RGR
Robert G Ruff
1000 Kings Hwy 192
Port Charlotte FL 33980

Call Sign: KJ4NDK
Charlie Robertson
1000 Kings Hwy 324
Port Charlotte FL 33980

Call Sign: KD4JIR

James F Bonnes
2100 Kings Hwy 388
Port Charlotte FL 33980

Call Sign: W2GZG
James G Timourian
2200 Kings Hwy 3L
Port Charlotte FL 33980

Call Sign: KK4GBB
David T Manolakos
1940 Kings Hwy 4
Port Charlotte FL 33980

Call Sign: KE4MKI
Lorne M Stone
2100 Kings Hwy 44
Port Charlotte FL 33980

Call Sign: KM4NQ
Jocelyn B Gunn
2100 Kings Hwy 725
Port Charlotte FL
339804243

Call Sign: N4QBO
Anthony Spano
2100 Kings Hwy 750
Port Charlotte FL
339804244

Call Sign: AF4BK
Margaret M Bosiak
2100 Kings Hwy 77
Port Charlotte FL 33980

Call Sign: KM4PY
Larry Rieck
2100 Kings Hwy 845
Port Charlotte FL 33980

Call Sign: N4QPL
Robert W Swirles
2100 Kings Hwy 854
Port Charlotte FL 33980

Call Sign: KN4AX
Harold T Blake
2100 Kings Hwy 867
Port Charlotte FL 33980

Call Sign: KC4AEA
Stanley R Pratt
Kings Hwy L1028
Port Charlotte FL 33980

Call Sign: K1NGC
Carl M Freeman
1000 Kings Hwy Unit 21
Port Charlotte FL 33980

Call Sign: KE4LMQ
Herbert V Stott
2100 Kings Hwy Unit 221
Port Charlotte FL 33980

Call Sign: WA8BQM
Charles R Wiese
1000 Kings Hwy Unit 319
Port Charlotte FL 33952

Call Sign: WB2UBX
Peter Koelemeyer
1000 Kings Hwy Unit 357
Port Charlotte FL 33952

Call Sign: KG4MAH
Leslie Reid
2100 Kings Hwy Unit 358
Maple L
Port Charlotte FL 33980

Call Sign: KG4MAG
Tim A Ramm
2100 Kings Hwy Unit 358
Maple L
Port Charlotte FL 33980

Call Sign: KM4PH
David R Bronson

2100 Kings Hwy Unit 665
Port Charlotte FL 33980

Call Sign: KC4OZL
James F Birch
2100 Kings Hwy Unit 84
Port Charlotte FL 33980

Call Sign: W4YUJ
Preston T Syme
21217 Knollwood Ave
Port Charlotte FL 33952

Call Sign: KG4ORS
Hulbert Cockram
2594 Lake Shore Cir
Port Charlotte FL 33952

Call Sign: KA2QKX
Victor B Callender
2607 Lake View Blvd
Port Charlotte FL 33948

Call Sign: KC4MKB
Georges Brun
365 Lambert St
Port Charlotte FL 33948

Call Sign: AA4ZN
Fred C Sisson
22224 Lancaster Ave
Port Charlotte FL 33952

Call Sign: KI4FAK
Michael K Hillman
22103 Landis Ave
Port Charlotte FL 33954

Call Sign: KC4PMI
Robert P Garneau
2090 Lantern Light St
Port Charlotte FL 33948

Call Sign: KE4ZZG
Kenneth J Starr

15204 Leipzig Cir
Port Charlotte FL 33981

Call Sign: K1FIL
Bernard B Hall
18490 Limberlos Ave
Port Charlotte FL 33948

Call Sign: KI4II
James A Hoffman
556 Lincoln Ave
Port Charlotte FL 33952

Call Sign: N1FFC
Dianne A Evans
584 Lincoln Ave NW
Port Charlotte FL 33952

Call Sign: K1CVP
Richard W Evans
584 Lincoln Ave NW
Port Charlotte FL 33952

Call Sign: KJ4RJZ
Paul J Saur
1061 Live Oak Cir
Port Charlotte FL 33948

Call Sign: WA8ZVJ
Edward C Howe
1162 Live Oak Cir
Port Charlotte FL 33948

Call Sign: KI4DLC
Jack A Ely
738 Lomond Dr
Port Charlotte FL 33953

Call Sign: KF4KHF
Daniel B Davis
13840 Long Lake Ln
Port Charlotte FL 33953

Call Sign: K3QBZ
Paul A Graves Jr

6321 Lori Ter
Port Charlotte FL
339816135

Call Sign: KB1GQW
Sandra A Dobbins
3310 Loveland Blvd Unit
1201
Port Charlotte FL
339806738

Call Sign: N1YEY
William L Dobbins
3310 Loveland Blvd Unit
1201
Port Charlotte FL
339806738

Call Sign: WB8LSV
Barry G Fluxe
1188 Lyle St
Port Charlotte FL
339521312

Call Sign: K8QI
Barry G Fluxe
1188 Lyle St
Port Charlotte FL
339521312

Call Sign: KB2FSL
Patrick J Elligott Jr
1210 Marlow St
Port Charlotte FL 33952

Call Sign: W4NJG
Marie K Manthe
3072 Mauck Ter
Port Charlotte FL 33981

Call Sign: W4NKE
Lucien M Manthe
3072 Mauck Ter
Port Charlotte FL 33981

Call Sign: KB3CNR
Louis B Roberts
585 Mayview Ave
Port Charlotte FL 33952

Call Sign: N8GQE
Kurtis D Truran
316 McCabe St
Port Charlotte FL 33953

Call Sign: KG4VKU
M J Shetron
18917 McGrath Cir
Port Charlotte FL 33948

Call Sign: KD4CMR
Susan M Duncan
23252 McQueeney Ave
Port Charlotte FL 33980

Call Sign: WB3CEB
Stefan E Hyatt
2266 Meetze St
Port Charlotte FL 33953

Call Sign: W4ZT
George A Ralston
4041 Michel Tree St
Port Charlotte FL 33948

Call Sign: W3PED
John W Berninger
3270 Middletown St
Port Charlotte FL
339527230

Call Sign: KF4BXW
Justin F Nichols
19705 Midway Blvd
Port Charlotte FL 33954

Call Sign: KF4YUE
Blaine O Ramsey
19835 Midway Blvd
Port Charlotte FL 33948

Call Sign: K4JDK
Tyrus R J Harris
21173 Midway Blvd
Port Charlotte FL 33952

Call Sign: KE4ZYA
Port Charlotte Junior ARC
23000 Midway Blvd
Port Charlotte FL 33952

Call Sign: KA4USQ
La Ree M Cook
202 Mk Quesada Ave
Port Charlotte FL 33952

Call Sign: KE4ZXM
Bradley T Gavin
1230 Mohawk Dr
Port Charlotte FL 33952

Call Sign: KF4NCO
Glenn A Bond
1293 Mohawk Dr
Port Charlotte FL 33952

Call Sign: AJ4NE
Glenn A Bond
1293 Mohawk Dr
Port Charlotte FL 33952

Call Sign: W4RFV
Tony Levenson
3543 Montgomery Dr
Port Charlotte FL 33981

Call Sign: KI4UPP
John W Leiss
20113 Mt Prospect Ave
Port Charlotte FL 33952

Call Sign: W4CJL
John W Leiss
20113 Mt Prospect Ave
Port Charlotte FL 33952

Call Sign: AC4CV
Gene A Robinson
23251 Mulligan Ave
Port Charlotte FL 33954

Call Sign: KE4JJQ
Gail E Glasspool
23355 Mullins Ave
Port Charlotte FL 33954

Call Sign: KT4MX
Walter O Glasspool
23355 Mullins Ave
Port Charlotte FL 33954

Call Sign: WD4MZV
Raymond R Frey Sr
690 Myra Ln
Port Charlotte FL 33948

Call Sign: KC4FIA
Alfred J Gagnon
142 NE Higgs Dr
Port Charlotte FL 33952

Call Sign: N8FFP
Restituto Antonio
23402 Nelson Ave
Port Charlotte FL
339543708

Call Sign: W4FFP
Restituto Antonio
23402 Nelson Ave
Port Charlotte FL
339543708

Call Sign: K1UU
Harold E Wyer
23494 Nelson Ave
Port Charlotte FL 33954

Call Sign: N4BOK
Carl B Chilldres

4198 Nettle Rd
Port Charlotte FL 33953

Call Sign: N3EPD
Anton E Zarour
2456 Newbury St
Port Charlotte FL 33952

Call Sign: KG4JGT
Howard Bollinger
2522 Newbury St
Port Charlotte FL 33952

Call Sign: K2YWI
Emory G Wall Jr
129 Northshore Ter
Port Charlotte FL 33980

Call Sign: KJ4EBI
Joanne M Mcaleney
3481 Norwick St
Port Charlotte FL 33952

Call Sign: WB2UFR
Robert M Sacilowski
23082 Nugent Ave
Port Charlotte FL
339543549

Call Sign: N1CEN
Oliver C Wilson
1987 Nurenberg Blvd
Port Charlotte FL 33983

Call Sign: N4IKN
Paul A Amodeo Sr
17079 O Hara Dr
Port Charlotte FL 33948

Call Sign: KG4ZPV
George M Cronin
3523 Ogden St
Port Charlotte FL 33948

Call Sign: KC7RFX

Joan Y Svardh
134 Oldenburgh Ct
Port Charlotte FL 33952

Call Sign: KA7AMC
Michael L Svardh
134 Oldenburgh Ct
Port Charlotte FL 33952

Call Sign: K4TDB
Martin E Lee
512 Orange Dr NW
Port Charlotte FL
339525124

Call Sign: K4EEL
Martin E Lee
512 Orange Dr NW
Port Charlotte FL
339525124

Call Sign: WB6NWY
Dennis R Shaw
3315 Osprey Ln
Port Charlotte FL 33953

Call Sign: W9ZCG
Dolan R Delaney
1673 Palace Ct
Port Charlotte FL 33980

Call Sign: KN8G
Donald M Ciccarone
2402 Pappas Ter
Port Charlotte FL 33981

Call Sign: KB4FKB
Richard A Angiolillo
230 Park St
Port Charlotte FL 33952

Call Sign: KA8ELU
Robert C Upham
26158 Paysandu Dr
Port Charlotte FL 33983

Call Sign: WA2HGW
Frederick M Quinn Jr
21309 Peachland Blvd
Port Charlotte FL 33954

Call Sign: W6FFP
Don R Morse
24123 Peachland Blvd
Unit C4 Pmb 312
Port Charlotte FL 33954

Call Sign: KD4AMS
Ronald D Oblinger
2352 Pellam Blvd
Port Charlotte FL 33948

Call Sign: K1IQP
Bernard J Hynes
4202 Perch Cir
Port Charlotte FL 33948

Call Sign: KD4MZD
Phillip B Rollock
117 Percy Ave NW
Port Charlotte FL 33952

Call Sign: KR4HB
John R De Baker
18234 Petoskey Cir
Port Charlotte FL 33948

Call Sign: N1ZJJ
Anthony P Marchetti
771 Phyllis St
Port Charlotte FL
339480000

Call Sign: WI1D
Stephen P Ruggieri
2233 Picnic St
Port Charlotte FL
339524154

Call Sign: WA4SYQ

William R Kadansky
2456 Picnic St
Port Charlotte FL
339524101

Call Sign: K4KKW
John J Mihall
3275 Pinetree St
Port Charlotte FL 33952

Call Sign: KF4MQN
John M Harrington
4311 Point Ct
Port Charlotte FL 33948

Call Sign: N2DLA
W Douglas Howland
3396 Port Charlotte Blvd
Port Charlotte FL 33952

Call Sign: AK4HZ
David P Mcguire
8 Prineville St
Port Charlotte FL 33954

Call Sign: K1WHY
Thomas L Erhardt
22243 Priscilla Ave
Port Charlotte FL 33954

Call Sign: K1SVF
Donald H Nash
1444 Pulaski St
Port Charlotte FL 33952

Call Sign: AB4JR
Arris J Geranis
22477 Quasar Blvd
Port Charlotte FL 33952

Call Sign: KC4DJH
Amy J Schelm
23460 Quasar Blvd
Port Charlotte FL 33980

Call Sign: N8EIB
Betty R Honisko
19505 Quesada 1013
Port Charlotte FL 33948

Call Sign: WO8M
James R Honisko
19505 Quesada 1013
Port Charlotte FL 33948

Call Sign: K4IB
Arie D Cook
20275 Quesada Ave
Port Charlotte FL
339521214

Call Sign: WA3DUX
James C Weaver
21224 Quesada Ave
Port Charlotte FL 33952

Call Sign: KF6DLY
Nicholas J Kurtz
12023 Ramona Ave
Port Charlotte FL 33981

Call Sign: K4VMS
Ricky N Kurtz
12023 Ramona Ave
Port Charlotte FL 33981

Call Sign: W4WZA
Donald B House
24000 Rampart Blvd 7
Port Charlotte FL 33980

Call Sign: K1PIN
Vincent G Caponera
14532 Ransom Ave
Port Charlotte FL 33953

Call Sign: WA8EIF
Stuart D Olbur
1263 Red Oak Ln
Port Charlotte FL 33948

Call Sign: KB9HPO
Paul J Bagby
1581 Red Oak Ln
Port Charlotte FL 33948

Call Sign: KB2TRN
Richard B Mallard
1627 Red Oak Ln
Port Charlotte FL
339483195

Call Sign: W4UGQ
John W Setliffe
20166 Renwick Ave
Port Charlotte FL 33954

Call Sign: W2IYO
David F Lewis
5364 Riley Ln
Port Charlotte FL 33981

Call Sign: KC4CAC
Claude D Marshall
110 Rio De Paz
Port Charlotte FL 33980

Call Sign: KD4UHO
William T Waters
2394 Risken Ter
Port Charlotte FL 33981

Call Sign: WA4MXK
Joseph T Manning Jr
18356 Robinson Ave
Port Charlotte FL 33952

Call Sign: W4INN
David P Senkpiel
505 Rose Apple Cir
Port Charlotte FL 33954

Call Sign: KI4QDW
Oliver U Pioquinto
560 Rose Apple Cir

Port Charlotte FL 33954

Call Sign: KD4MZC
Joseph P Brady
4161 Rosearbor Cr
Port Charlotte FL 33948

Call Sign: KF4IQD
Arthur D Dietz
173 Roselle Ct
Port Charlotte FL 33952

Call Sign: W1OBE
Edwin E Logan
885 Roseway Ter
Port Charlotte FL 33948

Call Sign: WA8BNO
William K Campbell
15556 Ruston Cir
Port Charlotte FL 33981

Call Sign: KG4BRQ
Ivan E Ewers
2000 S Chalkleaf Ct
Port Charlotte FL 33952

Call Sign: KK4LT
Richard G Brown
13435 S McCall Rd 110
Port Charlotte FL 33981

Call Sign: KC4RMQ
Jerry A Smith
1111 Salox
Port Charlotte FL 33952

Call Sign: WD8BXH
Charles F Deuser
222 Santarem Cir
Port Charlotte FL 33983

Call Sign: KJ4CRX
Brian L Carpenter
20439 Sapling Ave

Port Charlotte FL 33952

Call Sign: W4BLC
Brian L Carpenter
20439 Sapling Ave
Port Charlotte FL 33952

Call Sign: N4SBW
Phillip F Totten
10531 Sarasota Rd
Port Charlotte FL
339815168

Call Sign: K9KJH
Phillip F Totten
10531 Sarasota Rd
Port Charlotte FL
339815168

Call Sign: WD8PMB
Frank J Morse
1550 Schenley St
Port Charlotte FL 33952

Call Sign: KJ4ZHZ
William J Morse
1550 Schenley St
Port Charlotte FL 33952

Call Sign: K4IAS
Max H Dunlevy
134 SE Beeney Rd
Port Charlotte FL 33952

Call Sign: KD4ZRP
David Mc Kalip
283 SE Fields Ter
Port Charlotte FL 33952

Call Sign: KC4VMS
Joe Butler Jr
123 SE Graham
Port Charlotte FL 33952

Call Sign: WB4NCL

Bud B Shoup
165 SE Morgan Ln
Port Charlotte FL 33952

Call Sign: N4YIX
Dennis S Walker
104 SE Sinclair
Port Charlotte FL 33952

Call Sign: KC4ERH
Chalmer P Davidson
266 SE Tait Ter
Port Charlotte FL 33952

Call Sign: WA2OLA
Francis K Andrews
17094 Seashore Ave
Port Charlotte FL 33948

Call Sign: KF4FCC
Imelda Andrews
17094 Seashore Ave
Port Charlotte FL 33948

Call Sign: N1TFC
Denis A Dickinson
3480 Seminole Cir
Port Charlotte FL
339535611

Call Sign: W2HGF
Vincent C Patti
182 Severin Rd
Port Charlotte FL 33952

Call Sign: N1MAH
Louis E Nagy
4370 Shappell St
Port Charlotte FL 33948

Call Sign: K4EJV
Larrie A Eckman
17340 Shirley Ave
Port Charlotte FL 33948

Call Sign: W3TPW
Elbert H Van Houten
7563 Silage Cir
Port Charlotte FL
339812642

Call Sign: KE4NOU
Joseph D Pepe
931 Silver Sprgs Ter
Port Charlotte FL 33948

Call Sign: AJ4SX
Bernard Barink
9444 Singer Cir
Port Charlotte FL 33981

Call Sign: KA4ARO
Rickey L Hobbs
9286 Snapper Cir
Port Charlotte FL 33981

Call Sign: W3EZG
Gilbert G Borkenhagen
2345 Sofia Ln
Port Charlotte FL 33983

Call Sign: KD4SEN
John D Liggett
250 Spring Lake Blvd
Port Charlotte FL 33952

Call Sign: N4SWI
Jerry D Oglesby
3063 St James St
Port Charlotte FL 33952

Call Sign: KC4NUX
Aldo A Di Salvo
1486 Stamford St
Port Charlotte FL 33952

Call Sign: WA4KEF
Fred J Diedrick
504 Starlite Ln
Port Charlotte FL 33952

Call Sign: KI4YCX
Scott A Rhea
2565 Starlite Ln
Port Charlotte FL 33952

Call Sign: NK3H
Scott A Rhea
2565 Starlite Ln
Port Charlotte FL 33952

Call Sign: KG4OVF
Robert A Clark
2733 Starlite Ln
Port Charlotte FL 33952

Call Sign: K4KLQ
Dennis J Lazar
227 Stebbins Ter
Port Charlotte FL 33952

Call Sign: W4DNN
Dennis J Lazar
227 Stebbins Ter
Port Charlotte FL 33952

Call Sign: KJ4KPE
Ruth S Lazar
227 Stebbins Ter
Port Charlotte FL 33952

Call Sign: K4KLQ
Ruth S Lazar
227 Stebbins Ter
Port Charlotte FL 33952

Call Sign: KA4AWJ
Ray O Riddle
239 Stebbins Ter SE
Port Charlotte FL 33952

Call Sign: KA4AWK
Virginia E Riddle
239 Stebbins Ter SE
Port Charlotte FL 33952

Call Sign: KE4IUZ
Richard S Werley Jr
Stillwater Ave
Port Charlotte FL 33980

Call Sign: N8TVC
Gary R Chatfield
1010 Strasberg Dr
Port Charlotte FL
339521662

Call Sign: N8FEW
James S Karafa
2419 Suffolk St
Port Charlotte FL 33948

Call Sign: WA4DHF
Paul M Ignozza
337 Sunrise Ter
Port Charlotte FL 33952

Call Sign: KB4ISL
Elwood C Macgowan
23411 Superior Ave
Port Charlotte FL 33954

Call Sign: N4TMT
Robert Christiano
134 SW Colonial St
Port Charlotte FL 33952

Call Sign: KG4FRX
Joseph G Perez
128 SW Leland St
Port Charlotte FL 33952

Call Sign: KA4UHR
Michael E Draus
115 SW Peckham
Port Charlotte FL 33952

Call Sign: KF4IQC
J W Byrd
138 SW Seville Pl

Port Charlotte FL 33952

Call Sign: KF4HWG
John L Markwalter Jr
23301 Swallow Ave
Port Charlotte FL
339542548

Call Sign: WA6IKF
Gary K Gordon
4473 Sweetbay St
Port Charlotte FL 33948

Call Sign: KD4UTX
Devon Gardner
290 Tait Ter
Port Charlotte FL 33952

Call Sign: KD4UTY
Ron Hebert
290 Tait Ter
Port Charlotte FL 33952

Call Sign: KJ4LMR
Edgar W Buebel
3821 Tamiami Trl
Port Charlotte FL 33952

Call Sign: KN6XE
Benjamin J Rubright
Tamiami Trl
Port Charlotte FL 33952

Call Sign: KE1DC
Robert N March
214 Taunt St
Port Charlotte FL 33948

Call Sign: WD4LSD
Russell Hickman
22216 Tennyson Ave
Port Charlotte FL 33954

Call Sign: WD4DAF
Bobbie A Hickman

22216 Tennyson Ave
Port Charlotte FL
339543463

Call Sign: WX4DDH
David D Harris
2090 Torrence St
Port Charlotte FL 33948

Call Sign: K9MZN
Charles W Coulter
130 Valdiva St
Port Charlotte FL 33983

Call Sign: AF4KA
Fred Lopez
18303 Van Nuys Cir
Port Charlotte FL 33948

Call Sign: KE4FTX
David F Pray
20360 Vanguard Ter
Port Charlotte FL 33954

Call Sign: KD4PDJ
Carl C Grizzaffi
25383 Vantage Ln
Port Charlotte FL 33983

Call Sign: KE4RJY
Ken C Southwell
336 Waterside
Port Charlotte FL 33954

Call Sign: KG4MJM
Daniel A Wharton
488 Waterside St
Port Charlotte FL 33954

Call Sign: K4QCA
Ethel M Stover
22441 Westchester Blv Bd
1500 Apt A
Port Charlotte FL 33980

Call Sign: W4QC
Nelson K Stover
22441 Westchester Blv Bd
1500 Apt A
Port Charlotte FL 33980

Call Sign: KB1DQX
Edward A Grafton
22325 Westchester Blvd
Port Charlotte FL 33980

Call Sign: KA4AWU
Ruth M Long
22426 Westchester Blvd
Port Charlotte FL 33980

Call Sign: KA4AWT
William H Long
22426 Westchester Blvd
Port Charlotte FL 33980

Call Sign: W8AI
Frank T Lenc
23013 Westchester Blvd
Port Charlotte FL 33980

Call Sign: W4BEW
Elmer G Leachman
23033 Westchester Blvd
Port Charlotte FL 33980

Call Sign: WB4ITH
Walter F Hoettels
23033 Westchester Blvd
Port Charlotte FL 33980

Call Sign: AB4PL
Samuel R Curry
23033 Westchester Blvd
Apt C402
Port Charlotte FL 33980

Call Sign: WD4CUA
Harold W Hayward

23033 Westchester Blvd
Apt F508
Port Charlotte FL 33980

Call Sign: KA4CCC
Barbara C Howe
23053 Westchester Blvd
Apt R413
Port Charlotte FL 33980

Call Sign: WD4NSP
Jack L Howe
23053 Westchester Blvd
Apt R413
Port Charlotte FL 33980

Call Sign: K4XB
Robert C Allison
23033 Westchester Blvd C
412
Port Charlotte FL 33980

Call Sign: KI4GC
Leonard H Loufek
23033 Westchester Blvd
D316
Port Charlotte FL 33980

Call Sign: K4KNM
Lester C Berger
23033 Westchester Blvd
F203
Port Charlotte FL 33980

Call Sign: W8KQX
Robert L Pinkstaff
23033 Westchester Blvd
F302
Port Charlotte FL 33980

Call Sign: KN4BN
David G Weaver
23160 Wicker Ave
Port Charlotte FL 33980

Call Sign: N4XMB
Harriet C Weaver
23160 Wicker Ave
Port Charlotte FL 33980

Call Sign: KD4OMS
Kathryn F Wilson
7408 Widness Ln
Port Charlotte FL 33981

Call Sign: KI4CFB
William G Rudolph
11357 Willis Pl
Port Charlotte FL 33981

Call Sign: N2LRS
Donald W Hain
18033 Wing Ave
Port Charlotte FL
339489313

Call Sign: AK4NE
Donald W Hain
18033 Wing Ave
Port Charlotte FL
339489313

Call Sign: N8EQU
Catherine A Robertson
4256 Wood Duck Rd
Port Charlotte FL 33953

Call Sign: KG4SGG
James W Scanlon
2433 Woodyglen St
Port Charlotte FL 33948

Call Sign: AF4IS
Brice Jean Pierre
15216 Wymore Ave
Port Charlotte FL 33953

Call Sign: N4YEU
John E Wiseman
2200 Yeoman Ct

Port Charlotte FL 33983

Call Sign: KI4UAY
Robert C Hogue
1401 Yorkshir St
Port Charlotte FL 33952

Call Sign: KB4YL
Jeanne W Spica
1354 Yorkshire St
Port Charlotte FL 33952

Call Sign: AG4G
Robert A Spica
1354 Yorkshire St
Port Charlotte FL 33952

Call Sign: K2IIY
Donald A Duane
Port Charlotte FL 33949

Call Sign: KC4VTL
Walter G Henriksen
Port Charlotte FL 33949

Call Sign: W4WUN
George H Puterbaugh
Port Charlotte FL 33949

Call Sign: AA6JU
Karl H Berger
Port Charlotte FL 33949

FCC Amateur Radio Licenses in Punta Gorda

Call Sign: K8OST
Russell G Johnson
5840 Acla Vista Ln
Punta Gorda FL 33950

Call Sign: KD3KN
Arthur R Hinman
24300 Airport Rd Lot 166
Punta Gorda FL 33950

Call Sign: KD4PZQ
Julius L Forte
24300 Airport Rd Lot 50
Punta Gorda FL 33950

Call Sign: KB2PPN
Joseph M Kuzmiak II
8330 Alan Blvd
Punta Gorda FL 33982

Call Sign: KK4HQB
John Florit III
7243 Allamanda Ln
Punta Gorda FL 33955

Call Sign: K1AY
Christopher L Hallinan
4429 Almar Dr
Punta Gorda FL
339507796

Call Sign: KG4DSM
William B Clift
4710 Almar Dr
Punta Gorda FL
339507708

Call Sign: KE4GKJ
Andrew G Campbell
4510 Alta Vista Dr
Punta Gorda FL 33950

Call Sign: N4ISN
Dorothy M Campbell
4510 Alta Vista Dr
Punta Gorda FL 33950

Call Sign: KA8FFF
Lawrence E Fournier
26503 Angelica Rd
Punta Gorda FL
339550000

Call Sign: KT4EK

James P Forensky
3206 Antigua Dr
Punta Gorda FL 33950

Call Sign: KF4PXO
Maureen D Morris
3206 Antigua Dr
Punta Gorda FL 33950

Call Sign: KI4WGX
Frank J Kavanaugh
3306 Antigua Dr
Punta Gorda FL
339506370

Call Sign: KC6QWK
Joseph F Juiliano
1431 Aqui Esta 321
Punta Gorda FL 33950

Call Sign: KG4MSC
Tracie G Juiliano
1431 Aqui Esta 321
Punta Gorda FL 33950

Call Sign: K7CXW
Geahardt R Woster
1510 Aqui Esta Dr
Punta Gorda FL 33950

Call Sign: KB9UGB
John E Kelly III
2245 Aqui Esta Dr
Punta Gorda FL 33950

Call Sign: W1YVF
Harold N Gunther
2285 Aqui Esta Dr
Punta Gorda FL 33950

Call Sign: KJ4OIY
Raymond Negrycz
10191 Arrowhead Dr
Punta Gorda FL 33955

Call Sign: K2ZTQ
William D Kelly
10323 Arrowhead Dr
Punta Gorda FL 33955

Call Sign: NP2AO
Lawrence A Kurtz
10327 Arrowhead Dr
Punta Gorda FL 33955

Call Sign: WA2HTU
Albert L Shuhart Jr
3664 Aruba Ct
Punta Gorda FL
339508120

Call Sign: K4CPX
Stephen J Crow
3824 Aves Island
Punta Gorda FL 33950

Call Sign: KC1KE
Walter H Robertson
25170 Aysen Dr
Punta Gorda FL 33983

Call Sign: N9GHS
Gary J Berger
25932 Aysen Dr
Punta Gorda FL 33983

Call Sign: KF9DN
Charles C Veenstra
1133 Bal Harbor 1139
Punta Gorda FL 33950

Call Sign: W9YWR
Everett A Johnson Jr
777 Bal Harbor Blvd
Punta Gorda FL 33950

Call Sign: N4HPY
Barbara R Holland
801 Bal Harbor Blvd
Punta Gorda FL 33950

Call Sign: N4ALM
Clarence E Holland
801 Bal Harbor Blvd
Punta Gorda FL
339506509

Call Sign: KB9FJI
Helen I Veenstra
1133 Bal Harbor Blvd
1139
Punta Gorda FL 33950

Call Sign: WA7WPX
Bobby J Ward Jr
1133 Bal Harbor Blvd
1139 Pmb215
Punta Gorda FL 33950

Call Sign: N4TIX
Arthur J Anderson
1139 Bal Harbor Blvd 121
Punta Gorda FL 33950

Call Sign: N4ILJ
Jeanne T Anderson
1139 Bal Harbor Blvd 121
Punta Gorda FL 33950

Call Sign: KD4AO
Robert B Townsend
3640 Bal Harbor Blvd 313
Punta Gorda FL 33950

Call Sign: WA2MTS
Benjamin J Rubright
1133 Bal Harbor Blvd Ste
1139 309
Punta Gorda FL
339506574

Call Sign: KE4AOY
Robert M Stiffler
3830 Bal Harbor Blvd Unit
1

Punta Gorda FL 33950

Call Sign: N3TJG
Albert J Wiker
2000 Bal Harbor Blvd Unit
1021
Punta Gorda FL 33950

Call Sign: W4ONP
Howard L Grim
250 Bal Harbor Blvd Unit
113
Punta Gorda FL 33950

Call Sign: N3SUL
Paula Golden
3640 Bal Harbor Blvd Unit
525
Punta Gorda FL 33950

Call Sign: N3SUJ
Peter T Golden
3640 Bal Harbor Blvd Unit
525
Punta Gorda FL 33950

Call Sign: KF4CXD
Charles G Kindle
24238 Balearic Ln
Punta Gorda FL
339554015

Call Sign: N3DP
Donald A Pettross
315 Barcelona St
Punta Gorda FL
339835719

Call Sign: W3RMP
Rosabelle M Pettross
315 Barcelona St
Punta Gorda FL
339835719

Call Sign: N2XUW

Rebecca L Stockslager
25417 Barinas Dr
Punta Gorda FL 33983

Call Sign: N9WS
William E Stockslager
25417 Barinas Dr
Punta Gorda FL 33983

Call Sign: W2ESG
Larry C Schrader
4030 Bastia Ct
Punta Gorda FL 33950

Call Sign: N4QHQ
Mildred S Work
2755 Bay Ct
Punta Gorda FL 33950

Call Sign: N4KPW
Richard B Work
2755 Bay Ct
Punta Gorda FL 33950

Call Sign: KE4ADB
Penelope L Stiffler
3830 Bay Harbor Blvd
Unit 1
Punta Gorda FL 33950

Call Sign: WB2GIA
Paul F Lansing
2194 Bayou Rd
Punta Gorda FL 33950

Call Sign: AF4UQ
Paul F Lansing
2194 Bayou Rd
Punta Gorda FL 33950

Call Sign: N4SGA
Stanley B Smith Jr
135 Bayshore Ct
Punta Gorda FL 33950

Call Sign: W2DLK
Robert C Mc Intyre
2290 Bayview Rd
Punta Gorda FL 33950

Call Sign: KB8HL
Robert E Seltzer
2299 Bayview Rd
Punta Gorda FL 33850

Call Sign: KB8WCO
William E Atkinson
290 Belaire Ct
Punta Gorda FL 33950

Call Sign: WA4QPM
Robert J Walters
1719 Belle Ct
Punta Gorda FL 33950

Call Sign: K3YUN
Angelo J Drammissi
16446 Belo Ct
Punta Gorda FL 33955

Call Sign: K9BBT
Richard C Dickenshied
555 Belvedere Ct
Punta Gorda FL 33952

Call Sign: K4CR
Sherwood G Espenschied
33400 Bermont Rd
Punta Gorda FL
339829509

Call Sign: KF4BNA
Kenneth B Derr
46900 Bermont Unit 17
Punta Gorda FL 33982

Call Sign: KD4NBJ
James J Larkin Jr
3829 Bermuda Ct
Punta Gorda FL 33950

Call Sign: KC4PGP
James A Jones
122 Berry St
Punta Gorda FL 33950

Call Sign: KC0KDP
Cynthia S Harden
2057 Big Pass Ln
Punta Gorda FL 33955

Call Sign: KC0KDS
Ray Harden III
2057 Big Pass Ln
Punta Gorda FL 33955

Call Sign: K4TSL
Elwood P Sheetz
3065 Big Pass Ln
Punta Gorda FL 33955

Call Sign: WA2JGA
John F Quest
4032 Big Pass Ln
Punta Gorda FL 33955

Call Sign: W3WWQ
Carol A Ester
1857 Bimingham Blvd
Punta Gorda FL 33980

Call Sign: W3WQ
Kenneth R Ester
1857 Birmingham Blvd
Punta Gorda FL 33980

Call Sign: WA2TMN
Walter W Weisspfennig
24180 Blackbeard Blvd
Punta Gorda FL 33955

Call Sign: W8RKW
Burt F Reiniger
5205 Blackjack Cir
Punta Gorda FL 33982

Call Sign: KZ4K
Hans K Reiniger
5205 Blackjack Cir
Punta Gorda FL 33982

Call Sign: KB9JPP
Dan O May
1356 Blue Lake Cir
Punta Gorda FL
339835950

Call Sign: K8TT
Louis C Graue
1501 Blue Lake Cir
Punta Gorda FL
339835987

Call Sign: KF4GEK
Steven E Speer
161 Bodine St
Punta Gorda FL 33982

Call Sign: KD4UOJ
Patricia Poole
12052 Borax Ave
Punta Gorda FL 33955

Call Sign: KD4UND
Richard C Poole
12052 Borax Ave
Punta Gorda FL 33955

Call Sign: K4STL
Earl E Bates Jr
Box 801 Sunset Rd
Punta Gorda FL 33982

Call Sign: KJ4GPY
Elizabeth J Lambert
115 Breakers Ct 113
Punta Gorda FL 33950

Call Sign: W2KJJ
George B Riley

2391 Bremen Ct
Punta Gorda FL 33983

Call Sign: WA9NWX
Inez M Miller
10303 Burnt Store Rd 12
Punta Gorda FL 33950

Call Sign: N9CLW
Cliff L Stanis
10100 Burnt Store Rd 136
Punta Gorda FL 33950

Call Sign: KA3WDC
Frank L Blankenbuehler
15550 Burnt Store Rd 167
Punta Gorda FL 33955

Call Sign: KA9HPO
Gerald E Misener
15550 Burnt Store Rd Lot
45
Punta Gorda FL 33955

Call Sign: NZ1Y
Brad G Charbonneau
2162 Calcutta Rd
Punta Gorda FL 33983

Call Sign: WA2LCN
George J Porth Jr
1238 Canvasback Ct
Punta Gorda FL 33950

Call Sign: WN4YFD
George J Porth Jr
1238 Canvasback Ct
Punta Gorda FL 33950

Call Sign: NY4FD
George J Porth Jr
1238 Canvasback Ct
Punta Gorda FL 33950

Call Sign: WB2FYM

Carole G Polansky
1241 Canvasback Ct
Punta Gorda FL 33950

Call Sign: W2UIO
Edwin H Polansky
1241 Canvasback Ct
Punta Gorda FL 33950

Call Sign: N4ILN
Leonard Greene
1241 Canvasback Ct
Punta Gorda FL 33950

Call Sign: KC4JLO
Carl F Lannquist
300 Capri Isles Ct
Punta Gorda FL 33950

Call Sign: W8HTD
Wyatt E Mc Daniel
351 Capri Isles Ct
Punta Gorda FL 33950

Call Sign: KB3EAA
Jerry D Beard
Capricorn Blvd
Punta Gorda FL 33983

Call Sign: KB3GYO
Tara M Beard
Capricorn Blvd
Punta Gorda FL 33983

Call Sign: N6BUN
Roman A Sicho
24271 Captain Kidd Blvd
Punta Gorda FL 33955

Call Sign: N3RWK
Ruth E Kliment
1429 Casey Key Dr
Punta Gorda FL 33950

Call Sign: W3HZM

Joseph J Kliment
1429 Casey Key Dr
Punta Gorda FL 33950

Call Sign: WB4BEX
Richard M Manning
97 Castile Ct
Punta Gorda FL 33983

Call Sign: KB4MF
Joseph D Doyle
25169 Chiclayo Ave
Punta Gorda FL 33983

Call Sign: KG4NKP
James H Plummer
29295 Clark Dr
Punta Gorda FL 33982

Call Sign: KE4ZXL
Thomas K Crawford
29528 Clark Dr
Punta Gorda FL 33950

Call Sign: KB1EXX
Peter E Pitcher
27495 Cleveland Ave
Punta Gorda FL 33982

Call Sign: KJ4SMI
Thomas M Fischer
2709 Clyde Ave
Punta Gorda FL 33950

Call Sign: KA9QHF
Don G Coumbe
108 Colony Point Dr
Punta Gorda FL 33950

Call Sign: WA0JRO
Jan D Vanden Bergh
1 Colony Point Dr Unit
11C
Punta Gorda FL 33950

Call Sign: W9UYE
Gilbert C Hermeling Jr
1315 Columbian Dr
Punta Gorda FL 33950

Call Sign: WB2JOQ
James B Kantor
1318 Columbian Dr
Punta Gorda FL 33950

Call Sign: KJ4VDM
Lawrence J Mcdonough Sr
17370 Comingo Ln
Punta Gorda FL
339554448

Call Sign: AD4ZG
Louis M Aceti
26312 Copiapo Cir
Punta Gorda FL 33983

Call Sign: K8PUA
James E Hicks
26417 Copiapo Cir
Punta Gorda FL 33983

Call Sign: KB4ZQW
Todd M Puglise
460 Coronado Dr
Punta Gorda FL 33950

Call Sign: K8BTN
John D De Groot
140 Crescent Dr
Punta Gorda FL 33950

Call Sign: K4GPD
James A Bolliger
163 Crescent Dr
Punta Gorda FL 33950

Call Sign: WB4GPD
James A Bolliger
163 Crescent Dr

Punta Gorda FL
339505112

Call Sign: AA6WP
Dianne K Brooks
182 Crescent Dr
Punta Gorda FL 33950

Call Sign: N6VHI
Kenneth M Brooks
182 Crescent Dr
Punta Gorda FL
339505113

Call Sign: KI5TG
Lionel Seard
136 Cuiaba Dr
Punta Gorda FL 33983

Call Sign: WA3VQL
Robert C Moore
780 Deauville Dr
Punta Gorda FL 33950

Call Sign: K3KES
Thomas G Kessler
2200 Deborah Dr
Punta Gorda FL 33950

Call Sign: KC4RUJ
Charles G Sleichter Jr
2625 Deborah Dr
Punta Gorda FL 33950

Call Sign: N4XKG
Clarice J Forbes
1780 Deborah Dr 14
Punta Gorda FL 33950

Call Sign: N8JDB
James R Griffith
1890 Deborah Dr 2
Punta Gorda FL 33950

Call Sign: N8JDC

Margery B Griffith
1890 Deborah Dr 2
Punta Gorda FL 33956

Call Sign: K2ANK
Albert E Charters
1890 Deborah Dr 30
Punta Gorda FL
339508163

Call Sign: N4LYA
Carl P Mc Crillis
750 Del Ray Pl
Punta Gorda FL 33950

Call Sign: K4IRO
William G Chace
381 Delido Ct
Punta Gorda FL 33950

Call Sign: KB4TRN
Carolyn J De Bray
3463 Desoto Dr
Punta Gorda FL
339833525

Call Sign: K4KRJ
Thomas H De Bray
3463 Desoto Dr
Punta Gorda FL
339833525

Call Sign: WB2UKO
Joseph J Milazzo
3512 Di Leuca St
Punta Gorda FL
339507834

Call Sign: N3APH
Morton R Fleishman
3341 Diamond Key Ct
Punta Gorda FL 33955

Call Sign: KG9KB
Dean P Ayars

3530 Dipper Ct
Punta Gorda FL 33950

Call Sign: KI4EUK
Leo Hilke
257 Divinci Dr
Punta Gorda FL 33950

Call Sign: KC4YUD
James M Keir
26070 Dolman Ct
Punta Gorda FL 33983

Call Sign: KK4IDS
James T Bever
930 Don Juan Ct
Punta Gorda FL 33950

Call Sign: W4ZGD
James L Cadien
2809 Don Quixote Dr
Punta Gorda FL
339506351

Call Sign: N0EES
Ruth J Beye
2849 Don Quixote Dr
Punta Gorda FL 33950

Call Sign: KD4EII
Freddie T Clark
2853 Don Quixote Dr
Punta Gorda FL 33950

Call Sign: KD4EIH
Tom R Clark
2853 Don Quixote Dr
Punta Gorda FL 33950

Call Sign: KC4IXX
Patrick D Behr
120 Donna Ct
Punta Gorda FL 33950

Call Sign: WZ9L

Basil Willis Jr
3426 Dover Dr
Punta Gorda FL 33983

Call Sign: KC4LVA
Bonnie A Willis
3426 Dover Dr
Punta Gorda FL 33983

Call Sign: KM4XA
Richard A Warfel Jr
5601 Duncan Rd Lot 51
Punta Gorda FL 33982

Call Sign: KG4CLJ
Robert G Mason
411 E Grace St
Punta Gorda FL 33950

Call Sign: KA7NMB
John H Shields
25188 E Marion 47
Punta Gorda FL 33950

Call Sign: N8DVJ
John P Nehs
25188 E Marion C101
Punta Gorda FL 33950

Call Sign: KA4AEP
Victor H Campbell Jr
116 E Mc Kenzie St
Punta Gorda FL 33950

Call Sign: KH6LF
Parker N Blaney
2140 El Cerito Ct
Punta Gorda FL 33950

Call Sign: KI4SDE
Robert P Gosser Jr
617 Eleuthera Dr
Punta Gorda FL
339505836

Call Sign: W4RPG
Robert P Gosser Jr
617 Eleuthera Dr
Punta Gorda FL
339505836

Call Sign: W9NWY
David P Boland
712 Elisa Dr
Punta Gorda FL 33950

Call Sign: KA9CYD
Leona G Boland
712 Elisa Dr
Punta Gorda FL
339508024

Call Sign: WB4DSG
Ben E Pitts
624 Encarnacion St
Punta Gorda FL 33983

Call Sign: KT3TV
Roy C Pollitt
27031 Fairway Dr Unit A
Punta Gorda FL 33982

Call Sign: KJ4WZG
Michael C Williamson
26131 Feathersound Dr
Punta Gorda FL 33955

Call Sign: WA2ZHN
Eugene R Fiorot
26310 Feathersound Dr
Punta Gorda FL 33955

Call Sign: KF4PVA
Mary E Dixon
2463 Flora Ln
Punta Gorda FL 33950

Call Sign: KB9HKJ
William J Dixon
2463 Flora Ln

Punta Gorda FL 33950

Call Sign: KI4WHB
James W Beliveau
Garvin St
Punta Gorda FL 33950

Call Sign: N4FLG
Julian J Piurkowski
16085 Goldenrod Dr
Punta Gorda FL 33955

Call Sign: N3BEU
Donna J Chadburn
6800 Golf Course Blvd
E46
Punta Gorda FL 33982

Call Sign: K3JRO
Arthur R Chadburn
6800 Golf Course Bv E46
Punta Gorda FL 33982

Call Sign: AE4EV
Herman E Bandy Jr
4750 Green Woods Ct
Punta Gorda FL 33982

Call Sign: K0RTU
Kenneth J Van Patten
3321 Grenada Ct
Punta Gorda FL 33950

Call Sign: KB2KDE
Paul E Kennedy
3329 Grenada Ct
Punta Gorda FL
339506373

Call Sign: KF4LHQ
James C Rioux
2260 Gulfview Rd
Punta Gorda FL 33950

Call Sign: KE4UHT

John B Masters
2280 Gultview
Punta Gorda FL 33450

Call Sign: N2ALI
Vincent F Scotto
23465 Harborview Rd 634
Punta Gorda FL 33980

Call Sign: K4VFS
Vincent F Scotto
23465 Harborview Rd 634
Punta Gorda FL 33980

Call Sign: KB2EQ
Warren G Williams Sr
3055 Heights Ter
Punta Gorda FL 33983

Call Sign: W9RED
Eugene M Leazenby
115 Hibiscus Dr
Punta Gorda FL 33950

Call Sign: KE4EC
Donald E Frazier
135 Hibiscus Dr
Punta Gorda FL 33950

Call Sign: N4FWU
Marlis F Frazier
135 Hibiscus Dr
Punta Gorda FL 33950

Call Sign: KI4PYL
Marlis F Frazier
135 Hibiscus Dr
Punta Gorda FL 33950

Call Sign: K8CRX
Jimmy M Quail
178 Hilbish Dr
Punta Gorda FL
339828305

Call Sign: KG4NNL
Kevin P Chartrand
12460 Himalaya Ave
Punta Gorda FL
339552336

Call Sign: KJ4BPR
Octagon Wildlife
Sanctuary
41660 Horseshoe Acres Rd
Punta Gorda FL 33982

Call Sign: KA4ICG
Charles E Brown
1850 Hunter Creek Dr
Punta Gorda FL 33982

Call Sign: KE4AX
Owen C Wimpee
4007 Iola Ave
Punta Gorda FL 33982

Call Sign: KA2NGA
Leslie J Lev
1000 Islamorada Blvd
Punta Gorda FL 33955

Call Sign: N9WJN
John C Rue Sr
1201 Islamorada Blvd
Punta Gorda FL 33955

Call Sign: KJ4YYT
Louis L Hemphill
1307 Islamorada Blvd
Punta Gorda FL 33955

Call Sign: WB9VQD
Arthur W Komarek
1617 Islamorada Blvd
Punta Gorda FL
339551824

Call Sign: KK4BGU
Roderick B Brennan

801 Islamorada Blvd 25 A
Punta Gorda FL 33955

Call Sign: KD4SAX
Gerald P Tremblay
1373 Jacana Ct
Punta Gorda FL 33950

Call Sign: K4JUQ
James E Paul Jr
2005 Jamaica Way
Punta Gorda FL 33950

Call Sign: W4GYL
Lydia Quast
24119 Jolly Roger Blvd
Punta Gorda FL 33955

Call Sign: KH7EM
Eulalia P Hayden
27205 Jones Loop Rd Lot
9
Punta Gorda FL
339822381

Call Sign: K9ZFQ
Charles E Schenk
27110 Jones Loop Rd Unit
115
Punta Gorda FL
339822466

Call Sign: KJ4CIS
Wesley O Niccolls Jr
27110 Jones Loop Rd Unit
153
Punta Gorda FL 33982

Call Sign: WP4EKY
Bernardo Gonzalez
Valentin
27110 Jones Loop Rd Unit
163
Punta Gorda FL 33982

Call Sign: W2KDS
Kenneth D Sassadeck
1462 Kedron Ln
Punta Gorda FL 33983

Call Sign: KG4BSH
Donald C Ulrich
5061 Key Largo Cir
Punta Gorda FL
339554617

Call Sign: N4VVC
Thomas F Little
5035 Key Largo Dr
Punta Gorda FL 33950

Call Sign: N4RFU
Richard Greenwald
5077 Key Largo Dr
Punta Gorda FL 33950

Call Sign: KJ4TLM
Freerk (Frederick) S Vleer
4071 Key Largo Ln
Punta Gorda FL 33955

Call Sign: K4FSV
Freerk (Frederick) S Vleer
4071 Key Largo Ln
Punta Gorda FL 33955

Call Sign: W4PLL
Doyle D Thompson Sr
1546 Kinglet Dr
Punta Gorda FL 33950

Call Sign: KC4OVJ
John J Beamish
Kings Hwy
Punta Gorda FL 33980

Call Sign: KD4RLX
Harold M Kneller Jr
300 Klispie Dr

Punta Gorda FL
339504016

Call Sign: KG4WTQ
Julius Ehland
3929 La Costa Isl Ct
Punta Gorda FL
339508115

Call Sign: KG4CMY
Ann Z Shapiro
4090 La Costa Island Ct
Punta Gorda FL 33950

Call Sign: KG4CMX
Martin L Shapiro
4090 La Costa Island Ct
Punta Gorda FL 33950

Call Sign: WB8LHN
Eloise M Howe
2814 La Mancha Ct
Punta Gorda FL 33950

Call Sign: K2MLG
Bruce M Tompkins
2829 La Mancha Ct
Punta Gorda FL 33950

Call Sign: KB3DQL
Barry O Jollett
1120 La Salina Ct
Punta Gorda FL 33950

Call Sign: KD4SEO
Alric S Sutherland
805 La Villa Rd
Punta Gorda FL 33950

Call Sign: KI4RUS
Stephen D Summers
2130 La Villa Rd
Punta Gorda FL 33950

Call Sign: KF2A

Stuart C Pullen Jr
27491 Las Lomas Dr
Punta Gorda FL 33955

Call Sign: KA5YLM
Ginny Lea Duba
1303 Lindsay Ave
Punta Gorda FL 33982

Call Sign: N4RUJ
William C Seiberling
2795 Luna Ct
Punta Gorda FL 33950

Call Sign: AB4NO
Warren R Butler
26058 Luzon Ct Deep
Creek
Punta Gorda FL 33983

Call Sign: KJ4TMI
Robert G Fritz
571 Macedonia Dr
Punta Gorda FL 33950

Call Sign: K4RGF
Robert G Fritz
571 Macedonia Dr
Punta Gorda FL 33950

Call Sign: K4DES
David E Schall
619 Madrid Blvd
Punta Gorda FL 33950

Call Sign: WA6UEW
Martin E Tryon
3925 Madrid Ct
Punta Gorda FL 33950

Call Sign: W4WAZ
Martin E Tryon
3925 Madrid Ct
Punta Gorda FL 33950

Call Sign: KE4HFP
Marjorie L Noragon
9348 Mandy St
Punta Gorda FL 33982

Call Sign: KB4NOY
Conrad L Johnson
15553 Mapletree Dr
Punta Gorda FL
339551230

Call Sign: KA8UIF
Darla F Griswold
15490 Mapletree Ter
Punta Gorda FL 33955

Call Sign: KI4KHV
Daniel P Schaaf Sr
282 Maraca St
Punta Gorda FL 33983

Call Sign: WD8CCD
William H Rigby III
1310 Marathon Way
Punta Gorda FL 33955

Call Sign: KA1QMB
Eric K Woods
122 Maria Ct
Punta Gorda FL 33950

Call Sign: KG4SYB
Craig S Harger
25306 Marilia Dr
Punta Gorda FL
339835548

Call Sign: K0CSH
Craig S Harger
25306 Marilia Dr
Punta Gorda FL
339835548

Call Sign: K1BWT
Leonard F Poor

25188 Marion Ave F406
Punta Gorda FL 33951

Call Sign: N0AXQ
Frank C Gass
2821 Marlin Ct
Punta Gorda FL 33950

Call Sign: KG4KQW
Kenneth H Johnson
2049 Matecombe Key Rd
Punta Gorda FL 33955

Call Sign: KC8HZV
Margaret S Gutmann
2031 Matecumbe Key Rd
Punta Gorda FL
339554641

Call Sign: KD4GIL
Jami A Huppert
3150 Matecumbe Key Rd
Punta Gorda FL 33955

Call Sign: KB3MMC
David A Henry
3192 Matecumbe Key Rd
Punta Gorda FL 33955

Call Sign: KA8IGY
Robert E Gutmann Jr
2031 Matecumbe Key Rd
Punta Gorda FL 33955

Call Sign: KF4BXV
Harold W Howard
2731 Mayaguana Ct
Punta Gorda FL 33950

Call Sign: KG4MUS
Stanley W Davis Jr
507 Mayseilles Ct
Punta Gorda FL
339508030

Call Sign: K4VG
Russell J Schmidt
522 Medici Ct
Punta Gorda FL 33950

Call Sign: KI4NTB
Mary A Sanders
1344 Mediterranean Dr
121
Punta Gorda FL 33950

Call Sign: KI4USO
Rhonda K Lambie
12199 Minnesota Ave
Punta Gorda FL 33955

Call Sign: N4XJQ
Thomas A Lambie
12199 Minnesota Ave
Punta Gorda FL 33955

Call Sign: W0QBT
John R Nagel
384 Monaco Dr
Punta Gorda FL 33950

Call Sign: W8PCQ
James H Anderson
500 Monaco Dr
Punta Gorda FL 33950

Call Sign: N8XDG
William C Bareither
3530 Mondovi Ct 122
Punta Gorda FL 33950

Call Sign: W9JTB
William K Zeithammer
1111 Muscovie Ct
Punta Gorda FL 33950

Call Sign: N4ZNU
Jim E Cassell
1905 Myrtle Ave
Punta Gorda FL 33950

Call Sign: K4BLS
John E Brewer
7206 N Blue Sage St
Punta Gorda FL
339551104

Call Sign: K2IIN
Robert L Krieg
95 N Marion Ct 223
Punta Gorda FL 33950

Call Sign: WD4DXT
Maurice A O Donnell
819 Napoli Ln
Punta Gorda FL 33950

Call Sign: W4OGM
Thomas P Ward
1601 Narranja Ave
Punta Gorda FL 33950

Call Sign: KA1ZYF
Theodoros Bastas
1438 Navigator Rd
Punta Gorda FL
339836288

Call Sign: K3ZXL
Daniel P Schaaf Sr
27195 Neaptide Dr
Punta Gorda FL 33983

Call Sign: N8APA
Roy Λ Weekley
26028 Northern Cross Rd
Punta Gorda FL 33983

Call Sign: AB4KI
Antonia Commercio
2076 Nuremberg Bl
Punta Gorda FL 33983

Call Sign: NC3B
Leonard Michaud

1783 Nuremberg Blvd
Punta Gorda FL 33983

Call Sign: N6PBD
Marleen M Weinstein
13251 Oakwood Ct
Punta Gorda FL 33982

Call Sign: KE4SDD
Donald G Mayes Jr
33123 Oil Well Rd
Charlotte Corr Inst
Punta Gorda FL
339559701

Call Sign: K4ZVL
Walter L Thompson
26056 Olla Ct
Punta Gorda FL 33983

Call Sign: WA4YBG
Harvey J Mize
374 Omen St
Punta Gorda FL 33982

Call Sign: N5MAR
Charles H Cockrell
1336 Osprey Dr
Punta Gorda FL 33950

Call Sign: W9OFT
George M Sklom
25545 Palisade Rd
Punta Gorda FL 33983

Call Sign: KD4IZY
Guy H Willett
3711 Palm Dr
Punta Gorda FL 33950

Call Sign: KD4LVJ
Mary L Willett
3711 Palm Dr
Punta Gorda FL 33950

Call Sign: KJ4LMU
Kenneth E Martin
4420 Palm Dr
Punta Gorda FL 33950

Call Sign: KJ4LMS
Linda S Dobson
4420 Palm Dr
Punta Gorda FL 33950

Call Sign: N4BMU
Ted A Collins
29140 Palm Shores Blvd
Punta Gorda FL 33982

Call Sign: KT4VG
George R Withrow
2224 Palm Tree Dr
Punta Gorda FL 33950

Call Sign: KD4LUH
Ian M Smith
2343 Palm Tree Dr
Punta Gorda FL 33950

Call Sign: WA3RRJ
Phillip H Taylor
443 Panarea Dr
Punta Gorda FL 33950

Call Sign: WD8NWV
Steven A Schrock
27133 Partin Dr
Punta Gorda FL 33983

Call Sign: KK4HQI
Toby J Sheppard
27529 Pasto Dr
Punta Gorda FL 33983

Call Sign: KI4YCD
Carlos J Cardona
3417 Peace River Dr
Punta Gorda FL 33983

Call Sign: KJ4QXD
Kenneth C Rouleau
3673 Peace River Dr
Punta Gorda FL 33983

Call Sign: KB4KPV
Mary K Cox
24170 Peppercorn Rd
Punta Gorda FL 33955

Call Sign: KB4KRB
Thomas E Cox
24170 Peppercorn Rd
Punta Gorda FL 33955

Call Sign: KE4SJH
Marion J Martin
533 Philodendron
Punta Gorda FL 33955

Call Sign: K5TAS
William A Roussel III
1222 Pine Siskin Dr
Punta Gorda FL
339507644

Call Sign: W9DR
David R Ridge
1329 Pine Siskin Dr
Punta Gorda FL 33950

Call Sign: KC4JYD
Norman P Ketchum
28400 Plato Dr
Punta Gorda FL 33955

Call Sign: WA2DUK
Gino I Pinerolo
566 Port Bendres Dr
Punta Gorda FL 33950

Call Sign: N8TSC
Carole C Pehoushek
313 Portofino Dr
Punta Gorda FL 33950

Call Sign: W4TUT
Gregory S Morrisette
318 Portofino Dr
Punta Gorda FL 33950

Call Sign: KI4NTD
Joseph J Dlugosz
25895 Prada Dr
Punta Gorda FL 33955

Call Sign: KJ4DOZ
Hans J Hasenkamp
10487 Princess Ct
Punta Gorda FL 33955

Call Sign: KI4SDF
Robert P Gosser III
2391 Quirt Ln
Punta Gorda FL 33983

Call Sign: NJ2FL
Robert P Gosser III
2391 Quirt Ln
Punta Gorda FL 33983

Call Sign: K4WXL
Sidney R Tolbert
2399 Quirt Ln
Punta Gorda FL 33983

Call Sign: KI4WHA
William J Strobel
1355 Redbird Ct
Punta Gorda FL
339507624

Call Sign: KF4QFL
Hiram L Bajandas
29185 Riata St
Punta Gorda FL 33982

Call Sign: WB4CDJ
Robert D Brandt
508 Rio De Janeiro

Punta Gorda FL 33983

Call Sign: KJ4DOW
Brian L Miller
2250 Rio Dejaneiro Ave
Punta Gorda FL 33983

Call Sign: KG4KEX
Gerald Riseley
2534 Rio Largo Ct
Punta Gorda FL 33950

Call Sign: KB9GFD
Barbara J Swiader
2608 Rio Plato Dr
Punta Gorda FL 33950

Call Sign: KJ4KQV
John F Napoli
2630 Rio Plato Dr
Punta Gorda FL 33950

Call Sign: KB3LB
Matthew M Mc Girr
24380 Rio Togas Rd
Punta Gorda FL 33955

Call Sign: WB4FDR
Robert A Hoyle
761 Rio Villa Dr
Punta Gorda FL 33950

Call Sign: N8DDZ
John D Mc Kee
215 Rio Villa Dr 3003
Punta Gorda FL 33950

Call Sign: W1MIZ
Raymond A Minzner
215 Rio Villa Dr 3263
Punta Gorda FL 33950

Call Sign: N0KJD
Arline M Swecker
215 Rio Villa Dr 3296

Punta Gorda FL 33950

Call Sign: KF4RNT
William H Spinks
215 Rio Villa Dr 3365
Punta Gorda FL 33950

Call Sign: KI4WGZ
Douglas E Donovan
215 Rio Villa Dr Lot 3425
Punta Gorda FL
339507462

Call Sign: K3GRC
Fred D Day
4300 Riverside 184
Punta Gorda FL
339821723

Call Sign: WD9EWR
Russell W Walter
4300 Riverside Dr 196
Punta Gorda FL 33982

Call Sign: KF4DUU
Oliver V Hall
4300 Riverside Dr 84
Punta Gorda FL 33982

Call Sign: KJ4RVA
Jerry W Albert
1803 Rockland Rd
Punta Gorda FL 33980

Call Sign: KA9SLI
Fred H Meyer
25270 Roland Ln
Punta Gorda FL 33955

Call Sign: KC4JZJ
Bernard L Humphrey
2904 Roma Ct
Punta Gorda FL 33950

Call Sign: KJ4MUW

Francis A Walker
2447 Rosa Ln
Punta Gorda FL
339505013

Call Sign: N4YU
Henry W Braun
2472 Rosa Ln
Punta Gorda FL 33950

Call Sign: KD4UMZ
Duane L Christensen
25201 Rosamond
Punta Gorda FL 33983

Call Sign: N9JZG
Mark A Oliphant
25151 Rosamond Ct
Punta Gorda FL 33983

Call Sign: KF4KXQ
Sharon L Oliphant
25151 Rosamond Ct
Punta Gorda FL 33983

Call Sign: KA2EJT
William F Taylor
25167 Rosamond Ct
Punta Gorda FL 33983

Call Sign: KK4SB
John M Bahner
3525 Roseau Dr
Punta Gorda FL 33950

Call Sign: KG4ZSO
Joseph W Dennis
3280 S Shore Dr 85C
Punta Gorda FL 33955

Call Sign: K0GKJ
Eugene K Jurrens
3220 S Shore Dr Unit 22B
Punta Gorda FL
339551922

Call Sign: KF4HLO
Francis G Gendron
27430 S Twin Lake Dr
Punta Gorda FL 33955

Call Sign: KF4HLQ
Diana L Bailey
27430 S Twin Lakes Dr
Punta Gorda FL
339552320

Call Sign: KC8SIL
John H Frank
24 Sabal Dr
Punta Gorda FL
339505048

Call Sign: KE4BCQ
Carolyn M Potterton
95 Sabal Dr
Punta Gorda FL 33950

Call Sign: KD4CMN
Nancy C Rasmussen
423 San Carlos Dr
Punta Gorda FL 33950

Call Sign: KD4KVF
Wayne L Rasmussen
423 San Carlos Dr
Punta Gorda FL 33950

Call Sign: N4UHA
Bobby G Walker
1502 San Marino Ct
Punta Gorda FL 33950

Call Sign: KI4NTE
Virgil D Hemphill
1506 San Marino Ct
Punta Gorda FL 33950

Call Sign: KI4WGY
Thomas A Mcalear

1104 San Mateo Dr
Punta Gorda FL 33950

Call Sign: WA2JGC
Robert W Denman
1344 San Mateo Dr
Punta Gorda FL
339506311

Call Sign: K4RWD
Robert W Denman
1344 San Mateo Dr
Punta Gorda FL
339506311

Call Sign: KI4QPG
Matthew M Carpenter
207 Santarem Cir
Punta Gorda FL 33983

Call Sign: W4FAA
Matthew M Carpenter
207 Santarem Cir
Punta Gorda FL 33983

Call Sign: KI4PEV
Samuel C Carpenter
207 Santarem Cir
Punta Gorda FL 33983

Call Sign: K4BZZ
Samuel C Carpenter
207 Santarem Cir
Punta Gorda FL 33983

Call Sign: W8NQU
Robert L Goff
214 Santarem Cir
Punta Gorda FL 33983

Call Sign: WB4DTP
Edward Karl Jr
7360 Satsuma Dr
Punta Gorda FL 33955

Call Sign: N3CHG
John S Buckley
1216 Sea Breeze Ct
Punta Gorda FL 33950

Call Sign: W3IGM
Leroy R Weatherly
1447 Sea Fan Dr
Punta Gorda FL 33950

Call Sign: WS3U
Cynthia S Barrett
1312 Sea Horse Ct
Punta Gorda FL 33950

Call Sign: KE4RCS
Eredio J Munoz
341 Segovia Dr
Punta Gorda FL 33950

Call Sign: W5WFI
Clarence C Henderson
2816 Shannon Dr
Punta Gorda FL 33982

Call Sign: WA4EDB
Sybert A Browning
25517 Shore Dr
Punta Gorda FL 33950

Call Sign: K8VTJ
Abigail H Faerber
2411 Sierra Ln
Punta Gorda FL 33950

Call Sign: N4FLQ
Alan C Levin
2435 Sierra Ln
Punta Gorda FL 33950

Call Sign: KC4VKY
Donald C Bowen
2463 Sierra Ln
Punta Gorda FL 33950

Call Sign: N2IGV
Gwynne W Spencer II
2478 Sierra Ln
Punta Gorda FL 33950

Call Sign: N2QMP
Josephine A Spencer
2478 Sierra Ln
Punta Gorda FL 33950

Call Sign: WA1LLC
Robert D Richardson
316 Singapore Rd
Punta Gorda FL
339507527

Call Sign: KG4NKN
Virginia L Kadansky
1248 Slash Pine Cir 114
Punta Gorda FL 33950

Call Sign: KE4RFY
Richard E Lehman
460 Sorrento
Punta Gorda FL 33950

Call Sign: KK4BOU
Granville R Lecompte
445 Sorrento Ct
Punta Gorda FL 33950

Call Sign: KD4EIJ
Sandra B Lehman
460 Sorrento Ct
Punta Gorda FL 33950

Call Sign: K3NCL
Edmund H Smith Jr
3700 Spoonbill Ct
Punta Gorda FL 33950

Call Sign: WA3VHI
James D Hay
46900 SR 74 Unit 86
Punta Gorda FL 33982

Call Sign: N4NML
John R Godfrey
47900 SR 74 Unit 170
Punta Gorda FL 33982

Call Sign: N0AAK
Timothy W Bellows
3418 St Croix Ct
Punta Gorda FL 33950

Call Sign: W4SZ
Gene E Fuller
3437 St Croix Ct
Punta Gorda FL
339508142

Call Sign: K2YOI
William G Donaldson
3839 St Kitts Ct
Punta Gorda FL 33950

Call Sign: WA4GPQ
Julian Temple
26112 Stillwater Cir
Punta Gorda FL 33955

Call Sign: AI4RW
Julian Temple
26112 Stillwater Cir
Punta Gorda FL 33955

Call Sign: K2EBW
Rudolph T Bruno
26155 Stillwater Cir
Punta Gorda FL 33955

Call Sign: K2AYZ
Paul J Galburt
26158 Stillwater Cir
Punta Gorda FL 33955

Call Sign: N0RTE
John F Jensen
26335 Stillwater Cir

Punta Gorda FL 33955

Call Sign: KG4DYG
Sonia K Kuster
13482 Sulky Dr
Punta Gorda FL 33955

Call Sign: KC4ROI
Dawn E Scott
312 Sullivan St
Punta Gorda FL 33950

Call Sign: W8OJ
Danny R Hurst
3225 Sulstone Dr
Punta Gorda FL 33983

Call Sign: KI4DVB
Douglas C Jackson
Sunset Kcy
Punta Gorda FL 33955

Call Sign: KG4CLE
Merlin C Schaefer
3221 Sunset Key Cir
Punta Gorda FL 33955

Call Sign: KF8JA
Lowell K Shaffer
3389 Sunset Key Cir
Punta Gorda FL
339551971

Call Sign: KG4WSI
John M Campbell
Sunset Key Cir
Punta Gorda FL
339551970

Call Sign: WB2ITZ
Albert W Jex
2419 Sunshine Blvd
Punta Gorda FL 33950

Call Sign: KF4ALU

Dorothy B Jex
2419 Sunshine Blvd
Punta Gorda FL 33950

Call Sign: KA6RMK
Ronald H Boman
1207 Swan Ct
Punta Gorda FL 33950

Call Sign: KE4MKJ
George T Weschler
1230 Swan Ct
Punta Gorda FL 33950

Call Sign: KC4ROJ
Charles W Mc Abee Jr
5843 Swaying Palm Dr
Punta Gorda FL 33982

Call Sign: KJ4HIF
Barney D Mercer
504 Tabor St
Punta Gorda FL 33950

Call Sign: AC4NW
Richard V Allaire
2309 Talbrook Ter
Punta Gorda FL 33983

Call Sign: N8LDL
Joseph E Fiorini
12459 Tamiami Trl
Punta Gorda FL
339512711

Call Sign: K5CKO
William A Bell Jr
3941 Tamiami Trl 3157
Pmb 110
Punta Gorda FL
339507925

Call Sign: WA4RFH
Donald L Botten
6400 Taylor Rd 270

Punta Gorda FL 33950

Call Sign: KF4UOO
Murray A Cowan
6400 Taylor Rd Unit B11
Punta Gorda FL 33950

Call Sign: KA9AVM
Harold A Youngblood
70 Taylor St Apt 136
Punta Gorda FL 33950

Call Sign: N3AI
Neal R Haslam Jr
27225 Tierra Del Fuego
Cir
Punta Gorda FL
339835449

Call Sign: WA4UYW
Truman A Bass III
27581 Tierra Del Fuego
Cir
Punta Gorda FL 33983

Call Sign: KI4NZE
Fred H Landgraf
26205 Tocantins Ct
Punta Gorda FL 33983

Call Sign: WB3AHU
Charles D Martin
1128 Treasure Cay Ct
Punta Gorda FL 33950

Call Sign: KG4ELO
Charles B Lea
24150 Treasure Isle Blvd
Punta Gorda FL 33955

Call Sign: KM4MI
Kenneth M Gillroy
3307 Trinidad Ct
Punta Gorda FL 33950

Call Sign: N2LKU
Richard M Powell
3299 Tripoli Blvd
Punta Gorda FL 33950

Call Sign: WA8TVA
Orville L Hockensmith
2258 Triton Ter
Punta Gorda FL 33983

Call Sign: KB3DGW
Julienne V Brown
35 Tropicana Dr
Punta Gorda FL
339505018

Call Sign: KB3DGV
William S Brown
35 Tropicana Dr
Punta Gorda FL
339505018

Call Sign: KC1ZL
John C Leavy
43 Tropicana Dr
Punta Gorda FL 33950

Call Sign: KC4RUI
Stephen F Slaughter
69 Tropicana Dr
Punta Gorda FL 33950

Call Sign: N9AQD
John M Wuerz
71 Tropicana Dr
Punta Gorda FL
339505069

Call Sign: WD8PHK
Oscar J Dorr
181 Tropicana Dr Unit
1411
Punta Gorda FL
339501914

Call Sign: KC0JOY
Kevin J Beaver
57 Tucuman St
Punta Gorda FL 33983

Call Sign: W4PMQ
Samuel A Bruno
29499 Turbak Dr
Punta Gorda FL 33982

Call Sign: KI4SEV
Gregory H Dyer
1489 Ultramarine Ln
Punta Gorda FL 33983

Call Sign: K4PGD
Gregory H Dyer
1489 Ultramarine Ln
Punta Gorda FL 33983

Call Sign: WA6DBB
Mildred G Hicks
150 Uruguay Dr
Punta Gorda FL 33983

Call Sign: N2NKY
Warren T Mezger
17268 Vagabond Cir
Punta Gorda FL 33955

Call Sign: KE4RLW
Richard E Aldus
407 Valletta Ct
Punta Gorda FL 33950

Call Sign: KF4BDR
Donald R Young
431 Valletta Ct
Punta Gorda FL 33950

Call Sign: KJ4UNP
Ernest E Wharton
3525 Vasco St
Punta Gorda FL 33950

Call Sign: WB4FKE
Glenn E Roberts III
4211 Vasco St
Punta Gorda FL 33950

Call Sign: KG4QFO
Robert A Linehan II
258 Venezia Ct
Punta Gorda FL 33950

Call Sign: KB4NRJ
Catherine S Nelson
26476 Versaille Ct
Punta Gorda FL 33983

Call Sign: AA4KX
George E Nelson
26476 Versaille Ct
Punta Gorda FL 33983

Call Sign: KA8LSX
Kenneth R Morawski
419 Via Cintia
Punta Gorda FL
339505215

Call Sign: N2QIX
Susan L Vielhauer
2851 Via Paloma Dr
Punta Gorda FL 33950

Call Sign: KD4EIR
Alden P Gurney
816 Via Tripoli
Punta Gorda FL 33950

Call Sign: W9JAS
Stanley E Willard
824 Via Tripoli
Punta Gorda FL 33950

Call Sign: K9CQ
James D Puglise
2425 Via Veneto
Punta Gorda FL 33950

Call Sign: N4NAP
Lynne A Puglise
2425 Via Veneto
Punta Gorda FL 33950

Call Sign: WB2BNE
Alan C Grossman
2514 Via Veneto
Punta Gorda FL 33950

Call Sign: WD4CKH
Henry N Havard
2208 Via Veneto Dr
Punta Gorda FL 33950

Call Sign: KE4PIF
Joy E Speck
2507 Via Veneto Dr
Punta Gorda FL
339506337

Call Sign: W4MPJ
Robert C Speck
2507 Via Veneto Dr
Punta Gorda FL
339506337

Call Sign: KD4VSD
K A Kim Krieger
2090 Via Venice
Punta Gorda FL 33950

Call Sign: W2GYP
Maurice G Isenberg
2240 Via Venice
Punta Gorda FL 33950

Call Sign: KG4WHN
Joseph D Chickino
2295 Via Venice
Punta Gorda FL 33950

Call Sign: KI4AEQ
Regina E Chickino

2295 Via Venice
Punta Gorda FL 33950

Call Sign: KJ4WBN
Nelia D Neville
26359 Villa Maria Dr
Punta Gorda FL 33983

Call Sign: KJ4WBM
Stephen P Neville
26359 Villa Maria Dr
Punta Gorda FL 33983

Call Sign: WA2GGV
Jacqueline D Seeds
27052 Villarrica Dr
Punta Gorda FL 33983

Call Sign: KK4ECE
Dorothy K Nemec
27289 Voyageur Dr
Punta Gorda FL 33983

Call Sign: KK4ECF
Larry D Rand
27289 Voyageur Dr
Punta Gorda FL 33983

Call Sign: W4LER
Larry D Rand
27289 Voyageur Dr
Punta Gorda FL 33983

Call Sign: WA4NXJ
O Darwin Hillman
513 W Marion Ave
Punta Gorda FL 33950

Call Sign: KD4OHJ
Frances A Clymer
2521 W Marion Ave 612
Punta Gorda FL 33950

Call Sign: KD4OHI
Keith R Clymer

2521 W Marion Ave 612
Punta Gorda FL 33950

Call Sign: KC4VNG
Robert N Gillespie
1200 W Retta Esp D88
Punta Gorda FL 33950

Call Sign: KS4GV
Philip W Kay
1200 W Retta Esplanade
Punta Gorda FL 33950

Call Sign: N4YJZ
Bradford R Schultz
1200 W Retta Esplanade
D94
Punta Gorda FL 33950

Call Sign: KB8GXD
Michael R Donley
1200 W Retta Esplanade
Slip D91
Punta Gorda FL 33950

Call Sign: N4SVG
Daniel E Wohlers
37300 Washington Loop
Rd
Punta Gorda FL 33982

Call Sign: KD4VQM
Susan M Wohlers
37300 Washington Loop
Rd
Punta Gorda FL 33982

Call Sign: WA8GRG
Robert Rienstra
1477 Wassail Ln
Punta Gorda FL 33983

Call Sign: N0LNC
Terry L Merrill
1518 Wassail Ln

Punta Gorda FL 33983

Call Sign: KD4UAP
Lydia T Hellmann
15500 Water Oak Ct
Punta Gorda FL 33982

Call Sign: KC2MQQ
Stanley F Rosen
3768 Whippoorwill Blvd
Punta Gorda FL 33950

Call Sign: K4AZZ
Ruth E Brown
3786 Whippoorwill Blvd
Punta Gorda FL 33590

Call Sign: KG4UCL
Floyd T Kutz
18150 Wild Pepper Ct
Punta Gorda FL 33982

Call Sign: AA1GJ
Richard A Jensen
1368 Willet Ct
Punta Gorda FL 33950

Call Sign: AA6OP
Ken Wakabayashi
1368 Willet Ct
Punta Gorda FL 33950

Call Sign: W2OSZ
Ralph H Cranmer Jr
3398 Windmill Village
Punta Gorda FL 33950

Call Sign: KB3CFP
Donald C Brandt
2136 Wyatt Cir
Punta Gorda FL 33950

Call Sign: KF4HCH
Oscar L Revilla
24460 Yacht Club Blvd

Punta Gorda FL 33955

Call Sign: N4DMB
Herbie L Bullis
25146 Zodiac Ln
Punta Gorda FL 33983

Call Sign: KC4RUD
Christina A Fish
Punta Gorda FL 33951

Call Sign: KE4AAM
Jack Frankenthal
Punta Gorda FL 33951

Call Sign: K4IA
Edwin R Roller
Punta Gorda FL 33950

Call Sign: KE4FOK
Bradley K Taylor
Punta Gorda FL 33951

Call Sign: KJ4GGU
Bruce H Conklin
Punta Gorda FL 33951

Call Sign: KI4TUN
Christine K Fullom
Punta Gorda FL 33951

Call Sign: KI4TUM
Cliff K Fullom
Punta Gorda FL 33951

Call Sign: KJ4YBV
Dannela T Varel
Punta Gorda FL 33951

Call Sign: KI4WGW
George R Remick
Punta Gorda FL 33951

Call Sign: KF4HCI
John H Walker

Punta Gorda FL 33951

Call Sign: KJ4QAI
Neil T Flynn
Punta Gorda FL 33951

Call Sign: KI4PUA
Patric J Cockram
Punta Gorda FL 33951

Call Sign: NX3G
Thomas L O Grady
Punta Gorda FL 33951

Call Sign: WX4E
Charlotte Amateur Radio
Society Inc
Punta Gorda FL 33952

Call Sign: W4DUX
Peace River Radio
Association Inc
Punta Gorda FL
339510943

Call Sign: KB8YOE
Kenneth L Newton
Punta Gorda FL
339510999

Call Sign: KB1FQW
William J Clark
Punta Gorda FL
339512145

Call Sign: N1PI
William J Clark
Punta Gorda FL
339512145

Call Sign: KI4NTA
Rudy E Falkenberg
Punta Gorda FL
339512693

Call Sign: KE4ZMG
John T Feuchack
1361 Plover Ct
Punta Gorda Isles FL
33950

Call Sign: WB2CIZ
Ann C Santoro
1478 Raven Ct
Punta Gorda Isles FL
33950

Call Sign: WA2SCQ
Charles Santoro
1478 Raven Ct
Punta Gorda Isles FL
33950

Call Sign: KA9ZJT
Phillip J Tidler
288 Annapolis Ln
Rotonda West FL 33947

Call Sign: KJ4BBF
Dennis T Anderson
659 Boundary Blvd
Rotonda West FL 33947

Call Sign: K4BBF
Dennis T Anderson
659 Boundary Blvd
Rotonda West FL 33947

Call Sign: KE4SGK
Robert B Hudson
305 Boundary Blvd Apt A
Rotonda West FL 33947

Call Sign: AK4MD
Robert B Hudson
305 Boundary Blvd Apt A
Rotonda West FL 33947

Call Sign: KM4RF
Emery R Meszaros
237 Broadmoor Ln
Rotonda West FL
339471932

Call Sign: N4QFU
Frank J Konikowski
9 Bunker Rd
Rotonda West FL 33947

Call Sign: WA2LWM
Joseph V Black
211 Bunker Rd
Rotonda West FL 33947

Call Sign: WA2HMA
Donald W Dunlop
21 Bunker Ter
Rotonda West FL 33947

Call Sign: KB9QOB
Patricia A Kraemer
30 Caddy Rd
Rotonda West FL
339472216

Call Sign: KB9QOC
William F Kraemer
30 Caddy Rd
Rotonda West FL
339472216

Call Sign: N1KEN
John F Kelly Sr
73 Caddy Rd
Rotonda West FL 33947

Call Sign: WB2TCK

Joseph Traficante
41 Clubhouse Rd
Rotonda West FL
339472009

Call Sign: KE4NZV
Norman R Hall
22 Golfview Ct
Rotonda West FL 33947

Call Sign: W4JAC
John A Cerniglia
32 Golfview Ct
Rotonda West FL
339472229

Call Sign: W5SQX
Robert C Stroot
6 Golfview Ter
Rotonda West FL 33947

Call Sign: WA3GSA
Bruce T Herget
104 Jennifer Dr
Rotonda West FL 33947

Call Sign: NB3P
James G Reske
184 Linda Lee Dr
Rotonda West FL 33947

Call Sign: W1AMU
William H Stevens
51 Mariner Ln
Rotonda West FL 33947

Call Sign: WD9JAC
John A Cerniglia
195 Mark Twain Ln
Rotonda West FL
339472144

Call Sign: KD4NNC
Beverly A Estes
262 Mark Twain Ln

Rotonda West FL 33947

Call Sign: WB8RWW
Larry E Estes
262 Mark Twain Ln
Rotonda West FL 33947

Call Sign: KD4MMW
Renee C Estes
262 Mark Twain Ln
Rotonda West FL 33947

Call Sign: KB8BFW
Gerald L Schmidt
280 Mark Twain Ln
Rotonda West FL 33947

Call Sign: K4FIE
Kenneth S Hirsch
167 Medalist Rd
Rotonda West FL 33947

Call Sign: KC2JBW
James A Yellico
147 Medalist Rd
Rotonda West FL 33947

Call Sign: W4PHI
Clifton H Mc Cauley
7 Oakland Hills Pl
Rotonda West FL 33947

Call Sign: W4VV
Frank A Maren
1 Pebble Beach Rd
Rotonda West FL 33947

Call Sign: KB9YL
David J Daniels
66 Rotonda Cir
Rotonda West FL 33947

Call Sign: K8OGB
Michael N Gomola
221 Rotonda Cir

Rotonda West FL 33947

Call Sign: WA2WAH
Edward F Bauer
58 Sportsman Ct
Rotonda West FL 33947

Call Sign: W8KLL
Ernest A Gruenberg
19 Sportsman Rd
Rotonda West FL
339471928

Call Sign: KG4ZDX
Huston K Myers
47 Sportsman Rd
Rotonda West FL 33947

Call Sign: KE4UFT
Mark D Henry
59 Sportsman Rd
Rotonda West FL 33947

Call Sign: KE4UFS
Marty Henry
59 Sportsman Rd
Rotonda West FL
339471928

Call Sign: KF4KDI
Michael C Henry
59 Sportsman Rd
Rotonda West FL
339471928

Call Sign: WB3IVH
William B Raker
248 Sportsman Rd
Rotonda West FL 33947

Call Sign: KF4BIN
Chris D Combs
10 Sportsman Ter
Rotonda West FL 33947

Call Sign: KF4OGI
Us International Police
Assoc Southern Sect ARC
3429 1st Ave NW
Saint James City FL 33956

Call Sign: W2GOY
Kenneth J Koch
3980 Areca Dr
Saint James City FL 33956

Call Sign: KC4EAA
Richard F Davis
3573 Bayview Ave
Saint James City FL
339562211

Call Sign: KC4DZZ
Mona Lee Davis
3573 Bayview Ave
Saint James City FL
339562211

Call Sign: W3BVM
Charles E Kader
2891 Binnacle Ln
Saint James City FL 33956

Call Sign: WD8NDK
John S Borick
3058 Bounty Ln
Saint James City FL 33956

Call Sign: KC8BDW
James P Lehotsky
3084 Bowsprit Ln
Saint James City FL 33956

Call Sign: K2SXZ
Stephen F Vadas
3059 Bracci Dr

Saint James City FL 33956

Call Sign: NK9T
Robert L Cullen
2888 Buttonwood Key Ct
Saint James City FL 33956

Call Sign: KE4SML
Walter E Williams Jr
2357 Cherimoya Ln
Saint James City FL 33956

Call Sign: KE4JRV
James P Brennan II
3772 Citrus St
Saint James City FL 33956

Call Sign: KB4IZP
John Kilpatrick
4804 Curlew Dr NW
Saint James City FL 33956

Call Sign: KB4IZO
Isabell Kilpatrick
Curlew Dr Rt 2
Saint James City FL 33956

Call Sign: KC4HLZ
Kent D Stadlberger
3694 Dewberry Ln
Saint James City FL 33956

Call Sign: K8HIF
Richard M Dunlop
3966 Dewberry Ln Box
685
Saint James City FL 33956

Call Sign: WA4DOS
Scott D Simmons
5376 Fairbanks Dr
Saint James City FL 33956

Call Sign: K8DXE
Richard C Maier

5273 Flamingo Dr
Saint James City FL 33956

Call Sign: KA4PIR
Pine Island Radio
5273 Flamingo Dr
Saint James City FL 33956

Call Sign: N3DLC
Charles W Lester
3617 Gasparilla St
Saint James City FL 33956

Call Sign: KF4OHQ
Richard A Gamble
4660 Gulf Gate City
Saint James City FL 33956

Call Sign: WD8BKE
Michael T Barton
4404 Lake Heather Cir
Saint James City FL 33956

Call Sign: KA1CWC
Frances E Lever
2179 Lemon St
Saint James City FL 33956

Call Sign: KA1CWD
Ray C Lever
2179 Lemon St
Saint James City FL 33956

Call Sign: KD4NZB
Anthony C Diliberto
3795 Manatee Dr
Saint James City FL 33956

Call Sign: W4QJQ
William R Doctor
3458 Pinetree Dr NW
Saint James City FL 33956

Call Sign: K3NMY
Julian E Mc Carley

3752 San Carlos Dr
Saint James City FL 33956

Call Sign: KK4HAX
William A Conover
5021 Sand Piper Dr
Saint James City FL 33956

Call Sign: K8LIV
Verlin L Haywald
4837 Sandpiper Dr
Saint James City FL 33956

Call Sign: WB4NHW
Roosevelt Turner Jr
2597 Sanibel Blvd
Saint James City FL 33956

Call Sign: KF4DWI
Lois B Rhodes
3104 Skipper Ln
Saint James City FL 33956

Call Sign: KF4DWJ
Richard K Rhodes
3104 Skipper Ln
Saint James City FL 33956

Call Sign: N4ZOL
Martin F Coleman
3269 String Fellow Rd
Saint James City FL 33956

Call Sign: K6LXH
Phillip A Rosenberg
2467 Sycamore St
Saint James City FL 33956

Call Sign: KI4ZMC
Daniel R Nickels
3548 Tropical Point Dr
Saint James City FL 33956

Call Sign: N4PPR
Robert J Beale

Saint James City FL 33956

Call Sign: KD4CFG
Terry T Thompson
Saint James City FL 33956

Call Sign: KJ4SMJ
Rob L James III
Saint James City FL 33956

**FCC Amateur Radio
Licenses in Sanibel**

Call Sign: N4LF
Alex D Felker
920 Almas Ct
Sanibel FL 33957

Call Sign: WA9TUI
John D Petrikas
2477 Blue Crab Ct
Sanibel FL 33957

Call Sign: KF4NJT
James S Lewis
778 Cardium St
Sanibel FL 33957

Call Sign: KI4BAE
Terri S Cummins
800 Dunlop Rd
Sanibel FL 33957

Call Sign: KI4UQD
Cheryl A Waite
800 Dunlop Rd
Sanibel FL 33957

Call Sign: KI4UQJ
Dana J Raco
800 Dunlop Rd
Sanibel FL 33957

Call Sign: KI4LTZ
Michael R Cooper

800 Dunlop Rd
Sanibel FL 33957

Call Sign: K7MRC
Michael R Cooper
800 Dunlop Rd
Sanibel FL 33957

Call Sign: KI4BAF
Stephanie M Dowd
800 Dunlop Rd
Sanibel FL 33957

Call Sign: KG4AEL
Evanthia A Rodriguez
1012 E Gulf Dr
Sanibel FL 33957

Call Sign: KJ4GAX
Joseph P Bradshaw
223 Hurricane Ln
Sanibel FL 33957

Call Sign: N6IRZ
John F Jones
521 Lake Murex Cir
Sanibel FL 339575522

Call Sign: KD4GTF
Charles W Ringel
419 Lighthouse Way
Sanibel FL 33957

Call Sign: KF4LQL
Sanibel Emergency Radio
Unit
419 Lighthouse Way
Sanibel FL 339573903

Call Sign: KI4UQG
Nicholas A Brown
9032 Mockingbird Dr
Sanibel FL 33957

Call Sign: KA4PSJ

Leon D Bellamy
9428 Moonlight Dr
Sanibel FL 33957

Harrison S Condit
800 Sand Dollar Dr
Sanibel FL 33957

James T Ory
2100 Sunset Cir
Sanibel FL 33957

Call Sign: N6XRU
William E Wanamaker
5427 Osprey Ct
Sanibel FL 33957

Call Sign: N4TGT
John L Smith
958 Sandcastle Rd
Sanibel FL 33957

Call Sign: KA1JHL
Karen E Calkins Dr
2130 Sunset Cir
Sanibel FL 33957

Call Sign: KN4ES
Walter F Laforet
1119 Periwinkle Way 176
Sanibel FL 33957

Call Sign: WA4WDV
Alexander Mac Kenzie Jr
1036 Sandcastle Rd
Sanibel FL 33957

Call Sign: KG6TFX
David J Moore
948 Tarpon Bay Rd
Sanibel FL 33957

Call Sign: KB2JSV
Daniel J Bender
1119 Periwinkle Way 22
Sanibel FL 33957

Call Sign: WB2PDH
Robert W Orrell
1662 Serenity Ln
Sanibel FL 33957

Call Sign: KI4BEL
Steven B Smith
4117 W Gulf Dr
Sanibel FL 33957

Call Sign: KD5WNN
Harvey J Padewer
5744 Pine Tree Dr
Sanibel FL 33957

Call Sign: KF4QBD
Bethany J Highsmith
1705 Serenity Ln
Sanibel FL 33957

Call Sign: WB0JDA
Gilbert W Harris
4288 W Gulf Dr
Sanibel FL 33957

Call Sign: WA4AGJ
Everett E Ballard
1014 S Yachtsman Dr
Sanibel FL 339575013

Call Sign: KF4QBA
Dianna L Highsmith
1705 Serenity Ln
Sanibel FL 33957

Call Sign: W4JDA
Gilbert W Harris
4288 W Gulf Dr
Sanibel FL 33957

Call Sign: KG4ZCF
Coby A Amadio
5097 San Cap Rd
Sanibel FL 33957

Call Sign: KF4QBB
John H Highsmith
1705 Serenity Ln
Sanibel FL 33957

Call Sign: N9BOD
Michael I Miller
2737 W Gulf Dr Apt 136
Sanibel FL 339571259

Call Sign: KG4ZFJ
Matthew J Fannon
1421 Sand Castle Rd
Sanibel FL 33957

Call Sign: KC4GYJ
Scott D Mc Phee
2407 Shop Rd
Sanibel FL 33957

Call Sign: N9MQ
Michael I Miller
2737 W Gulf Dr Apt 136
Sanibel FL 339571259

Call Sign: KD4JNM
Mary K Condit
800 Sand Dollar
Sanibel FL 33957

Call Sign: WD9ATJ
James T Ory
2100 Sunset Cir
Sanibel FL 33957

Call Sign: K9DRJ
Robert R Arbuckle
2042 Wild Lime Dr
Sanibel FL 33957

Call Sign: KC4ZIJ

Call Sign: K4ORY

Call Sign: KI4IRB

Dave B Defonzo
1576 Wilton Ln
Sanibel FL 33957

Call Sign: KI4LTY
Albert C Smith Jr
Sanibel FL 33957

Call Sign: KI4IRC
George A Krivas
Sanibel FL 33957

Call Sign: KI4UQA
Holly A Vetter
Sanibel FL 33957

Call Sign: K2ORS
Jean P Shepherd
Sanibel FL 33957

Call Sign: KB4OZX
Joseph L St Cyr
Sanibel FL 33957

Call Sign: KI4UQI
Marcella M Stutsman
Sanibel FL 33957

Call Sign: W4SBL
Sanibel Emergency Radio
Unit
Sanibel FL 33957

**FCC Amateur Radio
Licenses in Sebring**

Call Sign: WB4DZN
William Snyder Sr
1500 11th Ave
Sebring FL 33872

Call Sign: KG4MCY
Nickolas Blooks
1205 5th Ave
Sebring FL 33875

Call Sign: K4LXR
Nickolas Brooks
1205 5th Ave
Sebring FL 33875

Call Sign: KG4JFP
Kathi L Jensen
4701 Adrienne St
Sebring FL 33872

Call Sign: K8MYO
Eldan E Burkholder Sr
28 Amos St
Sebring FL 338706837

Call Sign: W4FLA
Keith E Myers
8509 Andes Ct
Sebring FL 33876

Call Sign: WA4RB
Roy B Copeland Sr
211 Andretti Ave
Sebring FL 33876

Call Sign: NY4K
Billy R Gorsuch
1575 Arbuckle Creek Rd
Sebring FL 338706808

Call Sign: KD4BPK
Janet G Amon
6609 Ashton Dr
Sebring FL 33870

Call Sign: KD4CPF
Richard T Amon
6609 Ashton Dr
Sebring FL 33870

Call Sign: KE4NJE
Raymond D Mitchell
3314 Astoria Ave
Sebring FL 33875

Call Sign: KB4XJ
Darrell O Koranda
3022 Avery Ct
Sebring FL 338706816

Call Sign: W4LMX
John J Agee
2148 Banyan Way Box 46
Sebring FL 33872

Call Sign: WA8VEC
Michael P Gormley
4907 Barnum St
Sebring FL 33876

Call Sign: KJ4JUO
James O Terrell
3321 Bolide St
Sebring FL 33872

Call Sign: AJ4QO
James O Terrell
3321 Bolide St
Sebring FL 33872

Call Sign: N9AM
Richard G Spindler
1515 Booth Dr
Sebring FL 338725718

Call Sign: KC8WQR
Aaron P Menough
4604 Boston St
Sebring FL 33872

Call Sign: N4TO
Victor A Dubois
4400 Briarcliff Ave
Sebring FL 33875

Call Sign: N1NPG
Marcel A Lapierre
58 Cherokee St
Sebring FL 33872

Call Sign: KA6FDW
Debra L Chastain
304 Cherry Tree Dr
Sebring FL 33876

Call Sign: W4QV
William M Ambrose
4450 De Soto Rd 16
Sebring FL 33870

Call Sign: W4LMW
Anthony S Lake
1813 E Recreation Dr
Sebring FL 33875

Call Sign: K1RJR
Roland J Robert
6457 Columbus Blvd
Sebring FL 33872

Call Sign: N8NUH
Kimberly W Yeager
633 Denise Ave
Sebring FL 33870

Call Sign: KA4ZTU
Edward P Bertero
E Schumacher Rd
Sebring FL 33872

Call Sign: KG4INU
Joel R Gonzalez
4101 Cortez Blvd
Sebring FL 33872

Call Sign: N4HWG
Robert Gray
3811 Divot Rd
Sebring FL 33872

Call Sign: W4CBS
Donald L Roberts
308 Eagle Ave
Sebring FL 33872

Call Sign: W4GON
Joel R Gonzalez
4101 Cortez Blvd
Sebring FL 33872

Call Sign: AF4EY
William M Might
4115 Duffer Loop
Sebring FL 33872

Call Sign: K4IFH
Harry L Fish Jr
1916 Elf Dr
Sebring FL 33872

Call Sign: KD4HQN
James R Crum
1520 Corvette Ave
Sebring FL 33872

Call Sign: N0QJI
Robert L Singles
2766 Duffer Rd
Sebring FL 33872

Call Sign: KC4IQ
Anna L Justice
4005 Elson Ave
Sebring FL 33872

Call Sign: KN4DZ
Robert L Parker
6809 CR 17 S
Sebring FL 33870

Call Sign: KB9SDI
Edwin C Amsler
4032 Dunn Ave
Sebring FL 33875

Call Sign: N4NTV
Charles E Brady
4005 Elson Ave
Sebring FL 33872

Call Sign: N0HAO
Denise A Whitaker
6809 CR 17 S
Sebring FL 338765998

Call Sign: KJ4FS
Gene W Monroe
4306 Dunn Ave
Sebring FL 33875

Call Sign: K4EZM
Randall M Payne
4131 Elson Ave
Sebring FL 33875

Call Sign: KF4IER
William S Leftwich
7018 CR 17 S
Sebring FL 33870

Call Sign: KI4AQF
Gene F Durrance
10300 Durrance Rd
Sebring FL 33875

Call Sign: N3TND
Patrick W Elmore
1312 Emerald Ave
Sebring FL 33870

Call Sign: K2ECK
David H Tinkham
14 Daniel Rd
Sebring FL 33870

Call Sign: KB4CHS
Robert T Smith Sr
1510 E Circle Dr
Sebring FL 33872

Call Sign: KC4ITC
Carmen M Quinones
1704 Evergreen St
Sebring FL 33870

Call Sign: NY9Q
Miguel A Morales
1704 Evergreen St
Sebring FL 338701707

Call Sign: KA4LFI
Albert E Keenan
3422 Fairmount Dr
Sebring FL 33872

Call Sign: KA1AOE
Joseph W Brackett
2311 Flamingo Dr
Sebring FL 33870

Call Sign: KA6R
James B Wilbanks III
2003 Flower Ter
Sebring FL 33875

Call Sign: N8BMZ
Ray L Wynn
201 Garden Ter
Sebring FL 33876

Call Sign: WA4WUP
Stanley A Hutcheson
1934 Gardenia Ave
Sebring FL 33872

Call Sign: KT3O
Jo Anne M Angstadt
1926 Gardenia Ter
Sebring FL 33875

Call Sign: N3VVO
David M Rutt
1126 Ghana St
Sebring FL 33875

Call Sign: KB4HXG
Nancy M Asbury
3008 Going To The Sun
Sebring FL 33872

Call Sign: KK4RJ
Roland J Robert
5823 Golden Rd
Sebring FL 33875

Call Sign: WB9NOD
Eugene A Halvorson
3705 Golf Haven Ter
Sebring FL 33872

Call Sign: K0OFF
Everett R Ohrt
773 Golfside Ln
Sebring FL 33872

Call Sign: KI4HVP
Donald E Sicklesteel
3417 Golfview Rd
Sebring FL 33872

Call Sign: AA8QS
Larry L Ambuel
3412 Golfview Rd
Sebring FL 33875

Call Sign: W4AI
John R Beck
2790 Grace Ln
Sebring FL 33871

Call Sign: KT4HE
Robert W Eddleman
340 Grand Prix Dr
Sebring FL 33872

Call Sign: W2FQM
Frederick W Gieseking
510 Grapefruit Ave
Sebring FL 33870

Call Sign: K4HSC
Clara M Hennon
510 Grapefruit Ave Apt
13A

Sebring FL 33870

Call Sign: N4JOY
Christopher D Van Der
Kaay
926 Grey Fox Ave
Sebring FL 33875

Call Sign: KP4HYL
Heriangely Cruz
3303 Grouper Dr
Sebring FL 33870

Call Sign: KF4EXM
Charles V Vidaud
5931 Hammock Rd
Sebring FL 33872

Call Sign: AD4GI
Michael E Huylebroeck Sr
830 Harmony Dr
Sebring FL 33870

Call Sign: KC4SAV
Lynn D Roach
2333 Hartt Rd
Sebring FL 33870

Call Sign: W4EEP
Paul E Allyn
404 Hemlock Ave
Sebring FL 33870

Call Sign: KF4BQU
Brad W Phillips
280 Hendricks Way
Sebring FL 33870

Call Sign: AD4HB
Robert L Clark
1440 Hiawatha Ave
Sebring FL 33870

Call Sign: N4OCU
Donald W Swain

2400 Hidden Creek Cir
Sebring FL 33870

Call Sign: WB2KMH
Leon J Coffin Jr
5322 Highland St
Sebring FL 33870

Call Sign: KB2FZ
Roland G Roy
5911 Highland St
Sebring FL 33870

Call Sign: N9MC
Hugh C Mccartney
10921 Holly Dr
Sebring FL 33870

Call Sign: KG4RVU
Samuel B Pelot Jr
205 Holly Trl
Sebring FL 33875

Call Sign: KD4QKJ
Robert A Guris
204 Ibis Ave
Sebring FL 33872

Call Sign: KB4KRR
Paul Mayhew
3475 Ike Ave
Sebring FL 338754605

Call Sign: KC4VUB
Floyd J Hile
9080 Illinois Cir
Sebring FL 338705136

Call Sign: KF4YIA
Keith E Myers
211 Jay Ave
Sebring FL 33872

Call Sign: W2ERT
Clay H Nichols

321 Jay Ave
Sebring FL 33872

Call Sign: WA2DUY
Doris A Nichols
321 Jay Ave
Sebring FL 33872

Call Sign: K8HSN
Melvin L Palmer
2912 John L St
Sebring FL 33870

Call Sign: WW4EOC
Sean N Norris II
1877 Jones Dr
Sebring FL 33870

Call Sign: KB8LMW
Karl G Yeager
3807 Kearly Ave
Sebring FL 33875

Call Sign: W3CUH
T Kenneth Brown
760 Killarney Dr
Sebring FL 33872

Call Sign: KG4MLI
Stephanie L Hart
3311 King Dr
Sebring FL 33870

Call Sign: KE4TPL
Litton M Walker III
3710 King Dr
Sebring FL 33870

Call Sign: WD4KYW
James E Burris
7773 King James Dr
Sebring FL 33876

Call Sign: K4GEO
George C Sheaffer

2731 Kingswood Dr
Sebring FL 33872

Call Sign: W1HNU
Donald J Ryder
4726 Lafayette Ave
Sebring FL 33875

Call Sign: KF4RCL
Leon B Wiltsey Jr
4600 Lake Haven Blvd
Sebring FL 33872

Call Sign: KG4AHZ
Barbara M Hutchins
2034 Lake Josephine Dr
Sebring FL 33872

Call Sign: W2MAV
Frank D Hutchins Jr
2034 Lake Josephine Dr
Sebring FL 33872

Call Sign: W3SQA
Harold E Keller
404 Lake Josephine Shrs
Rd
Sebring FL 33875

Call Sign: N2WU
Andrew J Chapman
1015 Lake Sebring Blvd
Sebring FL 33870

Call Sign: N4OKB
Andrew J Large
14 Lake St
Sebring FL 33870

Call Sign: N4VNR
Diane K Large
14 Lake St
Sebring FL 33870

Call Sign: N4OKC

William E Large
14 Lake St
Sebring FL 33870

Call Sign: KE4TVI
David A Jensen
2581 Lakeview Dr
Sebring FL 33870

Call Sign: KB4FLE
Delton E De Laney
2615 Lakeview Dr
Sebring FL 33870

Call Sign: KE4CQA
Sharon M De Laney
2615 Lakeview Dr
Sebring FL 33870

Call Sign: KJ4IHQ
Garrett P Lee
2630 Lakeview Dr
Sebring FL 33870

Call Sign: K4LTM
Walter M Mc Dowell Jr
2131 Lakeview Dr Apt 510
Sebring FL 33870

Call Sign: KG4TQQ
Robert W Henderson
225 Lark Ave
Sebring FL 33872

Call Sign: N4RWH
Robert W Henderson
225 Lark Ave
Sebring FL 33872

Call Sign: KB4Y
Stephen L Foland
309 Lark Ave
Sebring FL 338723532

Call Sign: N2PCB

Charles Ortiz
2612 Lazy Days La
Sebring FL 33872

Call Sign: KA3ETO
Joseph A Hilinski
2605 Lazy Days Ln
Sebring FL 33872

Call Sign: WB4BHV
Roy H Rice
2606 Lazy Days Ln
Sebring FL 33872

Call Sign: K4SCT
Harold Sillman
3919 Leaf Rd
Sebring FL 33875

Call Sign: KF4SQS
Manfred R Zenk
861 Lemon St
Sebring FL 33870

Call Sign: WB4QVU
Florida Gulf Coast ARC
4504 Leucadendra Dr
Sebring FL 33872

Call Sign: KA4HBW
Dale W Mc Mindes
1113 Liberia St
Sebring FL 338755585

Call Sign: KB4DH
Roger W Thom
5317 Lime Rd
Sebring FL 338758040

Call Sign: WA9EJC
Darrell B Swank
111 Logan St
Sebring FL 33870

Call Sign: W4NVZ

Woodrow S Jackson
2908 Louis St
Sebring FL 33872

Call Sign: KJ4LK
Richard R Calhoun
318 Magnolia Ave
Sebring FL 33870

Call Sign: KI4LCQ
Robert S Curry III
3240 Maine Ave
Sebring FL 33872

Call Sign: KK4CYF
Lea A Curry
3240 Maine Ave
Sebring FL 338706500

Call Sign: KE4HDR
Gerald S Grasso
3348 Maryland Ave
Sebring FL 33872

Call Sign: KE4RRI
Sharon A Grasso
3348 Maryland Ave
Sebring FL 33872

Call Sign: K2IEC
Bernard F Pickering
3415 Maryland Ave
Sebring FL 33872

Call Sign: KE4CPN
William A Qualls
6723 Matanzas Dr
Sebring FL 33872

Call Sign: WA0NZI
Robert E Meyer
1 Matthew St
Sebring FL 33870

Call Sign: W1JLK

William A French
3208 Mayfair Ave
Sebring FL 338724423

Call Sign: W5RDH
Robert G De Hart
9051 Michigan Rd
Sebring FL 33870

Call Sign: KJ4QBM
Edelsa V Hernandez
460 Moon Ranch Rd
Sebring FL 33870

Call Sign: KJ4QBN
Julio C Hernandez
460 Moon Ranch Rd
Sebring FL 33870

Call Sign: N4FLJ
John P Payne
4526 Mundell Ave
Sebring FL 338707101

Call Sign: AI4JH
John P Payne
4526 Mundell Ave
Sebring FL 338707101

Call Sign: W4CWZ
John P Payne
4526 Mundell Ave
Sebring FL 338707101

Call Sign: KI4JVS
Sandra K Payne
4526 Mundell Ave
Sebring FL 338707101

Call Sign: WA4YUA
John S O Connell
1617 Myrtle Ave
Sebring FL 338702621

Call Sign: KF4ZYH

Vivian S Burton
1301 Nahaw Ave
Sebring FL 33870

Call Sign: KF4CEK
Wayne A Burton
1301 Nahaw Ave
Sebring FL 33870

Call Sign: KI4FSR
Alan J Holmes
1135 NE Lakeview Dr
Sebring FL 33870

Call Sign: N4ALF
Anthony S Kreski
3208 New York Ave
Sebring FL 338722533

Call Sign: W3GFQ
Elmer J Middleton
3225 New York Ave
Sebring FL 33870

Call Sign: W4URR
William D Youmans
3503 New York Ave
Sebring FL 33872

Call Sign: K4GRT
Sherman P Wantz
424 NW Lakeview Dr
Sebring FL 33870

Call Sign: W4JPA
Robert F Jarvis
2135 Oak Beach Blvd
Sebring FL 33875

Call Sign: N4WOH
Marie A Steele
6100 Oakland Rd
Sebring FL 33870

Call Sign: KB2HSQ

Randolph E Coffin
6509 Old Orchard Ave
Sebring FL 338768805

Call Sign: N4ZOH
Spencer H Thibodeau
2101 Orange Blossom Ave
Sebring FL 33870

Call Sign: KB4IQB
Bernard Wolkove
10234 Orange Blossom
Blvd S
Sebring FL 33875

Call Sign: KC4WFQ
Cecil C Robinson
2726 Orange Grove Dr
Sebring FL 33870

Call Sign: KK4CYD
Matthew S Pelot
300 Palmetto Dr
Sebring FL 33875

Call Sign: N4OXZ
Roger W Bohannan
4218 Palomino Dr
Sebring FL 33875

Call Sign: KD4DWX
Gordon E Churchward
3245 Paradise Path
Sebring FL 33870

Call Sign: KF4U
Kenneth E Freeland
208 Parkview Rd
Sebring FL 33870

Call Sign: KA1GVB
Margaret E Mitchell
3020 Parkwood Rd
Sebring FL 33870

Call Sign: W1PI
Clarence J Welsh
3036 Parkwood Rd
Sebring FL 33872

Call Sign: WG4M
Mildred M Roberts
511 Poinsettia Ave
Sebring FL 33870

Call Sign: N4CJ
Christopher J Page
312 Quail Ave
Sebring FL 33870

Call Sign: KI4KJJ
John Collier
1512 Penny Ave
Sebring FL 33870

Call Sign: KC4MHK
Cory H Imsdahl
2901 Pompino Dr
Sebring FL 33870

Call Sign: AI4JX
Christopher J Page
312 Quail Ave
Sebring FL 33872

Call Sign: W4PQ
Harry J White
727 Persimmon Ave
Sebring FL 33870

Call Sign: KI4CSY
Heather M Sparks
6416 Prince Ave
Sebring FL 33875

Call Sign: W2SR
Harry B Robinson
312 Quail Ave
Sebring FL 33872

Call Sign: KI4JVQ
Edgar A Porter
302 Pine Tree Ln
Sebring FL 33872

Call Sign: KF4VWR
John H Struck
1619 Prospect St
Sebring FL 33870

Call Sign: KD4DOW
Terry J Robinson
312 Quail Ave
Sebring FL 33872

Call Sign: KG4MRY
Edgar D Porter
302 Pine Tree Ln
Sebring FL 33872

Call Sign: W4IEV
Garold F Shepherd
1803 Prospect St
Sebring FL 33870

Call Sign: KI4IGX
Bennie E Hanley
2702 Queenswood Dr
Sebring FL 33875

Call Sign: AG4ZM
Edgar D Porter
302 Pine Tree Ln
Sebring FL 33872

Call Sign: K4CS
Clyde Scruggs
1803 Prospect St
Sebring FL 338707330

Call Sign: KE4EUW
Charles E Phillips
1820 Recreation Dr
Sebring FL 33875

Call Sign: KI4JVP
Jacquelyn J Porter
302 Pine Tree Ln
Sebring FL 33872

Call Sign: N4WRS
Norma J Scruggs
1803 Prospect St
Sebring FL 338707330

Call Sign: KA1GYW
Don J Welsh
232 Red Pine Dr
Sebring FL 33872

Call Sign: KE4CPZ
Derek J De Laney
2634 Pinewood Blvd
Sebring FL 33870

Call Sign: WD4BEE
Edward L Wanamaker Jr
226 Quail Ave
Sebring FL 33872

Call Sign: KJ4LI
John P Mills
558 Redwood Dr
Sebring FL 338756289

Call Sign: KD4YAU
Steven M Halkias
6832 Pioneer Rd
Sebring FL 33870

Call Sign: K8APY
Burton P Dennis
232 Quail Ave
Sebring FL 33872

Call Sign: KI4IML
Joe A Mize
1150 Rialto Ave
Sebring FL 33870

Call Sign: AI4KP
Joe A Mize
1150 Rialto Ave
Sebring FL 33870

Call Sign: KU4UA
Donald P Robenstine
1619 Ridge St
Sebring FL 33870

Call Sign: K0JLC
James A Williams
219 Robin Ave
Sebring FL 33872

Call Sign: N4KUT
Du Wane J Busse
221 Robin Ave
Sebring FL 33872

Call Sign: WB4QDL
Marilyn S Whiteley
124 Robinhood Ter
Sebring FL 33870

Call Sign: WB4QDM
Thomas A D Whiteley
124 Robinhood Ter
Sebring FL 33870

Call Sign: KC4OCP
Cirilo M Seralde Jr
343 S Commerce Ave
Sebring FL 33870

Call Sign: K4IDS
Eugene W Trumble
302 S Egret St
Sebring FL 33872

Call Sign: K9FAZ
Chester E Biter
856 S Eucalyptus St
Sebring FL 33870

Call Sign: KK4DSM
Matthew L Jensen
3906 Santiago St
Sebring FL 33872

Call Sign: KK4DSL
Michael A Jensen
3906 Santiago St
Sebring FL 33872

Call Sign: WD8OND
Graham W Paterson
4343 Schumacher Rd 107
E
Sebring FL 33872

Call Sign: KD4OB
John E Patton
1811 SE Lakeview Dr
Sebring FL 33870

Call Sign: K4WQB
William W Fulcher Sr
4400 Sebring Ave
Sebring FL 33872

Call Sign: WB8CDK
Donald R Pankuch Sr
4421 Sebring Ave
Sebring FL 33872

Call Sign: NT8Y
Anna A Wolfe
4514 Sebring Ave
Sebring FL 33875

Call Sign: W8JB
Floyd E Wolfe
4514 Sebring Ave
Sebring FL 33875

Call Sign: KG4NEA
Richard M Jacob
4834 Shad Dr
Sebring FL 33870

Call Sign: KF4YNL
D Renee Cullum
1130 Shadow Ridge Dr
Sebring FL 33872

Call Sign: N8IGX
Leonard W Wright
1131 Shadow Ridge Dr
Sebring FL 33872

Call Sign: N1ZTI
Elsie C Kenney
1132 Shadow Ridge Dr
Sebring FL 33872

Call Sign: N1LC
Robert G Kenney
1132 Shadow Ridge Dr
Sebring FL 33872

Call Sign: W4MOB
Everett L Trumble
1017 Shamrock Dr
Sebring FL 33870

Call Sign: N4OKR
Caroline N House
1319 Shamrock Dr
Sebring FL 33872

Call Sign: KG4PKC
Tristan C Stowe
127 Sharon Ave
Sebring FL 33875

Call Sign: AA1DJ
David G Douglas
4356 Skipper Rd
Sebring FL 33875

Call Sign: KA4HMK
Robert D Neal
2653 Skyview St
Sebring FL 33870

Call Sign: AA4ZQ
Robert Wood
29 Snook Dr
Sebring FL 33872

Call Sign: N3ION
Gerald G Bowen
205 Sparrow Ave
Sebring FL 338723272

Call Sign: W8QKV
Ernest E Coxson
236 Sparrow Ave
Sebring FL 33872

Call Sign: KD4AJO
Alexander A Mc Culloch
308 Sparrow Ave
Sebring FL 33872

Call Sign: AF4HV
Roy A Loweke
6937 Sparta Rd
Sebring FL 33872

Call Sign: K3FJF
Kenneth N Dale
7747 Spivey Ln
Sebring FL 33870

Call Sign: KU4LQ
Robert G Hay
549 Spoonbill Dr
Sebring FL 33872

Call Sign: W2RPX
Arthur J Mijon
332 Spring Lake Blvd
Sebring FL 338706146

Call Sign: KF4REH
Frank Rivera
1503 Springhill Ct
Sebring FL 33870

Call Sign: K2LG
Frank Rivera
1503 Springhill Ct
Sebring FL 33870

Call Sign: W4UUU
Eustache E Ames
1829 Stream Ave
Sebring FL 338756025

Call Sign: KV4IB
Eustache E Ames
1829 Stream Ave
Sebring FL 338756025

Call Sign: WB4UJU
Mortimer S Ryan
2517 Summit Dr
Sebring FL 33870

Call Sign: K2AKY
Frank Dobson
3723 Sunbird Cir
Sebring FL 338721438

Call Sign: KD4IVP
Louis J Drzewiecki
638 Sunbird Sq
Sebring FL 338723489

Call Sign: N8COI
Robert L Rizor
209 Swallow Ave
Sebring FL 33872

Call Sign: KU4RB
Donald F Rowe
5977 Thunder Rd
Sebring FL 33876

Call Sign: K7TJG
Roland G Roy
4071 Thunderbird Rd 10
Sebring FL 33872

Call Sign: KG4NDZ
Tracy A Rankin
4071 Thunderbird Rd Apt
2
Sebring FL 33872

Call Sign: AI4BD
Tracy A Rankin
4071 Thunderbird Rd Apt
2
Sebring FL 33872

Call Sign: KK2U
Tracy A Rankin
4071 Thunderbird Rd Apt
2
Sebring FL 33872

Call Sign: WB8DNE
Hiram W Brewer
2108 Timber Ln
Sebring FL 33872

Call Sign: KI4UMR
Lawrence J Mc Cauley
220 Timothy Rd
Sebring FL 33870

Call Sign: KF4DLF
Howard H Budd
256 Timothy Rd
Sebring FL 338706861

Call Sign: KF4DLG
Marjorie R Budd
256 Timothy Rd
Sebring FL 338706861

Call Sign: KE4BVF
Hector L Lorenzo
4714 Trout Ave
Sebring FL 33870

Call Sign: W8RUK

Lawrence E Geysbeek
1001 Upper Volta St
Sebring FL 33872

Call Sign: K9EHP
William S Coon
3800 Urbino St
Sebring FL 338722209

Call Sign: K3KIU
Richard P Keyser Sr
3901 Urbino St
Sebring FL 33872

Call Sign: KI4FJF
David A Onsted
4012 Urbino St
Sebring FL 33872

Call Sign: W9CWN
David A Onsted
4012 Urbino St
Sebring FL 33872

Call Sign: KG4MLF
Virginia S Dunn
6510 US 27 N
Sebring FL 33870

Call Sign: W8JMH
William R Talbott
1100 US 27 N 59
Sebring FL 33870

Call Sign: W3UGN
Donald P Lambert
11150 US 27 S 47
Sebring FL 33876

Call Sign: KK4HFZ
Tad S Serralta
813 US Hwy 27 S
Sebring FL 33870

Call Sign: KC4OCO

Mary June B Seralde
1821 Valencia Dr
Sebring FL 33825

Call Sign: N3BPC
Valentine O Clay
3009 Valerie Blvd
Sebring FL 33870

Call Sign: N8VCD
Arnold R Dilley
3910 Van Ln
Sebring FL 338705247

Call Sign: KI4MKU
Randall D Smith
1640 Van Pelt Rd
Sebring FL 33870

Call Sign: AF4HR
Dennis W Koranda
2701 Van Pelt Rd
Sebring FL 33870

Call Sign: KF4YHZ
Mary C Roberson
2702 Van Pelt Rd
Sebring FL 33870

Call Sign: AG4FD
Mary C Roberson
2702 Van Pelt Rd
Sebring FL 33870

Call Sign: KU4RS
Ronald L Roberson
2702 Van Pelt Rd
Sebring FL 33870

Call Sign: AF4SS
Ronald L Roberson
2702 Van Pelt Rd
Sebring FL 33870

Call Sign: KI4LCO

Roy E Snidow Sr
2126 Vantage Trace
Sebring FL 338728300

Call Sign: KE4YAV
Richard W Brown Jr
3809 Violet Ave
Sebring FL 33870

Call Sign: WD4HKN
Thelma D Chapman
109 W Center Ave
Sebring FL 33870

Call Sign: KI4HMY
Highlands County
Emergency Management
6850 W George Blvd
Sebring FL 33875

Call Sign: W4HEM
Highlands County
Emergency Management
6850 W George Blvd
Sebring FL 33875

Call Sign: KJ4FYZ
Highlands County
Emergency Management
6850 W George Blvd
Sebring FL 33875

Call Sign: WF4HEM
Highlands County
Emergency Management
6850 W George Blvd
Sebring FL 33875

Call Sign: KJ4VGI
Highlands County
Emergency Management
6850 W George Blvd
Sebring FL 33875

Call Sign: KA4LVE

Lance A Giller
8880 W Josephine Rd
Sebring FL 338727210

Call Sign: KI4FSS
Ryan A Mc Lean
4101 W Mulligan Ct
Sebring FL 33875

Call Sign: KI4VMI
Ryan A Mc Lean
4101 W Mulligan Ct
Sebring FL 33875

Call Sign: N9AVL
Wallace E Keller
329 Whip Poor Will
Sebring FL 33872

Call Sign: K1RUS
Valmore A La Flam
332 Whip Poor Will Dr
Sebring FL 338726249

Call Sign: K2HZV
Mervin D Anderson
517 Whip Poor Will Dr
Sebring FL 33872

Call Sign: N4NNI
Charles W Martin
1179 Whisper Lake Blvd
Sebring FL 33870

Call Sign: KC8XF
William H Rider
1184 Whisper Lake Blvd S
Sebring FL 33870

Call Sign: KA4SPQ
Virgil J Hock
2305 Whispering Pines Dr
Sebring FL 33872

Call Sign: KC8RB

James D Carbaugh
2760 Whistle Stop
Sebring FL 33872

Call Sign: KE4UNU
Richard K Strobel
1128 Wightman Ave
Sebring FL 33870

Call Sign: AG4ZN
Richard K Strobel
1128 Wightman Ave
Sebring FL 33870

Call Sign: KI4JVR
Sean N Norris
6108 Wilson Ter
Sebring FL 33876

Call Sign: N3VLK
John J Mckinney
2213 Woods And Water Ct
Sebring FL 33872

Call Sign: KE4FDM
Jim B Sanders
Sebring FL 33871

Call Sign: K4XX
Roland D Reed
Sebring FL 33871

Call Sign: KI4QIX
Joan M Frawley
Sebring FL 33870

Call Sign: KI4MZN
Edward A Frawley
Sebring FL 33872

Call Sign: W4HCA
Highlands County ARC
Inc
Sebring FL 33872

Call Sign: WA9JSX
Louis R Cass
Sebring FL 338711551

Call Sign: KA8WDT
Timothy C Willsey
Sebring FL 338711984

FCC Amateur Radio Licenses in South Punta Gorda

Call Sign: KI4CNE
Jerry L Davidson Jr
11187 4th Ave
South Punta Gorda FL 33955

Call Sign: NB4U
Jerry L Davidson Jr
11187 4th Ave
South Punta Gorda FL 33955

FCC Amateur Radio Licenses in Tice

Call Sign: KC4HAT
Marilyn L Staker
Tice FL 33905

Call Sign: WA4PSN
Phillip A Merritt
Tice FL 33905

FCC Amateur Radio Licenses in Venus

Call Sign: WD4HAM
Edward H Stephens
408 Grand Prix Dr
Venus FL 33960

Call Sign: KC4VMO
John J Stabler

215 Myrtle Bush Ln
Venus FL 33960

Call Sign: AA8JV
Phillip R Gonzales
215 Myrtle Bush Ln
Venus FL 33960

Call Sign: KI4UTK
Charles E Steele
47 Placid Farms Dr
Venus FL 33960

Call Sign: KI4IMM
Kye Ewing
20 Russell Ct
Venus FL 33960

Call Sign: KG4TNO
Albert O Ewing
20 Russell Ct
Venus FL 33960

FCC Amateur Radio Licenses in Wauchula

Call Sign: KB0PKG
Terry J Regennitter
2206 Alligator Alley
Wauchula FL 338738229

Call Sign: KI4SPH
Curtis M Bladen
1012 Blue Jay Rd
Wauchula FL 33873

Call Sign: KG4NNM
Kristina D Davis
509 E Palmetto St
Wauchula FL 33873

Call Sign: W4PEA
Kristina D Davis
1850 Heard Bridge Rd Lot
112

Wauchula FL 338732386

Call Sign: KI4MR
James A Braddock
112 Inglis Way
Wauchula FL 33873

Call Sign: KI4MU
Loraine C Braddock
112 Inglis Way
Wauchula FL 33873

Call Sign: K4QON
Jerald A Brush
1237 Louisiana St
Wauchula FL 338738765

Call Sign: KA4OKY
Robert W Williams
818 N Florida Ave
Wauchula FL 33873

Call Sign: WB9KAJ
Stewart Waxler
208 Orchid Ln
Wauchula FL 33873

Call Sign: N4JMX
Larry G Cook
301 Park Dr
Wauchula FL 33873

Call Sign: KG4KRQ
Dominic W Filice
323 Riverside Dr
Wauchula FL 33873

Call Sign: N6CUN
Joseph A Filice
323 Riverside Dr
Wauchula FL 33873

Call Sign: WD4CNJ
Robert W Bird
2246 Skp Way

Wauchula FL 33873

Call Sign: AB4GU
James A Dwyer
2212 Skp Way Skp Resort
Wauchula FL 33873

Call Sign: W4SAW
Ada S Walker
4086 W Main St
Wauchula FL 33873

Call Sign: N4EMH
Hardee Amateur Radio
Group
404 W Orange St
Wauchula FL 33873

Call Sign: KG4NUI
Hardee Amateur Radio
Group
404 W Orange St
Wauchula FL 33873

Call Sign: WA4GPK
Grady B Sheffield
Wauchula FL 33873

FCC Amateur Radio Licenses in West Fort Myers

Call Sign: KE4QNC
Harold K Williams
2616 Zoysia Ln
West Fort Myers FL
339172476

FCC Amateur Radio Licenses in Zolfo Springs

Call Sign: KB4BZI
Robert L Gill
Box 150
Zolfo Springs FL 33890

Call Sign: KJ4CL
Howard L Gilbert
Box 20
Zolfo Springs FL 33890

Call Sign: KF4LEA
Clyde W Barringer III
1564 Broadus Williams Rd
Zolfo Springs FL 33890

Call Sign: KF4LEB
David E Barringer
1564 Broadus Williams Rd
Zolfo Springs FL 33890

Call Sign: K3ODM
Frank E Whittam
3024 Clifton Bryan Rd
Zolfo Springs FL 33890

Call Sign: KA4DIU
William N Daniel
4650 Johnston Rd
Zolfo Springs FL 33890

Call Sign: AF4QM
William N Daniel
4650 Johnston Rd
Zolfo Springs FL 33890

Call Sign: WD4AQW
Gene H Archer
4012 Raccoon Rd
Zolfo Springs FL 33890

Call Sign: KG4TAA
Robert W Cole
Zolfo Springs FL 33890